PARTHESH THAKKAR PUBLICATIONS

THE ULTIMATE GUIDE TO IELTS SPEAKING

The ONLY book with IELTS Speaking Band Descriptors

Contents :

- 1200+ IELTS Speaking interview questions with answers.

- 1500+ IELTS Speaking interview questions for practice.

- **2250+ questions in total.**

- 170+ IELTS Speaking Q Cards (Part 2) with sample answers.

- 160+ IELTS Speaking Q Cards for practice.

- **340+ Q Cards in total**

- **Speaking Activities**

PARTHESH THAKKAR

First Edition: 2016   :   Third Reprint September - 2017

© Copyright 2016   :   **Parthesh Thakkar - 2007**

First Edition   :   2007

Second Edition   :   36th Reprint April, 2018

Revised Edition   :   2017

Published by   :   **Mr. Parthesh Thakkar**

Angel Edunext

304, Third Floor, The Grand Mall,
Opp. SBI, Nehrunagar to C.N. School Road,
Ambavadi, Ahmedabad - 380 015,
Gujarat, India.
Phone No.: 079 2630 5110, 079 3017 7464
Email: parthesh@angeledunext.com
Website: www.angeledunext.com

Distributed by   :   **MK Book Distributors**

1, Tulsi Complex, 2 Azad Society,
Ambavadi, Ahmedabad - 380 015, India.
Phone No.: 079 2676 3022, 079 2676 3012
Email: mkbooksd@gmail.com
Website: www.mkbooksd.com

ACKNOWLEDGEMENTS

I am very thankful to my wife, Vaishali Thakkar for her invaluable contribution to the creation of this book. I am also thankful to my little daughter, 'Sakshi', who has always shown me how to be diligent and energetic, through her innocent nature and playful disposition.

I convey sincere thanks to my parents, to Mr. Mohan Kirpalani, to my students: Dr Pragnesh Vaghela, Mr. J. G. Patel, Mr. Dipesh Trivedi, Mr. Ravi Patel, Mr. Janisaar, Mr. Dipen Adesara, Mr. Piyush Patel, Mr. Bhupendra Patel, Mr. Keyur Shah, Mr. Vipul Chaudhary, and all the others those who helped me at various preparatory stages of this book.

Finally, I am thankful to you for reading this book. I am sure it will make a creative and constructive contribution towards your preparation for IELTS Speaking.

Parthesh Thakkar

Author's Note

This book is meant for students at all levels of English language. It can be used both, as a self-study book, and as a classroom study guide. Candidates can use the questions given in this book to familiarise themselves with those questions that are usually asked in the IELTS Speaking test.

Most of the questions asked in the IELTS Speaking test are covered in this book. Further, this book is also useful for TOEFL iBT candidates for the first two segments of their Speaking test.

The first part of this book deals with an introduction to IELTS exam, the IELTS Speaking Assessment, Problems and Solutions in Developing Speaking Skills, and FAQs regarding IELTS Speaking. After that, the book is divided into three sections, which are related to each of the three parts of the IELTS Speaking Assessment.

I suggest that readers go through the introduction and assessment section before they start reading the questions and answers in this book. However, if the reader is already familiar with the assessment criteria, he/she may skip the introduction, and can start with Section I directly. I also suggest that readers go through the band descriptors and study them thoroughly, so that they may understand what the IELTS Speaking examiner is looking for, from them.

In this book, all the answers have been written using masculine pronouns (he, his, and him) for ease of reading. However, please replace these words with appropriate feminine pronouns (she, hers, and her) where applicable.

Finally, I suggest that readers use the ideas and opinions expressed in this book as reference only. Please do not try to memorise any of the answers given in the book.

I hope this book helps you in clearing your IELTS exam and fulfilling your dreams of studying or settling abroad.

Here's wishing you all the very best for your IELTS exam!

Parthesh Thakkar

Table Of Contents

Cue Cards with Suggestions, Followed by Follow-up Questions with Sample Answers and Practice Questions 259

Introduction to IELTS

What is IELTS?
IELTS stands for INTERNATIONAL ENGLISH LANGUAGE TESTING SYSTEM. This exam is designed to judge the English proficiency of candidates wishing to study or settle abroad.
IELTS is jointly managed worldwide by Cambridge ESOL, British Council, and IDP Education Australia.

Who can appear for IELTS?
Candidates who want to study in countries such as the UK, the USA, Canada, Australia, New Zealand, and Singapore can appear for IELTS. It is accepted in more than 110 countries, including most of the European Union.
Individuals who want to migrate to Canada, Australia, the UK, and New Zealand are required to take the IELTS exam as a proof of their English language proficiency.
A person needs to have a valid passport to appear for the IELTS exam.

What is the format of IELTS?
IELTS is available in two formats:

Academic IELTS and General Training IELTS.
Academic IELTS is for students who want to study abroad, and for professionals like doctors, pharmacists, and nurses who want to migrate to the UK, the USA, and Australia.
General Training IELTS is for candidates who want to migrate to countries like Canada, Australia, the UK, or New Zealand.

What is the format of the exam?
There are four tests in this exam; Listening, Reading, Writing, and Speaking.

LISTENING

Approximately 30 minutes + 10 minutes transfer time.
This test is divided into four sections and has a total of 40 items.
Students get a question booklet on which the questions are printed. A tape is then played and students write down their answers simultaneously, while the tape is going on.
Students get time to look at the questions before the listening test starts, and at the end of each section, to check their work.

	No. of Speakers	No. of Items (questions)
Section 1	2	10
Section 2	1	10
Section 3	2-4	10
Section 4	1	10

Discourse Types

Section 1: This is usually a conversation between two people regarding a general, everyday topic. It is conducted in two parts, wherein first you are given some time to look at the questions in this section, followed by listening to an example with the correct answer. Then, in the second part, the actual listening tape is played (including the example). Time: Approximately 4 minutes.

Section 2: This is usually a monologue (only one speaker) of a social functional nature, or an informational talk. It can represent a social or academic setting. It is held in two parts, where you get about 50 seconds to look at the questions. There will be no spoken example, but you can see a written example. Time: Approximately 3–4 minutes.

Section 3: This is usually a conversation between two to four people. It represents an academic, educational, or training-based situation. It is held in two parts, but there is no example on the tape in this section. Time: Approximately 4 minutes.

Section 4: This is usually a lecture or speech given as a monologue. It represents an academic, educational, or training- based situation. No breaks are given in between. In some cases there might be a written example. You may get a note, or a summary completion, or multiple choice questions, or a mixture of these question types. You get about 45 seconds to look at all the questions in the beginning of Section 4. Time: Approximately 4–5 minutes.

NOTE: As the Listening test progresses, the recording becomes more difficult. This does not mean that it becomes faster as it progresses. Instead, it becomes progressively complex and tests all the various aspects of the candidates' listening skills.

READING

Two Formats: Academic Reading and General Training Reading.
60 minutes and no extra time : 40 items.

ACADEMIC READING

	No. of Items
Reading Passage 1	13–14
Reading Passage 2	13–14
Reading Passage 3	13–14
Total	**40**

Reading passages are based on research material, case studies, and biographies, and they are argumentative. They are taken from journals, textbooks, or web sites.

With each passage, the test becomes progressively difficult.

GENERAL TRAINING READING

	No. of Items
Section 1	13–14
Section 2	13–14
Section 3	13–14
Total	**40**

Passages are taken from newspapers, magazines, catalogues, and from web sites. At least one section contains a detailed argumentative text.

WRITING

Two Formats — Academic and General Training.
60 minutes and no extra time: Two tasks in writing
Minimum 150 words are required for Task 1 and 250 words are required for Task 2.

Academic Writing
Task 1 — this includes either a bar chart, a pie chart, a line graph, a table, a flow chart, or a process, or a combination two or more of these, containing figures and details.
Task 2 — in this task a specific essay topic is given, about specific research areas, including but not limited to the environment, pollution, study, and science.

General Training Writing
Task 1 — for this task a short letter has to be written, either in a formal, or in an informal, or in a semiformal style.
Task 2 — here, an essay topic regarding day-to-day life is given. This could include subjects like the society, children, family, education, and lifestyle.

SPEAKING

The Speaking test is organised on a day other than the day of the main exam, which involves the Listening, Reading, and Writing tests.
11–14 minutes time: Three parts

Part 1

4–5 minutes
Introduction and Interview
In this part, the examiner introduces himself and verifies the test takers' identity. Then the examiner asks the test taker general questions on some basic topics such as home, family, work, studies, and other interests. To ensure consistency, questions are taken from a scripted examiner frame.

Part 2

3–4 minutes
Long Turn
Here, the candidate gets a Cue Card with a topic, about which he has to speak for 1–2 minutes. He gets one minute to prepare for the topic before he starts to speak. The examiner also asks one or two follow-up questions, when the candidate stops speaking.

Part 3
4–5 minutes
Discussion
In Part 3, the examiner and the test takers discuss issues related to the Cue Card topic in Part 2, in a more general and abstract way, and where appropriate, in greater depth.

16   **The Ultimate Guide to IELTS Speaking by Parthesh Thakkar**

IELTS Speaking Assessment

How is IELTS Speaking assessed?
Speaking is assessed on four criteria, as mentioned below.

Fluency and Coherence:
Fluency can be explained as the ability to speak at a normal speed, with natural continuity. The speech should be logically linked with the help of linking words, so that continuity is maintained, and listeners remain interested.

Fluency is often misunderstood as speed, but in fact, it has nothing to do with speaking fast. Fluency is one's ability to speak continuously at his natural pace, without taking unnecessary pauses, and without much hesitation.

Coherence is the ability to form a logical speech, where the flow of information is understandable, and appropriately connected. Among other things, coherence involves using proper linking words, pronouns, and intonation to maintain the meaningfulness and comprehensibility of your speech.

Lexical Resource:
Lexical resource can be explained as the ability to come up with appropriate words for specific situations while speaking, so that one's meaning, emotion, and viewpoint can be expressed properly.

For example: If you say, "The ship is swimming in the sea", here, you probably mean that the ship is moving on water, but the appropriate verb in this situation is 'sailing', and not 'swimming'. This is just a simple example to help you understand how you can use appropriate words in specific contexts. However, at times, it may happen sometimes that you may not be able to come up with the exact words to describe certain situations. At such times, you should still be able to communicate your general message, with its overall meaning intact, with the help of other words or expressions, to ensure that your speech remains continuous.

Grammatical Range and Accuracy:
Grammatical Accuracy can be explained as the appropriate and correct use of grammar while speaking, i.e. the use of proper tenses, verb forms, prepositions, and articles, along with other rules of grammar, while speaking.

Grammatical Range can be explained as the variety in sentence structures that the candidate can show during the test. The candidate should be able to show that he is comfortable with the use of different kinds of sentence structures, appropriately and correctly.

Pronunciation:
Pronunciation can be explained as the ability to speak clearly, so that the listener doesn't have to make special efforts to understand the speech. Listeners generally have to put in more effort to comprehend speech of candidates whose first language strongly influences their second language, i.e. English.

Assessment

Candidates are given bands out of nine in each of the four assessment criteria, and their average is considered as the final band score for the Speaking test.

For example, if an examiner gives bands for all four assessment criteria as mentioned below:

Fluency and Coherence	:	7
Lexical Resource	:	7
Grammatical Range and Accuracy	:	6
Pronunciation	:	8

Then the final band score of this imagined candidate would be **7.0**

IMPORTANT

IELTS Speaking and Writing Bands were awarded as full band scores (5, 6, 7, 8, and 9) only till June 2007. However, from July 2007 onwards, bands in Speaking and Writing started being reported as both, half and full band score, thus making it possible to get 6.5 or 7.5 bands in IELTS Speaking and Writing. Log on to **www.ielts.org** for more details and for newer changes introduced in IELTS Speaking and General Training Reading.

Solutions for the Common Problems in Developing Speaking Skills

i. Problem

I cannot speak at all. I have not studied in English medium, and I can't understand what to speak, because words come to my mind in my first language, only.

Solution

It is seen at times that candidates cannot speak in English at all when they start their IELTS preparations. If you become tongue tied, you need some practice in speaking English. This can be done at home. You can take any written or printed material in English, and start reading it aloud (reciting it) for ten to fifteen minutes, every day. This will help you in developing some familiarity with the language.

ii. Problem

I can't speak fluently in English. I hesitate a lot when I speak.

Solution

Fluency in speaking is an important tool to score high bands in IELTS. You can improve your fluency in English by practising more speaking. You can practise speaking with the questions from this book, either with a friend or classmate, or by yourself.

However, there is an important point I would like you to understand; fluency in English does not mean speed. Most candidates confuse speaking fluently with speaking fast. No, fluency doesn't mean speed. It means being able to speak naturally, in a rhythm, with a constant flow, which can be slow or fast, but must sound natural, and must not have major, unnecessary pauses.

Here, I would like to emphasise one more important point regarding pauses in speaking. There are two types of pauses in spoken English — positive and negative. Positive pauses generally don't reduce your band score, but negative pauses can affect your band score, negatively. If, for instance, you are speaking about an article you read in the newspaper, but are unable to recall the name of the writer of the article, and you take a pause of a few seconds here, just to remember this detail, then such a pause is understandable, and is not likely to reduce your rating in fluency. However, if you take a pause to search for language, such as appropriate words to describe a situation, then this is considered a negative pause, and it will affect your fluency rating.

iii. Problem

My grammar is too weak. I think I should improve my grammar before I start practising for IELTS Speaking.

Solution

Knowledge of grammar will certainly help you to score higher in IELTS Speaking. Thus, it is a good idea to learn grammar, either by joining some grammar classes, or by referring to a practice book. There is a separate list of English preparation books given at the end of this book for students who want to practise independently.

However, grammar is certainly not the only assessment criteria in IELTS Speaking, so, it is important for you to develop skills in other areas as well. Remember, IELTS Speaking checks your overall ability to communicate. For this, you should start your speaking practice, even before you start learning grammar. There are two benefits of this strategy. One is that you can develop fluency in spoken English, right from the beginning. The second is that when you start speaking English, you will come across many situations in which selecting the right tenses or words may be confusing, and here analysis of the confusing situations with the help of a grammar book or your tutor, can help you grasp things faster. Practical exposure to spoken English situations always helps in improving language skills.

iv. Problem
I understand all the questions in IELTS Speaking, but, at times I can't speak on some topics because I don't know anything about them.

Solution
Read up a lot on various topics or current affairs like pollution, politics, religion, festivals, education, lifestyle, children, social issues, marriage, travelling, and tourism. Such practice will give you multiple benefits in the form of an increase in your knowledge about various issues, enhancement in your vocabulary, and improvement in your reading comprehension skills.

However, it is not always possible for you to give perfect answers to all the questions in IELTS Speaking. Here, I would like to tell you that there are NO perfect answers when it comes to the speaking test. You are expected to state your opinion or belief about a given topic. If you don't know anything about the topic, you can speak about your personal experiences in life surrounding the topic, or you can even speculate about the answer. Your examiner will not check whether your speech is factually right or wrong, but, he will certainly check your level of spoken English on the four assessment criteria mentioned above.

*Remember one golden rule in IELTS Speaking; "How you speak is more important than what you speak."

v. Problem
I know what to speak, but when I start speaking, I just can't do it properly. I am concerned about my mistakes in speaking. I fear what others will think about me. In this process I can't speak fluently. Consequently, I lose my confidence.

Solution
You are facing this problem due to your lack of familiarity with the language. To overcome this problem, try to discuss everything only in English, both in your classes, and at home in your routine life. This will help you develop a familiarity with the language. It is also a good idea to group up with some candidates around your home or at your classes, to develop an interactive learning atmosphere with others who are also trying to master spoken English. Here, you can comfortably interact in English without worrying about others judging your speech. Over time this will help you get a grip on your spoken English.

You can also request your tutor to assess your speech and give suggestions to overcome your mistakes and weaknesses so that you may improve on them. Remember, your job is to speak English without thinking about others' reactions to your speech, because no one in this world is perfect.

---

vi. Problem

I can't speak for two minutes in Part 2 (Cue Card) of IELTS speaking.

Solution

The best way to improve your speaking in Part 2 is to record your speech every time you speak on a Cue Card topic. For example, select a Cue Card from this book, take one minute to think about the topic, press the record button of your music system, computer, or mobile phone, and start speaking on the topic. Stop recording when you finish speaking. Now, listen to the recording and analyse it on different criteria given in the table below. Give yourself a rating for each criterion on a band scale of 1–9:

Criteria	Rating (1–9)
Did I speak for two minutes?	
How many pauses did I make during the speech?	
How many pauses were negative and how many were positive?	
What grammatical mistakes did I make in the speech?	
Was my pronunciation clear?	
Did I use connectives and complex structures in the speech?	

Once you finish the analysis of your speech, speak again on the same topic and see where you have improved in comparison to your previous attempt.

If you speak for less than two minutes, think about the possible ways of extending your speech. For this, you can take help from the sample answers given in this book, also. Further, you can prepare a separate list of connectives commonly used in English and you can refer to that list on regular basis. Regularly referring to this list will certainly help you in bringing continuity to your speech and in holding your listener's interest.

Frequently Asked Questions about IELTS speaking

Q. Does the IELTS Speaking exam check the general knowledge of the candidate?

A. No, IELTS Speaking doesn't check the general knowledge of the candidate. It evaluates the candidate's proficiency in English on the four assessment criteria mentioned earlier. For example, your examiner will not ask you who the first president of your country was, but, he may ask you what qualities are required to be a good president of a country, or what you would do first if you were selected as the president of your country.

It can be understood from this example that the answer to the first question — who was the first president of your country? — needs to be given in the form of information or factual data, whereas the answers to the second and the third questions need only be given based on personal opinions.

Q. Can I mug up (learn by heart) some answers of possible questions before my IELTS Speaking exam?

A. It is a good idea to practise possible speaking questions before your Speaking exam. However, I suggest that you don't try to memorize the answers to any questions because IELTS examiners are well trained to detect whether a candidate is giving a natural answer or a memorized one. If you give a memorized answer, your examiner will immediately turn to a different set of topics and this might affect your assessment.

Q. Should I only wear formal clothes (shirt and tie) or traditional clothes (for e.g. sari for women) when I appear for my Speaking exam?

A. The IELTS Speaking exam is a formal situation. It is appropriate to wear formal clothes when you appear for the Speaking exam. However, remember an important point; your clothes will not make any positive or negative change in your Speaking band score. If you are a 6 band user, taking your Speaking exam in a tie and formal shirt will not help you get 7 bands. On the other hand, if you are a 6 band user, taking your Speaking exam in a pair of jeans and a T-shirt, or other casual wear will not reduce your band score to 5. In short, how you look is not going to be assessed; how you speak is going to be judged in the IELTS Speaking exam.

Q. In Part 2 of the Speaking exam, will the examiner take the Cue Card back from me when I start speaking?

A. No, the Cue Card stays in front of you till you finish speaking in Part 2. There is no need to return it to the examiner before you start speaking because the IELTS Speaking test judges how well you speak English and not how well you can prepare a speech and remember it.

Q. In Part 2, the examiner also offers a paper and a pencil when we prepare for the Cue Card topic, before we are told to start speaking. Is it compulsory for me to write some points on that paper? Will it be helpful to me in my assessment?

A. It is true that you get a paper and a pencil to make some points before you start speaking in the exam. However, it is not compulsory for you to write something on it. Your examiner doesn't see whether you have made points or not. This is not going to make any positive or negative impact on your assessment in the Speaking exam.

Q. Is there any specific band score allocated to Part 2 like 4.5 bands out of 9.0, or 3.0 bands out of 9.0?

A. No, there is no separate band score allocated to Part 2 of IELTS Speaking. The whole test is assessed on all four criteria mentioned earlier and the average band score is awarded to the candidate.

Q. Why is my Speaking exam recorded?

A. The Speaking exam is usually recorded for two reasons. First, the examiners worldwide are monitored only through this recording. So the recording helps in monitoring whether examiners are following the test format appropriately or not. Secondly, if a candidate is dissatisfied with his Speaking band score, he can apply for reassessment of the test. In this case, the Speaking exam recording is used to re-evaluate the Speaking band score of the candidate.

Q. Should I ask any questions to the examiner about my Speaking exam at the end of the assessment?

It is not advisable to ask any questions to your examiner before, during, or after your exam about your assessment or band score. There is no need for you to speak anything about your preparation also because examiners are not allowed to comment on your Speaking exam. So, they will not answer such questions under any circumstances. You are expected to only answer the questions that your examiner asks you. However, if you don't understand any question, you can request your examiner to repeat that question. But remember, they will not explain the question to you.

Q. Can I request my examiner to change the question if I don't understand it?

No, you can't ask your examiner to change the question if you don't know how to answer it. You have to try your best to answer the question by adding in your personal experiences about the question. What's more, if you ask your examiner to change the question, he may feel that you are trying to 'control' the Speaking exam, which may affect your band score negatively.

Q. Can I offer a handshake to my examiner?

No, you shouldn't offer a handshake to your examiner as it looks informal and inappropriate for the situation. However, if your examiner offers you a handshake, accept it immediately.

Q. Who is responsible for giving me my Speaking exam band score? — Is it the examiner who takes my Speaking interview, or someone else? Is it true that a group of examiners will assess my Speaking after my interview and give me a band score?

The examiner who takes your interview usually gives you a band score almost immediately after you leave the examination room. Each IELTS examiner is given a number and the same number will be printed on your IELTS result report card also. This fact also suggests that only one examiner (the one who takes your interview) is responsible for your Speaking exam band score.

Activities to Improve IELTS Speaking Skills

Activity 1

This activity can be done between 2–5 candidates.

First, the candidate must introduce himself. He should include the following in his introduction: name, family background in brief, city of residence, academic qualification, job, hobbies, and goals in life.

Other members listen to this speech and prepare 2–4 questions about each of the parts included in the speech. They may take help from the questions printed in this book. Once the candidate completes the speech, those who were listening to the speech are to ask their prepared questions. The speaker must answer all the questions one by one. The same activity is then repeated for every student in the group.

Benefits of this activity:

Candidates increase their familiarity with the language and also develop the skills needed to answer questions spontaneously. This ability further improves their confidence. This activity is extremely useful for students who have just started preparing for IELTS, and also for those who are at the beginner level in English language.

Activity 2

This activity can be done between 2–3 candidates.

Step 1: Select a Cue Card from this book.

Step 2: One of the candidates will start speaking on the topic given in the Cue Card. While speaking, if the speaker takes a pause for longer than 5 seconds, the second candidate must stop the first one and start speaking on the same Cue Card topic. Now, when the second speaker takes a pause for longer than 5 seconds, the first speaker must stop him and again start speaking on the same Cue Card topic from the point where he had stopped earlier.

The time taken for this entire activity depends on the number of candidates. If there are 2 candidates, it should take approximately 8 minutes, and if there are 3, it should take approximately 12 minutes.

At the end of the activity, the one who has spoken the most must be declared the winner.

Benefits of this activity:

Candidates learn to speak without long pauses. Their minds are motivated to work faster and prepare for the content in advance. This activity trains students to think faster, helping them to speak without hesitation and unnecessary pauses. This also helps students in gaining higher scores in the fluency criterion. Candidates are suggested to record the entire activity and to listen to the recording at the end of the activity. This will make them aware of the points on which they need to improve, thus enhancing their confidence.

Activity 3

This activity can be done between 2–3 candidates.

Step 1: Select a Cue Card from this book.

Step 2: One candidate will start speaking on the topic given in the Cue Card. During his speech, if he repeats a word or a phrase either immediately, or after a few sentences, the second candidate will stop him and start speaking on the same Cue Card topic. The first candidate must now listen carefully to the second one, and on noticing any repetition of words or phrases, he must stop the speaking candidate and restart his own speech from where he had left off earlier.

Benefits of this activity:

Some candidates have a natural tendency to repeat words and phrases. They tend constantly repeat themselves unintentionally, due to a lack of words to articulate their thoughts. This tendency can reduce their IELTS Speaking scores. On the other hand, the above mentioned activity provides the benefit of overcoming this tendency to repeat oneself. The second benefit of this activity is that it will encourage candidates to try to bring in some variety to the vocabulary that they use in their speech on a regular basis. This variety will eventually help in enhancing candidates' lexical resources, and in improving their scores in the speaking test.

Candidates may collect and prepare a list of words related to the Cue Card topic from various books and keep that list in front of them when they are practicing IELTS Speaking, so that they can incorporate new words from the list in their speeches. Candidates are advised to pick different topics for enhancing different skills by preparing a list of the skills assessed by examiners, from the IELTS handbook.

Activity 4

This activity can be done by 2 or more candidates.

Step 1: One candidate must select a Cue Card from the 'topic list' that he has prepared and start speaking on that topic. The candidate should be allowed to speak till he can do so fluently. However, if at any point during the process, he is unable to create a proper sentence, another candidate must start speaking on the same topic, and from the same point where the first candidate was unable to express himself clearly. The second candidate must speak instantly from the point where the first one hesitated because of a lack of language.

Benefits of this activity:

This activity is aimed to improve conversation repair skills in candidates. When one candidate hears another candidate speak on the same Cue Card topic from the point where he couldn't speak, he learns to repair the conversation and finds ways to not let it break owing to a deficiency of language, in future.

Section I

Questions and Answers for Part 1 of IELTS Speaking

Practice Questions for Part 1 of IELTS Speaking

Questions and Answers for Part 1 of IELTS Speaking

1. When do you get time to pursue your hobbies?

My hobbies are reading books and listening to music. I can pursue both of these at my workplace and at home. I take small breaks of a few minutes at my office to pursue my hobbies. However, I get more time for them at home, during weekends and on holidays.

2. How have your hobbies benefited you?

My hobbies have given me immense benefits. Reading books has given me a better insight to understanding life. I have learned and implemented the knowledge gained from books, both in my personal life and in my profession. This has enhanced my success on all levels. Next, music has always kept me fresh and energized, which is very important for someone in the teaching profession.

3. What type of hobbies do people of your generation usually have?

Among other things, people of my generation prefer to read books, listen to music, travel, and watch movies. Besides, there are a few new activities emerging as hobbies, too, such as surfing the internet, chatting online, and playing games on mobile phones and computers.

4. Why do hobbies keep changing from generation to generation?

I think changes in lifestyle and advancements in technology are instrumental in causing a shift in hobbies over generations. With each passing generation, these advancements offer more options to people to choose from, and to pursue. For instance, we can use the internet as a means to pursue our hobbies today; but this was not available at all, before a few decades.

5. What types of hobbies will the future generations have?

I think most hobbies of future generations will be based on technology. People will play virtual games, travel in space, explore the depths of oceans, make more friends online, and share their lives with them.

6. If you had an opportunity to pick up a new hobby, what would it be, and why?

If I had an opportunity to pick up a new hobby, I would learn to play a musical instrument — maybe a guitar, or a piano. I have a great affinity for these musical instruments, and even today I hold the artists who play such instruments in great regard. I will definitely learn to play them in future, if I get a chance.

7. How are hobbies useful to us?

Hobbies are useful to us in many ways. With hobbies, we can spend our time creatively, helping us gaining expertise in other areas of life, apart from our professions. At times, hobbies can also help us in earning fame and fortune. For example, a friend of mine likes to paint as his hobby. He is now able to sell his paintings and earns handsome amounts from them.

8. Don't you think hobbies are a waste of time?

I don't think hobbies are a waste of time. On the contrary, they enable creative utilization of our time. By pursuing hobbies we can actually develop our hidden abilities, which is very important for our all-round development.

9. Do you like to perform outdoor activities often?

Yes, I like to perform outdoor activities often. I enjoy being out in the open, and one with

---

nature. Outdoor activities allow me to rejuvenate myself in the fresh air, after a long day at work in a closed office.

10.Do you prefer indoor activities or outdoor activities?
This depends on the season and the weather. Where I come from, it stays very hot for most part of the year. So, except for the winters, I prefer doing indoor activities. In winters, however, I love to step out and indulge in outdoor sports and activities.

11. What are the options for outdoor activities in your city?
There are many options for outdoor activities in my city. People can go for walks and jogs, they can perform Yoga in open gardens, and they can play outdoor sports such as tennis, football, cricket, basketball, and volleyball. People can even opt to go for some bird watching just outside the city, and there are many good picnic spots nearby, too.

12. Is there a specific age limit for certain outdoor activities?
In my opinion, there is no age limit for any outdoor activity. I have seen many old people who are very fit and active, and many young people who are lethargic and unhealthy. I have seen very old people take part in strenuous outdoor activities such as long hikes and treks, and even mountain climbing, with as much gusto as youngsters. So, be it any activity, if one has a fit body and an enthusiastic mind, age is no limit.

13. Are you fond of bags?
Yes I am fond of bags. I like to buy a new backpack or laptop case every now and then. There are many options available in the market these days, which prompt me to keep changing the bag that I use. Bags are not just a utility item to me, but also a style statement. I think a good bag can add to the personality of the one carrying it.

14. Have you every purchased a handbag for anyone?
Yes, I remember purchasing a beautiful brown leather handbag for my mother when I was only 12 years old. I had saved up my pocket money for a few months leading up to her birthday, and found a bag that would suit her style and taste. The bag had many sections inside and a few handy side pockets as well. It was very hardy, too, and lasted a good few years.

15. What are some tips for selecting a bag for gifting?
The first thing to keep in mind while buying a bag is the gender of the person for whom the bag is being purchased. For women, handbags and purses are more suitable, while for men, laptop bags, messenger bags, and backpacks are ideal. Then, the choice of fabric is also important. Some people may be very fond of leather, while others may be completely averse to animal products. So, one must know the tastes of the person for whom the bag is being purchased. While gifting a bag, one should also keep in mind the age of the receiver, and buy suitable colours to suit their personality.

16. Are children's bags different from adults' bags?
Yes, children's bags are quite different from the bags that adults use. Children prefer bags which are more colourful and striking. They often go for multi coloured bags, or bags depicting their favourite superheroes and cartoon characters. These days it is easy to find school bags and hand bags for children, with any cartoon character of their choice. The quality of children's bags has also improved a lot in the last decade.

17. Do you think everyone dreams when they sleep?

Yes, in my opinion, and from what I have read, all of us dream when we sleep. Even animals tend to dream when they sleep. Babies who do not have fully developed brains are also believed to have dreams based on the things they have seen and heard through the day. Dreams help us sort out the events of our waking day, and also give us an insight into our subconscious.

18. Do you feel dreams have meanings that can be interpreted?

While dreams are sometimes simply repetitions of the activities that we have performed in our waking hours, at other times they can be metaphors for our life situations. These metaphorical dreams can be interpreted at times, and the interpretations can give us a better idea of the hidden thoughts and themes running in our subconscious.

19. Should we take our dreams seriously?

I have read about people who have dreamt of future events in their sleep, and then seen them manifest in waking life a few weeks later. In that sense, dreams may sometimes be meaningful and more like visions. In some cases, dreams may serve as warnings, cautioning the dreamer against possible future threats, too. At times, dreams also show the dreamer parts of him that need to be healed. We should take such dreams seriously.

20. What are some common dreams according to you?

I think dreams of chasing someone or being chased, dreams of falling, dreams of climbing hills and staircases, and dreams of flying are very common. These dreams can easily be interpreted as well, in context of the dreamer's waking life. Exam dreams are also fairly common, even with adults who have completed all their exams many decades ago. Most of these have something to do with anticipation, anxiety, the need for freedom, or the dreamers' efforts to reach their goals.

21. Do you play video games?

I play video games very occasionally, if a certain friend has purchased a new gaming console, or a new gaming arcade has opened up in the city. Otherwise, I am not too fond of playing video games, now. Also, I do not find much time for video gaming.

22. Did you used to play video games earlier?

Yes, until I got so busy, I used to play a lot of different video games with my friends. As children we used to play the basic versions made available by Nintendo and similar companies. Then, a few years after college we started playing multiplayer video games such as Counter Strike and GTA in gaming arenas and arcades. I must say, it was a lot of fun.

23. Are there any drawbacks of playing video games?

Most video games these days have amazing graphics and audio effects. The game play is very smooth and realistic, as opposed to how it used to be in video games from 20 years ago. So, the entire gameplay experience is very engaging and engrossing. Most games are addictive and very time consuming, too. So, if an office going person starts playing video games too frequently, either his career, or his sleep cycle is likely to get hampered.

24. Do violent video games affect children negatively?

Yes, violent video games can affect children negatively. Because video games are highly engaging due to their high definition graphics and sounds, children may become too engrossed and lose touch with reality. After long hours of game play, their impressionable minds may not be able to tell the difference between the virtual world and the real world, and they may replicate the violent moves of the video game in real life. This is known as becoming desensitised to violence and it can prove quite dangerous.

25. Do you help with housework at home?

Yes, I help with housework at home whenever I'm free, which is usually over the weekends. On other days I do not get the time to help with any housework, so we rely on our house help, who has been with us for many years now.

26. Do you enjoy housework?

I enjoy housework, because it helps me feel relaxed. I think housework is very therapeutic. Some activities such as scrubbing and cleaning tend to be very mechanical, thereby acting as stress-busters. Other than that, I also enjoy tending to our home garden, running errands like buying groceries from the nearby store, and fixing anything in the house that needs to be repaired.

27. Do all your family members help with the housework?

In my house everyone helps out with the housework to the best of their capacities and abilities. In spite of having a paid house help, no one in the house shirks their own responsibilities, and helping each other or tending to the house has become second nature to everyone. In their own little way, all my family members help with cooking, cleaning, gardening, repairing, maintenance, and shopping.

28. Do you play indoor games in your free time?

Yes, I play indoor games in my free time with family members and friends. I enjoy playing table tennis, snooker, and a variety of board games that are intellectually stimulating. We play a lot of Scrabble, Monopoly, and Scotland Yard post dinner on weeknights, and on weekends.

29. Did you play a lot of indoor games as a child?

I played a few indoor games as a child, but from what I can recall, I was always more fond of playing outside around the block or in my housing colony with my friends. We preferred games that involved a lot of running around. So, more than indoor board games, I used to play hide and seek, and catch.

30. Do children these days prefer indoor games over outdoor games?

If digital games and video games qualify as indoor games, then I think children these days by far prefer playing indoor games. Rarely do I see children out in the evenings running around after school, squealing with glee the way we used to. Gone are the days of playing in the sand without a care in the world. Now, children like staying indoors and playing on their tablets or phones in air conditioned rooms.

31. Is it enough for children to play only indoor games?

I think indoor games are good, depending on what kinds of games are being played. Board games and intellectually stimulating puzzles are usually better indoor games than digital video games, in my opinion. That said; playing only indoor games and avoiding outdoor games is not the healthiest way to be, for children. I say this because indoor games provide hardly any fresh air or exercise to the muscles during the crucial growing age of children.

32. What kind of shoes do you wear on a daily basis?

I wear formal leather shoes to work on a daily basis. I have two pairs, one in black, and the other in brown. I can match these with my outfits and belts, very easily. When I'm at home I prefer wearing comfortable open-toe loafers. While going out for a casual visit to my friends' and relatives' homes, I put on a smart pair of sandals.

33. Are you fond of buying new shoes frequently?

I like window shopping for shoes more than actually purchasing them. I am a careful user of shoes, so once I buy a pair, they last me for a long time. Another reason my shoes don't wear out very fast is that I buy good quality footwear only, even if it is a little expensive. But, I like purchasing new shoes for my family, as gifts.

34. Which is the most outrageous pair of shoes you've seen to date?

The most outrageous pair of shoes I've seen to date is a hideous pair of transparent heels, whose frame was made entirely out of thin metal wire. Mind you, these shoes were completely see-through, and one could clearly see the wearer's foot squirming for space inside the uncomfortable frame. The heels were four inches tall, and also transparent. The shoes were made out of glass-finish toughened acrylic, and were exorbitantly priced.

35. Do you buy shoes online?

I don't buy my shoes online, but some of my colleagues and friends order theirs online. I have realised that I'm not usually comfortable purchasing shoes without trying them out. However, for those who are very sure about their size, online shopping opens up lots and lots of options when it comes to shoes. One can select from hundreds of brands, colours, patterns, and shapes from the comfort of their house. A lot of companies these days have a very sound exchange policy if sizes don't fit. This makes online shoe shopping a convenient choice.

36. What difficulties did you face at your first job interview?

I was a little nervous as it was my first interview. I knew nothing about the company and the field as a whole. Moreover, as it was a walk-in interview, many candidates appeared for it, which made me even more sceptical about my chances of selection. However, I performed well and I was short listed by the interviewing panel for a personal interview. Finally, after a few days of my interview, I got an appointment letter.

37. How should a candidate prepare himself in order to succeed in a job interview?

The first factor that ensures success is demeanour. The candidate must appear for an interview in a polite, yet confident manner, and in formal clothes. The second important factor is to collect information about the organisation, the demands of the job and the expectations of the employers. I think such preparations help the candidate to perform well at the interview.

38. Do you think employees should be paid more if they work on weekends?

I believe that employees should be paid more for weekend work, because they usually save weekends for themselves and to spend time with their families. This comfort is sacrificed when employees work on weekends, so they should be compensated by being paid higher wages.

39. Do you plan your work schedule?   OR
    What are the benefits of planning one's work schedule?
I always plan my work schedule as it helps me in managing my workload and increasing my efficiency. I use a planner in which I write down the tasks I have to take up every day. This helps me in prioritizing my work and keeps me more focused on the useful tasks of the day than on trivial matters.

40. What are the benefits of doing a business over a job?
Doing a business gives us the freedom to experiment, and explore new ideas. It also gives us the independence to manage our time, as we are not bound like employees. Moreover, a business offers tremendous growth opportunities to the owner. On the other hand, jobs offer security and a less stressful life because jobs give fixed salaries. Besides, people doing jobs can completely get detached from their work concerns after leaving their office for the day, which is not possible for business owners. Still, looking at the growth possibilities and freedom, I think one should always opt to do his own business.

41. How do people in your area spend their leisure (free) time?
It depends on the age group. Children prefer playing games and watching cartoons. Housewives prefer watching TV and heading out for window-shopping. Youngsters like roaming around with friends or going to cafeterias and discotheques. Old people like to visit gardens and temples to pass their free time.

42. Where and when do you prefer meeting people?
I prefer meeting people at home, at restaurants, at some shopping mall, or at a movie theatre where we can spend enough time with each other and simultaneously enjoy other activities offered by the place we are at.

43. How do you greet foreigners?
I greet foreigners by saying hello to them or shaking hands with them, because, I think we should greet people in the way they are used to.

44. Is there any government or non-government organisation that helps visitors or international tourists?
I know about a government organisation called 'Atithi Devo Bhava' that helps international visitors in my country. They help tourists in various ways, like with hotel bookings, sightseeing, providing local guides, facilitating currency exchange, and so on. I really appreciate this idea because by offering support to international visitors we can make their sojourn easier and enjoyable, which encourages them to visit our country again.

45. Why do you think people choose to be social workers?
I think the feeling of compassion for the less fortunate is the prime motive behind those who opt to become social workers. Those who have a loving heart, and compassion to help other people who are facing difficulties, generally choose to work for the betterment of the society.

46. What qualities are needed in a good social worker?
The first and the most important quality is compassion. In addition, qualities like hard work, honesty, politeness, courage, communication skills, and motivation are also required in a good social worker.

47. How can society and the government support social workers?

The government can support social workers by giving grants, land, and other privileges to them. Moreover, government can also give awards to honour them. On the other hand, as a society, we can donate money to social workers and offer our assistance in their work. This could make them feel like they are not alone in their work.

48. What is the importance of religion in our life?

Religion acts as a guideline for us to lead a good life. It is a manual that should be followed to gain eternal peace, satisfaction, and happiness in life.

49. Which society is better to live in? — A single-religion society or a multi-religious society? Why?

I think a multi-religious society is much better than a single-religion society, because people in multi-religious societies tend to have better acceptance of, and more tolerance for other religions and their customs. It is often observed in single-religion societies that people do not get a chance to explore other religions, belief-systems, and their specialties. Whereas, in multi-religious societies, people can learn about, accept, and adopt many customs from each other. Ultimately, every religion leads to one common goal, and that is 'salvation'.

50. Why do you think some people prefer to live as religious saints?

I think only a few people can really delve into the depths of religion and unravel the mysteries of the soul. This is probably why those who have uncovered these mysteries become saints and feel like they should reach out to the world and spread their message and learnings. To do this more effectively, they become messengers of God and religion.

51. What can we learn from religious/spiritual people?

We can learn many things from them. We can understand various aspects of our religion and our life, and can implement this understanding in our everyday living. For any problems that we may face in life, we can go to them and seek out a solution from a religious or spiritual perspective. They can be an important part of our lives.

52. Which language do you prefer to write in?

I prefer writing in English, because these days, a majority of written communication is carried out in English, only. In addition to this, in my occupation as well as in most other professions, English is the most preferred medium of communication. Hence, I do most of my written work in English. However, when required, I do write in my first language, and in my national language, also.

53. What do you like and dislike about writing in English?

I like many things about writing in English. First, English offers a large variety of words that can be used in different contexts. Secondly, it is internationally understood and accepted. Because of this widespread acceptance of the language, writing in English makes my communication fast and effective. There is nothing that I dislike about the English language. However, I have found that some people face difficulties in spelling words correctly and in writing with grammatical accuracy because of the complexity of the language.

54. Are birthdays important in our life?

Yes, birthdays are important because they reminds us when we came into this world, and help us keep a tab of how old we are. I think birthdays act as milestones in any individual's life.

55. At what age, according to you, should one celebrate his birthday, and why?

When a child starts going to school, aged 4–5 years, his birthday should be celebrated. This is because these are the years when children start making many friends in their neighbourhood and at school. So, with their many new friends, children can enjoy their birthday celebrations to the fullest. What's more, people should also celebrate their birthdays in their old age because these are the years in which they often feel lonely. Birthday celebrations can bring them the company of others on their special day and help them get back in touch with old contacts.

56. How should people celebrate their birthdays?

It varies from person to person. I think we should celebrate our birthdays with our family members, friends, and relatives. On top of this, according to me, each of us should help at least one needy person on our birthday, so that we may receive blessings from those that we help, for our lives.

57. What activities do children like to do on their birthdays?

The first thing that every child likes to do on his birthday is to cut a cake. Besides, children like to play different games with their friends. They also like to dance, sing, and take photographs on their birthdays. Lastly, they like giving out return gifts to their friends who come for their birthday celebrations.

58. What changes have you observed in the ways that birthdays are celebrated in your city, over time?

In the past, on their birthdays people used to visit temples where they sought blessings from God, and religious mentors. They preferred to eat traditional dishes at home with their close family members. These days, people go out to restaurants or hotels with their friends to enjoy good food. Youngsters often arrange dance parties where they dance to the tunes of a D.J.

59. Do you like to visit beaches/seashores?

Yes, I like visiting seashores because the climate there is fantastic. What's more, I live in a city that is far away from sea. So, I get to take a break of 2–3 days from work, when I decide to visit the seashore. This is an additional reason for me to go out to the beach and enjoy with my family.

60. At what time of the year do you prefer visiting beaches?

I prefer visiting beaches in winter because the climate on seashores stays warmer and more humid compared to other inland areas, where the atmosphere in winter is cold and dry.

61. If given a chance, would you like to live at the seashore? Why?

I would certainly like to live on the seashore, because I like the climate there. I also enjoy various physical activities like jogging, sunbathing, boating, swimming, and beach volley ball, which can be enjoyed better on seashores.

62. What types of TV programs are more popular in your city/country?

People in my city/country like to watch social, cultural, and comedy based programs. However, reality shows like 'KBC' and talent hunt shows like 'Indian Idol' and 'SaReGaMa' are also becoming immensely popular where I live.

63. What are the advantages and disadvantages of watching TV?

Television offers many benefits. We get local, national, and international news on television almost instantaneously. We can also watch live sports, and other important events on it. What's more, along with watching movies, we can enjoy numerous programs based on society, lifestyle, general knowledge, religion, history, and science and technology.

On the flipside, watching television is a passive activity. It doesn't refresh our minds. On the contrary, we feel fatigued and lazy when we watch TV shows for too long. Moreover, excessive TV-viewing is also harmful to our eyes. Lastly, owing to the availability of international satellite channels, selection of proper programs suitable for viewers of all ages has become a difficult task as some of the programs tend to have offensive or disturbing content that can have adverse effects on the minds of the viewers.

64. What is the difference between Hindi and English movies?

There is a vast difference between Hindi and English movies. They differ in length, theme, content, and use of technology. Hindi films are 140–170 minutes long as opposed to English movies, which are 100–120 minutes long. Hindi movies are based more on culture, society, religion, and love, whereas English movies are largely based on science, space, fiction, fantasy, and romance. Lastly, Hindi movies are often musical; we can see 4–5 songs in a single movie on screen, whereas most English movies do not have songs on screen.

65. When did you start to learn English?

I started learning English when I was in school. After leaving school, I took up my tertiary education in English, and even now, I keep updating myself on the latest developments in written and spoken English by reading books and by visiting English teaching websites.

66. Did you want any change in your school uniform?

My school uniform was a white half-sleeved shirt, a pair of navy blue trousers, and white canvas shoes. It was comfortable for all students, and I was also satisfied with it. So, I never wanted any changes in my school uniform.

67. Should uniforms be made compulsory in schools?

Uniforms must be made compulsory in schools. It makes students feel united and equal. This feeling of unity and equality is a very important factor in learning good values according to me, as it gives a sense of equality in students' minds. It also helps them in interacting with each other in a better, more efficient manner.

68. According to you, which is better, school life or college life? Why?

Well, both have their own peculiarities, pros, and cons. But to me, college life felt much better, because at college we come out of the innocent world of school and enter the more practical, real world. College is where we learn the basics of conducting ourselves in our social, professional, and practical lives.

69. Which are the meeting places of teenagers in your city?

Teenagers in my city meet at restaurants, fast food joints, shopping malls, multiplexes, game parlours, and discotheques. Teenagers are attracted to the lively, youthful, and vibrant ambiences of such places.

70. How is a library useful to teenagers?

A library can be extremely useful to teenagers. They can read books on various subjects of their interest and satisfy their thirst for knowledge, which helps them in improving their academic performance. Moreover, they can also develop different aspects of their personalities by reading self-help books.

71. How would you collect funds for establishing and running a library?

There are numerous ways of collecting funds for setting up a library. We can go to big business houses or industrialists and persuade them to donate money for the library. We can also run campaigns in newspapers, radios and on television to urge people to donate generously. Lastly, we can request the government to fund the library, and once it is established we can request existing members of the library to support the funding program as best as they can.

72. What qualities or skills are required to become a good librarian?

The job of a librarian is interesting and demanding. A librarian must have very sound knowledge of all the titles of books, and the names of their authors which are available in the library. Further, he should be able to use the index system efficiently so that book utilization can reach and remain at optimum levels. Also, he should look for new titles which are released in the market from time to time, so that he can add those titles to his library. Lastly, he should be a good communicator so that his communication skills can inspire and encourage other people to use the library more often.

73. If given a chance, would you like to work as a librarian?

It is an interesting job. I think, if given a chance, I would certainly work for a library as a librarian. This will prove beneficial to me. To begin with, it will enable me to, stay abreast with the latest trends in the field of writing and publication. Secondly, I can stay in touch with many readers of various interests and age groups. Lastly, I will get excellent exposure to a vast number of books with which to quench my thirst for reading.

74. How should the student–teacher relationship be?

I think student–teacher relationship must be friendly and interactive. It is very important for both to understand each other to ensure smoothness in the learning process. If the student-teacher relationship is distant, learning becomes difficult and disturbed, and does not give students desirable academic results. I strongly believe that teachers who avoid, insult, or humiliate their students are doing injustice to the students, as well as to their occupation, because by staying inaccessible or unapproachable to students, no teacher in this world can teach efficiently.

75. Why do people visit gardens?

People visit gardens for a variety of purposes. In the morning, many people go to gardens for morning walks and for participating in laughing clubs. Children visit gardens for playing games, and elders go to gardens to pass their time with other people of similar age groups. We can also see sales and marketing executives arrange their on-field meetings in public gardens.

76. Do you like flowers?

Yes, I like almost all flowers; roses, sunflowers, carnations, and many other exotic flowers, because of their fragrances, vibrant colours, and refreshing appearances.

77. Do you give flowers to other people? If yes, when do you give flowers to others?

I give flowers to people I know on various occasions, like marriage ceremonies, inauguration events, and house warming parties, or when I visit someone who is admitted in a hospital. Moreover, I also give flowers to my friends and family members when they have exams, important interviews, or crucial meetings. At times I also give flowers to loved ones without any reason whatsoever, just to express my gratitude or affection for them.

78. What is the difference between an urban and a rural area?

There are many differences between urban and rural areas. They differ in size, infrastructure, available facilities, and climate. Cities are bigger compared to villages in terms of area. They have wider roads, flyovers, multi-storeyed complexes, and shopping malls, whereas old houses, narrow roads, and natural landscapes are usually found more often in rural areas. Lastly, the atmosphere in urban areas is more polluted and much noisier compared to the cleaner, healthier, natural, and more peaceful atmosphere in villages.

79. What are the advantages and disadvantages of living in an urban area and in a rural area?

Urban areas offer better facilities like continuous water supply, electricity, drainage, transport, and prompt health services. Moreover, cities also offer more employment opportunities and better quality educational institutions. However, urban life is faster, more stressful, and more affected by environmental pollution.

Rural areas have fewer facilities in terms of health, transport, employment, and education. But, people in these areas live in unity and warmth. What's more, the climate is also pleasant and pollution-free, and life is less stressful.

80. How do urban people perceive those living in the countryside?

I think people living in urban areas often perceive rural people as incompetent and rustic. They think people in rural areas do not live as privileged a life as themselves, and so more people are shifting from villages to cities. However, not all those who live in urban areas have these perceptions. Many city dwellers respect rural people and often help them settle in when they come to cities.

81. What are the consequences of more people migrating to cities from villages?

Large-scale migration of people from villages to cities is likely to cause an imbalance in both regions. As more people start to live in select small areas, they need more food, water, and shelter. This usually puts an extra load on the existing urban supply systems and causes cities to expand in unorganised patterns. Simultaneously, villages from which people migrate out, start regressing further, bringing in a huge disparity between urban and rural areas.

82. What should be done to prevent the migration of people from villages to cities?

The government must take active interest in this issue. It should provide all the facilities that cities have, to the villages, also. This includes continuous clean water supply, drainage, electricity, transport, road networks, hospitals, and quality education. When people start getting all these facilities in their villages, they will not migrate to cities. Only after this, can the fruits of national economic development reach every part of our country.

83. Why do people want to study/settle in other countries?

There are many reasons for which people want to study or settle overseas. In the field of education, I can say that some specialisation courses in management, science, and technology are taught better in foreign universities. Moreover, foreign education gives international exposure to the students, which helps them when they start their professional lives. Lastly, some countries like Australia offer options to overseas students to settle there. In case of immigrants other than students, I think they may want to take advantage of the stronger economies in some foreign countries, to increase their income and to improve their standard of living. Moreover, some countries offer open immigration to skilled people and they also offer benefits such as free education, medical aid, and unemployment allowances to citizens, which may not be available in the home countries of most immigrants.

84. What are the effects on host countries of many people going to study/settle there?

The host countries certainly enjoy major boosts in their education industry and related segments, because most universities charge higher fees from international students as compared to domestic students. The study environment of the country becomes more heterogenic, diverse, and competitive, thereby enhancing the education level of all students. In case of non-academic immigration, host countries receive skilled workers who help their economy grow more. Besides, host countries can also benefit from the cultures of the new people that come in. This ultimately helps in building a cosmopolitan, tolerant environment. However, a heavy influx of immigrants and students may affect the local job market negatively. Consequently, local people of the host country may face unemployment.

85. What are the effects on the country from which people go to study/settle in other countries?

There are many negative effects of this phenomenon of emigration. Firstly, the people who go to foreign countries to study pay high fees in foreign currencies, causing a net revenue loss for their home country because this is a non-recoverable, one way expense. Additionally, it is a well-known fact that skilled workers are needed everywhere. So, if skilled workers from one country migrate out, the economic growth of the home country often gets affected adversely.

86. Will this trend continue in the future as well?

I think the trend will certainly continue because everyone wants to lead a better life that offers social status, luxury, and security. In many countries of the world, such a life is not available, so those who are skilled and capable of migrating out will likely do so. Besides, the need for economic growth will also cause many developed countries to woo skilled people from developing or underdeveloped countries. So, from where I can see, this trend is here to stay.

87. When does rainy season start in your country?

Rainy season usually starts in the last week of May or the first week of June in southern India, and then spreads to other parts of my country.

88. Do you enjoy the rains or not?

I like the rains a lot. I like to go out when it rains. The climate becomes pleasant and soothing. I like to get wet in rain and feel the sensations of the raindrops on my face. All the trees, plants, buildings, and roads look new and fresh after a rainfall. I also enjoy going out with my family members to eat roasted corn and other traditional deep-fried dishes such as samosas and lentil fritters.

89. What do you feel at the end of rainy season?

I really miss the rains at the end of the season. So, I usually try not to miss any opportunity to step out and enjoy myself when it rains. However, on the flipside, the climate often becomes uncomfortable for most animals, and epidemics spread faster at the end of rainy season. Even so, I look forward to the onset of the next monsoon.

90. What is the difference between the rains in your city, in the past and now?

The intensity and consistency of rainfall has changed a lot now, compared to the past. These days we get ten to fifteen inches of rainfall in just two to three days, compared to the past when we used to receive consistent rainfall over many months of the entire rainy season. Moreover, the places which earlier used to get scarce rainfall now get high or average rains, and some of the areas where the rainfall used to be heavy earlier, now get average or below-average rains.

91. What factors affect the rainy season?

There are quite a few factors that affect the rainy season. One of them is environmental pollution. The cloud formation and condensation processes are affected by both, pollution in the atmosphere, and global warming caused by higher carbon emissions in the air. Over the years these emissions have increased substantially as a result of industrialisation and burning of fossil fuels. These factors disturb the weather cycles of many regions. Consequently, we have less rainfall in the rainy season and unexpected rains in the winter and summer.

92. What is the importance of the rainy season in your country?

Rains have great importance in my country. India is traditionally known as an agricultural country, yet, the irrigation system is not completely developed here. While I admit that other industries are also contributing to the economic growth of my country, the major proportion of population in my country is still dependent on farming and associated industries, even today. Apart from this, the population of India is also very high, thus calling for higher amounts of drinking water. Because of these reasons, the rainy season is of prime importance in my country.

93. What developments in agriculture have you observed in your country?

I have observed immense changes in the field of agriculture in my nation. Irrigation facilities have now come to cover most of the farmlands in my country. The government has started counselling farmers about the types of crops suitable for their land, and providing better quality seeds, fertilisers, and pesticides. Because of all these factors, we now get improved product yield as compared to a few decades ago. This helps in meeting the increasing food demands of our country better than before.

94. How can fertilisers be harmful to us?

Fertilisers can be harmful to us in many ways. If used excessively, they may mutate the composition of crops or contaminate them. Such crops, when eaten, can lead to serious diseases or disorders in humans and animals. Further, excessive use of fertilisers have a harmful effect on the soil. The soil may, over time, lose its natural fertility and in turn be rendered incapable of providing a good yield.

95. How can we prevent negative effects of fertilisers?

Moderation is key here. Farmers should avoid excessive use of chemical fertilisers, replacing them instead with natural alternatives like animal manure and compost. Moreover, governments can also ban harmful fertilisers and guide farmers to use natural fertilisers to increase their crop yield and to maintain soil health.

96. Why do people use so much plastic?

People use plastic because it offers many advantages. It is light, cheap, stable, and waterproof. All these qualities of plastic make it a preferred choice for packaging and for making an array of everyday objects ranging from a small from pen to heavy-duty furniture.

97. Are there any disadvantages of using plastics?

There are some long-term disadvantages of using plastics. They are non-biodegradable and they do not permit the exchange of air and water molecules through their surface. Now, as plastic doesn't decay naturally, it doesn't allow plant-life to sustain on the land where it is dumped as waste. This can affect the natural ecological cycle (food chain) of that area, which can lead to large-scale deterioration of the environment in extreme cases.

98. What are the causes of overpopulation?

There are three prime reasons behind overpopulation. The first is a lack of education. Uneducated people don't pay attention to family planning because they cannot understand the long-term effects of overpopulation on economy and environment. The second is poverty. Contrary to what we believe, the uneducated poor classes, feel that there should be more members in their families so that more people can earn and contribute to the income pool. The third is cultural conditioning. In many countries, it is a tradition to have more children per family. As this tradition is embedded in religious beliefs, it is hard for them to adopt family planning.

99. What are the consequences of overpopulation?

Overpopulation has frightening consequences for both, the earth and the society. It can inhibit the economic growth because governments of overpopulated nations have to spend a big chunk of revenue for satisfying the basic needs of their people, such as healthcare, food, water, and education. Next, many people remain unemployed in overpopulated regions due to a lack of available jobs. This often leads to a rise in crime rates in those regions. In my opinion overpopulation is a curse.

100. What are the consequences of riots on individuals and society?

It is well-known that common and poor people suffer most from riots. They lose their wealth, homes, and sometimes even their lives. What's more, victims of riots live a disturbed, traumatised life, which can influence their future generations negatively. This increases passive feelings of rivalry between different groups of society that may then explode into new riots even at the hint of a small conflict. On top of it, riot sensitive areas can never witness economic growth because big companies, investors, and even government bodies stay away from investing their money in the development of such areas.

101. What factors are responsible for the occurrence of riots?

I think the main reason for the outburst of riots is the spread of rumours. In sensitive situations, gaps in communication among people are often observed. These gaps make way for rumours and infuriate people, thus instigating violence. Moreover, I think the media is also accountable to some extent, because they keep showing images and recordings of the sufferers. Such footage reminds people from the suffering community of the atrocities they have been through, which in turn hurts them and influences them to extract revenge.

102. Do you think noise disturbs a person?

It is certainly true that noise can disturb people. Noise actually distracts our minds and doesn't allow us to concentrate on our work, which leads to irritation. As a result, the disturbance gets further magnified.

103. Do you think that noise pollution is increasing in the world?

Yes, noise levels are mounting in many parts of the world. Noise occurs in various forms at public places, like the sound of people talking loudly to each other, the sound of traffic and horns on roads, ad campaigns in the form of road shows. In addition, the increasing number of air planes also adds to the noise levels.

104. Why are birds important in life?

Birds are an important creation of nature. Their importance can only be understood by those who know the importance of nature. They are an integral part of our ecosystem. They eat small insects and reptiles, and by doing so, they help in maintaining a healthy and disease free environment.

105. What should people do to save birds?

First and foremost, we should stop killing birds for their meat, feathers, or nails. In addition, we should also stop others who are engaged in such activities, by informing appropriate government authorities about their operations.

106. What are the harmful effects of smoking?

Smoking is harmful to our health in a number ways. Smoke weakens the muscles of our respiratory system, which affects our breathing process. With prolonged use, smoking can cause cancer in smokers. Moreover, it can lead to impotence in males, and can cause health problems for pregnant women by inhibiting the normal growth of the baby in the womb.

107. Should the government ban tobacco products? Why?

I strongly favour banning of tobacco products. The government must ban all types of tobacco products. This will bring long-term benefits to the country. We will lead a healthier and more efficient life without tobacco. Some people argue that the government earns revenues in the form of direct and indirect taxes on tobacco products. However, the government also has to spend huge sums of money for the treatment of cancer patients.

108. Should celebrities endorse tobacco and alcohol products? Justify your answer.

I don't agree with celebrities endorsing tobacco and liquor products, because celebrities are role models for teenagers and youngsters. The youth is likely to get influenced by celebrity endorsements, as youngsters are sometimes unable to differentiate the good from the bad. I also assert that celebrities have some moral responsibility towards the society. Keeping this in mind, they should not misuse their popularity for money, by promoting harmful products.

109. How do people get into the habit of doing drugs and smoking?

Teenagers and youngsters take up smoking as a thrilling experience. They often try cigarette smoking or narcotics to quench their curiosity. However, many of them then get addicted to these substances. Working professionals take up cigarette smoking for a change or break from their work routine, in the beginning. Later though, in most cases they get addicted to it.

110. How should a neighbour be?

A neighbour should be friendly, cooperative, compassionate, and honest. His attitude towards others should be to live and let live. On top of it, a neighbour should not interfere in others' family lives or personal lives. We cannot enjoy spending time in our neighbourhood if our neighbours don't have such qualities.

111. How can you know what attitude your neighbours carry towards you?

As I said, their attitude should be to live and let live. We can judge their approach by observing their behaviour towards us. If a neighbour seems interested in borrowing things from our house all the time, or is too interested in our personal life, or turns away when we need help, we may assume that he is not a good neighbour. We should maintain a safe distance from such people.

112. When can neighbours be helpful?

It is said in my culture that neighbours are our first relatives. Our neighbours can be helpful to us in many areas of life. For instance, in case of emergencies like accidents, thefts, or illnesses, neighbours can be the best help because they can reach our house within seconds.

113. What type of problems might you face from your neighbours?

There are many problems that we might face from our neighbours. One of them is interference in our family matters. They often try to pry into what is happening in the lives of our family members by peeping in, or by visiting our homes on the pretext of resolving trivial issues. Apart from this, they may harass others by making too much noise, spreading rumours about people, or by throwing their garbage in others' compounds.

114. Are you punctual?

I always try to be on time for all my meetings and commitments. Whenever I feel that I am unable to reach somewhere on time, I always inform the concerned person about the reason, apologize to him, and request him for possible options to meet later.

115. What do you feel when someone doesn't remain punctual?

I don't like it if someone doesn't remain punctual. However, I don't get irritated or angry at them for it. I try to contact the concerned person to find out the reason for the delay, and I manage my spare time with some other work.

116. What factors can affect people in being punctual?

There are many reasons that may affect the punctuality of people. They might get caught up in traffic jams or their vehicles could break down. Some unavoidable work or emergency could crop up, too. I can list down many possible reasons for getting late. However, I feel that if we are unable to keep time, we must contact the person who is waiting for us and inform him about the situation, so that he can utilize his time for some other work.

117. Do you think that the new generation ignores elders?

In some cultures or in some families it is seen that youngsters ignore old people. I think such behaviour in youngsters is a reflection of the kind of behaviour they may have seen in the past, coming from their parents and influencers, when they were younger. However, this is not true for most families and cultures in my country.

118. What do today's youngsters expect from their elders?

Today's youth needs guidance in fulfilling their dreams in life. They are zealous and diligent in their approach, but they sometimes lack experience and self-motivation in the process of goal achievement. Here, they seek constructive support from elders, who are expected to direct them on the right path to success.

119. How important is it to study and understand the history of our country?

History informs us about the culture, lifestyle, religion, technology, and art that existed in bygone eras of the past. It is a legacy of humans through the ages, which we should all be aware of. Moreover, the study of history also prevents present generations from repeating past mistakes.

120. What are the leading industries in your country?

Before a few years, India was largely known as an agrarian country. However, in the last few years, other industries have flourished in India. Industries like automobiles, auto ancillaries, cement, steel, chemicals, pharmaceuticals, sugar, textiles, petrochemicals, fashion, entertainment, education, and hospitality are contributing to the economic growth of India. But, one sector has really outperformed the others in the last few years. That sector is Information Technology. It has supported other emerging segments like BPO (Business Process Outsourcing), KPO (Knowledge Process Outsourcing), and customer service call centres. All these fields are showing skyrocketing growth in their earnings. Their contribution to the GDP (Gross Domestic Product) is increasing year after year. It is now believed that India could become a global technology hub in the near future.

121. Should industries be globalized?

Yes, industries ought to be globalized. There are lots of benefits of this. First, industries can target international consumers, which in turn will enhance the profitability of the company. Secondly, the understanding of the management about various trends in international markets will also increase, enabling them to enhance the quality of their products, thereby also helping their domestic customers. Lastly, international exposure always enhances the reputation of the industry and attracts foreign investments, enabling companies to pay more taxes. This increases the national revenues, and also capacitates companies to pay more dividends to their shareholders. In short, it is a win-win situation for both, the domestic consumers and the companies, if industries become globalized.

122. How can we develop the economy of India?

The economy of India is already developing with a cumulative GDP growth of around 9% per annum, which is higher than that of most developed countries. Still, a few necessary steps need to be taken to develop further. The government should develop the infrastructure in all regions of the country. This can be done by developing road, rail, and air transport networks throughout the country. Next, electricity, potable water, irrigation, and telephone services must be made available in every corner of the country. Last, government must provide education to people, because only educated people can help the economy to grow at a better and more sustainable rate than this.

123. What are the consequences of unemployment?

Unemployment is the cause of many problems. Because of unemployment, people become dissatisfied with the government, and may turn towards illegal activities to earn money. This situation can give birth to terrorism in extreme cases. What's more, unemployment disturbs the communal harmony among different sects in society. To top it, skilled people start migrating towards better countries. This process is called brain drain, and it is very harmful to any country.

124. Do you keep goals in your mind for the future?

I prefer keeping short-term goals of 1 to 2 years in mind. I don't believe in long-term goals of 10 or 12 years. I have found that keeping short-term goals gives me a stress free, flexible, and practical approach to my work, which ultimately increases my efficiency.

125. How do you define happiness?

To give a universal definition of happiness is next to impossible, because the perception of happiness is different for different people. I think it is a reaction of one's mind to an external situation, based on the inner condition of one's thoughts and feelings. In this sense happiness is a momentary response, because as we all know, any reaction of the mind cannot sustain for longer than a moment. To me, happiness is a part of our consciousness. We should try to search for it within, not outside.

126. How can a person remain happy in life forever?

It is impossible to remain constantly happy through one's entire lifetime, if the consideration is based on the general perceptions of happiness that we carry. This is because, happiness is only a momentary reaction. However, happiness can be transformed from a mode of reaction, to a state of being. This state of being happy can then be extended to eternity. For example, a flower gives its fragrance to its surroundings till it withers. It is fragrant in itself, without caring about the external world and its opinions. Happiness as a state of being is similar. One needs to be happy within themselves irrespective of the opinions of others, and by adopting a non-judgmental approach to the events of life.

127. Do you think money brings happiness in your life?

Money brings comfort, luxury, social status, a sense of security, and psychological gratification in life. If someone associates such things with happiness, then from his standpoint, money brings happiness in life. However, I personally don't associate money with happiness, so I don't agree with this notion.

128. How can a person balance his job and social life?

The best way to balance one's job and social life is to learn to prioritise tasks and to be fully involved in each action, while performing it. Sometimes we see people carry their social lives to their work places, and worrying about work while socialising, thus disrupting both. We should learn to prioritise our work over our social life when required, and vice versa. By doing so, we can easily balance both.

129. How do you help with household work?

I often help my family with household work. I help in doing odd jobs around the house, such as maintaining and repairing equipment, arranging cupboards, going to the bank, and paying utility bills for the telephone and for electricity. I also take care of the vehicles at my home by taking them to their service centres, inflating tyres, and refuelling. I also teach my child a few school subjects and reduce my wife's workload.

130. What is the difference between the present leaders and the past leaders?

There is a vast difference between the present leaders and the past leaders. Leaders of the past adopted the right principles in their lives and remained loyal to those principles throughout their lives. They even sacrificed personal and financial benefits to follow their moral values. In comparison, most present day leaders adopt exactly the opposite strategy. They first attract people towards themselves by claiming to be staunch followers of moral values and portraying themselves as being dedicated to the countrymen. Then, when they achieve political heights, they don't hesitate to compromise on those morals to derive personal benefits.

131. What are the advantages and disadvantages of becoming popular?

The benefits of becoming famous include social status, recognition, money, power, influence, and respect in the society. Popular personalities may have many fans or followers. However, such personalities often have to sacrifice their individuality and privacy. This is because they are constantly under pressure to maintain their public image in society. For this they often have to do things against their personal wish to sustain their popularity by upholding the expectations of their fans. In short, popular people have to live their lives bearing the burden of maintaining their public image.

132. If given a chance to meet a famous personality, who would you meet, and why?
It has to be Mr. Amitabh Bachchan. I want to meet him and talk to him about his past career experiences in times of crises. I think he is one of those rare celebrities who can transform themselves with time, ageing gracefully, and yet remaining at the top. To me, he is not only an actor, but also a legend.

133. What is capital punishment? Is capital punishment useful in controlling crime?
Capital punishment is the same as a death sentence. To some extent, it is useful in controlling crime because it instils the fear of death in people, which is a major motive to avoid committing crimes.

134. Compare the old buildings in your city with the new buildings.
Buildings in the past were small, low-rise structures compared to the high-rises of the present with their big blocks, and many wings. In the past buildings were more spacious with better natural lighting and air circulation than the new ones. In contrast, though, the new buildings in my city depict better space utilization. Here, natural lighting and air circulation are often ignored because of the availability of electricity and air conditioning. Moreover, buildings in the past were made up of limestone, sand, and wood whereas modern buildings are made up of RCC (Reinforced Cement Concrete), cement, and steel. Lastly, in the past, people used wooden and stone carvings to decorate buildings, but now builders use glass, aluminium, and other fabricated materials for the same purpose.

135. What are the benefits of prayers?
The best advantage we can derive from offering prayers is relaxation. When we pray, all our thoughts are directed towards the process of praying. This takes our focus away from our daily tensions, stresses, and worries, and brings calmness and relaxation to our minds. The experience of praying can prove helpful when it comes to resolving difficult situations in life, because during and after prayers, we can assess situations with better mind sets and from different viewpoints. In addition, prayers set positive energy fields around us, which help us in staying strong and connected to our intuition, in turn helping us discover the best possible ways to lead better lives.

136. Is there any difference between the ways in which people prayed in the past, when compared to the present?
In the past most people offered prayers as per their religious scriptures. They would sing and recite hymns scripted by poets of yore, in temples or in groups. People these days do still use such methods, but I also see many devotees making silent, individual prayers instead of singing and chanting out loud. They may utter some words aloud, but those are their own; not from any scriptures.

137. People often pray for others. How helpful is this according to you?
Praying for others is always good for all the individuals involved. Those who pray for others feel a sense of fulfilment and satisfaction in their minds. On the other hand, the

people for whom prayers are being offered feel strong, contented, and cared for. Thus, when prayers are offered for others, they forge and strengthen the bonds in relationships between people.

138. Should we make prayers compulsory in schools and colleges?

It is necessary for students to remain calm and silent, and to channelise their energies to the higher power that we call God, for some time during their day. Prayer is useful in connecting students with their inner peace. This promotes virtues like maturity, responsibility, compassion, and honesty in students. So, it should be made compulsory for students to offer prayers at the beginning of each day.

139. Should we make singing the national anthem compulsory in schools and colleges?

Yes, we should make singing our national anthem compulsory in schools and colleges. When students sing the national anthem, they are reminded of the importance of their nation, its greatness, their heritage, and their duties towards it. I think regularly chanting the national anthem stirs and strengthens patriotic emotions in students, too.

140. Do you think we will have a terrorism-free society?

Looking at the present scenario, this notion appears too optimistic. But nothing in this world is impossible. I believe, when we have religious, economic, and racial harmony in the world, we will have a terrorism-free society, because when living in a world of equality, there will be nothing for which people would need to kill others.

141. What are the advantages and disadvantages of space research?

Space research is the quest to find out the mysteries of our universe. Space research gives us information about other planets, stars, and galaxies. It also helps us in protecting our people by evacuating and relocating them on time when threats like comets and asteroids are identified. On the other hand, it is expensive, time consuming, and futile at times. Space exploration consumes valuable non-renewable fuel resources of the earth. This is the reason some people argue that rather than wasting money on space research, we should use the funds for the betterment of the poor and the needy of our own planet.

142. If given a chance, would you like to travel in space? Why?

I would definitely take the opportunity. Since I was a child, I have longed to see how the earth looks from outer space. Moreover, I would also be able to see other planets and stars more closely while traveling in space. This feeling itself is likely to be very exciting; this trip to outer space could prove to be an experience of a lifetime for me.

143. Do you think one day we will be able to live on Mars or on the Moon?

It is difficult for me to make such a prediction because to date, no evidence of life on Mars or on the Moon have been found. But, going by the way science and technology are progressing, the chances of scientists finding ways for humans to inhabit other planets, appear bright.

144. Did you visit any art exhibition or museum when you were a child?

Yes, I visited a few museums and art exhibitions when I was in school. I had some interest in art and history back then, so I always participated in such visits organised by my school. I also made it a point to observe art works of my schoolmates that were displayed in my school.

145. How useful is it for children to visit such places?

It is immensely useful that children visit such places. To me, those who have even a little interest in art and history, should visit art exhibitions and museums. This might increase their interest towards the arts in general, and it could motivate them to bring out their hidden talents and show them to the world.

146. Is bicycle riding safe in your city?

Bicycle riding is reasonably safe in my city. There are thousands of people who use bicycles to travel from one place to another in my city, and they do so happily. Sometimes I read about bicycle riders meeting with accidents or mishaps in the newspaper, but all in all bicycle riding is quite safe where I come from.

147. What kinds of people ride bicycles in your city?

People of all age groups ride bicycles in my city. School children use them to go to their schools. Youngsters use bicycles to reach their workplaces, and often, for daily physical exercise to stay fit. Middle aged and old people also ride bicycles for similar reasons where I stay.

148. What changes have you seen in bicycles in the last few years?

Bicycles have become fancier and more rider-friendly in the last few years. We can see bicycles available today in all frame sizes and wheel sizes, with many speed gears, and we also get to see variants with tubeless tyres. Many other attractive features such as GPS devices and fitness trackers are also included in bicycles to attract more people towards riding them.

149. Do you think there should be separate tracks for bicycles on roads?

It is indeed a great idea. Many countries in Europe have done this. We should have separate tracks for bicycles on roads in order to provide safety to riders, and to encourage more people to ride bicycles. This also facilitates our environment, because if more people use bicycles, human transportation will cause lesser pollution, thus safeguarding the earth against the negative effects of global warming.

150. Why is it preferred that children ride bicycles?

Children love riding bicycles because it is the first step in their lives towards learning how to ride a vehicle. Additionally riding a bicycle is safer than most motorised vehicles, and also convenient for short distances. To top it, children are not licensed by the government to drive any motor vehicle until they reach a certain age and clear the driving standards. These are the reasons why bicycles are the preferred choice for children.

151. Why do some people buy farm houses?

People buy farm houses to enjoy leisurely weekends or holidays on their own property, in their own way. Farm houses are usually away from cities. They offer views of the countryside, along with a pollution free atmosphere, thereby promoting peace of mind when visited. Some people use farmhouses for recreation, some use them for pursuing their hobbies, some use the setting to relax by themselves, while others use farmhouses to spend quality time with their family members.

152. Is this a new trend or an old one?

This trend is very old. The difference is that earlier only royals and aristocrats bought farm houses for their recreation and relaxation because transportation to distant farmhouse locations was not very good or secure in the olden days. However, these days, faster and safer transportation systems allow more people of varying income groups to buy farm houses and visit them for leisure.

153. What are the possible disadvantages of buying a farm house?

Buying a farm house does have some disadvantages. First, they are expensive to buy or build. Secondly, they need to be maintained regularly just like regular houses. For this, we have to spend some more to hire trustworthy staff to maintain the house in our absence.

154. If given a chance, where would you buy a farm house?

I would certainly buy a farm house if I get the opportunity. I like the idea of living in the countryside, in a noise-free and pollution-free area, where I can seek closeness with nature. I think in the near future, I will be able to buy a good farm house for myself.

155. Some people keep an aquarium (fish-tank) in their house. Why do they do this and do you think it is good or bad?

In my view, there are two main reasons behind keeping an aquarium in the house. First, some people have a hobby of keeping colourful fish in an aquarium, and tending to them, to enhance the beauty of their house. Second, according to some ancient beliefs, fish are considered holy and capable of enhancing prosperity. It is also believed that when a fish dies in an aquarium, it takes away any impending danger on the household upon itself and saves the owners from mishaps.

156. Many people follow various ancient systems like Feng Shui or Vaastu. Do you agree with these beliefs?

The extent to which these systems are followed depends a lot on the beliefs of the people who follow them. However, I don't deny the underlying science behind both the systems of architecture and home decoration. They are based on the principles of energy movement in a space, and they outline ways to determine the good and bad consequences of different kinds of energy movements, according to the interior and exterior arrangements of a structure. We could make certain changes in the interiors of our house or office in order to make the structure compliant with the guidelines given by these systems.

157. Is it true that the populations of some countries are happier than those of other countries?

It depends on the criteria used for the consideration. If we consider wealth as the criteria for happiness, some countries like the US and the UK will be ranked happier than developing countries. However, if we consider other more qualitative criteria like family and social bonding, religious beliefs, and spiritual and yogic advancement, then some eastern countries may have an upper hand on the west. So, it may be true that the populations of some countries may be happier than others, varying based on the criteria considered to measure happiness.

158. What is the case with the population of your home country?

In my view, the population of my country is very happy if I consider religious, social, spiritual, and yogic advancement, because India is the pioneer for many spiritual, religious, and yogic movements, which were intended to uplift the spiritual consciousness of people. Many people in my country follow the procedures and guidelines given in these ancient scriptures and they do find much satisfaction in their lives.

Practice Questions for Part 1 of IELTS Speaking

1. Could you tell me your name? (Or) By what name can I call you?
2. What do you do at present?
3. What are your academic qualifications?
4. What are your future plans?
5. Why are you taking the IELTS?
6. To which country do you plan to go?
7. Why have you selected that country?
8. Which course are you going to study there? (For academic students only)
9. Why have you selected that course? (For academic students only)
10. How will your future plans help you and your family?
11. How will your qualification help you in your future?
12. Where have you studied? (Or) Where do you study at present?
13. How good is the place where you currently study or have studied?
14. Where do you work presently?
15. Why have you chosen that job?
16. How did you get that job?
17. How helpful is your education in your present job?
18. What are the products or services offered by your company?
19. How many hours a day do you work?
20. What are your job responsibilities?
21. What skills are demanded by your job?
22. Are you satisfied with your job? (Or) Would you like to change your job if given a chance? Justify your answer.
23. Can you describe your routine?
24. What are your hobbies?
25. How did you take up your hobby?
26. Who motivated you to take up your hobby?
27. Do you use a camera?
28. Where can you use your camera?
29. Do you like to meet people?
30. Do you meet foreigners in your area? (Or) Where can you meet foreigners in your city?
31. Do you do any social work?
32. How do you feel when you do some social work?

33. Is there any government or non-government organisation that handles social work near you?

34. Give your opinion — can an individual do social work better or can an organisation do it better? Why?

35. Do you have any experience working with a social worker?

36. What are the advantages and disadvantages of a single religion/a multi religious society?

37. Do you have any experience with a religious/spiritual saint?

38. Tell me something about the latest news that you read or heard.

39. Do you like cooking?

40. Who cooks food at your home?

41. From whom have you learnt cooking?

42. What food items do you like to cook?

43. Could you describe your typical traditional food dish?

44. Which meal is more important to you — lunch or dinner? Why?

45. Do you write anything?

46. What kind of writing do you do?

47. What are the benefits of writing?

48. How often do you go to eat at restaurants?

49. Do you like to visit parks or amusement parks? Why?

50. When do you like to visit a park?

51. Describe your last visit to a park or an amusement park.

52. What activities do you/people do in a park?

53. Why do children like to visit amusement parks more?

54. Do you celebrate birthdays?

55. What do you prefer — celebrating birthdays with friends or with family members? Why?

56. How much should a person spend on birthdays?

57. Are you fond of travelling?

58. What type of places do you prefer to visit?

59. Describe your last travel/excursion.

60. How often do you visit seashores?

61. What do you feel when you visit seashores?

62. What activities do people/you do at beaches?

63. Do you like to watch movies? What type of movies do you watch?

64. Which language do you speak generally?

The Ultimate Guide to IELTS Speaking by Parthesh Thakkar

65. Did you wear a uniform to school?
66. Do you think uniforms should be made compulsory for all days of the week in schools?
67. What were the main subjects that you studied in your school/college?
68. Could you describe your college life?
69. What were the meeting places of teenagers in the past?
70. Is your city good for youngsters?
71. Where did people in the past meet each other?
72. Is there a garden near your area?
73. How often do you visit it?
74. What do you do there?
75. Do people give flowers to each other on festivals?
76. Which flower is used more in your country?
77. How often do you visit your native place?
78. How is the life of people there?
79. Where do you prefer to live — in a city, or in a town/village? Why?
80. How is today's life different from that of the past?
81. Which lifestyle is better — the one which your grandfather had or the one which you have? Why?
82. How will your children's lifestyles be different from yours?
83. Why do people use so much plastic?
84. How can we solve the problem created by the usage of plastics?
85. What should the governments do to stop riots?
86. Do you often come across places that are noisy?
87. Can you show me the direction to your home from here?
88. How can we prevent the harmful effects of smoking?
89. Is marrying necessary in life?
90. What difficulties can an unmarried individual face at later stages in life?
91. Which is better according to you — a love marriage or an arranged marriage? Why?
92. Do you like having visitors/guests at your home?
93. How do you greet guests/visitors at your home?
94. What places in your city can you show to a domestic/foreign visitor?
95. How often do you visit your relatives?
96. How often do you meet your neighbours?
97. What is the difference between a neighbour and a friend?
98. What do elders expect from the young generation?

99. What are the effects of TV on the new generation?

100. What does success mean to you? (Or) Can you define success?

101. How do you plan to achieve your goals?

102. How/why do famous people impress/influence us?

103. Should a person visit a library regularly? Justify your answer.

104. How often do you pray to God?

105. Where and when do you pray?

106. Have you ever prayed for someone else? If yes, when and why?

107. What are the reasons behind the rise of terrorism these days?

108. What should governments/people do to curb terrorism in the world?

109. Why do you think people become terrorists?

110. What will happen if terrorism spreads to all parts of the world?

111. Should governments spend large sums of money on space research?

112. Describe any wall of your house. (Please note that this question can be asked as a 2 minute Cue Card also.)

113. Should we celebrate a 'Bicycle Day' every year?

114. Will such events motivate people to use bicycles more?

115. Some people also buy residential properties in foreign countries. Is this good or bad?

116. Does the expression of happiness differ from culture to culture?

117. Do you believe that modern farming methods are harmful to domestic animals?

118. What can a person's leisure time activities tell us about his personality?

119. What will the possible comments of future historians be, about the way we are living now?

120. Are the people of the country you want to go to happier than the people of your home country?

Section II

Cue Cards with Sample Answers
followed by Follow-up Questions with
Sample Answers and Practice Questions

Cue Cards with Suggestions followed by Follow-up
Questions with Sample Answers and Practice Questions

Cue Cards with Sample Answers and Suggestions followed by Follow-up Questions with Sample Answers and Practice Questions

1. Speak about a person who has just moved to a new home.

You should say

- **Who this person is**
- **When he moved to the new home**
- **Why he decided to move homes**

How did he feel about moving to the new home?

One of my friends recently moved from his ancestral bungalow in the old part of the city, to a brand new three bedroom flat in a newly developed area. He had lived in the ancestral bungalow ever since he was born, and that house itself was over sixty years old. Although it was beautiful, and the part of the old city where it was located was very quiet and peaceful, the structure was no longer sturdy. My friend and his family had started noticing signs of damage and dilapidation in the structure since a few years, and eventually they got around to consulting some engineers. The engineers advised them to vacate the old bungalow for safety reasons, because the structure had become so weak, it could topple at the mildest of tremors.

After searching high and low across different areas of the city, my friend invested in an under construction residential apartment scheme that was launched by a reputed builder in the city. He had seen a sample house before paying up, but it was going to take a few months for his new home to be ready and handed over to him. About a year ago he took possession of the new house, and became the proud owner of a beautiful, big flat overlooking a public garden in a serene area surrounded by open meadows.

It took him a while to organise, pack, and then to transport the contents of his ancestral bungalow to the new house. But, he felt very happy about the move. In the process, he also managed to unclutter a lot. He is really pleased with the ambience and vibes of the new house, and his entire family came together to make the new house a home, thereby strengthening their bond.

Follow-up Questions & Answers:

1. Have you ever moved homes?

Yes, I have moved once, from my childhood home to the current apartment I live in. My childhood home was an enjoyable place, but the structure had become old and weak. It was dangerous to continue living there, and so we shifted to a new home in the same locality when we got the chance. I moved homes with my entire family, and we still live together. The best part is, because we are in the same area as before, I get to stay in touch with all my childhood friends without any difficulty. I am also familiar with all the places around me, which makes life quite convenient.

2. Was it an emotional experience when you moved into a new home?

It was certainly an emotional experience when I moved into a new home. I had spent my entire childhood and college days in the old house, and it felt like I was bidding goodbye to all those memories by leaving the home. I realised in the process that I had become very attached to a non-living object. Even my family members felt a little sad about leaving the old house. However, moving to a new home was an exciting prospect and it uplifted our spirits tremendously.

3. Does it help to decorate the interiors of a new home just like an old one?

For people who are very attached to their old home, decorating the new home like the old one may help ease the stress and tension. However, I do not think this is a healthy pattern to follow. One must learn to let go of the old in life, when something new and better enters. If we keep holding on to our past, we cannot enjoy our present to the fullest. Decorating a new house differently brings in excitement and positive energy into the lives of the entire family.

4. What makes a house a home?

The people living in the house make it a home. The emotions of those who decorate the house, plan its structure and interiors, set up the furniture, cook there, study there, and play there, infuse the house with movement and energy. They invite life to a non-living structure through their laughter and tears, through their joys and sorrows, through free flowing conversations and shared meals. The people living in a house give it a soul and make it a home. Without them, a house would simply be an empty, clinical structure. Caring for and nurturing each other in a house makes it a home.

5. Is it easier to move homes today, than it was a decade ago?

Yes, it is easier to move homes today, than it was a decade ago. This is because we have large agencies today that are adept at the business of packing and moving. A decade ago, these agencies existed, but they were not as efficient or effective, owing to unavailability of large vehicles and know how. Earlier, the residents of a house had to physically pack all their belongings and get them transported to their new house personally. One would have to make many rounds in small vehicles to get the task completed. Today, movers and packers can be hired for the same. They come with enough packing material, including cartons of different sizes, and large transport vehicles. They do all the packing for the customer, under his supervision, and even help in setting up the contents in the new house.

2. Describe a situation where you needed to use your imagination.

You should say

- When you needed to use your imagination
- What you accomplished by using it
- How your imagination helped you

Were you pleased with the results of using your imagination?

A few years ago my family and I decided to move homes, and I booked a three bedroom apartment in an upcoming scheme, in a nearby locality. The exteriors of the building were beautiful, but the interiors were left empty, for home owners to design as per their individual requirements. So, there emerged the need for me to use my imagination. I needed to sit and visualise what I wanted my home to look like, how I wanted the floors to be, what kinds of fittings I wanted to use in the rooms and bathrooms, where I wanted to arrange furniture, what kind of furniture I wanted to purchase; the list was endless. To be honest, I did not even know where to begin. So I started off by taking suggestions from all my family members as regards their likes and dislikes. Keeping those in mind, I hired an interior designer to help me execute my project and translate my imagination to reality.

I described to the designer how each room looked in my mind's eye, and he drew rough sketches as I spoke. He gave me his own inputs at each stage, and especially pitched in when it came to the minute but important details, such as space utilisation and ease of access around the house. Then, as I fine-tuned the more detailed aspects of the home interiors using my imagination, the designer used advanced CAD software to make my creativity come to life. I was very pleased with what I saw on his computer screen. We sat together and worked out things that needed to be changed, and additions that needed to be made. The paint for every room was worked out, the sofas and beds and all other furniture had been decided upon, and within no time, the home interiors were ready. The flat was just waiting for us to move in. The night we shifted in, I almost got no sleep because I was thrilled at how beautifully the home interiors had panned out, based on my imagination. I realised that night how the seed of every creation lies in imagination. Every hour I had spent thinking about how I would do up my new house had been worthwhile.

Follow-up Questions & Answers:
1. Is imagination inborn, or can it be cultivated?
I think imagination is inborn. All of us have the capacity to imagine and dream, since our childhood. Some of us may lose it by not using it. At times, people may be pressured into not using their imagination by their education system or the authority figures in their lives; but, to begin with, each of us has the capacity to imagine. Imagination can also be cultivated by encouraging freedom of thought and expression among people. Those who feel threatened to express themselves gradually lose the capacity to imagine. Those who feel safe in their environment can retain their imagination and use it to live life creatively.

2. How does imagination help?
Imagination is the seed which gives birth to every idea in the universe. The first step towards creating something is to imagine it. When one imagines something in a lot of detail with a lot of focus, one tries to find way to make it manifest. Then the journey towards acquiring knowledge and information begins. This journey brings ideas to fruition. Imagination thus helps in inventing and innovating, be it in the field of science and technology, or art and literature. Our ability to imagine has helped our species survive for so long, in spite of not being the strongest, fastest, or stealthiest mammals to walk the earth. Imagination helps us build tools and procedures to speed up our work and protect ourselves. It helps us build constructs to entertain ourselves and create interesting things.

3. Which occupations or professions require the maximum use of imagination?
The field of art in my opinion requires the maximum use of imagination. Artists try to

create something new each day, for which it is necessary to be able to imagine. Even to create an abstract painting, one needs to have tremendous capacity to imagine. Painters, writers, musicians, and actors, all need to tap into their imagination and stay tuned to it throughout their lives, especially while they are working, in order to extract the best kind of art from within themselves. Secondly, scientists also need to use their imagination to invent, innovate, and to solve complex technical problems and glitches.

4. Were you more imaginative in your childhood, than you are now?

Yes, I think I was definitely more imaginative in my childhood than I am now. I used to cook up interesting stories with make believe characters all the time. I even created imaginary situations with my friends as we played new games each day. Each time I sat with a sketchbook and some crayons, I painted the sky any colour I liked. In my imaginary world, I saw flowers in rainbow palettes and grasses that were purple. The waters could be pink, and the sun didn't have to be yellow. I could make up rhymes and tunes, and I even used to pen poetry like a pro. In my childhood, I did not feel the need to explain and define my creations to anyone, not even to myself. As I grew up, I started questioning my imagination, and I saw it dwindle considerably.

3. Describe a place where you like to relax.

   You should say

- **Which place this is**

- **When you visit it**

- **What you do there**

Why does it help you relax?

When it comes to relaxation after a long day at work, most people I know would opt for their living room sofas, or nearby gardens and parks. I, on the other hand am a little different in this aspect. I love to admire the night sky. As the sun slowly sets and makes way for the subsequent moonrise, I enjoy watching the canvas of the sky turn orange, pink, purple, and eventually pitch black. I cannot stop marvelling at the cyclical nature of life, and the stars in the night sky take me to a deeply philosophical place within my own mind.

So, naturally, I like to relax on my terrace. My building has a common terrace, but hardly anyone ever frequents it. I am a regular visitor there. After work, on days when I crave tranquillity and me-time, I head up to the terrace with a comfortable rug, and lay down on it to absorb the magnificence of unending skies. Sometimes I just rest my elbows on the sturdy parapets and watch the sun fade away beyond the city skyline. Soon after, with alarming regularity, thousands of birds start chirping and cawing, and when I look up, I see them flying across the sky in beautiful flight patterns. They are countless in number, and the chirping seems incessant. Most people I know have an aversion to this noise, but to me it is relaxing. No sooner have the birds settled in to roost for the night, than the sky turns a little darker, and the streetlights turn on one after the other — a message to drivers to turn on their headlights.

These everyday activities free my mind from the stresses and anxieties of the day. When I see the mundane day-to-day hustle bustle of traffic from my terrace, the bird's eye view assures me that no matter how hard situations get, I can remove myself from them, and return with renewed gusto each morning. The sight of the setting sun balances my biorhythms and ensures that I get a good night's sleep. The solitude allows me to get in touch with my inner self, giving me immense peace of mind. Some of my best ideas have come to me while relaxing on that terrace.

Follow-up Questions & Answers:
1. Is physical relaxation more important than mental relaxation?
I think both kinds of relaxation are equally important for the human body to function optimally. Relaxation of the physical kind provides wellbeing and balance to the physiological systems of the body, while mental relaxation calms the mind and refreshes it. In the larger scheme of things, I have noticed that a person can be physically exhausted and still remain happy, but a person who is mentally exhausted finds it difficult to be happy. So, in my opinion mental relaxation is a little more important than physical relaxation, if one has to choose.

2. Do you get enough time to relax during the week?
Yes, I get enough time to relax during the week. I have quite a disciplined schedule, which I stick to each day. Seldom do I waver from this schedule. This helps me feel less stressed, and also assists me with time planning and management. Every day, I schedule enough time for meal breaks and for sleep after work. I even make sure that I find time to meditate and go for walks without fail. In spite of working for more than fifty hours a week, I manage to get enough time to relax, because I chalk out my time-slots carefully.

3. Do youngsters today find less time to relax?
From what I have observed, many youngsters hardly find any time to relax, other than the few hours that they sleep. Because of excessive work pressures and a very competitive work environment, the youth today is always in a race to outdo someone, either to ensure business success or to ensure job security. Increasing materialistic aspirations urge many youngsters to stay on the move constantly, even at the cost of their meal breaks and sleep times. Further, socialising has increased a great deal these days as compared to a few years ago. Amidst work and partying, very few young people consciously find time to sit by themselves and relax in solitude.

4. What are the side effects of not getting enough relaxation?
There are many side effects of not getting enough relaxation. Without relaxation the body tend to stay in 'fight-or-flight' mode. This is very stressful on the organs and organ systems. It leads to imbalances in physical functions, causing chronic ailments and lifestyle diseases. At a mental level, a lack of relaxation can cause issues like insomnia or hampered sleep quality. These sleep disorders in turn lead to severe weight disorders, irritability, rage, and even depression. Not getting enough relaxation also affects one's creativity and potential negatively, thereby reducing their productivity.

5. Some people find listening to music very relaxing. Do you feel the same way?
Listening to music is a very passive activity for most people. One can sit back on a couch or lie down in bed and tune in to good music to calm the mind and soothe the senses. Once a playlist is started, or a radio station has been tuned into, the listener does not need

to apply any effort, focus, or concentration to the process of listening to music. One can even drift off to sleep as soft music plays along in the background. I feel the same way about music. If I play soft tunes, I can relax very easily. I have noticed that music helps me breathe slower and deeper. It also rejuvenates my mind and instils positivity in me. However, if one listens to very fast or loud music, it may prove counterproductive.

◆ ◆ ◆

4. Describe a time when you prepared for a happy event.
   You should say
- What the event was
- How you prepared for it
- Who helped you with the preparations
How did the event eventually turn out?

Many years ago, I stared my business out of a small office near my house, and with dedicated efforts, my team and I made it quite a success. So much so, that we began to run out of space to accommodate clients and new staff. The time had come to move to a new office. We started looking for office spaces, and not before long, we narrowed down on a new commercial building in the city centre. The office was purchased, and the interiors were done up to suit the business type, and my personal taste.

But, one thing had been nagging me since I decided to move. I was a little wary of losing out on clientele owing to the sudden change of location. We had started telling all our customers about the impending change of location a few months in advance, but I knew this much would not be enough. I also needed to make sure my business became well known in the new area. So, we decided on hosting a grand inauguration for the new office. I prepared for it with much gusto and enthusiasm alongside my team. I was ideating, planning, coordinating, and executing, altogether! My team helped with fine-tuning all the small and big details. Once I had selected a cuisine, the office staff helped me select a good caterer, and managed all the bookings and food arrangements. They helped me arrange space for seating our guests, and also sent out invitations, and tried hard to ensure a high turnout of people. My family assisted me in narrowing in on the chief guest for the ribbon cutting ceremony, and the building management took care of valet services.

I was personally in charge of all the decorations, checking on the lighting, and last minute tidying up. My relatives took charge of handing out brochures to people while simultaneously ensuring that all the guests were entertained. My neighbours had assisted in preparing neat little baskets full of goodies for all the attendees, a week in advance. The event started at nine in the morning, and went on till noon. It turned out to be very successful, and we were all very pleased when the guests bid us farewell with big smiles on their faces.

Follow-up Questions & Answers:
1. Are you good at event management?

I am good at all kinds of management tasks. Event management is one of them. I am very good at people skills and communications. In addition, I am also a very good planner. My mind is organised, and I know the art of staying calm even in apparently stressful situations. I know how to find ways around glitches, and how to turn unfavourable situations around to my benefit. All these skills make me good at event management.

2. Do you think certified courses in event management are helpful?

Yes, certified courses in event management concentrate on this particular aspect of management, as opposed to a broader MBA programme. In these courses, one gets the chance to study in detail all that goes in to managing different types of events with different numbers of attendees. One learns how to arrange entertainment options, food options, and security measures to manage crowds. In these courses, students are also taught how to deal with different agencies and people to get tasks done on time, with perfection.

3. Have you hired an event manager for any private function?

Yes, on the occasion of my cousin's wedding, we had hired a very good event manager. The main reason for doing so was that we were looking to organise a destination wedding far from home. We knew it would be difficult for us to personally get everything in order on time for our guests to arrive. Many things needed to be taken care of, such as guest accommodations, welcoming them, taking care of their various needs, organising decorations, venues, photographers, entertainers, and caterers for the various functions. The event manager took care of everything based on our guidelines and requirements, and the wedding proceeded without a glitch.

4. Are event managers only available for happy events?

Today, event managers are available to manage all kinds of events. Event managers can be roped in to handle unemotional business events, formal conferences and dinners, seminars, and political campaigns and rallies. In fact many people hire event managers to organise funeral services and to do the needful while they deal with their grief in peace, without being bothered about arrangements and formalities.

5. Describe an electrical gadget/tool/machine that you use at home.

   You should say

- **What this electrical gadget/tool/machine is**

- **What functions it serves in your home**

- **Who uses it the most at home**

Are you satisfied with it, and would you recommend it to others?

We use a lot of electrical gadgets at home, in order to keep up with the changing times and to make our lives easier. Some of these are television sets, a microwave, an oven, an electric grill, and air conditioners.

However, the one electrical gadget that we cannot live without is our refrigerator. The annual range of temperature in my city is very broad. This means that while winters get quite cold, summers become excruciatingly hot. With the mercury soaring steadily for at least six months every year, a good quality refrigerator becomes a must in every household. We use our refrigerator to store fresh fruits and vegetables, to make and dispense ice cubes, to store our juices, breads, milk and milk products, and bottled sauces and dips. We even store dry fruits, some spices like cinnamon, nutmeg, bay leaves, and vanilla, and various ice creams in our fridge.

We have newly purchased this 654 litre refrigerator from Samsung because of its various functional features. This fridge has an in built technology to keep food fresher for longer, and it is lined with an anti-bacterial mesh, as well. It is a two door fridge with an ice dispenser, and a water dispenser on the outside. The fridge has smart sensors which sense any sudden changes in climate and change the inside temperature accordingly, to keep food safe for consumption.

My wife uses the refrigerator the most at home, because she manages most of the cooking. She is very pleased that our new fridge has many compartments which help her organise different food items neatly and category-wise. This ensures that opposing food odours do not mingle. She can store many jars of jams, pickles, and sauces in the shelves that line the refrigerator doors, too.

All of us at home are very happy with this refrigerator, so I would definitely recommend it to friends and relatives who are looking to buy a new fridge or do up their kitchen. In fact I am so pleased, that I am considering buying a similar model for my farm house.

Follow-up Questions & Answers:

1. Are humans dependent on electrical gadgets?

I think humans are completely dependent on electrical gadgets today. In fact, most of us would feel handicapped without gadgets such as the television, our mobile phone chargers, refrigerators, air conditioners, water heaters, lights, and fans. Our music systems, grooming accessories, and sometimes even our stovetops depend totally on the availability of electricity. Industries and manufacturing plants would come to a halt without electrical gadgets. What's more, the world would regress in the absence of computers!

2. Are electrical gadgets used more in urban areas than in rural areas?

In developed nations, electrical gadgets are used just as much in rural areas, as they are in the urban areas. However, in my country, many rural areas still do not have access to electricity 24 hours. So, most rural dwellers use fewer electrical gadgets than the urban dwellers. Electricity is quite expensive, and so are electrical gadgets. Because the rural economy of developing countries is usually agrarian, people seldom have disposable incomes to spend on electrical gadgets. They are still seen as luxury items in many places, and hence used less frequently in villages.

3. Would you be willing to live completely off the grid for a few days?

I would look forward to living completely off the grid for a few days. It would be lovely to disconnect from all electrical and electronic devices, for a while, in order to retreat into a calm, serene, atmosphere, where the hum of gadgets and machines does not interfere with the sounds of nature. It would be a life of more awareness, more physical activity, and lesser distractions from one's goals of self-actualisation. However, I think I would only be able to live that way for a while. After some days I would want to return to a comfortable life made more convenient by electrical gadgets and machines.

4. Name an electrical gadget/machine that you would be unable to spend a day without.

Since I live in a very hot city, I think I would be unable to live without the air conditioner for a single day. Where I come from, days tend to be hot even during the winters, at times. Summers are excruciating, and the scorching heat often kills people. Dehydration is commonplace, and sun strokes happen to people every now and then. In such conditions, if I were to live without an air conditioner, my entire day would be spent sweating profusely, cursing the heat, and not being able to work at all. Productivity in my office would come down manifold, and I would remain irritable throughout the day.

6. Detail a method that helps you save money.
   You should say
- **What this method it**
- **How you learnt about it**
- **How it helps you save money**
Do you follow this method regularly in practical life?

I am very good with budgeting and saving money. At the beginning of each month I put a fixed amount of money into my daughter's fixed deposit account. Then, my family and I allocate money for various different expenses. During the month, whenever we spend money we always preserve the bills and receipts. Once the month draws to a close, we tally all our expenses, and put all the saved money in another fixed deposit account. We also make it a point to check if we have overspent anywhere, or if there is scope for better planning.

Early in life, I learnt the importance of saving money, budgeting, and even investing it correctly. My father has always been a very shrewd investor, and he started giving me pocket money from the young age of ten years. At the beginning of every month I would receive fifty rupees from him, and I was allowed to spend that money any way I liked. There was only one condition — I needed to keep track of where I spent how much. My father taught me to maintain a little diary, and I did as I was told.

Every time I made an expense — be it on candies and chocolates, or on stationery, or on entry tickets to the children's park — I wrote down how much I had spent. At the end of each month I would calculate how much I had saved, and hand it over to my father. He would give me a small percentage of interest on that amount, and that is how I learned all about saving and investing money.

Using this technique, I have already managed to save more money than most of my peers who have a similar income to mine. In fact, all our expensive electronic and electrical gadgets, and a lot of our domestic as well as foreign trips get funded from the interest we earn on our investments. Having seen the benefits of saving money first hand, I follow this method regularly in practical life.

Follow-up Questions & Answers:
1. Is it important to save money?
Yes, it is very important to save money. A penny saved is a penny earned, as the old

saying goes. That which we save, we do not have to strive to earn again. Further, if we manage to save enough money when times are good, we will be able to sail through tough times brought on by circumstances out of our control. Saved money can also be turned into smart investments which can fund our retirement, health care, education, and travels.

2. How much percentage of income should a person save each month?

This is a very personal decision, depending upon one's individual reasons for saving. If one is saving without a particular goal in sight, then even ten percent of his income can qualify as sufficient savings. If however, someone is saving with the goal of investing systematically, or with the goal of making big expenditures at a later stage in life, then he may need to save more money each month, in order to achieve his goals at the earliest.

3. Do people in your country have a habit of saving money?

People in my country most certainly have a habit of saving money. Most people I know have fixed savings plans in place since the time they start earning. The culture of saving money has kept the economy of my country quite stable as opposed to those of other countries, even in times of extreme international economic upheaval. When markets become recessionary, people in my country are able to tap into their savings and get by comfortably, until circumstances improve. Children have grown up seeing such examples for generations, so saving has become more of a culture here, than just a habit.

4. What do you usually save money for?

I usually save money for travelling and retirement these days. I am very fond of exploring new places, and even though I don't have enough time for that right now, once I retire I would like to tour the whole world with my family. I have seen most of the places within my country, so I save money with a view to travel abroad at leisure, maybe rent holiday homes for longer holidays, or event set off on luxury cruises at whim.

7. Describe a foreign food dish or special meal that you have had.
    You should say
- **When you had this meal**   *unusual meal*
- **What this meal consisted of**
- **Who made it for you**

Did you enjoy the meal?

I've had many wonderful, delicious meals in my life, and this includes both Indian, and foreign dishes. Partly, this is because we like to eat out and experiment with different cuisines. Also, my wife is a very good cook, well versed with many cuisines, and she often tries out new recipes from across the world.

The most recent, very special foreign meal I had was in France, when I visited there with my family. We were in Paris for a holiday, and decided to head out to a highly recommended roof top restaurant. A few of my friends who had already been there were raving about the amazing authentic food options available there, and their large wine menu.

typical

The moment we entered the restaurant and stepped out from their lounge area onto the terrace seating, we were enchanted. The fragrance of fresh French food was wafting from the kitchen, and the potted plants and veils lining the terrace took us back to eras bygone. Little marble fountains shaped like cherubs covered the corners of the large terrace, and the minimalistic flooring complimented the sprightly yellow fairy lights beautifully. Standing near the railings we saw the sun set as we ordered bowls of classic French onion soup and a fruity red wine with deep notes of honey and cedar.

The view from the terrace as we sipped our wine was mesmerising; all of Paris lit up like a piece of paradise. When the maître d' noticed that our soup bowls were empty, we were served a tray full of avocado tartines and cottage cheese crepes for starters. These were dishes we hadn't tried before, but ever willing to experiment, we dug in. Suffice it to say, the memory of those dishes still makes my mouth water. The starters were followed up with a rich spinach and ricotta quiche for mains. Before we knew it, we had guzzled down our bottle of delicious wine alongside our dinner! It was time for dessert and along came a server, bringing fluffy Belgian chocolate soufflé garnished with basil leaves.

The chef had outdone himself in catering to our request for a delicious, vegetarian four course French meal! That night became memorable because of the meal, and I remember sleeping like a log afterwards.

Follow-up Questions & Answers:
1. Do you like experimenting with different cuisines?
I enjoy experimenting with different cuisines from time to time. It gives me a lot of satisfaction when I indulge my taste buds with new dishes from across the world. During my childhood my city did not have any multi-cuisine restaurants. So, when I was first introduced to global cuisines, I was astonished at the variety of foods human beings from different parts of the world ate. Now, I try different cuisines to better understand the cultures of different places. I also enjoy tasting desserts from international cuisines.

2. Which is your favourite cuisine?
I am a self-confessed foodie. So, it is difficult for me to select just one cuisine as a favourite. I am very fond of Indian food from different states. Punjabi cuisine is my constant go to, when it comes to Indian food. Sometimes when we go out to eat, I really enjoy authentic Chinese food. Rice noodles, noodle soups, various stir fries, dipping sauces, Manchurian platters, and fried rice make for delicious meal options. Chinese cuisine, in fact is quite varied, and I discovered this only when I first went to an authentic Chinese restaurant in Mumbai. Before that I had only tried a watered down, altered version of this cuisine at local delis.

3. What are desserts of your local cuisine like?
Indian cuisine has more of sweet dishes than desserts. The difference between the two is that sweet dishes are eaten along with the main meal, and desserts are eaten after the main meal as a separate course. Indian traditional food sciences say that sweet foods must be taken along with the meal in moderate quantities in order to ensure a balanced intake of nutrients and 'taste-groups'. These sweet dishes are seldom served chilled. They are either given steaming hot, or at room temperature. The dominant ingredient in them is clarified butter, which makes them absolutely sumptuous. Other ingredients commonly used in sweet dishes in India are dry fruits such as cashews, almonds, pistachios, and

spices such as cardamom, saffron, and nutmeg.

4. What do you usually eat for breakfast?

I eat lots of different foods for breakfast. In fact, I wake up quite hungry each morning, so my breakfast is the heaviest meal of my day. Some of the things that I enjoy for breakfast are stuffed flatbreads served with yoghurt dips and pickles, toasts with different cheese spreads, savoury waffles, stir fried cottage cheese, fruit salads, and fruit juices. At times I indulge in large proportions of fried breads with spicy curries as well. Some of my family members like eating packaged cereals, but I am not too fond of them. One thing that is a necessity for me is my pot of steaming hot coffee to go with my morning meals.

8. Talk about a small business venture that you would like to start up in the future.

   You should say

- **What business venture this is**

- **When you would like to start it**

- **Why you want to be involved with this venture**

Will you require any additional qualifications for starting up this business venture?

If I start up a small business in future, it will definitely be a small restaurant. I have always been fond of trying out different dishes and tasting new cuisines. My family is full of good cooks and all of them would be able to help me out with executing this venture successfully. My restaurant will serve fresh food, largely made out of organic, locally grown produce, in order to promote healthy eating. I will consult leading nutritionists to prepare my menu, so as to include delicious, balanced meal options for diners to indulge in.

I would like to start this venture after retiring from my primary business, when I have a lot of leisure time on my hands. By then, I will have visited many restaurants and cafes all over the world and gathered knowledge about the ins and outs of the restaurant business. The main reason behind wanting to be involved with this venture is that a restaurant business can be run by the entire family, together, as one unit. It is a business that is guaranteed to give good returns in a city like mine, which is full of foodies, provided I can execute it correctly.

I have sound knowledge of the business model and I even have good friends in the hospitality industry who can offer me guidance at every step of the process. Further, if I decide to rent out a commercial space for my restaurant instead of buying it, the initial investment is also not too high.

I don't think I will require any additional qualifications for starting up this business venture. I will make sure I hire good chefs and trained servers. Apart from this I am a very good manager, good with money, and also great at people skills. These qualities of mine will make up for my lack of qualifications in the field of hospitality.

Follow-up Questions & Answers:
1. Do people in your city eat out a lot?

People in my city are very fond of food; at least the people I meet most frequently are. Food is a high point in everyone's life here. I come from a dry state, so people don't socialise over alcohol in my city. That leaves us without pubs or bars to hang out at. So, in their free time, people frequent cafes and restaurants and indulge their taste buds with different snacks and meals instead. Today, we have many hawkers, delis, mini vans, cafes, bistros, restaurants, and large hotels serving everything from breakfast, brunch, and lunch, to evening snacks, dinner, and even midnight meals. No matter what time you step out of home, you are guaranteed to see lots of diners in and around various food joints in my city.

2. What kinds of restaurants make the most money, according to you?

I think diners that serve fast food make the most money. They work on the principal of serving very tasty food, very fast. The interiors of such diners are often coloured very bright, thereby enhancing the appetites of customers and encouraging them to eat quickly and leave. So, every day these restaurants serve large numbers of people. They earn their money through quantity, more than presentation, ambience, and other attributes that restaurants capitalise on. Apart from fast food joints, very high end fine dining restaurants also earn a lot, because of their delicate presentation, exotic food options, beautiful ambience and interiors, and most importantly, the huge profit margins on each of their dishes.

3. Is it advisable to have a very large menu in a restaurant?

I used to think it is very good to have a large menu in a restaurant. When I was younger, maybe in school, I loved looking at large menu cards full of lots of food options to select from. As I grew older though, I realised that such menus are not feasible in the long run for the restaurant management to work with. In many cases, extensive menus simply have lots of items with minor differences listed down, to make the menu cards appear larger. In other cases, where a restaurant is genuinely trying to serve up too many different dishes, it becomes very difficult for the owners to plan and manage the inventory. Too many chefs also need to be employed to cope up with cooking different cuisines and dishes. Freshness of food often gets compromised when the menu is too large and the management feels bad about wastage. Eventually, either the quality of food suffers, or the profitability of the business suffers.

4. Is it easy to acquire funds to start up a new business in your city?

My city is full of entrepreneurs and investors willing to invest some of their money in promising business ventures. These venture capitalists gauge the business idea, the business model, its feasibility, and the projected returns on investment, when someone approaches them for funds. If they are convinced, they fund the venture either at very low interest rates, or often free of interest, in return for partnership in the firm or simply profit sharing. Banks in the city also give business loans to start ups, but this process is a little tricky because it takes too much effort on the part of new entrepreneurs to convince banks to fund their ventures.

9. Describe an instance when you were very close to a wild animal.

You should say
- Which animal it was
- Where you encountered it
- How you felt when you saw the animal

Would you like to experience this again?

Many years ago when I was in the second year of college, our department organised a tour to Kanha. Kanha is a national park in central India, famous for its huge tiger population. The forest is one of the largest in India, and home to many different species of animals. It is a self-sustaining ecosystem full of symbiotic and predatory relationships between animals.

We were a group of twenty students who had signed up for the tour, and our college had put us up in a hotel very close to one of the entrances of the forest. The next morning, we woke up very early, a little before sunrise, in fact, and got ready for our jeep safari into the wilderness. The twenty of us assembled into five jeeps, bubbling with excitement. For the first hour and a half we saw a lot of deer, sambar, wild boars, monkeys, and exotic birds. However, we spotted no tiger. The guide in our jeep kept looking for pug marks to ascertain the location of any tiger that might be in the vicinity. Unfortunately, he couldn't spot any, and we only had permission to spend about forty five more minutes in the forest for that morning. Just when we had given up, we heard some monkeys hoot and squeal in fright as they jumped from branch to branch. This was followed by the cries of birds, and we could sense that something was up. The animals were alerting each other to danger.

As we looked here and there with bated breath, suddenly out of a thick, green overgrowth on the left, emerged a majestic tigress! Her bright orange coat was striking, and her eyes were almost hypnotic! She stood in front of our jeep and turned to face us. We were all left speechless, and the warning cries of the jungle slowly subsided. My heart was beating in my throat, and all I felt was a deep sense of fearful reverence for the beautiful tigress before me.

I would love to experience such a sighting again, and plan on going there once with my family in the near future.

Follow-up Questions & Answers:
1. Are you afraid of wild animals?
I would not say that I'm afraid of wild animals. Of course, if a wild animal were to attack me or chase me, I would run for my life. But, in general when I visit animal reserves, national parks, or wildlife sanctuaries, sitting in the open jeep, or on elephant back, or even in a canter, I don't really feel afraid of wild animals. I have seen many large, aggressive bears, huge packs of wild dogs, sly wolves, stealthy cheetahs and hyenas, and even tigers on the hunt, on my trips to forest reserves. On these occasions I was awe-inspired more than afraid. The sight of wild animals is so breath-taking, that fear takes a back seat when the mind knows that one is sitting in a vehicle, quite protected.
2. Do you think we need to increase the forest cover globally?

I feel very strongly for this cause of planting more trees and increasing the forest cover globally. Forests are dwindling at scary speeds internationally because of increasing industrialisation and deforestation for agriculture and mining. This is leading to an increase in global temperatures, better known as global warming, causing many species of animals to become endangered or extinct. Ecosystems are getting disturbed and food chains are breaking because of a lack of forest cover. If we manage to increase the forest cover all over the world, we will be able to bring down the negative effects of global warming and reinstate many endangered species, thereby balancing out food webs.

3. What is your opinion on hunting?

Hunting is an unjustified act of extreme cruelty in my opinion. No one has the right to decide the fate of another life form for sport. When humans hunt other animals for sport, we display our arrogance and insensitivity towards other life forms. We display that we are not worthy of being at the top of the food chain, when we misuse our power of handling tools by killing animals and birds without reason. Today, there are many food options, and many sport options that people can indulge in and enjoy, without harming anyone in the slightest. Killing animals for any reason other than self-defence is an act of unintelligence, because only an unintelligent creature would destroy his own ecosystem and planet.

4. What can a country do to promote wildlife tourism?

The prerequisite for wildlife tourism is to have sanctuaries, safe havens, and large natural habitats where different animals can live, forming predatory and symbiotic relationships with one another, depending on the characteristics of their species. Such sanctuaries can be created by starting massive tree plantation, leading to the organic development of diverse ecosystems through the process of natural succession. The government must then take necessary measures to protect the forests themselves and the animals living inside, from human interference. Once these measures are in place, forest safaris can be started, and these can be promoted internationally using the internet and other direct marketing platforms such as travel fairs, television ads, and magazine ads.

10. Describe an activity that is a little expensive.

   You should say

-   **What the activity is**
-   **Why it is expensive**
-   **Where it is carried out**

Why do you like performing this activity?

With the advent of various adventure sports involving a lot of equipment, people have started taking a keen interest in many expensive outdoor activities. One expensive outdoor activity that I enjoy a lot is embarking on road trips. The good thing about road trips is that while they are a little expensive, they are not prohibitively costly. Going on a holiday in one's own car can be costly for many reasons. The first is the cost of fuel.

Depending on the distance one wants to cover, refuelling needs to be planned out, and a considerable amount of money needs to be kept aside for the purpose. The second expense is that of getting the car serviced very often if one tends to go on too many long journeys. The third expense comes in when it is time for maintenance and replacement of parts. It is advisable to replace the battery, the clutch plate, and the tyres at regular intervals if one goes out on a lot of road trips. These replacements are quite costly, yet unavoidable.

Road trips are carried out all over the world by people who are fond of driving. There are many who do not personally like to drive, and yet prefer to travel by car than by any other means of transport. Such people hire a chauffeur for their road trip, thereby incurring an additional cost. Scenic routes are the most popular choices for road trips, so roads that are lined by trees on either side, or lush green fields, or even tall mountain ranges tend to be frequented by driving enthusiasts.

I really enjoy going out on road trips because a big car can accommodate my entire family comfortably. We have the liberty to make as many halts as we require along the way, without major restrictions. My entire family can enjoy the beautiful sights on the way to our destination, and we end up having many interesting conversations, too. The best part about going on road trips is that we can organise our very own little picnic on the way, anywhere we like.

Follow-up Questions & Answers:
1. Are all fun activities expensive?

All fun activities need not necessarily be expensive. One can get immense enjoyment and pleasure even by indulging in simple and inexpensive activities. Many people have hobbies that are purely talent based, requiring very little equipment. Activities like playing or listening to music, painting, sculpture and pottery, going on walks and jogs, mountain climbing, swimming, and hiking are a lot of fun, and they are not too expensive either depending on the area in which one is living. When we choose activities that are accessible in our locality, they turn out to be quite affordable.

2. What can your government do to make your chosen activity less expensive?

Road trips are expensive for most people across the world, except for those living in oil rich countries. The government in my country is already doing a lot by providing vehicle fuel at highly subsidised rates. If the government further improves the conditions of roads in certain rural areas and facilitates the flow of traffic better, people will be able to drive cars consistently at economic speeds, thereby reducing the consumption of fuel in the long run.

3. Which other activities do you enjoy, which are a little expensive, other than the one you mentioned?

I am very fond of horse riding. Owning a horse can be very expensive, so the other option for me to enjoy horse riding is to register with a stud farm, or to sign up for riding classes and expeditions. The sign up fees for such activities involve fees for the maintenance of horses that are used, and for safety measures and guidance. Due to this, horse riding is a little expensive. However, it is not too costly, and most people with steady incomes can enjoy this activity from time to time.

4. Does the activity you spoke about earlier require any special skills?

I mentioned going on road trips, earlier. This activity does require certain skills on the driver's part. The driver needs to have very good control of the steering wheel, and also needs to be adept at driving. He needs to be patient enough to manoeuvre through traffic jams skilfully without losing his cool. Further, the driver needs to be able to remain alert throughout the journey, to avoid any mishaps. He must also be good at reading maps and using the GPS in the car or on his smart phone.

11. Talk about an unusual/interesting thing that you recently did in your free time?
    You should say
-   **What you did**
-   **When you did it**
-   **With whom you did it**
Why do you think it was unusual or interesting?

Recently I was in Europe on some business, when I tried my hand at Snapchat for the very first time. My daughter had installed the app on my smart phone a while ago and urged me to start using it repeatedly, but I had kept procrastinating.

Now, I had finished with all my meetings in Vienna that evening, and decided to retire early to catch up on lost sleep. But as fate would have it, the effects of jetlag were more powerful than my determination to sleep. My biological clock had not managed to synchronise with the new time zone, and I lay awake in bed, staring at the ceiling. After an hour and a half like that, I picked up my phone and decided to read some articles online. In the process I noticed the little ghost icon of Snapchat staring back at me, and a certain curiosity made me open it up.

It was 4 am, but before I knew it I had taught myself the ins and outs of the app, and even started using it. I was a pro at inserting filters and sending out snap chats. What I figured out was that this new messaging system was in fact quite sophisticated, and also fun to use. While exploring its features, I didn't even realise when sleep took over.

It was very unusual for me to use an app like that, because I don't normally experiment much with messaging services. I am one of the last few to adopt a new technological innovation, if at all. When my daughter had first told me about the app, I had just politely nodded and then mentally dismissed the notion of ever using it, thinking it was just something that teenagers liked to play with. You can imagine my surprise when I found myself hooked to it in the span of just one sleepless night.

Follow-up Questions & Answers:
1. Are you wary of trying out new things in life?

I am not at all wary of trying out new things in life. In fact, I think that exploring new activities and pastimes can give rise to new interests and hobbies. Further, when I try out new things I invariably learn new skills and expand my own horizons. Trying out new things keeps me entertained, young at heart, and updated with new international trends.

When I learn something new, I feel more confident about myself, and there is a satisfaction that comes from understanding new concepts and acquiring new technical skills.

2. Who inspires you most to try unusual/interesting things?

Young people and teenagers around me inspire me most to try and try unusual /interesting things. Teenagers are the risk takers, innovators, and adopters of new products and technologies in any society. They are the first to try out new technologies, new inventions, and upcoming fashion trends. When I speak to them or see them exploring something interesting or unusual, I automatically feel the urge to go and seek more information from them regarding what they are doing. They inspire me to step out of my routine chores from time to time, to keep myself entertained.

3. Can unusual activities be dangerous?

Sometimes certain unusual activities can be dangerous, if not practiced carefully. Some unusual pastimes such as motorbike and car stunts can be life threatening even if all the necessary precautions are taken. Then there are other current unusual activities such as getting permanent tattoos, which may not necessarily be dangerous, but can have far reaching consequences that one needs to live with, long after the activity has been completed. Activities like trying out new software, applications, and games are not exactly dangerous, but are often highly addictive. Some of these involve taking a lot of personal pictures constantly, which can induce narcissism or self-esteem issues.

4. What is the best time to try out unusual/interesting things?

The best time to try out unusual or interesting things is when a person is holidaying, or relaxing in his leisure time. At such times the mind is completely stress free and relaxed. This makes a person more receptive to new ideas, and learning new things becomes very easy. When relaxed on holidays, there are very few or no interruptions. This encourages people to talk to lots of people and explore unusual things. Then, because of availability of extra time, one can practice these newly adopted interesting activities and master them as well. This is probably why there is a growing trend of people trying their hands at art, photography, and music when they are holidaying.

◆ ◆ ◆

12. Talk about a product you have planned to buy in the near future.	 OR	**13. Describe a machine or equipment that you would like to buy.**

OR

14. Talk about a kind of electronic device you would like to buy.

You should say
- **What the product is**
- **What it looks like**
- **When you plan to buy it**

Why do you want to buy this product?

Sample Answer:

I have always been lured by fancy, attractive electronic gadgets with versatile functions and uses. The chase for the best electronic device appears to be endless, with new products becoming redundant in no time after they are launched. The next electronic device that I would like to buy is the Apple iPad Pro from Apple Inc. This device is essentially a tablet computer, better known as a tab, and its variants come in two sizes — 12.9 inches, and 9.7 inches. Apple calls the iPad Pro a super computer, because it been designed to facilitate next generation personal computing needs with ease, thanks to its new capabilities and enhanced portability. I would like to purchase the 12.9 inch model, as this size is impressive to look at and more comfortable to use. In addition, it costs just a little bit more than the 9.7 inch model. I want to buy the Apple iPad Pro over any other tab because it offers the best quality display and graphics, a very use friendly interface, a responsive touch screen, and speedy functioning. The 12.9 inch iPad Pro offers the highest screen resolution in comparison with any other Apple products. The screen adjusts itself to all kinds of light conditions making usage easy on the eyes. This creates a unique experience, similar to viewing a sheet of paper as opposed to the artificial glare of a computer screen. This is not all; this tab also has high fidelity speakers on all four corners. The device automatically orients higher frequency sounds to the top speakers, making game play and listening to music all the more engaging. When I first heard about all these features I thought the computer might have a low battery life, but in spite of its very high processor speed, the iPad Pro 12.9 has a 10 hour battery life!

All these features of this tab make it the perfect next purchase for me. This is an ideal electronic device to buy, according to me, and I feel it will help me a lot in my work, even when I am travelling. Furthermore, when I extract it from my bag, it will grab all the right kind of attention and help elevate my status in the eyes of clients and business associates.

15. Talk about the film that you saw last.

OR

16. Talk about your favourite movie.

   You should say
- **When and where you saw it**
- **Whom you saw it with**
- **What the story was like**

What did you like about the movie?

Suggestions:
Candidates often start thinking and selecting their favourite movie. I suggest, if you are not sure of a single favourite, it is better to speak about the one you saw most recently.

Sample Answer:
There are a number of movies releasing every week in Hindi, English, and other vernacular languages in my country. They range from action, thrillers, and science fiction, to comedy, romance, history, and even art. I often go to watch movies in different theatres in my city. The film that I would like to talk about today is 'PK'. I saw this movie

with my family at a multiplex near my house. It is the story of an alien who comes to earth with a group of other aliens, and gets stranded. Furthermore, he loses the only device with which he can communicate with his spaceship. The movie follows his story as he tries to find that device in every possible lace. In the process he makes many people of different religions question their blind religious beliefs and fanaticism. PK manages to do all this in a classic, endearing style, underpinned by his childlike innocence. The role of PK is essayed brilliantly by Aamir Khan, who is known as a perfectionist in the film industry. In the movie, Anushka Sharma plays the role of his friend, Jaggu, and eventually his unrequited love interest. She essays the role of a journalist who helps PK find his device. The interesting thing about PK was that people on his planet had no concept of clothing, religion, or verbal communication. They exchanged information simply by holding hands, through mental communication. He expected a similar level of maturity from people on earth, but instead he found corruption and lies everywhere he went. PK was most astounded to find that some people on earth killed others in the name of religion, and he was even more shaken up to find that a self-proclaimed god man who was worshipped by thousands of people, was in fact responsible for stealing his communication device. With the help of his Jaggu, PK starts finding ways to expose the god man as a fraud, and retrieve his device.

In the process, PK challenges the god man to a debate on Jaggu's news channel, and he accepts the challenge. It gets decided that the winner of the challenge would get to keep the communication device. PK gives his all in the debate that ensues live on TV, but towards the end it seems as though he is going to lose to the god man. Just when the audiences appear to be giving up their faith in PK, he comes up with a trump card, and saves the day. This movie is actually a blend of comedy, satire, and philosophy of life. The director has successfully given the message that all religions preach the same tenets of peace and honesty, but the preachers of different religions contort the messages of their holy books, and lead followers on the wrong path. The climax of the movie also makes viewers consider that true love may not always be about possessing the one we love; that there is so much more to loving someone than simply spending our entire lives with them. In conclusion, I think PK is a complete, unique, must watch movie that not only teaches us, but also touches us.

17. Speak about your favourite artiste/musician, or singer.
    You should say
-   The name of the artiste/musician, or singer
-   What skills he/she possesses
-   What qualities make the artiste/musician, or singer stand out
Why is he/she your favourite?
Sample Answer:
My favourite singer is the late Mr. Kishore Kumar. He was a legend of the Indian music industry. During his career, he sang songs for most of the contemporary actors of his

time, because his voice suited them all on screen. He sang thousands of songs for Hindi and Bengali cinema. It is a really tough task for a layman like myself to describe the technical qualities of his voice, and the versatility that he possessed in his art. He was able to mould his voice according to the demands of the lyrics, his music directors, and the situations portrayed in the film on screen. His voice was equally effective in romantic, sad, fast, classical, and folk songs. This is the reason, that even today after almost 20 years of his death, his songs are played on the radio on public demand, and many upcoming singers in singing contests still sing them. Moreover, many of his songs are rehashed and presented afresh with remixed sounds to satisfy the newer generations' thirst for a combination of fast music along with a high quality, soulful voice. Kishore Kumar won countless awards for his singing during his lifetime.

There were three important qualities in him that made him superior to others. The first of these was his ability to work at different levels in different roles. He was the only artist in Hindi cinema who worked as an actor, a comedian, a film director, a music director, and a playback singer. He was the only singer in the day who managed to sing a song in both, male and female voices, for a Hindi film. Last, but not the least, the most striking feature about him was his spontaneity. He did not have any formal training in music and he never did 'riaz' (practice of singing) at home. He was a readymade singer served to this country on a silver platter; a true legend. I salute his greatness. I am also thankful to nature for gifting such a precious artiste to my country.

18. **Speak about an international/national celebrity, or personality who is controversial.**
    You should say
- **The name of the personality**
- **What he does for a living**
- **How that personality/celebrity is controversial**
What is your opinion of this personality/celebrity?

Sample Answer:
There are many celebrities, who willingly or unwillingly keep courting controversies during the spans of their careers. Many celebrities in fact are more famous for their controversies than for their actual achievements in life. While the list of controversial celebs is actually endless, today I would like to speak about the man who was elected President of the USA in 2016. The 45th President of America, Mr Donald Trump is a very successful businessman, too, and has featured in television shows as well, before campaigning for his presidential role. Almost all his television appearances have made headlines in his earlier days, but this is not what makes him a controversial personality in my eyes. Trump truly started courting controversy when he decided to run for President. He started making the most outrageous statements in public, started saying things that no politician had said before on an international platform. He unabashedly went on to criticise immigrants and refugees, blamed them for the lowered employment of American citizens, and even went so far as to say that if he became president, he

would see to it that America was rid of its immigrants. This statement was not only discriminatory and insensitive, but also went against America stood for. In fact, the USA is a nation of immigrants, Donald Trump being one of them. In fact Trump's own wife was also an immigrant. This mentality and negative attitude towards people won him many brickbats and he became an international talking point.

Further, Trump went on to make racist and sexist comments on international TV, regularly and repeatedly. He kept tweeting insensitive one-liners online, which ensured that he got likened to a loose cannon. He even went on to say that he would build a big wall between the USA and Mexico, and that he'd make the Mexicans pay for its construction. Soon, he became a trending topic and memes about him started surfacing. People started making fun of his appearance, his mannerisms, his loose talk, and also started questioning his intelligence.

It appeared for the longest time that Trump had no chance at winning the election, because he was so controversial, and so unlike all the other highly polished, politically correct Presidents of the USA. To everyone's surprise, as the elections drew closer, Trump managed to amass the support of many Americans. The number of people willing to vote for him kept increasing in spite of his exponentially disrespectful public speeches and statements. Eventually, he became the President of the USA, and even now he continues to court controversies.

However, everyone should be given a chance to prove themselves without being judged, and Mr Trump is no exception.

Follow-up Questions & Answers:
1. How did you come to know about the controversies created by this person?
I came to know of Donald Trump from the TV, initially, and then I followed up on news of the American elections in newspapers and on the internet. I have always been interested in political debates and discussions, so I managed to gather some information on Trump's latest controversies every now and then from my circle of friends, too.

2. Do celebrities deliberately create controversies at times?
Yes, sometimes celebrities do create controversies to stay in the limelight in the media. Sometimes, they intentionally spread rumours of accidents, affairs, break ups, or similar issues, as the media pays more attention to such scoops. This coverage also reaches people faster and grabs their attention. This is the reason, just before the release of a film or a music album, they intentionally create such controversies in a pre-planned manner. They also drag in other people, organise press conferences, and give provoking statements to garner public attention. Sometimes, some media men also take an active part in encouraging and supporting pre-planned controversies because they get monetary benefit in return.

3. Do you think celebrities/personalities create controversies intentionally? If yes, how?
Celebrities create controversies for many reasons. First, they try to catch the attention of people through their antics so that their popularity amongst the masses increases quickly. Secondly, they create controversies to bring monetary benefits to their forthcoming projects like films or live events. Through these controversies, they get the desired coverage and popularity, which helps them in achieving their goal of attracting more business for their projects.

4. Do you think controversies really have a positive impact on their careers?

It is difficult to answer this question. However, considering the present lifestyles of people and the cultural changes in society, I think controversies do help celebrities in getting a boost in their market value. Today's success parameters have changed; they focus a lot on the market value of a celebrity also, along with their qualities and talents. Considering this, I must admit that celebrities do get short term revenue based benefits by creating controversies or being involved in them. On top of it, in today's fast moving life, people actually do not remember issues and controversies for long. Soon after a big controversy, their minds become fresh and ready to welcome another controversy, and to boost the market value of the celebrity.

5. Do you believe that the media gives more importance to the controversies of celebrities rather than their achievements?

Yes, it is true to a certain extent. Most newspapers, magazines, and television channels want to increase their circulation or viewership. In this race, they must present something different, spicier, and more attractive each time, in order to get more business. Unfortunately, controversies do attract the immediate attention of people and, hence, are used to gain more business by media houses.

6. Has the popularity of international celebrities increased or decreased in your country in the last few years?

The popularity of international celebrities has increased in my country in the last few years. These days, people talk about international celebrities, more than ever. International celebrities from various fields such as sports, films, music, politics, and business are given more attention by the media and the people of my country.

7. What are the reasons behind the rise/fall in the popularity of international celebrities in your country?

There are two major reasons behind the rise/fall of international celebrities in my country. The first is globalization. It has enabled people to keep updating themselves about international lifestyle and culture themes. In addition, this has also increased the study of English language across people of all age groups in my country. The second reason is the outstanding economic growth of my country in the last few years. This boom in the economy has attracted many international investors and entertainers to penetrate into the Indian market and develop it as one of their potential big earners. So, the popularity of international celebrities has risen in my country.

Practice Questions:

1. Why do people have more interest in such controversial news?
2. Which is a better medium to receive international news?
3. What kinds of people are more interested in knowing about international celebrities?

19. Speak about a positive change in your life.

    You should say

-   **When it happened**

- What the positive change was
- What you learned from it, or how it changed your life

What brought about this positive change in your life?

Suggestions:
Candidates can speak about any experience that has had a positive impact on their lives; for example, a failure in an exam could have inspired them to work harder and made them better at studies.

Sample Answer:
'A moment or an event can sometimes change our lives'. This saying was only a theoretical concept for me before I received the results of my 12th grade prelim exams in school. I was a happy-go-lucky person, and was not too dedicated to my studies despite all the constant prodding from parents and relatives. I received a lot of appreciation and compliments in my school life for my adaptability and my ability to understand and grasp study concepts. I knew that I was in an important year, which would decide my future career. Still, I was taking it casually, and for me, it was all fun and games till I received the results of my preliminary exam just before a month and a half of my final board exams. I was shocked to see that I only received a 55% score in my main subjects. I remember feeling very sad, depressed, and frustrated; so much so, that I started cursing myself for my score, because I knew that if I had worked hard, I could have managed better results. I wanted to hide from my friends, my teachers, and even my parents. When I went home, everyone was waiting for my results. I felt guilty and sorry on looking at their expectant eyes, because I knew that soon they would be unhappy. Tears started streaming from my eyes and I could not utter a word. Seeing this, my father understood the situation. He sat with me and he explained to me that nothing was lost because I still had 45 days more to prepare, and that much time would in fact be enough for me to improve my results. He restored my confidence and motivated me to do as best as I could. I changed my attitude from that moment on, and worked to my best abilities in those 45 days before my final board exam. I was a little sceptical about the results as I waited for them, but in the end I scored a distinction in my 12th grade. I was really happy that day. I took my parents' blessings and conveyed my gratitude to my father. Had he not handled the situation well on the day I scored badly, I wouldn't have got a good final result, which was a major stepping-stone for my career. I learned to be sincere and proactive about my studies, from that event and I scored well throughout my graduation years. That day was a turning point in my life.

Follow-up Questions & Answers:
1. Do you still consider it a positive change in your life, or not?
Yes, I still consider it a positive change in my life because I learned the importance of dedication from that moment on, which has proved helpful to me in all walks of my life.
2. How has it changed your life?
It has made dramatic changes in my life. I became sincere, dedicated, and proactive in my approach towards my studies, and other aspects of my life. This change in attitude helped me in sharpening my ability to work hard and adapt to situations, which ultimately increased my self-confidence. I also learned to be alert and receptive, and to

take appreciation only as a part of life, so that I might not become overconfident about any aspect of my life again.

3. What are the social changes happening in your country?

There are many social changes happening in my country. Lifestyles, family systems, customs and traditions, and ways of celebrating festivals and ceremonies are undergoing major transformations. All these aspects of our society are being influenced by western culture. I think we are witnessing an important social transformation in the history of this country, which will bring many new changes in our social system in the future.

Practice Questions

1. How can rapid changes affect individuals?
2. What should we do to face these changes?
3. What changes do you anticipate (predict) will happen in your life/society/city/country?

20. Talk about s story/tale you heard in your childhood.

You should say

- **What the story was**
- **Who told it to you**
- **When they told you the story**

What is the message/moral of the story?

Sample Answer:

I heard and read many stories in my childhood. My parents and grandparents told me many stories about various aspects of life. Here, I would like to talk about a story that I heard from my grandmother when I was seven years old. This is actually an incident from the great epic Mahabharata, where the Pandavas and Kauravas went to learn archery and other skills in the hermitage of Draunacharya. As we all know, Arjuna was the expert in archery, among the Pandavas. One day the mentor, Draunacharya, asked all the candidates to sit under a tree. He then kept a wooden idol of a bird on one branch of that tree and informed all his disciples that they had to target the eye of the wooden bird and hit it with their arrow. After that, he called each student one by one and asked each of them what they could see. Varying replies started coming from students, one after the other. Some could see the whole sky, some saw the whole tree, while others saw the branch on which the bird was kept. On hearing their answers, the mentor didn't allow any of the candidates to hit the target. Finally, he called Arjuna and asked him the same question. Arjuna, unlike the others claimed that he was able to see nothing but the bird. On hearing this, the mentor asked him the same question again, and this time Arjuna focused a little more and said that he saw only the eye of the bird, and nothing else. Listening to this, the mentor immediately handed the bow and arrow to him and permitted him to take a shot. Arjuna was successful in hitting the eye of the wooden bird. The moral of the story is — 'we should learn to be focused on the goals in our life. If we are focused on the target, and not on other trivial things, we are bound to succeed'.

Follow-up Questions & Answers:

1. What other stories do you remember from your childhood?

I heard plenty of stories in my childhood. While I don't remember many of them today, I can still recall stories from the Ramayana and Mahabharata, the anecdotes of Akbar and Birbal, fables from the Panchtantra, tales of Chanakya, and the stories of our struggle for independence that I heard from my grandfather. He used to tell me his first-hand experiences from when he took part in the fight for freedom for our country. He also participated in the 'Quit India Movement' in 1942.

2. What is the role of stories/tales in the development of a child?

Stories play an important role in the development of a child. They help a child to imagine anecdotes in his mind, which is the first step to developing the child's creativity. Another important benefit of telling stories to children is that through these tales we can impart knowledge of our culture, traditions, moral values, and religious beliefs to them. Such knowledge forms the basis of a child's personality. Lastly, storytelling often satisfies the curiosity of children, and enhances their mental growth.

3. What are the benefits of grandparents telling stories to children in the family?

This is one of the best ways to pass on the cultural heritage of one's family and community to the offspring. What's more, this tradition is practised most in joint families, because in such families, grandparents get to spend more time with their grandchildren on a daily basis, and storytelling serves as a constructive way for grandparents to pass their leisure time, while simultaneously keeping an eye on the children.

4. What is the difference between the stories of the past and the present?

In the past, stories were based on history, tradition, religion, and moral values. But stories these days are largely based on fantasy, fiction, and super natural characters or superheroes, examples being, Barbie, Superman, Spiderman, and Pokémon.

5. How do stories affect youngsters/teenagers?

Stories can have life-changing effects on both, youngsters and teenagers. Stories can divert their minds to religion, culture, and patriotism. There are incidents in all societies of teenagers changing the direction of their lives towards positive activities after hearing influential stories or parables.

6. Do you think children have lost their interest in stories?

No, I don't think children have lost their interest in stories. However, I do admit that they have more entertainment options these days, and so, their interests have changed in terms of the subjects of stories. Now, they prefer listening to stories about fantasy lands and fairies, rather than old parables. But that doesn't mean they have lost interest in stories.

7. Should schools organise story-telling competitions? Why?

Yes, schools must organise story-telling competitions for many reasons. First, participants develop their public speaking skills through story-telling. Secondly, they have to read and understand many stories to be able to select and tell a single story on stage. This preparation actually improves their reading comprehension skills, which can help them in their academic subjects, too. Lastly, by organising such contests, schools can identify children with extraordinary oratory skills and mould themselves into even better orators of the future.

Practice Questions
1. Can story books serve as ideal gifts for children?
2. How can a teacher tell a story?
3. Should schools use stories as a method of teaching?
4. What are the advantages and disadvantages of using story-telling as a teaching method?

21. An expensive thing that you had wanted to buy for a long time and were able to buy.

You should say
- **What that thing was**
- **How long you waited**
- **How you bought it**

In what ways is it useful to you?

Suggestions:
Candidates can speak about computers, houses, offices, mobiles, motor bikes, jewellery, and other similar big purchases.

Sample Answer:
I was desperate to buy a house for a long time. It was getting difficult for me to buy the perfect house because we were in a dilemma as regards whether to change our area of residence, or not. I live in a joint family and a majority of my relatives and friends lived in the same area as myself. We tried hard to find a flat that was spacious enough for six members and had good facilities, including parking spaces. Finally, one builder introduced a new scheme near my home. It was a low-rise apartment with 3 bedroom flats. The site plans and structure of the building looked perfect for us, and fit all our requirements, but was priced much higher than what we were prepared to pay, owing to the recent boom in real estate in our city. I knew that the builder had bought the plot at a high rate himself, and was confident that the building would be made according to the latest trends in interior decoration and construction. We were sure we wanted to buy that house, and hence, we started arranging money for it. However, it was doubtful if we would be able to buy it before it gets sold to someone else, because of the gap between our budget and the property price. Meanwhile, a dispute happened between the builder and the original land-owner, and the dispute went to court. It went on for almost 12 months, and we could arrange the required money in the meantime. We booked the flat through a bank loan, and we also sold our old flat to pay for the new one. Finally, after a long wait of almost 2 years, we were able to buy a house that was simply perfect — awesome, spacious, and in the same area as my previous residence. My parents were also happy as they had lived in the same area for many years and were averse to moving away from there. This house is very useful to me because we all now have enough space to store our stuff, and to live in comfort and luxury. I like my home very much.

Practice Questions
1. Do you still use that thing? (OR) Do you still live in that house?
2. What is the difference between the attitude of parents and children towards saving money?

22. Tell me about an interesting/important letter you received.

You should say
- **When and where you received it**
- **Who sent it to you**
- **What the contents of the letter were**

How did you react to it?

Sample Answer:

I would like to talk about the first appointment letter I received in my life. It was 1996 when I completed my graduation, and I wanted to take up a job in the marketing field where I could interact with different types of people and have the opportunity to sharpen my communication skills. I had applied to a multinational company for the post of a marketing executive. Fortunately, I was called for an interview where I found that many candidates were in the race for the job. It was my first interview and I was not completely confident, nor entirely satisfied with my preparation. However, seven days after the interview, when I was sitting at home, a letter from the company was delivered to my doorstep, and I felt a rush of excitement. I immediately opened the envelope, and to my surprise, it was an appointment letter for the post I wanted. The letter contained an offer of appointment, along with the terms and conditions, my job responsibilities in detail, and the date of reporting to the company. The management had also mentioned the salary, which was a little more than what they had offered me at the time of the interview. Along with this letter they offered me a free rail ticket to the company headquarters, where I would have to go to take the pre-job training for seven days. I jumped with joy and instantly called up my father and my friends to inform them about the appointment letter. I was very happy that the company had selected me and offered me an attractive salary. I will never forget that moment in my life because that letter was the first step from where I started my professional life.

Follow-up Questions & Answers:

1.Have you preserved that letter?

Yes, I have had that letter laminated and have kept it in a separate file with my other important documents, at home. Even today, whenever I want to relive old memories, I open that file and read the letter and try to recall that day of my life.

2.Did you expect that letter?

Honestly speaking, I didn't expect that letter, because I saw many competent and experienced candidates applying for the same post, while I was a fresh graduate at that time. Despite that, the company selected me for the job. Later, I was informed that I was found suitable on all selection criteria that the management had deemed necessary for the role.

3.What are the advantages and disadvantages of emails?

Emails offer more benefits than drawbacks. They are a fast, cheap, accurate, safe, and reliable medium of communication. In addition, we can easily transfer large amounts of data in various forms including photos or graphics, through emails. However, it does have some drawbacks. To access emails, the users need to know at least the basics of English, and computer operations. Moreover, it is a mechanical way of communication,

---

where people don't use handwriting. Unfortunately, some people also misuse emails for fraudulent purposes, and for spreading viruses.

4.Do emails affect the writing abilities of people?
I think emails do affect the writing abilities of people to some extent. With emails, people have to use the computer keyboard only, which makes them so computer-addicted, that they then tend to avoid using pen and paper, and even when they do, the quality of their writing is often inferior in terms of intelligibility, and language, because of a lack of practice.

Practice Questions
1. For what purposes, do you think people use emails?
2. What are the advantages or disadvantages of SMS?
3. Do you use a computer, or a laptop for emails?
4. What type of emails do you generally send/receive?
5. What difficulties do you face when you write a letter?

23. Describe a three-day holiday you enjoyed.

   You should say
- **Where you went and when**
- **What preparations you made for the holiday**
- **With whom you went there**
What was your overall experience like?

Sample Answer:
I would like to talk about my visit to Mount Abu. Last January, I went to this hill station with my family. Before I begin, I must say that my current occupation is quite demanding. It doesn't allow me to take too many holidays. I had to prepare one month in advance to organise my work schedule. After that, I inquired with different travel agents who offered package deals for families to Mount Abu. I selected the most suitable package with all the facilities we wanted, and eventually we set out on our holiday. We reached Mount Abu in about 5 hours, checked in at our hotel, rested for a while, and then left for the market. The market is very close to the famous 'Nakhi Lake'. We enjoyed boating in the lake, and then we set out to shop for some traditional garments and winter wear. We also took a few photos of each other with my camera; but the most amazing aspect of our trip was the atmosphere there. The sky remained clear and cool breezes blew throughout the day. We had our lunch at a good restaurant in the market, roamed around a little more, and then returned to our hotel in the evening.

Next day, we went out for some sightseeing. We saw popular places near the city like the very tall 'Guru Shikhar" peak, the peaceful Bhramakumaris' centre, some beautiful gardens, the famous Delwada Temples, and the very scenic Sunset Point. The atmosphere was stunningly beautiful and energizing throughout the day. We then came back, and on the third day, we took some rest, roamed about the city, and bought some souvenirs from local vendors. After that, we started our journey back home, already determined to visit again, soon.

It was a refreshing trip that filled me with zeal, enthusiasm, and energy by the time I returned home. A year later, today, when I see photos of that trip, I still experience the refreshing feeling from back then.

Follow-up Questions & Answers:

1. What type of activities do people enjoy on holidays?

It depends a lot on the type of destination they visit. When people go to the seashore, they like indulging in activities like sunbathing, swimming, boating, and beach volleyball. When they visit hill stations, they may enjoy adventure activities like skiing and paragliding, or more leisure activities like hiking to various peaks, or enjoying sunrise and sunset points. In short, people like to do something different and exciting when they are out on holidays.

2. Should we plan our holidays in advance?

It is advisable that we plan our holidays in advance, so that we may not face hardships in booking tickets, looking for accommodation, and finding our kind of food, at the last minute. Usually, we go on holidays to relax and to experience something new. But, if we waste our time at such places looking for lodging and boarding facilities, it defeats the purpose of relaxation. Instead, it becomes a mechanical experience for us. I have realized, that planned holidays are enjoyed more than unplanned ones, especially if we are headed to distant places, because our advance planning makes us stress free and relaxed.

3. Should we prepare a budget before going on holidays?

This is an important aspect of holiday planning. We ought to plan our budget for all events and places we plan to visit and enjoy. This financial planning enhances our enjoyment a great deal. In addition, it also helps us in spending money on only those things that are necessary, which is especially important, because we often feel tempted to buy many trivial, useless things when we are holidaying.

4. Do you plan holidays on your own, or do you hire the services of a travel agent? Why?

That depends on the destination I want to visit. If I know the place, the hotels, and the average rates of accommodation there, I don't hire a travel agent. But if I plan to visit a distant place for the first time, I prefer hiring the services of a travel agent.

5. What are the services provided by a good travel agent?

A good travel agent always offers value-for-money services. He provides flexible and economical packages. The hotels offered by him are safe, well maintained, and near the downtown areas. Moreover, good travel agents provide a tour manager who can also work as a tour guide when required.

6. Are tour guides necessary during holidays?

Tour guides are necessary only at the places which have historical, religious, or archaeological significance. They can explain to us the history of such places, and also suggest important locations in and around our destination, that are worth visiting.

7. What are the benefits and drawbacks of giving holidays to employees?

Employees need holidays for a variety of reasons like satisfying their personal and family needs, as well as their social obligations. What's more, they also need a break from their work to avoid a feeling of monotony in life that may otherwise reduce their efficiency. I don't think there are any major drawbacks of giving holidays to employees. However, too many holidays certainly affect the output of the company and disturb the work environment, because other employees have to carry the additional workload of their absent colleagues.

8. What types of jobs are offered by the holiday/hospitality industry these days?
The hospitality industry offers a number of jobs in a variety of categories. These jobs range from tour guides, hotel staff, restaurant staff, and travel agents, to local artisans and craftsmen. This massive industry also creates job opportunities in dependent fields, such as airways and railways.

Practice Questions
1. Do you think that holidays should be given to employees?
2. What benefits are provided by the tourism industry to the nation?
3. What types of problems are faced by travel agencies?
4. What are the advantages and disadvantages of traveling alone and traveling in a group?

24. Describe a hotel you stayed at.
  You should say
- **The name and location of the hotel**
- **Where you went, and when**
- **What facilities were offered by the hotel management**
What was the highlight of the hotel you stayed at?

Sample Answer:
Today I would like to speak about a hotel called Atlantis, The Palm. This hotel is located in UAE's international hub of business and tourism, Dubai. I stayed there a year ago, when I went to Dubai on a leisure trip with my wife and daughter. Atlantis is a five star hotel spread over a very vast 1 km area, facing the grand Arabian Sea. It has won many awards in the field of hospitality for its outstanding ambience, luxury, and service delivery. Not only does Atlantis have many rooms, it also has many categories of rooms. Apart from the regular deluxe rooms, this hotel offers ocean rooms that overlook the sea, palm beach rooms that overlook the magnificent Dubai skyline, executive, regal, and terrace club suites, each of which come with dedicated concierge services. These suites are ideal for families because they are huge in size, with enough space for 3 people per room. They have balconies which are perfect for sunbathing, and for dining in the open. Each room has humongous attached bathrooms with beautiful glass panels, very luxurious showers, and in built bath tubs to facilitate relaxation.
Apart from these beautiful regular rooms and suites, Atlantis, The Palm also has some very unique accommodation options for those willing to shell out a few extra bucks. One such option is the 220 square metre big Presidential Suite, truly fit for a king, because of tis perfect blend of luxury and prestige. Another unbelievable room option is the Underwater Suite, which gives guests the feeling of living under the sea. These rooms

have toughened glass panels fitted in them, which give a beautiful view of the local marine life. For those who opt to stay at the Atlantis, the hotel offers amazing activities such as dolphin viewing, visiting their Lost Chambers Aquarium, which is like entering a parallel world of fish, far removed from this one, and entry to the Aquaventure Waterpark, rated number one in the Middle East and Europe.

Atlantis, The Palm also has a state of the art spa and rejuvenation centre, replete with the best of spa services and packages from across the world. It also offers salon services, yoga, and other fitness options. Further, this hotel has a dedicated kids' area where children can enjoy their trip to the fullest without getting bored, while their parents immerse themselves in more relaxing leisurely activities. As far as food is concerned, the Atlantis has 15 restaurants, each one catering to a different cuisine, with a different ambience. Whether you have a craving for authentic Chinese cuisine, or you want to indulge in rustic Italian flavours, the Atlantis has it all. For children looking to eat American fast food, too, there are options available.

Further, guests can go shopping at the Atlantis, play sports, go for a swim either in the many pools, or in the sea, and can even opt for yacht cruises or helicopter tours of the area. All in all, this is a hotel I would recommend to everyone, as a must visit, at least once in a lifetime.

Follow-up Questions & Answers:

1. What types of hotels are available in your country/state/city?

All types of hotels, ranging from those with 3 star ratings to those with 7 star ratings, are available in my city. However, hotels catering to corporate and banquet activities are found more frequently in my city, because more big businesses are coming up, in and around. They tend to build their offices within the city, so their meetings, seminars, conferences, and training sessions are held in various nearby hotels. Next, the trend of organizing marriages and other cultural functions in hotels is in catching on, these days. This is the reason why hotels catering to marriages, ring ceremonies, and other social functions are also coming up in my city. This trend is seen in almost all the cities in my state.

2. Do you think hotels should organise cultural or religious events in their premises?

Yes, I think it is a good idea. Hotels should organise cultural events in their premises. This could help them in gaining a presence in the local community and staying in the limelight. In addition, visitors who are interested in local culture and religion are more likely to select these hotels over others, thus giving a business advantage to the hotels in question. To top it, locals also benefit from cultural and religious events organised nearby. I think this is one of the most direct routes for local people to gain from the hospitality industry.

3. What challenges are faced by the hotel/hospitality industry today?

The hospitality industry faces lots of challenges from various sources. One of them is a lack of government support in its development. The government in my country levies high taxes on hotels, resorts, and other leisure establishments. This forces them to increase their prices when it comes to customer service. In addition, it also reduces their profit margins and inhibits their growth. However, the biggest challenge that the hotel industry in my country faces these days is terrorism. Terrorism threatens local and international visitors against visiting popular tourist places, causing a big dip in the revenues of the hotel industry. I would like to assert here, that the government must take active and result oriented steps to curb terrorism in the whole country.

4. How has the hotel industry in your country grown in the last few years?

Thanks to globalisation, economic growth, and a boom in the IT sector, the hotel industry in India has flourished in last few years. More international visitors are coming to India now, than ever before, for business purposes. As India is gaining a good reputation internationally, many foreigners are coming here to stay, to travel, to study, to work on projects, or to conduct research on the lifestyle, culture, religions, ancient scriptures, and even the food here, in India. To top it, the average income of my countrymen has also increased substantially in the last few years. This has made it possible for more people to go for regular visits to popular, recreational places such as hotels and restaurants, giving a boost to the hotel industry as a whole.

5. Do you think more taxes should be levied on international tourists who stay in hotels in your country?

I am against it personally. I think when international tourists come to our country, they give our nation the privilege to host them, by selecting it as a preferred travel destination over other countries. In doing so, they bring foreign revenue to our country's economy. Considering this, it is not good on our part if we levy additional taxes on international visitors. However, the exception to this is, if a region or a place depends entirely on visitors or tourists to sustain its economy. In such cases, the authorities may consider levying additional taxes on international tourists to increase the revenue from tourism, if the region is already underperforming on economic grounds when it comes to its other industries.

6. What is the difference between the hotels located in hill stations and the hotels located in big cities?

Hotels located in hill stations and tourist spots normally focus on entertainment, and tourist support services and facilities. They tend to focus more on leisure, because that is the main purpose of people visiting their hotel. On the other hand, hotels located in big cities focus more on corporate and banquet services. They try to facilitate business visitors and upgrade their facilities accordingly.

7. If given a chance, would you prefer working in hotel? If yes, at what post and why?

It is tough for me to decide whether or not I would like to work in a hotel. However, I think if I get the chance, I would like to work as a manager, or a chief of divisions such as customer care and marketing, where I can communicate with people and keep updating my soft skills from time to time. In addition, I would also like to train the hotel staff in honing their communication skills and soft skills.

8. What steps should hotels take to prevent terrorist attacks?

Hotels must have tight security systems in place, with well-trained security guards, and electronic security devices like CCTV (Close Circuit Television) cameras, laser movement detectors, metal detectors, and finger print identification machines. Such preventive measures will surely help in restricting the entry of any unwanted persons or terrorists, and help the management in catching any culprits from within the hotel premises. In addition, such security measures also prevent local criminals or thieves from entering the hotel premises.

9. What effects do terrorist attacks have on the hotel industry?

Terrorist attacks have an extremely negative effect on the business of the entire hospitality industry. Tourists and families avoid visiting hotels in the fear of being attacked by terrorists. In addition, the employees seem to stay away from working in those hotels or cities that are prone to terrorist attacks. Further, the hotel management has to spend more money on installing enhanced security measures. All these factors can create a big reduction in revenue generation of business across the industry.

Practice Questions:

1. What did you enjoy most during your stay in that hotel?
2. How was the service of that hotel?
3. Do you have any suggestions for the hotel management or staff?
4. How does the government of your country promote or support the hotel industry?
5. How important is it for hotels to offer facilities like swimming pools/gyms/conference halls/theatres/yoga and meditation centres? (This is not a single question; this is a combination of 5 questions in one).
6. What skills are required to work in a hotel, according to you?
7. How can the government help hotels in improving their security?
8. Do you think hotels should hire private security guards to fight against terrorist attacks?

25. Describe a large organisation you know.

    You should say

- **The name of the organisation**
- **How and what you know about the organisation**
- **What products/services that organisation offers**

What was the role of the founder in making the organisation successful?

Sample Answer:

I would like to speak about Reliance Industries, today — probably the largest and the most diversified business organisation of my country. I came to know about Reliance because of my interest in the stock market. Because I am also a shareholder of Reliance Industries, I study their annual reports regularly. I also read about the company in newspapers, and online. It was founded by Mr. Dhirubhai Ambani. He started this organisation as a textile manufacturing unit in Mumbai, and then went on to diversify into various business segments like petrochemicals, petro products and refinery, fabrics, yarns, infrastructure, power distribution and production, mobile services, financial services, and retail. Now, the entire group has been divided into two parts, under separate managements, but both parts collectively, are still amongst the fastest growing business groups in the world. Their growth is reflected in their financial results also. As I mentioned earlier, Reliance was founded by Mr. Dhirubhai Ambani. He first went to Mumbai, from Gujarat simply to trade in commodities. But, his vision and hard work helped the company grow in leaps and bounds, beyond anyone's imagination. He courageously led his company on the path of growth, and consistently gave value to its shareholders. Reliance has recently launched one of the largest oil refineries of the world, in India. What's more, the company has also started a chain of grocery stores named Reliance Fresh, and jewellery showrooms named Reliance Jewel, all across India. It holds the number one position in terms of market capitalisation in the Indian stock market, today.

Recently, I was happy to learn that even in the current recessionary times, Reliance is showing positive growth and hiring more employees to support the economy of India.

Follow-up Questions & Answers:
1. If given a chance, would you like to work for that organisation?
It is a privilege to work with such an organisation. Many engineers and technicians aspire to work with Reliance group, and to pursue their career with the company. This is because Reliance has a very good reputation and strong market presence amongst competitors, across its entire range of products. Such organisations give better job satisfaction to their employees. I must admit, if given a chance I would certainly serve this organisation if their requirements match my skill set. It is a matter of pride for any professional to be associated with Reliance group.

2. What is more important when it comes to the brand recall of an organisation — the name of the company, or the products/services they offer?
Well, it depends on the range of the products that the company offers. Many a time, we remember the products first, and then the company name comes as an afterthought. For example, if we talk about televisions, most of us can easily recall SONY, or LG, or Samsung by association with their good quality TVs. However, there are many companies that do not manufacture popular consumer goods, but still manage to be popular among the general public, because of a variety of other reasons. Infosys, for example, is a leading software services provider that offers its services to corporate clients, only. Rarely does one come across retail or individual users of Infosys products; still, its name is easy to recall.

3. What are the benefits of working with such organisations?
Such organisations offer threefold benefits— the first being remuneration. They offer higher pay packages to their employees compared to small or medium sized organisations. The second benefit is job satisfaction. It is a matter of privilege for employees to work for such companies as it improves their social status, while also providing better facilities in the workplace. Finally, working for such organisations offers high growth prospects because the ladder of hierarchy is often longer than in small businesses. This actually provides enough promotion opportunities to employees, to grow in their career.

4. Why do some organisations work in night shifts?
There are two major industries where working in night shifts is common. One is the manufacturing industry, where they keep their machines on round the clock to get the maximum possible output, to enhance their productivity and profitability. The second is the ITES (IT Enabled Services) sector, fuelled by call centres, which work in night shifts because they have to attend real time calls from customers across different time zones. Many customers call in from western countries like the USA, Canada, and the UK. These countries move far behind the Indian standard time, and hence their day starts when our

---

evening begins. This is the reason why call centres have to work in night shifts to serve clients.

5. Are any bad effects noticed on the health of those workers who work in night shifts?
At times it is observed that those who work in night shifts disturb their normal body clock, and attract diseases or disorders related to this disturbance. They might face high stress, headaches, eye problems, and sometimes even muscle related issues. However, with proper exercise and other healthy habits, such problems can be taken care of.

6. Do you think working in night shifts should be banned? Justify your answer.
No, I don't think working in night shifts should be banned, because it is not a sensible decision, considering the contribution that the manufacturing and service sectors provide to the society and the economy. More people are likely to get jobs, tax collections could rise, and more employee satisfaction and success is also likely to be noted in the near future, provided we don't ban working in night shifts. Besides, there are many essential services like transportation, electricity, telecom, and power that are the lifeline of any economy. Here, it is necessary for some employees to work night shifts.

7. What is the difference between government organisations and private organisations in your country?
There is a huge difference in government organisations and private companies in India. Government organisations normally have fixed rules and procedures to follow, and they run under the monitoring of government employees. We can find at least one government organisation in almost every city or town in our country. The availability of some types of government organisations can vary from region to region sometimes. For example, we may not find manufacturing units run by the government, in big cities. The same is true for private sector companies, also. However, private sector companies are run either by a small group of select people, or an individual in a leadership position, making the procedures faster and swifter while also allowing for urgent modifications in procedures, when needed.

8. Why is the working style in government organisations slower than that of private organisations?
The working style of government organisations is generally slower, because of many reasons. The government gives unconditional job security to its employees. This often makes them complacent, and thus less efficient. Promotions are also based on seniority as opposed to merit. This hinders the overall performance of government organisations. In addition, government organisations have more hierarchy levels compared to private ones, which might frustrate some employees from time to time, if lines of authority are not clear. On the other hand, private sector companies only acknowledge performance, and give incentives and promotions on merit only. This is the reason why employees in private organisations are concerned only about their performance. This kind of set up ultimately enhances the output of the company.

9. How do large organisations help the society/country?
Large organisations help the country and the society in various ways. They directly help the society by recruiting more people from the community, thus reducing unemployment. They also directly help the country by contributing more tax revenues to the system, and to boosting the national economy. However, there are many indirect benefits, also. Some organisations run their own welfare trusts or social service organisations as part of their

CSR. They help poor and needy people, by giving jobs and money for education. In addition, some of them have started opening their own schools, colleges, and hospitals. Thus, a large organisation committed to making a positive impact on the society can prove to be a valuable asset for the country.

Practice Questions
1. Have you visited the premises of that organisation?
2. Why don't some people work with large organisations?
3. Are there any disadvantages of large organisations to individuals/society/the country?

26. Describe a historical place or a historical monument you have seen.
   You should say
- **When and where you saw it**
- **How that place was**
- **What the historical significance of the place/monument is**
What is your overall opinion of the place/monument?

Sample Answer:
India has a reputation of being rich with historical places and monuments scattered across her length and breadth, because this land has supported many civilizations, races, and religions through time. Here, I would like to talk about one of the Seven Wonders of the World, the Taj Mahal. I visited this place two ago years with my family. Located in the north of India, in Agra city, the Taj Mahal is well-known as a symbol of love. It was built during the reign of the Mughal emperor Shah Jahan, in loving memory of his beautiful wife Mumtaz. This monument is a masterpiece of art and architecture. It is a mausoleum built on the tomb of queen Mumtaz on the bank of river Yamuna. Made up entirely of white marble, its ceiling has a big dome in the centre, under which the tomb is situated. The tomb is surrounded by pillars of white marble decorated with amazing artwork. In the evenings we can see dancing fountains with multi coloured lights. This arrangement further enhances the beauty of the place. The splendour of this place cannot be described in words because the greatness of this monument surpasses language. It can only be experienced by visiting. I was thrilled by the vibes inside the Taj Mahal. They are astonishing, even though the construction is almost 400 years old. It took more than 20 years for thousands of workers and craftsmen to complete the structure. In my opinion, the Taj Mahal is the best monument in the world that symbolizes both, art and love.

Follow-up Questions & Answers:
1. What is the history linked to that place/monument?
This monument was built in the loving memory of Queen Mumtaz Mahal. There are some other interesting facts related to the Taj Mahal, too, apart from the motive behind its construction. What stands out is that it took 22 years' time to complete the construction of the Taj Mahal, in around 1648 AD. It was constructed entirely using white marble, and this heavy weight material was carried from about 180 miles away, to the construction

spot, with the help of around one thousand elephants. It is said that more than twenty thousand workers used their skills to build this masterpiece, and after its completion, the awe-struck Emperor Shah Jahan ordered the hands of all the artisans to be chopped off, so that such a monument could never be constructed again. It is also estimated that if the same monument were built today, it would cost billions of dollars.

2. How important are historical places/monuments in our life?
Historical places are very important in our life. They are legacies of our past, which can be passed down to the future generations, along with the great stories they hold. We can study the history of the world better with the help of such monuments. We can also learn about the lifestyles, cultures, religions, and traditions of the past.

3. What are the threats posed to historical places/monuments, today?
The first threat is pollution. Both air and water pollution affect the appearance and structure of historical monuments. For example, a few years back, I read in a newspaper that the Taj Mahal is turning off-white in colour because of the air pollution caused by the nearby industries. The second threat is the visitors themselves. Visitors often do not maintain discipline, and they either misuse such places or damage them. Lastly, an emerging danger is terrorism. Terrorists target historical monuments for various reasons; case in point being, how a few years back, terrorists in Afghanistan destroyed large statues of Buddha, masterpieces of Buddhist art, and texts on history, and spirituality, in a fundamentalist, fanatic outburst.

4. What should governments/individuals do to protect such places from pollution?
Governments should impose strict rules for preventing pollution-related damage to historical places. They should also install security measures to protect such places from vandalism by visitors and antisocial elements. Simultaneously, individuals can behave responsibly when they visit historical places. They should not damage any features of monuments, and should also maintain cleanliness in the area, by using dustbins, and not littering.

5. Should the government develop the infrastructure of historical places, or should they be maintained as they are? Why?
This is a debatable question. However, I think the infrastructure of the monuments and the surrounding areas should not be changed, because if local buildings are converted into hotels and restaurants, local people will have to shift to other places. And without the local people and local structures, the overall charm of the place will get reduced to a great extent. The monuments will look isolated and dull if the surrounding areas are changed. Hence, to keep the original effect and combination intact, governments should not develop the infrastructure of historical places. Ultimately, the architecture, art, and the ambience of the place are more important than infrastructure development, because these historical masterpieces are instrumental in attracting tourism to the area.

Practice Questions
1. Are there any other historical places that you have been to?
2. Should the government sell parts of historical monuments to private companies?
3. Should government hire private companies to manage the security of historical places, or not?

---

27. Describe your visit to a religious place.

  You should say
- **The name and location of the place**
- **When you visited the place**
- **Who you visited with**

What did you like there?

Sample Answer:

I have visited many religious places in India. I have also visited religious places of religions other than mine. However, here, I would like to talk about 'The Golden Temple' (also known as Harmandir Sahib) located in Amritsar, Punjab. I visited this place a few months back with my family. Though I don't follow the Sikh religion, I have huge respect for it. I had wanted to visit 'The Golden Temple' ever since I read the Guru Granth Sahib, which influenced me deeply. This temple was originally a place to meditate, for saints who sought enlightenment. It is said, that initially, a lake was created there, and because of the purity of the place, the water in the lake was referred to as 'Amrit', the elixir of immortality for the Gods. Consequently, the entire city is now known as Amritsar. Sometime around the 17th century, Guru Arjan Sahib installed the newly compiled Guru Granth Sahib in this temple, and since then, followers of the Sikh religion have been reading it regularly as their holy book. The temple has been constructed in the middle of a lake, and its outer walls are coated with real gold. This is probably the only temple of its kind in the whole world. Unlike most temples in India, which have just one entry, we can enter The Golden Temple from all four directions. However, in my eyes, it is not the temple structure or the golden coating that distinguishes it or makes it unique. According to me, the positivity, purity, and holiness of the temple is far greater than its aesthetic beauty. When I first entered the temple corridor, my heart was filled with bliss. I felt as though I had walked into a special place. The peace, the vibes of the place, they were so powerful that I felt pulled into an instant meditative state, from the very moment I entered. From the bridge that connects to the main shrine, we can see a clear reflection of the temple in the lake water. Not only is this sight very soothing to the eyes, but it is also a blissful experience as a whole. I had seen pictures of The Golden Temple reflected in the water in many photos and movies in the past, but seeing it first hand was simply awesome. I then went to the main shrine, where the original Guru Granth Sahib is placed, and sought blessings from the Almighty. I must say, my visit to The Golden Temple was really memorable.

(I personally recommend all the readers of this book to go and visit at least once.)

Follow-up Questions & Answers:

1. What is the importance of such places in our society?

Such places are prominent in our society and hold immense importance amongst the community. They encourage the followers of a religion to gather at one place to participate in religious rituals and processes aimed at improving their lives. In addition, such places also help in creating religious awareness among people of other cultures and countries. This helps in the overall growth of the town or region where they are located, thereby improving the quality of life of the local people who follow that religion.

2. Do you think such places help people in getting connected to their religion?
Such places are of prime importance in our society. They serve as a link between the religion, and the people. People can visit such places and imbibe the virtues and spiritual preaching of the religion, by following the processes enlisted within, to enrich their consciousness. To top it, such places also give an identity to religious followers, and help them associate faster with each other, and stay in touch with their religion.

3. Should we motivate children to visit such places regularly?
Yes, children should be motivated to visit such places regularly, so that they may understand the virtues of their religion. In addition, we can inculcate the values and importance of our culture, along with its rituals and religious practices, in the minds of our children, from an early age, so that they may feel encouraged to follow the religion throughout their lifetime.

4. What kinds of people visit such places often?
People of all ages and genders visit such places. Followers of the religions propagated by such places also visit these institutes and spend time there. To top it, many seekers of peace, consciousness, and spiritual enlightenment also visit these religious places to add something to their search.

5. What did you feel after visiting that place?
I didn't want to leave The Golden Temple, once I had stepped inside. I felt like I was in a heavenly place; the bliss, the peace, the positivity of that place was so powerful that I felt ecstatic, and strongly connected to the temple. I must say, if I get a chance, I will visit The Golden Temple again.

6. What should the government do to protect such places?
Such sacred places need to be protected and maintained, too. They need protection from criminal and terrorist activities. The government should provide armed security to protect such places from criminals. In addition, the government should also provide electronic equipment like metal detectors to catch those who hide weapons under their clothes.

7. Should you follow any procedure before entering such religious places?
Yes, we should keep our shoes outside the temple premises on a shoe rack, before entering. This is so that the dirt and dust stuck to the soles of our shoes stay out of the sacred areas. In addition, many shoes are made of leather, and it is believed that leather articles should not be carried inside holy places. Moreover, we should wash our face, hands, and legs, to clean ourselves before entering the temple. Finally, we must cover our head with a turban or a cloth before entering a Sikh temple, because in Sikhism hair is considered to be one of the holy gifts given to us by nature.

8. What is the importance of following these procedures before entering such places?
Such procedures have been followed in our culture since ages. It is important for us to clean ourselves, and to not carry any animal products like leather with us inside the temple, as they are considered unholy. This is because leather is made from animal skin, and thus, believed to contain negative energy vibrations. There is one more reason according to me; when we clean ourselves and keep our shoes outside, our minds gets ready to feel the place. We can actually put a break to the multitude of thoughts that we have carried with us to the temple, and focus on prayers with a quiet, open mind. To top it, when we clean ourselves, we are sending a message to our subconscious mind that we are now pure and ready to receive God's blessings, better. This enhances our feeling of

oneness with our God in the temple.

9. Do people of other religions also visit that place?
Yes, people who follow other religions also visit such places. However, it depends a lot on their faith in the place in question. If one believes that the holiness of a place is worth experiencing, irrespective of its religious associations, then he should visit holy places belonging to other religions, too.

10. Should photography or videography be allowed at such places? Justify your answer.
I am personally against it. There is no need to permit photography or video recording at such places, because photos and videos commercialise a place. People sell photos and videos of such places to those who live far away, and while this looks good on the surface, it actually weakens the intent of people to make personal visits to these places. Secondly, the replicas or photos are often kept in houses as a show pieces only, which, according to me, is not very respectful towards the religious place.

11. Do you think local authorities should give special facilities to the people who come to visit religious places?
I think it is a good idea. Local government authorities should definitely give some special facilities to those who travel long distances to visit religious places, in order to make their visits more convenient. They can give facilities like better public transport systems, better electricity supply in guest accommodations, and some economical guest houses for those who wish to stay there for a few days. What's more, the government should also take effective steps to secure visitors from frauds and criminals. Such facilities often motivate people to visit the venue repeatedly.

12. Should the government offer special transportation facilities to such places?
Yes, if possible, the government should arrange special routes for popular religious places. The government can organise special bus and train routes exclusively for those who wish to visit these religious destinations. This helps visitors in avoiding the excessive hassle that often occurs during long distance travel.

Practice Questions
1. Is there any history linked to that place?
2. If given a chance, would you prefer buying a house near that place?

28. Describe a memorable event in your life.
   You should say
- **When and where the event took place**
- **What happened on that day**
- **What feelings you experienced**
Why do you remember that event?
Suggestions:
Candidates can speak about events like marriages, festival celebrations, winning prizes in competitions, school or college farewell parties, or any other events when they were honoured in public.

Sample Answer:
I have been a part of many important and memorable events, in my life. However, today I would like to speak about my college 'welcome party'. It was organised on our second day of college, in the college hall, in 1993. I had a flair for handling announcements, and managing other anchoring related activities since childhood, but I had never made any serious attempts to hone my talents or use them, until this event happened. On the first orientation day of our college, seniors came to our class and announced that there would be a 'fresher party' the next day, and that we were all invited to it. When I reached the venue, I noticed that the party was quite exciting, and everyone was enjoying the company of their new college mates. After a while, some seniors went on stage and started performing their rehearsed comedy acts and dances. Suddenly, there was an announcement that the anchor for the rest of the event, a student from the senior class, had been unable to attend the party because of personal reasons. On hearing this, one of the professors gave the students an open invitation to host and manage the event, if any of us wished to. I gathered some courage and went on stage. It was a new and exciting experience for me. I used my in-born talents skilfully that day, and everyone present enjoyed the event. The professor who had invited us to anchor the event, came to me in the end and appreciated me for my endeavours. After that, I anchored many college functions, but the first experience was the most outstanding for me. Being able to make the event an enjoyable affair for all the students and professors, gave me a lot of confidence and satisfaction. I still remember that event, and even today, whenever I want to relive my college days, I make it a point to see photos of that event.

Follow-up Questions & Answers:
1. What is the importance of ceremonies in our lives?
Ceremonies are important for personal, social, and religious reasons. When we celebrate ceremonies, we can enjoy the event in many ways that make pleasant, lifetime memories for us. Moreover, ceremonies serve as an excuse to meet our friends, relatives, colleagues, and neighbours. These gatherings help us in strengthening the social bonds we share with others. Furthermore, ceremonies also keep us in touch with our religion because we often follow a set of religious rituals on such occasions.

2. How has the attitude towards marriage changed in the last few years?
The attitude towards marriage has considerably transformed in the last few years. People now avoid getting married at an early age, which is a good development, because getting married after settling in one's career gives maturity to the relationship, enabling the couple to enjoy their life better. Child marriages and caste marriages are gradually disappearing from the society because of rising levels of education, and an awareness of the benefits of attaining stability in life. People don't hesitate to get married to the person of their choice, these days and this can prove to be the right decision for many. This is because most people these days prefer to get married after 25 years of age, when they are sure of what they want and can better understand their responsibilities and commitments towards each other, as well as towards other aspects of life.

3. What kinds of national/international events make headlines in your country?
There are many political, financial, and strategic developments happening in my country, which make headlines. In addition, important sports events, major accidents, epidemics,

important developments in the field of entertainment, and big news about other industries also earn their space in the headlines. Apart from this, visits of a political foreign delegates to my country, comments made by international leaders about our country, and acts of terrorism also grab the headlines.

4. Should we make a record of all the memorable events that take place in our life? How?

Yes, I think we must keep a record of all the memorable events of our life in the form of photos and videos. This record becomes an invaluable asset for us in future, because they hold our past memories, milestones, and life achievements.

Practice Questions

1. Will there be any change in the importance of ceremonies in people's lives, in the future?
2. Do men and women have different attitudes towards marriage?
3. What type of issues does the media in your country pay more attention to?

29. Describe some news about your family that gave you happiness.

You should say

- **What that news was**
- **When and where you got it**
- **Why it was important**

How did you react to the news?

Suggestions:

Candidates can speak about any news regarding their family members, such as childbirth, a new job, a new house, an engagement or marriage, a promotion at work, or the setting up of a new business.

Sample Answer:

I live in a family oriented culture, which means we have a higher emotional attachment towards each other, as compared to other cultures of the world. This is the reason behind the intensity of our feelings of happiness and sadness, for events happening in the lives of our relatives. Today, I would like to talk about my aunt, who got her US visa in March 2002. My aunt lived in a house separate from ours, and contributed heavily to her home finances from a very young age. She took up a job immediately after her graduation, to support her father in educating his other two children. She even delayed her marriage in a bid to fulfil her duties towards her family. Her family always refused financial help from us and other relatives, because of their high self-esteem. With time, one of her younger brothers graduated in management and got a good job, after which their finances started improving. Then, in 2001, my aunt got married to a businessman, who was a US citizen. He then went back to USA and sent his wife the required papers so that she could enter the country. However, we all know that at the time, the most infamous terrorist act of 9/11 had rocked all of America, and made them very conservative and defensive in issuing visas. My aunt was denied entry twice for no concrete reasons. She was getting frustrated and depressed because of this development. The rest of us were also getting worried for her. I was more concerned about her because I felt she was very genuine and deserved to get a chance to start her life afresh struggling for so many years. Finally, her husband came back to India and presented himself at the embassy. He was able to convince the visa officer that he was indeed married to my aunt, after which she got the visa. I was at my home on that day, waiting for my aunt's call from Mumbai. I was anxious, and had been praying to God to help her. Finally I received a call on my mobile and got the good news. We all were very happy for her because now she would be able to join her husband in the US. I immediately went to the temple and thanked God for His kindness. Later, we went to meet my aunt at her home, with sweets and gifts to express our happiness. All in all, this news made me extremely happy.

Follow-up Questions & Answers:
1. What news can be surprising?
Any unexpected news is often surprising, be it winning a competition, getting very good grades in exams, getting a good job in the first few attempts, or winning a lottery or lucky draw. We often feel high levels of happiness when we hear such unexpected news.
2. What was the importance of that news for you?
That news was of immense importance to me, as I had a lot of respect for my aunt, and held her in high regard because she had helped me in the past, when I was a student. To top it, because she was a family member, that news became all the more important to me, and brought on a sense of relief.
3. Which is the best medium for getting news — the newspaper or the TV — and why?
In the context of instant news, television is the best medium. We come to know of any development in the world within just a few minutes of its occurrence. However, if we want detailed information about events, we should rely more on the next day's newspaper.
4. Which medium do people use for communication, in your city? Why?
People in my city use mobile phones for communicating with each other, because mobiles provide instant connectivity. With mobiles, we can convey our message immediately and directly to the concerned person, within seconds.
5. Which is the best medium for communication, according to you?
That depends on the type of communication. If it is a short message for a local person, I think the mobile phone is the best medium. But if I have to communicate with someone in another state or country, I think emails or messenger services prove to be better platforms.
6. What will the main medium of communication be in the future, and why?
I think, in future, people will be using a combination of the internet and mobile phones as the main mediums for communication, because internet calling is quick, convenient, and inexpensive. Of course, we will continue to use regular mobile phone networks to communicate with each other in our own areas or cities.

30. Describe a public holiday celebrated in your country.
   You should say
- **When it is celebrated**
- **Why it is celebrated**

- **What people do on that day**

What do you do on that day?

Sample Answer:

There are a number of public holidays in my country that can be categorized as national, religious, and cultural holidays. People in my country celebrate almost all holidays in different ways. Here, I would like to talk about the Independence Day celebrations that take place in my city every year on the 15th of August. This is the day our country gained freedom from the British rule, in 1947.

Celebrations take place across many venues in every city, but the main celebration is organised in the Capital of my country, New Delhi, where the Prime Minister and the President begin the flag hoisting ceremony and follow it up with patriotic speeches. After that, military officers are ceremoniously awarded medals for their special contribution to the country. Most people watch this event live on television, at home. However, I go to the main celebration venue in my city — a lake near my home — where the Chief Minister and the Mayor salute the Indian flag early in the morning. After the flag hoisting ceremony, we all sing our national anthem together. This is followed by various cultural programs depicting the spirit of patriotism, and the glory of our nation. Some sports competitions are also organised in the afternoon, and the honourable Chief Minister distributes the prizes to winners. We sing our national anthem once again before the sunset, and then a separate session of fireworks is organised, which garners many spectators from the area. Till a few years ago, I, too, used to take part in some sporting activities like hockey and cricket. However, now I go to the venue only to see the event, and the celebrations.

Follow-up Questions & Answers:

1. Some people say that there are too many public holidays in your country. Do you agree with them?

I live in a multicultural country and our motto is 'unity in diversity'. We believe in giving respect to all cultures and religions, and hence the number of public holidays here, is higher than in other countries of the world. I support this notion of allowing holidays for people to celebrate their important religious days. So, while I do admit that there are too many public holidays in India, I would also like to add that we have a six-day work week here, as opposed to the customary five day week that the west enjoys. On average, in spite of the numerous public holidays we celebrate, we work for more days when compared to most other countries.

2. What are the other important public holidays celebrated in your country?

Apart from the Independence Day, we celebrate other national holidays, like the Republic Day, Gandhi Jayanti, and other birthdays of prominent freedom fighters like Nehru and Sardar Vallabhbhai Patel. We also celebrate festivals like Diwali, Navratri, Eid, Onam, Pongal, and Christmas.

3. Do all the people in your country celebrate all these holidays?

All the people in my country take an interest in the celebration of all holidays, in general. However, the interest levels of people differ when it comes to religious holidays. Here, people belonging to various religions celebrate their respective holidays with greater involvement, than those of other religions, who don't take that active an interest. This is understandable because not everyone is aware of rituals and traditions of religions other than their own.

4. What is the importance of public holidays?

Public holidays are very important. They serve as a break from our work or studies. Their celebration also increases the importance of the day and the event in our mind. In addition, this brings people of similar cultures closer to each other and makes them feel united. What's more, units of the leisure, hospitality, and entertainment industries such as cinema halls, recreation centres, holiday resorts, restaurants, and amusement parks, all get a boost in their business on such days. This is good for a growing economy like India.

5. Is it important to celebrate anniversaries or special days?

According to me, special days and anniversaries are milestones in the journey of life. Often, when we look back, we remember these milestones more than anything else. Hence, it is very important to celebrate such days, in order to make them memorable for the future. In addition, their celebration also gives us an added boost of energy and inspiration to move forward enthusiastically in life.

6. What do you prefer — a five day working week, or a six day working week — and why?

I personally prefer a five day working week because we often have personal, social, and family commitments in life, and many of these commitments are necessary to address. Now, if we get only one holiday per week, it becomes difficult for us to balance various aspects of our lives.

7. Do you think people/governments waste too much time, energy, and money on the celebration of festivals or public holidays?

At times it seems like governments waste money on the celebration of public holidays, because such events are celebrated with great pomp. This involves a lot of government expenditure on the celebration itself, as well as the management of other administrative aspects such as safety and security of large crowds. I think some part of this money should instead be diverted towards other essential requirements of the nation. People, at an individual level, on the other hand also waste too much money on celebrations by using them as an excuse to show-off their financial status in society. But, this doesn't happen very often, as the wastage of money and material is usually restricted through proper event management.

31. Speak about a competition/contest you took part in, in the past.

    You should say

- **When that competition/contest took place**
- **What the participants had to do**
- **How you performed**

What kind of reactions did you receive from others?

Sample Answer:

I would like to speak about an extempore competition organised by my daughter's school, two years ago. It was actually a surprising event for all of us. We went to attend a function organised by the school, for both, parents and students. The function was organised at the cultural hall in the school premises. Here, the school management came up with some surprising activities for the students, as well as the parents. The principal explained the importance of public speaking, and to emphasise it, he introduced a surprise extempore contest for parents. He invited some parents to participate in the contest, and decided to select topics for them to speak on. I raised my hand, along with 15 other participants. Finally, we were all asked to go on stage one by one, and each of us was given a topic by the principal. I must say, it was a tough call to judge our speeches, from the competition perspective, as everyone did really well. As a participant, I quite enjoyed it. The topic I had to speak on was — teaching children in English medium schools. I instantly started my speech and spoke for a few minutes in front of the 500 strong audience. I organised my thoughts well, and was able to deliver the content clearly and emphatically. Everyone applauded my speech. At the end, the principal declared me the winner of the contest and everyone gave me yet another big round of applause for my performance. The principal, teachers, and the audience were all very happy in the end because the entire function was aimed at increasing parent-school interaction. My daughter was also very happy about my win; she jumped with joy, and rushed to me to give me a hug. Many parents came to me later, and congratulated me on the win. I have won many other contests in the past, but I will not forget this contest throughout my life.

Follow-up Questions & Answers:
1. Does the presence of our family members help in our performance? Why?
Yes, the presence of our family members gives us mental support and motivation. We can actually perform better in the presence of our loved ones, because their feelings add energy to our performance.
2. Should such competitions/contests be organised regularly in all parts of your country?
It is not a bad idea. It will actually strengthen the bonds between schools and parents. This, will subsequently be helpful to the children. In addition, this will also help people in expressing and sharing their ideas and opinions with others on a public platform. Finally, these kinds of contests will also motivate children to perform better in the competitions organised for them at school level.
3. What are the advantages/disadvantages to the people who participate in such competitions/contests?
I don't think there is any direct or indirect disadvantage to people entering such contests. On the contrary, it benefits them in many ways, by providing them an opportunity to share their ideas with others, enhancing their confidence levels, and helping them to gain recognition and a good reputation among their friends, relatives, and the society.
4. Some schools give prizes to all the participants in contests/competitions. Is this a good or a bad practice?
It is indeed a good practice to give out prizes or mementos to all the participants. School children are vulnerable and sensitive. When they prepare for a contest, they do it with all their heart, and so, at times, they tend to get emotional if they don't win the competition. Thus, in order to prevent them from getting frustrated, some schools give a prize to every participant. This keeps students motivated to perform even better in the next contest.

1. Did your family members remain present to see your performance?
2. Do you think such competitions also improve team spirit among the people?
3. How did you feel after the competition?

32. Tell me about an important sports arena in your hometown.

You should say
- What this sports arena is called
- Where it is located
- What sports facilities it has

What makes this sports arena important?

Today I would like to talk about a relatively new sports arena that has been developed in my hometown. In a well-known area known as Kankaria, famous for the Kankaria Lake and Kankaria Zoo, a new sports complex has come up just a while ago, called 'The Arena'. Its location makes it quite easy to find and also easily accessible to citizens. This sports arena has many facilities and state of the art sports equipment for players and enthusiasts. It has badminton courts, a basketball court, card room, fitness studios, fitness centre, infinity pool, squash centre, multi-sports pitch, a six lame shooting range, a room for medics, four tennis courts, a volleyball court, a football field, and many table tennis tables, too.

The arena even offers good food in its cafes. There is ample seating for audiences to enjoy national and state level sports tournaments, and all sports areas are built according to international standards. It is the first of its kind sports arena in the entire nation, and what makes it even more important is that the international kabbadi world cup was hosted there recently. It drew a lot of people, and everyone who visited only had good things to say about the complex. Crowd flow, emergency situation management, and safety and security features have all been implemented with a lot of care and painstaking attention to detail.

In fact the sports complex is multi-storeyed, so it can host multiple events at the same time, too. I have yet to visit this arena, but I plan to do so very soon.

Follow-up Questions & Answers:
1. Does your hometown have many sports arenas?
My hometown has a handful of sports arenas; not too many. However, so far these have proven to be good enough to accommodate sportspersons and encourage new talent to try their hands at different sports. In future, my hometown could become more sports friendly and new sports arenas might have to be built to facilitate the growing sports culture.

2. How does access to sports help a society?
Access to sports helps a society in many ways. It encourages people to try their hands at physical activities in their leisure time. It motivates children to play games and get physical exercise from a young age, thereby cultivating healthy lifestyle habits and

---

patterns. Further, it can facilitate the feeling of team-play and unity among members of the society. When a society is pro sports, youth tend to find creative ways to channel pent up energy, and thus become less likely to fall into traps of alcoholism and substance abuse.

3. Should elderly people play sports?

Elderly people should most definitely play sports in every society. Cultures in the Far East — places such as Japan — are very pro sports. One can find elderly people playing interesting physical games in parks everywhere, if one visits Japan. Those who are very fit go on regular morning and evening jogs, and even play intensive sports, there. This is probably the secret behind their longevity and good health. If elderly people play sports, they are less likely to need the services of physiotherapists, because their muscles will not degenerate due to lack of activity. In the long run they will remain less physically dependent on others, and feel more confident about themselves.

4. Can certain indoor activities be classified as sports?

Yes, some indoor activities can be rightly classified as sports. If an activity involves a fair amount of use of strategy, and is sufficiently competitive, it can be called a sport. Games such as chess, snooker, pool, squash, and gymnastics are already categorised as sports, internationally. On the other hand, playing video games and arcade games need not be classified as sports because they are often passive in nature, and work on the principles of simulation, as opposed to active involved gameplay.

33. Describe a sports event you have seen.

You should say

- **Where and when you saw it**
- **Who came with you**
- **What you enjoyed most, there**

What was the final outcome of the sporting event?

Sample Answer:

Last year, I went to see a cricket match between India and Pakistan at the Motera Cricket Stadium in my city. I went there with three of my friends. We reserved our seats by buying the tickets well in advance, to avoid any last minute hassles. We reached the stadium almost two hours before the match started, so that we would get to see the players practicing on the ground, and take their autographs. The atmosphere was electrifying and thrilling, and it became increasingly exciting as the match progressed. We cheered a lot for our team, and enjoyed each and every moment of the match. I liked the performance of my favourite batsman Sachin Tendulkar, in that match. He played a wonderful innings of 110 runs to help India put up a challenging total of 329, for Pakistan to beat. Sachin played some classic shots across the ground. He was set and aggressive, right from the first ball. To top it, he bowled extremely well and took three important wickets of Pakistan. His efforts multiplied the enjoyment of spectators. I had taken my mobile phone and digital camera along, to capture some exciting moments from the match. Finally, India won the match, and Sachin was declared the 'man of the match'. We stayed there until the end of the prize distribution ceremony, after which we left for our homes with wonderful memories of the match.

34. **Describe a piece, or a set of furniture that you have seen or you use.**

    You should say
-   **Where the furniture is**
-   **How it is useful**
-   **What it looks like**

What do you like about it?

Sample Answer:

Furniture is one of the most important parts of the interior of any office or house, because it decides the utilization of the space. I would like to talk about a complete set of furniture that we bought about three years ago, for our drawing room at home. This set of furniture consists of two sofas, two tables, two chairs, and a decorative wooden cabinet. We bought it from a reputed furniture mall in my city. The sofas and the chairs have a brownish fabric that goes well with our drawing room's wall paint. The sofas are big enough to fit ten people comfortably, and the table is wooden, with a glass top. It is one of those big tables with rollers under its legs, so we can move it easily to serve refreshments and snacks to our guests. It is very useful to us in our everyday life, because all the members of my family can sit together and spend time with each other. The most helpful and attractive part of this furniture set is its wooden cabinet. It has a television case, two big glass show cases with shelves, two wooden storage cabinets with doors, and four drawers. The wood of the cabinet is polished with a brownish finish, and it is big enough for our television, music system, and other important daily use things. I have arranged some photo frames in the glass show cases, alongside some prizes that my daughter has won in various competitions. She also likes to play with many toys, so we have given one wooden cabinet to her, to store her toys. What's more, the material used for this cabinet is very high quality and attractive. I really like this set of furniture because not only is it an integral part of our house, but now it has also become an important part of our lives.

Follow-up Questions & Answers:
1.Who selects furniture in your house?
We all take an active part in selecting furniture for our home. However, we pay more attention to the person who is going to use each piece of furniture, than the others. For example, we always give more respect to the opinions of my mother and my wife when we buy anything related to the kitchen. We also listen to the likings of my daughter when we buy things for her use.

2.What is the importance of furniture in our home and office?
Furniture is very important, both at home and in the office. We can ensure comfort, convenience, storage, and optimum usage of space and electricity, with good furniture. I think furniture is an essential part of any construction in today's life.

3.How different is today's furniture from that of the past?
There are marked differences between the furniture of the past, and the furniture

available today. Today's furniture has a combination of utility, style, and luxury. We can have trendy shapes, vibrant colours, and different materials like steel, plywood, aluminium, and plastic, today, compared to the past, when only wood was used to make furniture.

Practice Questions
1. What is the difference between home furniture and office furniture?
2. Should we use different furniture at home and at office?

35. **Speak about a decision made by a person, company, or country, which you disagree with.**
    You should say
-   **What this decision was**
-   **Who was responsible for making the decision**
-   **Why you disagree with it**
What should have been done instead, according to you?

There are many decisions made by many people, businesses, and nations every day all over the world. I may agree with many and disagree with many, but I rarely voice my opinions or delve too much into these choices. However, if a decision is made at a large scale by a multinational company, or by a nation, then the effects of such a decision are far reaching, and often impact many stakeholders. The stakeholders of major national decisions are often not just the citizens of the nation in question, but also other nations all over the world. National level decisions impact investments globally, and move international stock markets considerably.

One such decision that was taken recently was the Brexit. Brexit essentially stands for Britain's exit from the European Union. I disagree with this decision made by the British parliament and the British citizenry, for quite a few reasons. The European Union is a body I hold in great esteem for the manner in which it has brought together many European nations under one umbrella to facilitate tourism and trade. I think that when two or more nations share trade and tourism relations, there is little or no scope for them to end up in conflict with one another. Should conflicts arise, they are resolved quickly, keeping trade in mind. In the long run such an establishment becomes an antidote to war. When Britain was considering leaving the EU, it asked its people to vote in favour or against the move, and the poll result was to be the primary deciding factor in the matter. When it was found that the majority of the British populace was in favour of Brexit, the move was executed quite swiftly. However, the vote was split nearly halfway! Only a few more people were in favour of Brexit than those who were against it. I disagree with this decision because I think it is more divisive than inclusive. As a race we should strive to surpass boundaries and borders instead of building new ones. In my opinion, there should have been a re-election after a while, and more consideration should have been given to the matter at hand.

Follow-up Questions & Answers:

1. Are you good at decision making?

I consider myself quite good at decision making. A large part of managing a business like mine is the decision making process. Every time I am faced with options, or I'm faced with a dilemma, I clear my mind, look at the pros and cons of the possible choices that lie before me, and take the decision that is most likely to benefit everyone involved. At times I have made incorrect decisions, but I am able to resolve any negative consequences brought on by them. I try to learn from them and use them as references to make good decisions in future.

2. Is good decision making an inborn skill or is it learnt?

Good decision making is one of those skills that can easily be learnt. Most people are not born with much more than basic decision making skills. As we grow up we are faced with different situations each day, where it becomes necessary for us to take complex decisions. Once we start working, decision making processes have to become more rapid, as the world is moving at a very fast pace. Further, when a person gradually makes his way to the top in his field of work, he gradually acquires better decision making skills. He learns from his mistakes and improves upon them over time. This is how good decision making skills are acquired.

3. Have you ever made a really bad decision in life?

I have made some bad decisions in life, whose consequences I realised much later. When I was about fifteen years of age, I had a favourite great uncle who lived in another city. I used to play with him a lot as a child. However, as I entered my teens, other things started occupying my mind, and spending time with my great uncle didn't seem much fun anymore. Earlier I would visit him every now and then, and spend a lot of time with him during vacations, but slowly I stopped visiting him completely. He would often call and invite me home. I would always accept the invitation, but when it was time to go visit him, I would be busy with my friends, and would ditch him. The year I turned seventeen, this wonderful man passed away, and only at his funeral did I realise how bad my decision to not meet him when he called was. I miss him till date, and wish I hadn't cancelled on him so often.

4. Do governments need to be more careful about their decisions than individuals?

Governments certainly need to be more careful about their decisions than individuals. When individuals make decisions they usually end up impacting only themselves, or their nearest family members. At the most they may impact a few friends. In context of one's career, an individual's decisions may impact those who work with him or under him. This is why large companies have decentralised management, so that one person's decisions cannot impact too many people all at once, lest he make a mistake. Governments, on the other hand are responsible for millions of citizens of a nation. If they make a bad decision, lots of people are likely to suffer tremendously.

36. Elaborate on an instance when you spent time with a child.

    You should say

- **When this happened**

- Who the child was
- What the experience was like

Did you learn anything from it?

A few months ago one of my friends had to rush out of town on short notice on some important business, along with his wife. They have a daughter who was four years old at the time, and it was not feasible to take her along. So, I offered to babysit her at my home. Before heading to the airport, they dropped her off at my place, and very confidently and unhesitatingly she walked straight in and made herself comfortable on my sofa.

Then and there, she had won my heart with the simplicity of her actions. There were no formalities involved; she was at ease at her uncle's place. She had only met me twice before and we had hardly interacted, but nothing was worrying her. I was touched by the level of trust she showed, and by how quickly she considered me one of her own. There were no judgments on her part, and she was not concerned about me judging her.

No sooner had she settled, than she asked my wife for a glass of lemonade with an endearing smile. Then, she politely yet firmly told me that she wanted me to help her fill her colouring book. She extracted it from her little bag along with some crayons, and we started colouring. For an hour we kept colouring, not a word exchanged. I was taken aback by her focus on the task at hand. She was enjoying herself thoroughly in a task as simple as colouring, without any expectation of reward or return.

As she sipped her lemonade, she went on to tell me all about her kindergarten, her favourite teacher, her friends, and the games they played. After every few sentences, this little child would laugh heartily with a twinkle in her eyes. Her childlike innocence and ability to find joy in the smallest of things surprised me!

I learnt a lot from her that day. I learnt that it was not necessary to take everything in life seriously. I learnt to be in the moment instead of thinking about the past or worrying about the future. I realised that this in itself was meditation of the highest form. I learnt that if we avoid unnecessary judgments and hypocrisy in our interactions with others, we can derive so much more value from them. That day I decided to make her my role model, and every time I am faced with a sticky situation, I try and think about how that little child would have reacted to it. Astonishingly, my problems start seeming much simpler when I look at them from her perspective.

Follow-up Questions & Answers:

1. Are children more innocent than adults?

Most of the time, children are way more innocent than adults. They live life from moment to moment, staying completely in the present. They have no care for the future, and no grudges from the past. They forgive easily, and do not have preconceived notions and prejudices towards people and situations. Children do not manipulate like adults, and they do not hide under any garb of hypocrisy. Sometimes though, some children may be a little sly, if they have had to deal with an unpleasant early childhood. But, this is rarely the case.

2. Do children need the company of adults to remain entertained?

Children usually know how to keep themselves entertained. These days, even if children accompany their parents outside, they carry their own games or colouring books, to keep themselves busy. A lot of children today are happy playing games on their parents' smart phones, without anyone else's company. Children are very imaginative, and they seldom get bored because they know how to create their own games and pastimes. They mix with others of their age group easily without judgements. So they don't need the company of adults to remain entertained.

3. Why are some children more reserved than others?

Just like adults, children also have individual personalities. While some children like socialising and mixing with different people, there are others who prefer spending more time with their parents, grandparents, and a handful of friends, only. A lot of times we assume that these children are shy and reserved, but not socialising may simply be a personal choice. Adults and teachers around these children may feel they are shy or under confident, but in reality they may be very confident, and yet prefer to not mix a lot with strangers.

4. As a child, what games did you enjoy playing?

As a child I used to play lots of indoor and outdoor games. Every day after school I would freshen up and run out to play with the other children who lived around the block. There were many boys and girls of my age group who gathered there every evening to play. We enjoyed games such as catch, hide-and-seek, and badminton. We would race on our little bicycles, and explore the common areas. If we found a sandpit somewhere near an under construction building, we would build sand castles together. Often we even continued our games when it was raining. If the weather became too bad I would retreat indoors and colour in my sketch book or play board games with my friends.

37. Elaborate on a time when you were not allowed to use your mobile phone.

   You should say

- **When this happened**

- **Where you were**

- **What you did in that situation**

How do you feel when you are not allowed to access your mobile phone?

We were planning a family trip to the US a while ago, and I needed to get a visa. Since the US embassy does not provide visa interview facilities in my city, residents usually travel to Mumbai or Delhi for the purpose. Now, the rest of my family already had valid visas, so when my interview call came, I travelled to Mumbai all by myself and proceeded for biometric scanning even before checking into my hotel. Since I had been picked up at the airport by a friend's chauffeur, I left my mobile phone with him.

The next day, I was scheduled to go for the personal interview to a different building. Now, I had taken a regular taxi and headed there, but I'd totally forgotten to leave my mobile phone in my hotel room. Carrying around had become so much of a habit that it felt like an extension of my arm, and if I didn't feel its weight in my pocket, a sense of incompleteness would keep biting at me.

Now, I was already at the gate of the venue when I realised that I shouldn't have carried my phone along. I looked around and saw others in a similar predicament handing over their phones to auto rickshaw drivers for safekeeping. I could have done the same, but the prospect of giving my phone to an auto rickshaw driver wasn't comforting at all. For all I knew, he'd walk away with it and I'd never be able to find him in Mumbai.

A brilliant idea struck me then. I walked over to a nearby five-star hotel and requested the receptionists there to please safeguard my phone. They took a small fee for the service, but also gave me a receipt so I could reclaim the phone at the end of my interview. It worked out well for me. Suffice it to say, at the end of the interview I got both, my visa and my phone.

When I am not allowed to access my phone, I must admit, I feel a little handicapped. My phone has become a little bit of a safety net and a constant companion over the years. But, I can manage without it for short spans of time.

Follow-up Questions & Answers:

1. Do you use your mobile phone a lot?

Yes, I use my mobile phone a good deal. Earlier, when I did not have a smart phone, I only used to extract it from my pocket to make or receive phone calls. I seldom used the SMS facility on my phone, unless I had an important message to convey to someone urgently. Since I have started using a smart phone, I use it for a lot of different things. I make phone calls, send messages to friends and relatives using free messaging apps, I enjoy videos and picture messages, share music and photographs, surf the internet, check my emails, and often even book movie and travel tickets using my mobile phone.

2. Do you feel handicapped without your phone?

I must admit, I do feel handicapped without my phone. It has become a constant companion of mine. In fact, these days, it is rarely stashed away in my pocket or bag. I access my social media account a few times every day using the phone, and I make several phone calls and send out regular emails to lots of people. If one day I forget my phone at home, a lot of work comes to a standstill or at least slows down drastically. If the battery of my phone dies down, I cannot access my calendar and have to rely on my memory to recall my schedule for the day. I have stopped memorising phone numbers, too, because I store contact details in the mobile phone instead.

3. Are children using mobile phones these days more than they should be?

Children these days are in fact more addicted to their mobile phones than adults. Many teenagers I see are into the habit of clicking selfies and uploading them on social media constantly. There is a certain fear of missing out embedded in their psyche, which makes them keep sending messages, with or without reason to their friends. They need to constantly stay in touch with their contacts in the virtual space. In fact, in many cases their dependence on phones has increased so much that virtual contact has started replacing physical contact. Even children as young as three and four prefer playing virtual games on their parents' phones as opposed to playing real games.

4. Do you play games on your mobile phone?

I do try out new games on my phone if someone recommends them to me. I download them from time to time and play them for a while. Then I delete them or simply get bored of them. Unlike most people I meet these days, I do not tend to get addicted to virtual games. After some time I find them exhausting, and too much exposure to the coloured graphics of these virtual games tires out my eyes completely. I have also noticed that they are a complete waste of time. Unless I download engaging puzzle games, I feel like I am adding no value to my life by spending precious work hours on game play.

◆ ◆ ◆

38. Describe a toy/game you played with in your childhood.

You should say
- Who gave it to you, and when
- Special features of the toy/game
- How you played with it

Why is that toy/game, your favourite?

Sample Answer:

Toys and games are real assets in childhood. Every child has his own kingdom of games, toys, gifts, and other possessions, which are not too valuable for grown-up people. I used to play with many toys when I was a child. However, the game I played most with, was a board game called 'Business'. I had tremendous interest in managing and saving money since my early childhood. I used to keep a separate money bank for me at home, and save money to buy important things for myself and my family members. Seeing this interest of mine, my father gifted me this board game, on my eighth birthday. 'Business' was an old, Indian version of the famous board game, 'Monopoly', designed by an Indian company. Up to 5 players could play this game, and one player was required to play as the banker, responsible for giving out loans to the players. As the game moved on, players would earn or lose money. It was an exciting and interesting game, where we had to earn money by buying property and then earning rent on it from other players to pay back bank loans. I liked the game so much, I would play it with my friends for hours. At times, the game would last so long, that we would have to pause for the day, take an account of our respective positions, and continue where we left of, the next day. This game taught me important lessons in financial planning, and strategies that could actually help us in surviving through difficult conditions in life. I experimented a lot while I played the game with my friends and family, and I learned a handful of strategies from them, as well as from my experiments. This ultimately enhanced my interest and performance in the game. I have still preserved the board game at home. I assert that every child should be familiarised with this board game and its importance, so that he may learn to manage money well, when he enters the real world.

Follow-up Questions & Answers:

1. What is the role of toys in a child's development?

Toys are like companions for children. In today's society, we can see families where both parents work, and many of them have one child only. In this situation, toys can be a child's best friends. They keep children engaged in some creative activity, preventing the feeling of isolation or loneliness. Apart from this, toys help children in developing some important life skills, such as taking care of their possessions, sharing things with friends, sportsmanship, and learning to be tolerant of, and cooperative with others. Some knowledge- based or education-based games help children in learning specific skills in a

---

fun filled manner. In short, toys are an important part of a child's life.

2. What types of toys are popular these days?

Boys these days like video games, and other interactive games, more than board games. They also like games surrounding famous cartoon or action characters like Pokémon, Batman, and Spiderman. Girls on the other hand, like to play with teddy bears, dolls like Barbie, and games centred around cartoon characters such as Dora the Explorer, or the Minions.

3. What type of toys will be available in future according to you?

Interactive electronic toys will be more popular in future. Toys that can move and follow commands from a remote control will be highly appreciated because they appear lively, make various sounds, and have attractive lighting fitted on their body.

4. What type of toys would you gift to a child?

I prefer gifting toys in which children can use their creativity, get entertained, and acquire some knowledge, also, while playing. There are many games and assembly sets available in the market that teach spelling, maths, or other creative skills, like building blocks. Moreover, I also prefer games involving puzzles, musical instruments, or clay art, because they help children use their intellect and imagination constructively.

Practice Questions

1. Describe other toys that you played with, as a child.
2. Who used to buy toys for you in your family?
3. What kinds of toys were popular when you were a child?
4. Was there any toy that you dreamed of having when you were a child?
5. Is there any difference in the preference of toys between boys and girls? Why?
6. Many people prefer spending more on books, than on toys for their children. Do you support this? Why?
7. How many hours a day should a child spend with toys, according to you?

39. Describe a situation where you received important advice from others.

You should say

- **When you got it**
- **From whom you got the advice**
- **How important it was to you**

Did you do anything special in return, for the person who gave you the advice?

Sample Answer:

We keep receiving advice from others all through our lives. But, sometimes, we receive some pieces of information or suggestions that can actually change many things in our lives, and enable us to pick new directions. I also received one such advice when I completed my graduation. I was in a dilemma regarding whether to join my father's business, or to do something on my own. In this situation, I started both! I started going to my father's office for a few hours every day, and I also started applying for jobs. However, because I was not sure of the specific kind of job I wanted, I applied for different types of jobs. One day, I met a senior from my college, who was doing a marketing job at the time. We went to a restaurant to catch up on our old college memories. I shared my career confusions with him, in the course of the conversation. He understood my problem very well, and started telling me more about the role of 'marketing executive' that he was engaged in. He explained, that by getting involved in a marketing job right after graduation, one could get a chance to dip his toes in the good, constructive, and challenging experiences of life, job settings, and society. He also added that a good marketing job in a good company could help a person imbibe qualities such as persuasion, convincing power, and strong communication skills, along with an understanding of different types of people and their mind-sets. To top it, we can improve our spoken English in a marketing job. After listening to him, I decided to try for a job in the field of marketing. I was selected by a multinational company as a marketing executive, and I started working for that company. While doing that job I realized that there were lots of hardships faced by those who moved about wearing a tie, looking otherwise happy and confident. Soon, I learnt many skills of communication and persuasion, and I also improved my spoken English, because I had to promote my product to the elite classes of society. I was able to understand the mind-sets of the rich and upper middle class segments, which really helped me later in my life, and is still helping me, today. Receiving this piece of advice at such an important phase of my life, proved invaluable for me. Later, I gifted a wonderful wristwatch to my college friend as thanksgiving for giving me such a precious piece of advice.

Follow-up Questions & Answers:
1. What do today's youngsters follow more — the advice of their friends, or their family members?
It depends on the situation. If youngsters want to buy clothes or vehicles, or are looking to take up a job temporarily, they may give more importance to the advice of their friends, but if they want to take important decisions about their life, regarding marriage, career, or studies, they tend to give much consideration to the advice of their family members.
2. Do you think people should go to counsellors for advice?
Yes, if required, people ought to go to counsellors for advice, because counsellors are competent professionals, who have more knowledge about various aspects of life than laymen, and more importantly, can provide their clients with an objective view-point, regarding any situation. Generally, we keep viewing our situations with a highly subjective mind, from a first person point of view. So, with our emotions involved in the equation, we may not be able to come to a conclusion in case of a dilemma. However, if a third person gives us some proper, objective advice, we can get excellent clarity regarding our problem, and find the best possible solution.
3. Should a counsellor be a trained and qualified person, or not? Why?
Yes, I think counsellors must be qualified and trained professionals. What's more, they should be highly experienced in their field, so that they can give clients the benefit of their qualification as well as their experience. Sometimes, I have observed that the advice of an experienced person proves more fruitful as compared to the advice of a qualified professional who is still a novice.

Practice Questions

1. Is there any other occasion when you received advice from your family/friends /relatives?
2. In which situations do you take advice from your family members?
3. Do you take advice from people other than your family members? If yes, in which situation, and if not, why?

40. Talk about an event in history that took place in your country.
   You should say
- **What this event was**
- **When it took place**
- **What was the outcome of that event**
Is the event inspirational in your opinion?

I would like to talk about the Battle of Saragarhi here. This battle is considered one of the most inspiring last stands in history. Saragarhi was a post which connected two British Indian forts near the border area of Afghanistan. Here, 21 Sikh soldiers of the 36 Sikh Regiment fought an army of over 10000 Afghans, and managed to kill 600 of them. Eventually they became martyrs to enemy bullets, after putting up a valiant fight. This battle took place on 12th September, 1897 in Tirah, which became part of Pakistan after the Partition.

The odds were stacked 1:476 against the Sikhs, and they knew very well that the mud walls of the fort would not be able to stand for long against the attacks of the invading Afghan forces. They had the option of retreating without putting up a fight, but they chose not to, under the leadership of Hawaldar Ishar Singh. Earlier that morning when they had seen the Afghan forces coming towards their post, the Sikhs had signalled to the colonel stationed at nearby Fort Lockhart for reinforcements. Unfortunately, the colonel was not able to send any reinforcements at such short notice.

Very sure of their victory, the invaders tried to entice the Sikhs to surrender, but even in the face of certain death the brave Sikhs kept fighting, firing rounds after rounds of bullets to the best of their abilities. That day, 21 brave Sardars managed to keep 10,000 invaders at bay for 3 hours. This gave the stationed colonel some time to call in reinforcements and save the fort.

Today, in honour of these lionhearted Sikhs, 12th September, 1897 is celebrated as Saragarhi Day. Three gurudwaras have also been built to commemorate the sacrifice of the Sikhs. In my opinion, this event is very inspiring, not only for me, but for all my countrymen. Such bravery is rare. There are very few people who can lay down their lives deliberately for a cause that is not their own. Such noble and honourable deeds by the Sikh community have made them worthy of all the respect that the nation can bestow on them.

Follow-up Questions & Answers:
1. Are you interested in history as a subject?
Yes, I quite like history as a subject. I used to enjoy history lessons even during my school years. There was a phase when I started enjoying history so much that I seriously considered taking up archaeology as a subject during my undergraduate studies. Tales of royalty, invasions, wars, and love are strewn across time and space in the pages of history books. Studying history has always felt like reading interesting stories, to me. I get lost in the glorious sagas of ancient times, and long after I am done reading, those stories continue to occupy my mind.

2. Which was your favourite subject in school?
In school I used to enjoy humanities the most. So, history, civics, and geography were of course some of the subjects I liked. But, my favourite subject was English. I appreciate languages a lot, and I consider literature an art form. My English teachers throughout school were very well-read learned women who managed to get me very interested in the language by encouraging me to read lots of good books. By the time I was seven, my grammar had become perfect, even though English is not my mother tongue. This even brought on a lot of appreciation from various people, making me want to study it more.

3. How does knowledge of history help us?
Knowledge of history tells us more about our roots, about our past, where we come from, and what our journey as a species has been like, through time and geography. History shows us how far we have come since the time we evolved into humans. It gives us an insight into the good and bad decisions taken by influential people through time. As a species, we can learn lessons on ethics, morality, free will, and humanity by browsing through history books. Knowledge of history teaches us to be more tolerant to people who appear different than us, speak in different languages, and follow different religions. This helps people from across the world treat each other with respect, and accept the planet as a global village. In the long run knowledge of history can help prevent wars and establish peace across the world.

4. What is the difference between mythology and history, according to you?
History is a representation of factual details in the form of chronologically arranged stories and anecdotes. History does not contain legends that have not been proven, or stories that have no proof to back them up. History is based on documented evidence that has been passed down from generation to generation over time. Mythology on the other hand is full of legends and stories that are not backed by any proof. In fact, mythological stories are usually full of supernatural characters that have never actually been documented in reality. Myths take place in surreal landscapes, and in mythical stories the heroes and heroines perform feats that normal humans cannot even think of performing. Mythology is full of seemingly imaginary tales about deities and demons, while history contains stories about real people who walked the planet at some point in time.

41. Speak about a family member who made you proud.

   You should say

- **Who this family member is**

- **What he did to make you proud**

- **How you showed him your appreciation**

Are you in touch with this family member?

I have a younger cousin brother who I've always been very close to. As children we used to play together a lot, and he would often come to me for guidance regarding his life. I remember that he had always been a very good student, and most of the time he would manage to get brilliant grades in school. This streak continued well into his 10th grade. However, in 11th grade when it was time to select a discipline from among Science, Commerce, and Arts, he got very confused. He went to many of our relatives for guidance, and he even came to me. Even after listening to everything we had to say, he would go back home just as confused as he had come.

Then, one of his friends asked him to sit and pen down his life goals, and the steps necessary to achieve them. No sooner had he done this than he picked the Science stream, and embarked on his mission. He wanted to work for Google! I was impressed by the way he tackled subjects like Physics and Chemistry inspite of not being interested in them. He treated them not as hurdles, but as stepping stones towards his ultimate goal. A few years back, he managed to snag a very good job with Google in Canada. When he shared the good news with me, I was speechless. Such a young boy and so much dedication! I hosted a party for him, to celebrate his success, and invited all his friends, and all our relatives. We even invited some of his tutors and mentors who had helped him along the way. This was my little way of showing him how much I appreciated his efforts.

Today he is still working with Google at a very good post, and is enjoying life to the fullest. I am very much in touch with him, and he even makes it a point to come down to India and visit us every year. At other times we stay in touch through video calling, and exchange gifts during festivals.

Follow-up Questions & Answers:

1. Are you in touch with most of your relatives?

I am fond of socialising and have been very close to most of my relatives since my childhood. So I make it a point to stay in touch with them. I still learn a lot from my relatives every time I speak to them, and I am genuinely interested in knowing about their lives, as well as in sharing details of my life with them. I have video conferences over the weekends with relatives who are abroad, and I regularly meet up over dinners and lunches, with relatives who live in the same city.

2. Do you show your appreciation to people easily?

I am a very expressive person. If I see someone doing a good job, or succeeding at something, I am quick to appreciate them. If someone has acquired a new skill or is adept at a task or activity, I truly feel like appreciating their efforts. I think appreciation is a very good tool for encouraging people to excel in life. I am generous with showering praises on people. Not just my family and friends, even if I see a good street musician playing a nice melody, I go forward and appreciate his efforts in my own small way. The world today needs encouragement and motivation. So, I am not one to be economic with words and gestures of appreciation.

3. What is the role of family in one's success?

A person's family is his closest support system. The first people a person is acquainted with in life are his immediate family members. They are his primary caretakers, and their behaviours shape a person's character to a very large extent. People rely on the opinions of their family members, because they trust them to be kind, yet honest. When a person sets a goal for himself, if his own family does not support him, he is quite likely to leave it halfway or fail at it. On the other hand, if his family encourages him, helps him get over initial bumps and failures, and motivates him to continue with his efforts, he is quite likely to succeed. So the role of a family is very crucial to one's success in life.

4. Can pride in one's achievements lead to problems?

A certain amount of pride is necessary to maintain a good pace at work, and to stay motivated enough to achieve one's life goals. However, if self-pride exceeds certain boundaries it can quickly turn into overconfidence. An overconfident person is seldom likeable to others. Further, it is a quality that is known to cause a person to stumble and make mistakes due to carelessness. Those who are confident stay motivated, but those who are overconfident become arrogant and prudish. They take others for granted, and gradually alienate their own support system.

42. Talk about a well-paid job that you think you would be very good at.

You should say

- **What this job is**
- **What tasks it entails**
- **Why you think you would be good at it**

Have you had any experience in the field?

One job that I am very sure I would be good at is Career Counselling. There is a dearth of good career counsellors in my city, and there are many youngsters today who need it, especially because of the growing competition and increasingly fast life. Many people come to me seeking advice regarding their careers and life paths, and I am able to assist their decision making quite well. This job would indeed be well-paying because of the immense value it adds to a person's life.

The job essentially entails helping youngsters select the correct educational course at undergraduate and post graduate levels of study, based on their interests, talents, and skills. The key here is to help people identify what they would like to do in life, in order to become successful while also enjoying their work.

The next step is to help them select the right country for the course of study that they have narrowed in on, and then to assist them in selecting the correct college or university. Once these bases are covered, they can manage their own career path quite well, and job offers start pouring in for people who have graduated with good certification, diplomas, and degrees.

The reason I think I would be good at this is that I have sufficient experience of the same, thanks to my current business. Further, I am very good at reading people and understanding their motivations in life. Once I speak to someone for a while, I can gauge their strengths and weaknesses. I know how to help people capitalise on their plus points, and diminish their negative qualities. My good communication skills help me with this to a large extent.

Follow-up Questions & Answers:
1. Do you prefer doing a job or a business?
I prefer doing business over doing a job personally. This is probably because I am well established in my business now, and the journey has been very fulfilling for me. In my earlier years I have done a few jobs, and they taught me many essential life skills. Had I been asked this question ten years ago, I might have said that I prefer a job over a business. But, today I understand how rewarding my business has proven to be, in spite of all the initial struggles.

2. What are the advantages of doing a job, over owning a business?
There are quite a few advantages of doing a job, over owning a business. The first advantage of doing a job that comes to mind is, in a job the employees can remain quite tension-free as regards the overall functioning of the business. All they need to concentrate on is their own job profile, and the completion of individual and team tasks assigned to them. After work hours, they need not worry about what happens to the business's assets or liabilities. If for some reason the business even shuts down, the employees usually have other options available in the market.

3. What are the advantages of owning a business, over doing a job?
Owning a business gives the entrepreneur sufficient freedom to plan other things in life without worrying about whether or not he may get enough holidays. An entrepreneur can manage to find time for himself and his family members more easily than someone who is doing a job. So, there is more scope for personal growth and for indulging in leisure activities, travelling, or exploring hobbies if one owns a business, instead of working under someone.

4. Are more youngsters these days opting for jobs over businesses?
I think a lot of youngsters are opting to do jobs over starting up their own businesses today, because international markets have become very volatile and dynamic. It is very difficult for start-ups to grow at a steady pace today. This means that breakeven takes longer these days than it used to earlier. By consequence, banks and moneylenders are not very eager to fund new businesses at low interest rates. This makes the entire environment to start up a new business quite non conducive. In such a scenario, most youngsters understandably find it more feasible to opt for a job instead of starting up their own business.

43. Elaborate on a life plan of yours that is not related to work or study.
   You should say

- **What this life plan is** ~~would tour~~ *besides*
- **How you would fulfil it** *my own* ~~fond of travelling~~
- **Why it is important to you** *fond of travelling*

By when do you think you can bring this plan to fruition?

One life plan of mine that is very close to my heart is to do with my retirement. It is motivated by the fact that I do not want to spend my retirement in the hustle bustle of the polluted city. After working very hard for many years in my career, I would like to buy a plot of land in a serene area a little bit on the outskirts of the city, where the air is clean, and natural ecosystems thrive.

In this countryside property, I would like to have my own little farm where I can grow organic fruits and vegetables, in order to share with my family and friends. In this property, I want to build a small, cosy cottage, like one of those holiday homes we often see on TV. My lifestyle would be very pro-nature there, and I would spend many hours meditating and enjoying good music with my family.

I plan to build a small pyramid structure there for hosting group meditation sessions every day, in a very inclusive manner. These sessions would be open and accessible to all. I want to do this in a bid to raise the collective conscience of humanity. The next step would be to involve myself in providing social services to the community around me for their wellbeing, and also to uplift them.

This is very important to me because I see many people today who are not living their lives as happily as they otherwise can, simply because of mental blocks, and lack of me time. I think a meditation centre in the countryside would be a blessing to people, and it would be my small way of giving back to the community.

In the next fifteen years, I think I can successfully bring my plan to fruition.

Follow-up Questions & Answers:
1. Is retirement planning important?

Yes, retirement planning is very important according to me. If a person plans well in advance for his retirement, it can turn out to be a very enjoyable phase of life. Someone who starts making a list of things he would like to do during his retirement, he can start saving money accordingly and invest it in the most profitable manner possible. Retirement planning also takes into account expenses that may have to be incurred for healthcare and in case of other unforeseen emergencies, apart from just a person's leisure activities. If sufficient planning has been done in advance then emergencies and healthcare expenses will not leave any dents in the retiree's savings, thereby enabling him to live his life to the fullest in the absence of a steady flow of income from a job or business.

2. Why do people make some life plans keeping in mind their retirement?

There are many things that each of us wants to accomplish in life, many places that we want to travel to, and many activities we want to try our hands at during the course of our lifetime. However, we all only have limited time on our hands, and most of it is invariably spent on running around to earn money. While we are working to earn money, it is very difficult to find sufficient time to travel the world or indulge in our hobbies to our heart's content. So, we make some life plans especially with retirement in mind. For instance, it is not feasible for most people to detach from society and work stresses and retreat into the hills while they are in their thirties or forties. However, this is a real possibility for many people, after they retire.

3. Is it necessary to have a companion to fulfil one's life plans?

It is not always necessary to have a companion to fulfil one's life plans, be they related to relaxation, travel, or any other hobby. However, having a companion by one's side while enjoying one's free time, trying out new activities, seeing new sights, and trying one's hands at interesting hobbies can definitely make things much more pleasurable. If a person has a good, steady companion by his side that he can rely on, he is more likely to remain engaged in life. If we have someone to share our joys and sorrows with, we can live life more deeply and more passionately. We can involve ourselves in each task with our hearts and souls. Life plans that are fulfilled alone can seem hollow in comparison to those that are shared with a partner.

4. Have you prepared a bucket list of things to do before you die?

I have prepared a mental bucket list of things to do before I die. This list although, is not set in stone. I keep subtracting things from it and adding new things to it, from time to time. One thing that remains constant in this list is my plan to build myself a country home with an attached farm. Another constant in my bucket list is travel. A new addition to my bucket list is my desire to go skydiving at least once. Sometimes I manage to achieve certain things earlier than planned. When that happens, I do not strike the item off my list. Instead, I just replace it with another brand new desire.

44. Describe an occasion when you received good service at a restaurant or a shop.

   You should say

- **Where you received good service**
- **What the service entailed**
- **How you reciprocated**

Does providing good service help increase business?

In winter last year, I went out to a new restaurant in the city with my family. The restaurant specialised in serving authentic Punjabi food, and we were a lively bunch of 10 people. On looking at the menu, we all got excited and started ordering our food as the confused waiter quickly penned things down.

Then halfway into our starters, someone realised that all the curries we'd ordered would be quite similar to each other, because they all had cottage cheese in them. So, we summoned the waiter again and asked him if he could change the order a little. Because our curries were almost ready, the waiter rushed to bring the manager. The manager patiently listened to our problem, even though the bunch of us was speaking together. He then told us not to worry, and assured us that he would change our order to bring us different curries with varied flavours.

We were very thankful that he cancelled and replaced three of the curries for us, even though they were already cooked by the time we requested the cancellation. Further, the curries that they served us were delicious, and each one had a different base, with unique ingredients.

What's more, when the bill came they did not even charge us for the three curries we had ordered initially. We were touched and impressed. In reciprocation, we did eventually pay for the three curries, and got them packed to donate to the needy. We also wrote a very good feedback for the manager, and some people from our group put up very good reviews of the restaurant online.

I think providing good service definitely helps increase business, because happy customers spread good word of mouth. This encourages other people to visit the shop or restaurant, as well.

Follow-up Questions & Answers:
1. Did you visit this shop/restaurant again?
Yes I visited the restaurant many times after that day. In fact, I even recommended it to my friends and other relatives. We hosted a few office parties there, as well. We are now on such good terms with the management that they have agreed to cater at our next house party in spite of being overbooked throughout the month. By now, I think I must have tried every dish on their menu, and believe me, each time their service delivery just keeps improving.

2. Have you ever gone out of your way to provide good service to your clients?
I often go out of my way to provide good service to my clients. Especially in the initial years when I started my business, I remember going above and beyond my means to assist my clients. There were days when we would keep our office open well beyond 9 pm, and then still be available on the phone till as late as 11 pm. Even now, if a client really requires our services urgently on a holiday, I make sure that someone is available to help out the client, either at the office or through remote assistance.

3. In what industry is good service extremely crucial, according to you?
Good service is important in every industry today, because markets have become very competitive. However, one industry where providing good service is absolutely crucial is the hospitality industry. Internationally, hotels, flights, restaurants and travel desks function on the basis of service delivery alone. Their main product offering is their service to those looking for a good time. They need to ensure at every step of service delivery, that clients are provided the best experiences at the best rates constantly and consistently. If this goal demands going out of their way at odd times of the day and night, then that too needs to be done. Failure to accomplish this is likely to result in bad reviews, negative press, and consequently, lowered revenues.

4. What are the consequences for a business if it fails to provide good service to consumers?
If a business fails to provide good service to consumers, they may lose those customers. What's more, unhappy customers are most prone to spreading negative word of mouth. This will deter new customers from trying out the business's product offering. Over time it will create an opportunity for competitors to capture the market by capitalising on the business's failure to deliver good service. Once market share has been lost to a competitor, it is very difficult to recapture it. By consequence, the business that has failed to provide good service to consumers suffers losses or has to make peace with selling their products and services at lower costs to survive in the market.

45. Describe a trait of your personality that is special to you.

You should say

- **What it is**
- **How it distinguishes you from others**
- **How you have used this trait**

How have you benefitted from this trait?

Sample Answer:

I learnt one fact early in my childhood; that every person has something special in his personality. If he manages to identify that speciality, he can achieve great success in life. While there are many qualities in all of us, there is always that one special trait that stands out amongst others, and my special trait is persistence. I can confidently say that I am a persistent person, because I have never given up in any difficult situation in life. I faced many difficulties through my childhood and my college years that might have forced many others in my place to give up their efforts, and surrender. However, instead of giving up, I viewed those difficulties as stepping-stones to future success. My analyses of temporary failures and setbacks, and my faith in the self were two supporting pillars that always enhanced my persistence in life. I have seen people giving up on important projects in their lives, because of a lack of persistence, and later repenting or regretting their decision. Worse still, they may even develop an inferiority complex when they see other more persistent people achieve those things in life that they once wanted to. Apart from helping me in achieving success in various aspects of my life, my trait has taught me many important lessons, too. It has given me unshaking faith and confidence in myself, and in the divine.

(Here, I would like to recommend a book to all the readers to develop positive thinking and persistence. The title is 'Power of Your Subconscious Mind' by Dr Joseph Murphy. I hope this book will help those who want to nurture their dreams, and fulfil big ambitions in their life.)

Follow-up Questions & Answers:
1. Is there any disadvantage of that trait?
No, I have never noticed any drawback of persistence in my life. But, I have observed the development of a subtle egotism in some people, who achieve success through persistence. They develop the feeling that they are capable of doing anything in this world, if they have persistence and, with such a mental setup, they may not evaluate certain tasks properly, and consequently, they may not get the desired results.

2. What personality traits should one have, to achieve success in life/business?
There are many qualities needed to achieve success in life and business. Some of them are persistence, a positive and adaptive attitude, honesty, hard work, competitiveness, and an ability to envisage future outcomes.

3. Are there any personality traits that are specific to a culture/religion?
There are a few religions and cultures in which we find some specific traits. For example, Punjabis are very hardworking, Rajasthani Rajputs are aggressive and trustworthy, and the people of Gujarat are good entrepreneurs. However, because of globalization and uniformity in education, these specific traits are losing their dominance, and now we can

see a fusion of cultures, in which people have a mix of many traits in more or less, the same proportions. This is a good sign for the overall growth of the country.

4. Is there a personality trait that is specific to your culture/religion?

I belong to the Hindu religion. Hindus are believed to be highly religious, polite, and assertive. Hinduism is the only religion in the world that has countless branches and sects, where people worship different Gods and Goddesses. We also worship the cow as our mother, because we believe that man is the only animal in this world that drinks the milk of other animals — primarily, the cow. We regularly visit temples in our routine life, and we give immense respect to those engaged in working for the welfare of the society, such as priests, teachers, doctors, and farmers.

5. Do you think people with similar qualities attract each other?

I think it is true that people with similar qualities attract each other, because we often feel attached to our traits, and also identify with them. When we find others with similar qualities, we get intrigued by them, and feel as if there is a point of connection between us and them. This feeling often attracts people with similar qualities to each other.

Practice Questions

1. Is there a quality/trait you want to develop in yourself, in future?
2. How do you think you can acquire that trait?
3. How will that trait help you in your life?
4. How will that trait be helpful to your family members?

46. Describe an important city of your country.

   You should say

- **The name and location of that city**
- **What facilities are available there**
- **What the importance of that city is**

What is it like to live there?

Sample Answer:

There are many important cities in my country. They are all centres of different activities that contribute to the economic growth of the nation. I feel, the most important among them is Mumbai, formerly known as Bombay. It is one of the four metros of my country. Mumbai is the financial capital of India, and it is an important financial centre of Asia. It is one of the largest cities of the world, both in terms of population and area. It is important to the nation because it is the commercial centre for many businesses. The majority of multinational, international, and domestic companies have their head offices in Mumbai. In addition to this, both major stock exchanges of my country — the NSE and the BSE — are also located in Mumbai. What's more, the world's second largest film industry, known as Bollywood, is also situated in Mumbai. We can find many film studios there, too. Next, it is the busiest port of my country, and is very important because of it is connected to most ports of the world. Moreover, it holds the reputation of being India's first offshore oil drilling base, known as 'Bombay High'. Apart from this,

Mumbai is now home to different communities of my country. It is known as the city that offers the most employment opportunities in India. We can find people of all regions and religions in this city. Mumbai has an important contribution in the tax collections of India, which indicates that it plays a phenomenal role in our present economic growth. This city has given a reputation and an international identity to the country. It is indeed a privilege to live in this city.

Follow-up Questions & Answers:
1. What facilities should the government provide to people who live in big cities?
Government must provide all the basic facilities like water supply, electricity, drainage, road networks, and housing, to those who live in big cities. Apart from these basics, the government should also provide higher quality of education, recreation, hospitality, banking and its related services, and a proper supply of essential commodities like milk, vegetables, fruits, oil, and gas. Latest healthcare systems, and international and domestic airports are also required in big cities, as they are necessities for city dwellers.
2. What facilities should the government provide to people who live in small towns or villages?
People need all the basic facilities mentioned in the previous answer, irrespective of where they are living. Apart from this, they need irrigation facilities, market yards for the sale of the commodities they grow in their farms, better roads, and sufficient rail links to all nearby cities and towns.

Practice Questions
1. Which are the other important cities of your country?
2. Would you like to settle in that city if you get a chance?
3. What is the difference between life in a city, and life in a village?
4. Which areas of your city are the best to live in, according to you, and why?

47. Elaborate on an interesting house or apartment that you have visited.
   You should say
- **What makes this house or apartment interesting**
- **When you visited it**
- **What you liked most about this house or apartment**
Would you like to live in such a house or apartment for a while?

On a recent trip to Cambodia, in the midst of our long temple trails, we happened to pass by a very interesting looking community dwelling. This dwelling had little cottages built on trees, supported by stilts emerging from the ground. The moment we saw these treehouses from the street, I had to go inside and get a closer look.
Each treehouse had different interiors, and some even had trees growing through them. The furniture was made entirely from recycled wood, and the entire property was powered by alternative sources of energy, such as windmills and solar panels.
The best part about these treehouses was that they overlooked a dense forest. The views

The Ultimate Guide to IELTS Speaking by Parthesh Thakkar

were simply breath-taking, and the chirping of birds made the ambience very pleasing. Thanks to the forest around, the overall temperature in the area also remained quite cool, albeit a little humid. We happened to visit in December, and still had a few days of vacation pending. So, I went to inquire if any of these houses were available on rent for travellers like me. It turns out that they do rent out to tourists at a reasonable price. However, these houses were not easy to access for the elderly, and I was travelling with my parents who would not have been able to climb up twisted ladders and staircases. Access to the nearby city was another concern. It was difficult to find taxis in the area, and food options were very limited for vegetarians.

Nonetheless, some day I would like to live in such a house for a while. Who knows, I meet even build something like that for myself someday.

Follow-up Questions & Answers:

1. Have you seen any other interesting houses?

Yes, I have seen a few other interesting houses other than the ones I already mentioned. On my travels I have had the chance to see stone cottages, log cabins, and make shift tent dwellings, too. I have seen people living in modified caravans and in forest cabins. What's more, I have even seen a few glass houses! One of these was entirely transparent, and the home owners did not seem to be too insistent on having heavy or dark curtains either. The few rooms that were visible from the street did have curtains, but these too were quite see-through. I would label such a house highly unusual and interesting.

2. Would you like to spend a few nights in an unusual resort?

I think I would enjoy spending a few nights in an unusual resort. If I got the chance to live in an underwater room, or in a transparent igloo under the starry night skies, I would most certainly give it a go. As long as the experience is considerably safe, I would even like to spend a few nights in tented accommodations right in the middle of a dense forest. Living in an unusual forest would give me the chance to enjoy something new without the hassle of actually managing or maintaining the structure itself.

3. If you were to build an unusual house, what would it be like?

If I were to build an unusual house, I think I would build a stone cottage or a log cabin in a densely wooded area. In a clearing near the house, I would grow my own vegetables and fruits. The house would be my sanctuary, with warm, earthy interiors that are conducive to meditation and relaxation. I would assign some space to create a study inside that house, which I would stock with my favourite books. The log cabin or stone cottage would also have a beautiful garden adjacent to it. I would use this garden to socialise and conduct community activities.

4. Are there many interesting or unusual homes or apartments in your city?

My city does not have too many interesting or unusual homes or apartments. Most homes in my city are built along standard guidelines and ideas, with only a few variations depending on the choices and tastes of home owners. Of late though, some people have started building huge mansions and palatial homes on the outskirts of the city. Buildings have started becoming equipped with swimming pools, and a lot of people have started buying homes adjacent to golf courses, too. Apart from this, it is not very easy to get the necessary permissions from authorities to build out of place or wonky homes. Treehouses, glass homes, and other structures that are deemed unsafe by the government cannot be

---

built without resistance in my city.

◆ ◆ ◆

48. Elaborate on a book you want to read again.

You should say
- **The name of the book**
- **What it is about**
- **Why you want to read it again**

Would you recommend it to others?

One book that I can keep reading time and again is the Bhagavad Gita. The Bhagavad Gita is a profound dialogue between two characters of the famous Indian epic Mahabharata. These characters are Arjun, a brave warrior and expert archer of the Pandava clan, and Krishna, an incarnation of Lord Vishnu of the Hindu pantheon. The Mahabharata war was fought mainly on horseback, on elephants, and on foot. Arjun the archer had a fine chariot, and Krishna was his charioteer during the war. At the beginning of the war, Arjun was in a strange predicament as he was faced with all his cousins, his teachers, and even his own grandfather. Unable to bring himself to kill them, he dejectedly drops his weapons.

Krishna then begins a dialogue with him, where he counsels Arjun, and gives him lessons on righteousness, duties, sins, and rights. As Arjun asks questions, Krishna replies, and eventually inspires Arjun to wage the war.

At first glance, the Bhagavad Gita may simply be an interesting read. But, as one delves deeper, profound truths of life start emerging from the text. It had been written poetically in 700 verses. One can relate to Krishna's teachings at every stage in one's life. Whether the reader is young or old, the teachings of the Gita are applicable to him, if he attempts to contemplate on them.

If a reader reads the Bhagavad Gita in a sad frame of mind, his grief will deepen till it transforms into solace. If a reader reads it in an angry frame of mind, his anger will turn into rage and then transform into forgiveness. If one reads the Bhagavad Gita in confusion, he will become further confounded and entangled, until he reaches the root of his confusions and finds understanding. For a reader who explores the Gita in a happy and content frame of mind, even enlightenment is possible.

The Bhagavad Gita is like a life guide, and so it keeps appealing to me repeatedly. Each time I read it, I learn something new, I find a deeper meaning. Life feels simplified, and answers become available to me of their own accord. In our age of constant dilemmas and confusions, I recommend the Bhagavad Gita to every seeker who wishes to understand the self and the universe.

Follow-up Questions & Answers:
1. Do you often re-read books?
I seldom re-read books. Once I am done reading something I don't usually keep going back to it, unless the book in question is an encyclopaedia or a reference book. The Bhagavad Gita that I mentioned earlier is an exception. So, I feel compelled to re-read it.

It is very difficult to actually write a book that is interesting for readers to browse through time and again, over and over. Most books do not have such profundity to offer. So, I usually read each book only once.

2. Which author's books are best for reading multiple times, according to you?

Some of my friends and acquaintances enjoy re-reading books by Paulo Coelho, Amish Tripathi, and J.K. Rowling repeatedly. The Harry Potter series by J.K. Rowling and The Alchemist by Paulo Coelho are classic examples of books that people keep reading over and over, from time to time, without getting bored. They claim to learn something new from the works of these authors, just as I manage to gain something new from the Bhagavad Gita every time I read it. There might be some substance to these claims, since I have heard many reliable people endorsing these authors with fervour.

3. What kinds of books can be read only once?

Thrillers and detective stories can be read only once, in my opinion. The fun of reading thrillers and detective stories is in the mystery. Once the book has been read, the cat is out of the bag and the mystery is solved. Nothing remains to look forward to, once the mystery is solved. If I know already who the murderer is in a thriller, or in a detective story, there remains little more in the novel that can grab my interest. While romance novels and adventure stories can be read multiple times, thrillers and detective stories are one time reads.

4. Why do people re-read self-help books?

Humans as a species have an inherent need to constantly evolve psychologically and mentally. Each of us wants to become better tomorrow than we are today. We have immense potential to keep improving ourselves, and to achieve more each day. We have tremendous capacity to enhance our intellect, and polish our good qualities, while consciously diminishing our negative traits. This is what sets us apart from other species that walk this planet. People read self-help books to become the best possible versions of who they are. Reading a self-help book once gives a person insight into what he can do to better himself. Reading it again helps him internalise the messages conveyed by the book in question. Reading it repeatedly then helps him focus on individual aspects of the book, so as to actually derive maximum benefit from each chapter.

49. Describe different types of laws in your country.

   You should say

-   **Which laws people obey**
-   **How effective these laws are in maintaining order**
-   **What differences there are, between previous and current laws**

Which laws do people tend to break frequently, in your country?

Sample Answer:

There are two major categories of law in my country — criminal law, and civil law. Criminal laws protect citizens of my country from violent crimes like murder, terrorism, and dowry harassment. Civil laws cover offences pertaining to income tax, sales tax, traffic, and company laws. Laws in my country are updated from time to time, and the changes are known as amendments in the law. There is a lengthy procedure for amending or creating any law at the state or national level.

According to me, laws in my country are reasonably effective in maintaining law and order. I firmly believe that the efficiency of a law depends upon the clarity provided in its clauses, and the awareness prevailing about that law, among the general public. Here, the support of the police and the judiciary are essential in maintaining a crime free state. Over the last few years, as we can see, many new laws have been introduced in response to the call of the hour, such as laws against cyber-crime and domestic violence. The former is being used to protect the online privacy and safety of internet users in my country, because cyber frauds involving hacking of email accounts, banking accounts, and credit card accounts are increasing with each passing day. The domestic violence law has been introduced to protect women, children, and other vulnerable members, from aggressive and violent members of their own families.

In my country, I have observed that many people obey laws, and live as law abiding citizens. However, there are some people who often disobey anti-piracy laws and tax laws. Unfortunately, piracy is a black mark on our country. It is slowly gripping the entire art and entertainment industry, including music and books. People often 'rush' to buy cheap, pirated books and CDs just to save some money, but they don't understand that the money they pay for pirated books and CDs goes to the mafia groups operating the network, and not the author or artist who has worked hard behind creating the book or music album. In addition, we all know that the more we strengthen the mafia financially, the riskier they will prove to our country and society.

Follow-up Questions & Answers:

1. Do you think it is only the government's responsibility to maintain the law and order?
No, I totally disagree with this. It is not just the government's responsibility to maintain law and order. I firmly believe that as civilians, we are also equally responsible for maintaining the law and order in our country. If we see any unlawful act being carried out by anyone, it is our moral and constitutional responsibility to inform the police about that activity, so as to stop it immediately. At times, it is necessary that we bring illegal activities to the notice of the media, so that other people can also be aware of the goings on in society, and help in preventing them in future.

2. Do you think the people of your country are aware of the laws?
Unfortunately, this does not hold true for most civilians. Knowledge of laws can be best imparted at school and college level, but many children in India, even today, don't attend schools, and many grownups have also not completed basic schooling, here. This is the reason that lack of awareness about simple and common laws regarding income tax, sales tax, and even traffic still persists to a considerable extent in my country.

3. What is the role of individuals in maintaining law and order in the society?
Individuals can play a vital role in maintaining law and order. First, we should update ourselves regarding the laws in our region and country, and then we should obey them diligently. Secondly, we should educate our family members, friends, neighbours, and relatives, and insist that they also obey the laws. Apart from this, we should actively participate in government programs aimed at enhancing legal awareness among people. I believe that laws are made by us and for us; if we follow them, we can lead better, safer,

and happier lives ahead.

Practice Questions:
1. Are you satisfied with the system of law and order in your country?
2. Do people break/disobey laws in your city?
3. What kinds of laws are broken more often in your city?
4. Do you think the study of laws should be made compulsory in schools and colleges? Why?
5. Do you think illiteracy is also responsible for the increasing number of crimes?
6. Do the people give due respect to judges and lawyers in your country?
7. What are the positive and negative aspects of the law and order system of your country?

50. Describe an open street market of your city.

You should say
- **Where it is located**
- **When you go there**
- **What you enjoy there**

With whom do you go there?

Suggestions:
Candidates can speak about any open market where they can find vendors or small shops selling vegetables, books, garments, and second hand items.

Sample Answer:
Open-air markets are actually an age old system across all human cultures, originally conceptualised to facilitate trade in commodities. Initially, trade was carried out through the barter system in open street markets, but with the advent of currency, money became the accepted medium for buying and selling goods and services. While open-air street markets were very popular for many centuries, in the 21ˢᵗ century, their importance has declined with the entry of organised business houses and proprietors in the form of shopping malls and supermarkets. Now, open street markets have a grip over trading in a very limited range of items. However, they are still the preferred choice for commodities like fruits, vegetables, and other economical items. I do visit one open street market in the central area of my city quite frequently. It is a well-known book market, which assembles at Gandhi Road. At this market, one can find books on every subject, from the enclosed bookshops, as well as from roadside vendors. I first visited this market as a fresher in college. I went there to buy some second hand reference books, whose brand new versions were very costly. I was able to buy them at very low prices there, because they were pre-used. The whole place is chaotic, and the traffic is a big problem there. In addition, we often don't find parking spots near the market, so we have to park our vehicles at a significant distance, and walk down. However, the varieties and titles of the books available at this place make all the hardships we face in reaching there, worthwhile. I have bought many old journals on science, medicine, and English language from the

---

Gandhi Road book market. Sometimes I also buy books on subjects like spirituality and philosophy, from there. Many college students from different streams of study — both from my city, and from surrounding cities — visit this market at least twice a year to buy the prescribed text books for their studies. There are more than fifty enclosed bookshops, and an even greater number of street vendors in this market. I usually visit this place once a month, and I especially make a visit here when I am looking for a reference book that is not available in the bookshops in my area. Generally I visit this market alone, but at times I go with my friends, if they, too want to buy some books for themselves.

Follow-up Questions & Answers:
1. What is the difference between shops and street markets?
There is a considerable difference between shops and open street markets. We get ordinary and unbranded goods at open markets, whereas shops sell branded and packaged items. Also, shops offer facilities like after sales services, warranties, replacement of goods, bills, and credit card payments. Open markets don't offer such services.

2. How many types of open markets are found in your city?
Open markets are found in all the areas of my city, now. Most of them offer many varieties in just one product category. For example, markets like Palica Bazaar offer all types of fashionable garments at cheap rates. The Law Garden area clothing market only offers traditional clothes for men and women. In the same area, we can find a big food market which is packed with food carts selling Indian fast food dishes, as well as Indian versions of famous Chinese and Italian dishes.

Practice Question
1. What do you prefer — open markets or shops — and why?
2. What do youngsters think about the open markets of your city?

51. Describe the stage of your life which you enjoyed the most.
   You should say
- **What your age was**
- **How you enjoyed it**
- **Where you lived**

How different is that stage of your life, from your present life?

Sample Answer:
Even today, I remember my college days with nostalgia, because those were the days that I enjoyed the most in my life. I spent three years in college, and in those three years I learned a lot, improved a lot, and enjoyed my life in the best way possible. That was a time in my life when I lived with maximum resources, and minimum responsibilities. I had a very large group of friends. We all met every day at college, and did lots of activities together. We were all sincere in our studies, too. None of us got less than a first

class result in our exams and yet, we enjoyed parties, movies, discos, concerts, sports events, picnics, excursions, and adventures, without compromising on our mischief and fun. We also used to get involved in charitable activities every now and then. I was lucky enough to live with my parents while I studied, and make friends from the same city. This is the reason why many of us are still in touch, even today. I enjoyed that time most because, as an individual, I grew at the fastest pace ever. When I entered college I was not too confident, not too mature, and was often sceptical of building strong relations with friends. However, the initial days of my college helped me in balancing my personality. I then sharpened my unique qualities and turned them into virtues. I became an essential part of my friends' group. I maintained strong relations with all my friends in many creative ways.

However, that stage of my life is not very different from my present life for two good reasons. First, the self-development process I outlined is still going on. In the course of this process, I get the support of my family members, relatives, and colleagues, and I am able to reciprocate creatively, too. Secondly, though I have many responsibilities in the existing set up of my life, I have learned to enjoy them without perceiving them as problems. Instead, I perceive them as opportunities to contribute to my family, and to the world.

◆ ◆ ◆

52. Describe the happiest day in your life.

You should say

- **What that day was, or what the occasion was**
- **What happened on that day**
- **How happy you were**

How did you react to the situation on that day? (OR) How did you celebrate that day?

Suggestions:

Candidates can speak about their selection in their first job, their first appointment letter, their marriage or engagement day, winning a prize or a competition, a chance meeting with an old friend, a picnic with friends, etc.

Sample Answer:

The happiest day of my life was 30th April, 2000. This was the day my wife delivered a baby girl, and I became a father. It was an auspicious moment for me when I saw my new born baby girl for the first time. She was crying when I first saw her. Her crying was turning her face a tender reddish pink. She had kept her eyes and fists closed. The corners of my eyes also became wet with happiness, when I set my eyes on her for the first time. My body and mind brimmed over with joy as soon as I took her in my hands. That was an ecstatic moment for me, and the ecstasy lasted throughout the day. Thrilled and overjoyed, I thanked the doctor and her assistant nurse for the safe delivery of my child. After that, I went to see my wife as she had been transferred to her room by then. I gifted some flowers to her and thanked her for giving me the most invaluable gift of my life. I could not take my eyes off my new born daughter as she lay sleeping beside her mother, taking deep breaths. Later, I called my friends, relatives, and neighbours, and gave them the good news. I also bought sweets to distribute to all the visitors who came to see my wife and daughter, the staff members at the hospital, and the other patients, there. On that day, I also felt some changes coming over myself. Suddenly, I felt more responsible and more conscious. I also felt grateful to the Almighty, who gave me this opportunity to take care of, and nurture a new life on earth. It was certainly the happiest day of my life.

Follow-up Questions & Answers:
1. What makes you happy in life?
Everything that is good for me, my family, and mankind, makes me happy. I don't believe in giving a conditional and emotional response to the situations in my life. I firmly believe that complete acceptance of everything in life makes us eternally happy.

2. How do you celebrate the happy moments of life?
It depends a lot on the situation. Generally, I go to restaurants or ice cream parlours with my family and friends to celebrate happy moments. I also take photographs of those who are present there.

3. Do you do anything to cherish the memory of that event/day/occasion?
Yes, that day is actually the birthday of my daughter. So, I give her some gifts every year. We also invite her friends and classmates home, and arrange a small party, on that day. What's more, I also always make it a point to buy return gifts, for my daughter to give to her friends, at the end of the party. She gets very happy on her birthday. In fact, she starts making plans for the celebration weeks in advance! Her happiness at the celebration actually enhances our happiness, too.

4. Do wealth and material possessions play any role in bringing happiness in life?
Material possessions and wealth offer luxury, comfort, and convenience. People often associate their happiness with luxury and comfort. Such people may feel happy with wealth. However, in a bid to buy happiness, some people may adopt unethical ways to attain wealth. This is the reason why happiness bought in exchange for money is short lived. Hence, it is important to understand that money and things cannot bring long lasting happiness in life.

5. What factors are responsible for the well-being of a person?
There are three factors important to the well-being of a person. They are physical, psychological, and financial stability. Physical stability relates to the health of the body. Psychological stability relates to the health of the mind; and financial stability is related to the monetary support available to a person in order to survive and grow in this world.

53. Describe your favourite bird.
   You should say
-   **The name of the bird**
-   **Where, and when you get to see it**
-   **Why you like it**
What is unique about this bird?

Sample Answer:
Birds are a beautiful creation of nature. They are helpful to us in many ways. It is difficult to pick one favourite bird, but here, I would like to speak about the national bird of my country — the peacock. I like the peacock because it is one of the most beautiful birds found in my country. It is a large multi coloured bird that cannot fly very high in the sky, and it can only jump a few meters above the ground, owing to its body mass. It is found in every part of the country, but it prefers to stay in remote areas. In cities, peacocks are often found in open grounds, gardens, and farms, where human interference is minimal. Peacocks live on insects, flowers, and fruits. They have a beautiful bunch of tail feathers, which make them extremely unique. Peacock feathers are colourful, and also considered holy as per Hindu mythology, because Lord Krishna is believed to have adorned his crown with a peacock feather. The peacock also has a crown on its head, because of which it has been labelled 'the king of birds'. In addition, we can also find white peacocks in some parts of my country. White peacocks look even more gorgeous, and stunningly attractive. In the monsoon season, peacocks dance in the rain and spread out their tail feathers to attract peahens (female peacocks that don't have tail feathers like their male counterparts). This sight of the dancing peacock is a wonderful scene to watch. Peacocks also have a melodious voice that they use to call out to their group. This sound is heard most during sunrise and sunset.

Follow-up Questions & Answers:
1. Is bird watching a useful activity, or a waste of time?
Bird watching is a fascinating activity for those who are interested. But, I admit, it is a waste of time for most people. However, we should be thankful to birdwatchers for providing us with amazing information, interesting trivia, and documentaries on birds so that we may be able to learn more about these beautiful creations of nature without actually going out on field to observe them first hand.

2. Do birds give any message?
Birds give us the message of enjoying our lives to the fullest, by living in the present. Most birds are always active and playful. They give us the same message of being diligent, while still remaining playful and stress free. This is why, when we see any bird engaged in its natural activities, we feel refreshed and relaxed.

3. Should we eat bird meat? (OR) Should we consume bird products?
I am against the use of all bird products. We must avoid using such products as much as possible because we have no right to kill any bird to satisfy our needs. However, some people justify this as essential in some regions, where vegetarian food sources are in short supply. I think we should always think about the survival rights of birds, also, when we argue about our own survival rights. Apart from this, many people hunt and kill birds just for fun, or as an exciting leisure activity. They also eat and use bird products, to introduce some novelty in their routine lives. I assert that such killing of birds should be banned.

4. Should we keep birds in our house?
We can keep a bird in our house if it gets familiar and intimate with the family members of its own accord. Also, while we may take care of the bird for as long as it wants to live with us in the house, we must not confine it to a cage for our personal interests. Birds

have as much right as humans to live a life of freedom.

5. Have you had any memorable experience with birds?

I haven't had any personal experience with birds. However, a friend of mine had a parrot at his home that once saved his house from theft. One night, two thieves broke into my friend's house, and the parrot made some noise to alert my friend and his family members. All the members of his family woke up from their sleep, and caught the thieves.

Practice Questions
1. Which other birds are your favourites?
2. Name some birds that are found in your city.
3. How are birds useful to us?
4. What should the government do to protect birds?

◆ ◆ ◆

54. Describe a long car journey you went on	OR	**55. Talk about an adventure tour you want to plan in the future.**
56. Talk about a memorable journey that you made by car.	OR	**57. Describe a road trip that you remember well.**

You should say
- **Where you went**
- **What you did at this place**
- **Who you went there with**

Why did you decide to embark this journey by car?

Today I would like to talk about a very long car journey to Laddakh that I embarked with a group of nine friends a few years ago. Laddakh lies in the eastern part of Kashmir, towards China, and unlike Srinagar, its beauty lies in its dryness, instead of greenery. The temperatures in Laddakh remain too low for most part of the year, for any vegetation to really thrive. In fact, the car routes to reach this hill station only open up for four months each year. Since a regular sedan is simply not fit to brave the treacherous road of this region, we decided to drive there in two mountain-worthy SUVs. The goal of our road trip was to enjoy the beauty of nature, and to appreciate the sheer grandeur of the Himalayas in all their glory, while braving the elements. To cut a long story short, we had planned to rough it out, camping style. We'd researched a lot before embarking on our road trip, and decided to go by car, because everyone we'd consulted told us that if we went to Leh by plane, and then drove around, our bodies would not have enough time to slowly get acclimatised. This could lead to sickness, fatigue, and exhaustion — all three of which we wanted to avoid. That sorted, we packed our sleeping bags, collapsible tents, torches, lots of warm clothes, mosquito repellents, and some dry snacks. We started out from Ahmedabad, where all of us live, and drove to Delhi, first. This stretch was quite uninspiring, to say the least, thanks to the traffic, horns, and the July heat. After a night halt at a hotel in Delhi, we carried on early next morning to Manali. This drive, too, was very long and tiring, but unlike the drive to Delhi, it was very beautiful, and the sights had us all staring out our windows with bated breaths. All this while, we took turns at the wheel, so that we'd maintain both, speed and safety. After spending one night in a hotel in Manali, we got back on the road and drove all the way to Sarchu. With each passing hour on our journey to Sarchu, the temperature kept dipping. While Manali was cold, everything beyond kept getting exponentially freezing. When we stepped out of our cars in Sarchu to pitch our tents, there wasn't a soul in sight; no dogs, no trees, not even any insects! The temperature was below 0 degrees centigrade, and we could feel the wind chill touch our bones. Somehow, we managed to pitch our tents and sleep, before once again hitting the road. This time we drove for a few more hours and reached our destination, Leh! From there we went to many different places within the Laddakh region, pitched our tents, sat around bonfires, cooked our own meals, and let the beauty of Kashmir sink in. When it was time to drive back to Ahmedabad, none of us were ready to leave.

Follow ups:

1. Why do people like to have private cars?
People like to have private cars because they give them the liberty to travel anywhere they like, at any time they want. Private cars offer privacy, because people usually only travel with friends and family members in private cars. They also allow us to travel comfortably, at our own speed and temperature settings, while listening to music of our choice, at any decibel we want to. Further, they allow people to carry large amounts of luggage that public transport often doesn't allow.

2. What are the differences between bicycles and private cars?
Bicycles are powered by mechanical energy that the rider generates by peddling, in order to make the bicycle move forward. Private cars run on motorised engines that are powered by heat energy which is generated through the combustion of fuel. Because of this, cars move faster. Further, bicycles require the rider to maintain his balance, in order to avoid falling. Cars have four wheels, so they manage to remain balanced without any effort from the driver. Cars offer more privacy because they are enclosed, and can have other features such as music systems, air conditioning, and comfortable seats.

3. Is it a good thing that everyone has their own cars?
It is good that everyone has their own cars, because this allows everyone greater freedom of movement, and faster transport. However, there are some disadvantages to everyone owning cars. If the number of cars starts equalling the population of a place or exceeding it, then the roads can become too congested, pollution levels ca rise phenomenally, and the frequency of accidents may increase, too.

4. How to buy private cars in India?
Buying private cars in India is fairly easy. One must research a little bit regarding the cars available in his budget. The next is to select between an SUV, a hatchback, and a sedan, depending on the pre-decided budget. One can even opt for a crossover. Once this decision is made, one needs to visit various car retail showrooms, view different models first hand, check the interiors and exteriors, and take those cars on test drives. This helps people shortlist the cars they like best. After this, showrooms provide comparison charts between similar models based on their individual specifications. After viewing these, one can decide on a car, and either make a complete down payment by cash or cheque, or opt

for easy car loans with affordable EMI options.

5. What's the difference between men and women's preferences in cars?

Men tend to prefer cars with powerful engines, masculine appearances, great music systems, and large frames. They like darker colours like blacks, browns, and dark greys. In some cases men prefer smaller sporty, too, because of their capacity for speeding. In these cases they like snazzy reds and bright yellows, too. Women, on the other hand tend to pay more attention to the mileage of the car, they prefer delicate feminine looking cars with smaller frames, comfortable seats, good safety features, and high responsiveness. They tend to go for whites, pastels, and silvers, more than dark masculine colours.

6. What will cars be like in the future?

In future cars will be smarter. They will run on alternative energy sources, such as solar powered batteries, low levels of thermal electricity, and wind energy. They will look snazzier and will produce lesser greenhouse emissions. Over time they will also become cheaper and more accessible to the masses. Further, in future we are likely to have driverless cars that run completely by themselves, dodging obstacles and even parking without the help of humans.

7. Do many families own private cars in India?

Lots of families own private cars in India. The numbers have only been increasing steadily since cars were introduced in India, even before independence. People here have always been fond of good cars, and since the public transport systems are not always in the best of condition, a lot of people prefer to travel in private vehicles. What's more, these days easy EMI options have made it easy for most people to own cars.

Discussion
- Why do you still remember that trip?
- How did you feel after finishing it?
- How did you get the idea for this journey?
- Why did you go by car?
- Did you consider public transport a feasible alternative?
- Why do people still prefer using cars?
- Do they think about the environmental damage caused by car usage?
- Is there any difference between watching faraway places on TV, and visiting them personally?
- Does travelling harm the environment in any way?
- Should people travel less to save the environment?
- How can these issues be resolved?
- Do people think more about money, or the environment?

58. Speak about something that you want to learn in the future (e.g. a subject, a language, computer skills, a sport, or a musical instrument).
   You should say
-   **What it is**

- Why you want to learn it
- How you want to learn it

How will it be useful to you and your family members?

Sample Answer:

Learning is a lifelong process, according to me. I believe in staying engaged in learning different things through my life. However, one important thing which I have always wanted to learn was a musical instrument — may be a piano, or a guitar. When I was a teenager, I used to attend many concerts, live musical performances, and musical nights, where I used to watch musicians play the key board, or the guitar. The liking, the affection, the attachment that I have towards these musical instruments is so deeply ingrained in me, that I find it difficult to verbalize. I feel waves of excitement gushing through my body when I see professional musicians playing these instruments. I did try to learn these instruments when I was in college, but, because of some unavoidable circumstances, I couldn't master them to a competent level. I want to learn to play a musical instrument masterfully, because I believe that music is one of the best ways to express our emotions to ourselves, and to the world. There are other means of expressing emotions, also, but I have always felt a strong inclination towards these instruments. I want to see myself playing a musical instrument in the presence of my family members and friends. I also want to learn to play a musical instrument for relaxation, because, to me, it is a type of meditation. One can replicate the ecstatic feeling of a meditative trance, while playing a musical instrument. This skill will be really helpful to us as a family, also, as good music soothes our senses, and strengthens the bonds between family members. However, I don't want to pursue a career in music, nor do I want to earn money from playing musical instruments. I only want music in my life as a means to obtain peace of mind and relaxation. I want music to serve as a good medium to express my emotions. In addition, I want to share the benefits of music with my family members, friends, and relatives, and inspire them to pick up an instrument, too, for their own betterment.

Follow-up Questions & Answers:

1. How will your present education help you in your future learning?
2. What extra skills will you require to learn that thing?
3. Do people of your age learn such skills in your country?
4. What skills should we learn at later stages in life, according to you?
5. What skills should the younger generation learn, in order to grow well in the society?

59. Describe an occasion when you received many visitors at your home.

   You should say
- **What that occasion was**
- **Who the visitors were**
- **What arrangements you made to receive them**

How did you feel about receiving the visitors?

Sample Answer:

Well, in Indian culture, it is very common for us to receive relatives, friends, and neighbours on many occasions. Here, I would like to talk about the day I turned 32 — 11th May, 2008. My wife had organised a surprise birthday party for me. It was a Sunday; and I had woken up early in the morning feeling good about the day. However, to my surprise, I didn't receive too many birthday wishes from my friends and relatives. While I found this unusual, I set the thought aside, and decided to plan a small celebration with my family members. I got ready, went to the temple, and prayed to the Almighty as I do each year on my birthday. When I came back, I was surprised to see a large crowd of all my friends and relatives waiting for me at home. Everyone welcomed me warmly and wished me a happy birthday. At first I couldn't believe my eyes, or understand what was going on, but, when I saw my wife smiling at me, I realised that she had arranged everything secretly. I immediately thanked her; and then I cut the cake, received gifts, more warm wishes, and heartfelt blessings from my relatives, friends, and elders. After that, we all went for a small picnic at a club located on the outskirts of the city. All these arrangements had been made by my wife. On reaching there, we played lots of outdoor and indoor games. The children who had accompanied us, also enjoyed playing various games with each other. Then, we saw a movie in the theatre located within the club. This, too, had been booked in advance by my wife. After watching the movie, we all enjoyed dinner in the sprawling club lawns. The menu that night was laden with all my favourite dishes. It was a day of happy surprises for me. I thanked my wife from the bottom of my heart for organizing such a wonderful event, exclusively for me. I felt special, delighted, and grateful to everyone who came by to make it a memorable day for me.

Follow-up Questions & Answers:

1. Do you think the visit of people is necessary on such occasions?

Yes, it is said that man is a social animal. So, the company of other people in good and bad moments in life, is necessary for most of us. The joy of a celebration multiplies when we celebrate the occasion with our friends, family members, and relatives. Their presence actually makes the entire celebration more memorable, and enjoyable.

2. What did you feel when people visited your place?

Seeing so many people at my place on my birthday made me feel like I was on top of the world. Everyone was bestowing me with good wishes, greetings, and gifts. I was overwhelmed, seeing their emotions for me, and their joy on my behalf. I felt privileged, because I realized that there are many people who care for me, and are happy to participate in a celebration meant for my birthday.

3. Some people get important occasions recorded on video. Do you think this is a good practice?

It is a good idea, provided we hire a professional videographer to record the occasion. We can view such video recordings in future, when we want to refresh our memories. However, if we record videos ourselves, we often cannot enjoy the celebrations to the fullest, in real time. So, it is a good idea to hire someone to record important occasions. What's more, a professional videographer can give us a very high quality video recording, as compared to an amateur.

4. What is more enjoyable, when it comes to reliving a memory, — a video recording of the occasion, or a photo album — and why?

I think, both are good mediums for refreshing our memories. However, photo albums are often handy, and can be seen anywhere, anytime, whereas video recordings can only be seen on television or on a computer, making it a little more cumbersome to view them.

Practice Question

1. How did you greet them?
2. Did you wear special clothes on that occasion? If yes, describe them. If no, why?
3. What other facilities did you offer your visitors on that occasion?

60. Describe your favourite game/sport.

　　You should say

- **What the game is, and how it is played**
- **When you learned to play it**
- **Who taught that game to you**

What do you enjoy about the game?

Suggestions:

Candidates can speak about any indoor or outdoor game that they like to play, either alone, or with their friends.

Sample Answer:

In India, people pursue many sports like soccer, hockey, tennis, snooker, and cricket. However, my favourite sport is cricket. It is also the most popular sport in India. In India, cricket is not just a sport; instead, it is more like a religion for a majority of Indians. Cricket can be played as a one-day match, and as a five-day test match. It is played between two teams consisting of eleven regular players, and one extra player in each team. One team bowls first, and the other team sends two of its players to bat on the ground. Two umpires on the ground, and a third umpire sitting in the pavilion, observe the game. I learned cricket when I was a child. I used to play cricket in a big ground near my home with the boys from my area. I haven't taken any formal training in cricket, because I only wanted to play it for fun. I didn't aspire to be a professional cricketer in life.

Cricket is one of the most exciting sports in the world. Even a one-day match sometimes runs for as long as eight hours. The most astonishing feature of cricket is its uncertainty. It is full of ups and downs. We, as viewers, generally cannot predict what might happen next in the match, and that is what keeps us stuck to our seats, ensuring that we constantly remain interested in the match. I often go to see cricket matches live in the stadium in my city, with friends and family members.

---

61. Describe your favourite jewellery/ornament.

OR

62. Describe a gift you bought for someone, that took you a long time to choose.

OR

63. Speak about a gift you recently gave someone.

You should say

- **How it looks**
- **What materials are used in it**
- **How you acquired it**

Why do you like this jewellery/ornament?

Sample Answer:

I would like to talk about a jewellery set that I gifted my wife on our last marriage anniversary. This is a set consisting of one diamond necklace, one uniquely shaped diamond pendant, one pair of diamond earrings, and one ring for her ring finger. The metal used in this set is 18k white gold, weighing approximately 30 grams, while the total weight of diamonds is around 20 cents.

It was a very tough task for me, to buy such a precious and valuable gift. Hence, I started my planning many weeks in advance. When the occasion came, however, another difficulty arose; I didn't have any experience in buying ornaments or jewellery. It was really difficult for me to decide on the shop, and the article that I wanted to buy. Finally, I called up my cousin who worked for a reputed jeweller in the city at that time. I went alone to his shop, as I wanted the gift to be a surprise for my wife. After an almost 2 hour long selection process, I finally decided on this diamond set for my wife.

I liked this set because I find the combination of white gold with diamonds very appealing. In addition, I planned hard and also devoted a lot of my energy into selecting it. But, the main reason this jewellery set is special to me, is the happiness that I saw on my wife's face when I gifted it to her. She was overjoyed and ecstatic on seeing it. She immediately wore it and showed it to me. The gift was perfectly suited to her personality. And now, that gift has become one of the best pieces of jewellery in her collection.

Follow-up Questions & Answers:

1. Is there a difference between jewellery and ornaments?

Yes, I think jewellery is made up of metal that has stones like diamonds in it, while an ornament is made up of metal only. It doesn't have any stone or jewel in it.

2. Why do you think people wear jewellery/ornaments?

In many cultures ornaments are worn as a tradition. They are used as a symbol to depict the social or personal status of a person. Apart from this, most people wear ornaments because they like to look fashionable and different. Furthermore, some people wear coloured gem stones because of their astrological beliefs, too.

3. Do people wear different jewellery on different occasions?

Yes, people wear different jewellery on different occasions. They wear their most exclusive, expensive, and trendiest jewellery when there is a marriage ceremony in the family. Nowadays, ornaments and jewellery are available in different shapes, colours, and varieties, so they can even be matched with different coloured clothes. This is another reason why people wear different jewellery on different occasions.

4. What factors should we consider before buying jewellery or ornaments?

There are many factors that we should take into account before buying expensive jewellery or ornaments. The first is our budget. It is often seen that people see articles that are costlier than their budget, and get confused when it comes to their final selection. The second is our requirement. We should look at and try only those articles, which we would like to buy. For example, people often waste their time in trying out necklaces when they want to buy bracelets.

5. Should children wear jewellery? Why?

Children should avoid wearing jewellery in their routine lives, because they are soft targets for thieves. It is often seen that thieves steal ornaments and jewellery from children, and in this process they may even harm children at times.

Practice Questions

1. Who likes to wear jewellery more — men or women? Why?
2. On what occasions do people wear jewellery in your country?
3. Is there a religious/cultural importance of jewellery/ornaments?

64. Describe your favourite restaurant.

   You should say
- **The name and location of the restaurant**
- **What you eat there**
- **The special features of the restaurant**

Why do you like it?

Sample Answer:

I often go out to eat at restaurants with my family and friends. I have visited almost every restaurant in my city, but I like 'Agashiye' the most among them all. This restaurant is situated in the 'House of MG', at a point where the old city merges with the new city. The House of MG is in fact a hotel famous for its old world architecture and ornate interior décor. In keeping with the overall theme of the hotel, the interior design of its restaurant 'Agashiye' is also reminiscent of Ahmedabad from the 1800s. The art installations and furniture lining the passages that lead up to the dining area are inspired by the pol-style heritage architecture that is characteristic of the Mughal ruled eras that my city has witnessed. 'Agashiye' literally means 'on the terrace', and in keeping with the name, the restaurant is situated at the top most level or terrace of the 'House of MG'. Terraces hold a special place in the hearts of locals of my city, because since time immemorial locals have used terraces as gathering spots to sit and spend time with neighbours, friends, and family members. The famous festival of Uttarayan which is a favourite among locals is also entirely celebrated on terraces across the city. 'Agashiye' is very popular among frequent visitors to Ahmedabad, and among the locals, and all the credit for this goes to its amazing menu and its execution. The restaurant serves an array of authentic, traditional Gujarati food in beautiful crockery to its diners, and is capable of catering to large groups, too. This is especially important in Ahmedabad, because even though people here have started living in nuclear families now, they still tend to hold family close to their hearts, and hence make it a point to meet in large groups frequently, to stay in touch and keep the feeling of community living alive. Whenever I go to 'Agashiye', I eat their spicy sweet *kachoris, dhoklas,* and *khaman,* followed by the traditional Gujarati *thaali.* In fact, my entire family enjoys these dishes. An important factor that makes this restaurant more likable is their prompt service, the friendly welcoming attitude of the servers, and their uncompromising stance towards hygiene and cleanliness. I recommend this restaurant to everyone who visits my city. I can confidently say that anyone who visits here once is sure to visit again.

Follow-up Questions & Answers:
1. What facilities should be provided by a good restaurant?
Apart from good quality food and prompt service, restaurants should provide comfortable sitting arrangements, air-conditioning, adequate lighting, spacious waiting lounge, soothing music in the background, free home delivery, and an option to pay by credit card. All these facilities can make our visit memorable, and encourage us to visit the restaurant again.
2. What types of restaurants are more popular in your city?
Multi-cuisine restaurants are more popular in my city. People in my city often visit restaurants with their friends and families. Hence, restaurants that serve a variety of dishes can easily cater to varied tastes and satisfy everyone's food cravings.
3. How will the restaurants of the future be?
I think many restaurants of the future will be theme based, and multi-cuisine to give diners a different or unique dining experience, and to cater to the tastes and moods of a variety of people.

Practice Questions
1. Which other restaurants are your favourites?
2. What do you prefer — going to restaurants with friends or family members? Why?

65. Speak about a person you know who is a good cook.
OR
66. Describe someone you know who cooks good food.
   You should say
- **How you know the person**
- **When you met this person**
- **What food items this person cooks well**
Which is your favourite dish, from the ones this person cooks?

Suggestions:

If candidates don't know someone who is a good cook, then it is better for them to simply speak about their mother, grandmother, sister, or aunt.

Sample Answer:

I am a food fanatic. I like to eat a variety of foods, even in my daily routine. For this reason, I have also developed a keen sense of analyses when it comes to people's cooking skills. From my experience, I can say that my wife is indeed a very good cook. However, when I met her for the first time, I was not aware of her cooking skills. She can cook all our traditional, cultural dishes, including sweets, desserts, vegetables, and chapattis. Apart from this, she also adeptly cooks other Indian foods from Punjabi, Rajasthani, and South Indian cuisines. To top it, she is great with cooking dishes from Italian, Mexican, Thai, and Chinese cuisines, too. She has a great sense of mixing just the right ingredients, most optimally, to enhance the taste of any dish. I have also observed another virtue of hers, apart from her way with flavours; whenever she cooks, she pays special attention to ensuring that everything prepared in her kitchen is healthy and hygienic for the entire family.

We often invite our friends and relatives home for dinner, and I feel proud of her when they all appreciate the food we have served. She also updates herself from time to time, by reading about different food recipes in books, magazines, and on the internet. What's more, she has also participated in many cooking shows on local television channels. Moreover, I have also seen that she uses all cooking equipment efficiently to support herself, and to prepare food efficiently. Often, our relatives and friends consult her regarding dishes that they want to serve to their guests, in upcoming functions and parties.

Finally, I want to say that, whenever she cooks, she does it with all her skill, and all the love that she has for my family and me. It is said that food prepared with love tastes even better. Whenever I eat dishes prepared by her and compare them with similar dishes made by others, I can immediately tell the difference. Her food is always better, by far. I am thankful to her for her interest in cooking, and to nature for gifting her such fascinating skills.

Follow-up Questions & Answers:

1. Do you think cooking programs on television also help in adding some variety to our daily diet at home?

Yes, I think cooking shows on television help women in learning about newer food and ingredient combinations, and about various dishes from different cuisines and cultures. Many shows also provide fusion recipes, which contain a combination of foods from different cultures, tastefully served together. Such shows help in enhancing the knowledge of interested cooks. They also increase the general public's awareness of latest food trends in various cities and cultures.

2. Should we teach cooking as a subject in schools?

Teaching cooking skills in schools is not a bad idea. However, it is practically not possible for schools to have a kitchen to use as a laboratory because it would turn out to be expensive. A cooking lab needs a lot of space, students and teachers need to invest a lot of time behind each class, and it may prove to be a little risky because children would end up dealing with gas-based or electric stoves, and ovens. Inexperienced students may harm themselves or others unintentionally, if they do not handle the equipment properly. To add to this, schools have to hire special trainers who can teach cooking. Hence, considering such factors, I assert that cooking cannot be taught in schools.

3. What are the benefits of learning farming skills?
I believe that we should learn only those skills which are going to be useful to us in our life. Farming is such a skill that most people would never need in their life, because even if one has to change his or her vocation, there are numerous options available for entrepreneurs other than agriculture. What's more, farming technology changes with time, and so, it is also possible that the skills we acquire today may not be useful to us at all when we actually decide to pursue farming as a career.

Practice Questions
1. What was your reaction when you tasted the food dish prepared by her for the first time? (If you speak about someone other than your family members in the Cue Card, this question is applicable)
2. Do others also like the food items cooked by that person?
3. What dishes do you normally demand from that person?
4. How can someone come to know about different varieties of food items in your country? (Through restaurants, parties, hotels, recipe books, TV shows, friends and relatives, and the internet.)
5. Preparation of food starts from farming, do you think we should also teach farming skills to school students?
6. What electronic equipment are used in cooking these days?
7. What are the advantages and disadvantages of using electronic equipment in cooking?
8. Have you ever used any equipment for cooking? If yes, what and when?

67. Describe an incident which frustrated/disappointed/shocked you.
　　You should say
- **What happened**
- **How it affected you**
- **What your reaction was**

Were you able to make things better?

Sample Answer:
I would like to talk about a real life incident of mine, here. After the huge success of my book on speaking, I was receiving lots of feedback about the book from various users, trainers, and educators across the country. However, in May 2008, I received a phone call from a book seller based in Patiala, Punjab. He warned me about a conspiracy against my book. He informed me that some antisocial elements had duplicated my book completely. They had scanned the entire book, used inferior quality of paper, ink, and a cheap

printing process, after which they had launched it in the market. The pirated book looks almost the same as the original one and it was sold at 30–40 percent discounted rates from the MRP of my book. I couldn't believe my ears and I requested him to send me a copy of the book. He was kind enough to do so, and when I received a copy of the book, I was shocked to see that it was in fact an exact duplicate of my book. Only if we kept both, the original and the duplicate alongside each other, was it possible to make out the difference between them. The duplicate was smaller and thinner in size, compared to the original book, and the quality of printing was far inferior in the counterfeit version. The last feature that I noticed was the paper quality; the duplicated book had a far inferior quality of paper to the original. I was really shocked to see this. I was unable to believe that someone's creativity could also be exploited by criminals, with the help of technology. I decided to do a thorough research on the issue, and I came to know that some cheap book stores that sell books near bus stations, railway stations, or on foot paths, sold these pirated copies of my book. These people simply copied the book, reprinted it, and were gaining the profits of my many years of hard work. It affected me in two ways, one of which was financial. As, they started selling duplicate books at lower costs, the sales of the original book were affected. Secondly, I was hurt emotionally; I lost faith in the capability of the law of our country when it came to taking care of such problems. However, I met a top level police officer in Punjab, and he took an active interest in the entire problem. We caught the culprit and took legal action against him.

Practice Questions
1. What did you do after that incident?
2. Did you learn anything from that incident?
3. What kinds of incidents disappoint us in life?
4. How are family members helpful in handling such incidents?
5. Does culture play any role in the way we handle difficult situations?

68. Speak about an occasion/event that was important to you, for which you reached late.
   You should say
- **What the occasion was**
- **When and where the occasion was**
- **What happened that day**
What did you learn from this incident?

Sample Answer:
Since my childhood, I have learned that I should always reach on time, so that I never disappoint others. However, here I would like to speak about an occasion when I was late for something. It happened when I was in the last year of my college. A very good friend of mine had got a student visa for Canada, and he was packing his bags for the trip. I went to his home to help him with his packing, and other last minute things. Soon we were done and he left for the airport. However, in his haste to get going, he forgot an

important folder full of documents at home. On his way to the airport, he remembered the folder. I, on the other hand, had an important submission to make at my college, which I had planned to get done with before going to the airport. My friend called me from the airport, and requested me to bring those documents to the airport at the earliest. I acted promptly, went to his home, collected the folder, reached my college, and handed in my submission. All things sorted, I left for the airport, but as fate would have it, my bike got a flat tire. I panicked big time, and even though another friend of mine offered me his bike to go to the airport, I denied his help thinking I would be able to manage with my own bike. I took my bike to the nearest mechanic, got it repaired, and rode to the airport. I was afraid I would be late, and at the same time I hoped to make it in time. However, I could not inform my friend what had gone on, as there were no mobiles those days. On the way I met with a traffic jam, a closed railway signal, and a minor accident, because I was riding too fast. Finally, I reached the airport, where I saw my friend waiting for me. The moment I saw him, I sighed with relief, and explained everything that had happened. However, my friend asked me to relax and told me that the flight had been delayed by an hour. On hearing this, I relaxed a little, and gave him his documents before he left for Canada. However, had the flight not been delayed, my friend would have missed it, because he could not have travelled without those documents. This occasion taught me an important life lesson — that I should accept help in emergency situations, instead of trying to do everything on my own, so that I may get things done on time; otherwise, I will have to face difficulties.

Practice Questions
1. How important was that occasion to you?
2. What were the reactions of others, to you?
3. Should we apologize if we are late? If yes, how?

69. Speak about your favourite flower.

   You should say
- **Its name**
- **How it is useful**
- **What it looks like**
Why do you like this flower so much?

Sample Answer:
Flowers are wonderful creations of nature. Nature conveys messages of love, beauty, peace, harmony, and endurance through flowers, to the whole world. My favourite flower is the rose. I like the red rose the most, because I find it more beautiful than any other flower. While red roses are found all over India, the special species of red roses that are bigger, and have more petals, come from the northern parts of my country. We offer flowers to offer our respects, and to worship our gods and goddesses in temples. The red rose is a symbol of love, and hence it is used by lovers to express their love for

each other. Apart from this, the red rose is always in high demand on special days like Valentine's Day, Teacher's Day, or Mother's Day, when many people across the world give red roses to each other to express their feelings of love, appreciation, and respect. I like the red rose because in spite of being a small, delicate flower, it gives us nature's message of beauty and love. It tells us that while love is eternal, external beauty is transient. We should not consider just superficial attraction, when developing relations with people. The red rose also teaches us lessons in peace, harmony, and oneness. It gives its fragrance to one and all, without discriminating between humans, animals, or birds, encouraging us to also let go of our prejudices. It also gives us the message of endurance. A rose has many thorns, yet it brings beauty and fragrance to our space. It tells us to endure the pains caused by external circumstances, and continue to spread the message of love in the world. I think nature has made this flower not only beautiful, but also mysterious. The more we try to understand it, the more we fall in love with it.

Practice Questions
1. Is there any other flower that grows more in your city?
2. Where are flowers grown in your city?
3. When did you last receive a flower as a gift?

70. Describe a shop near your house
You should say
- **Where it is located**
- **What facilities are available there**
- **What you like about the shop**

What is the staff there like?

Sample Answer:
The shop I would like to describe here is a gift shop in my area. It is located on the ground floor of a high-rise shopping complex that receives lots of visitors each day. Even though the shop is not very big, the way they have arranged their display, with a multitude of articles is appreciable. They sell all types of greeting cards, artificial flowers, chocolates, and various gift articles like showpieces, perfumes, imitation jewellery, photo frames, wrist watches, and toys. One thing I like about the shop is that many new items appear there, first before they become available in other outlets. It is an old shop, and I have bought many things from thereto gift to my friends and relatives. This shop is air-conditioned. The staff members of the shop are cooperative, friendly, and well informed about the selection patterns of people of different age groups. What's more, they also offer free gift packing and free home delivery services. They also accept credit cards. The owner of the shop Mr Haresh Shah is a friendly man who maintains good relations with all his regular customers. He also accepts suggestions from customers with a smile, and tries to implement them whenever possible. I have seen many gift shops open up and shut down in months, in my area, but this shop has been able to do better business consistently with the passing of time. I think the credit for this goes to the owner,

who is constantly engaged in giving a better product mix to his customers.

Follow-up Questions & Answers:
1. What types of shops are found in your area?
All types of shops can be found in my area. There are shops selling garments, gift articles, groceries, commodities, electronics, food, and even sweets, where I live. One can also find outlets of international food chains like McDonalds, alongside small, privately owned shops, in my area.

2. What are the advantages and disadvantages of having local shops in your area?
Local shops offer innumerable benefits to the people of my area. They sell products of all varieties and categories at competitive prices, so people in my area can select from a huge array of goods in stores, and buy what they like at affordable rates. In this way, local shops offer people a lot of convenience when shopping. On the other hand, some local shop owners who sell niche products often don't have competitors, if there are only local shops all around. They are then known to charge higher prices compared to their counterparts in other areas. This can prove a little disadvantageous at times.

3. What do you generally shop, for your home?
I generally don't go out to buy things for my home, but occasionally I buy groceries, dairy products, fruits, and vegetables.

Practice Questions
1. What are the differences between commercial buildings, local businesses, and shopping malls?
2. If someone wants to open a shop in your area, what types of shops can they open?

71. Describe your favourite season.
   You should say
- **The name of the season, and during which months it stays**
- **What climatic changes happen during this season**
- **Why you like that season**

What do you do to enjoy the season, in your free time?
Sample Answer:
In India, we do not experience different seasons for equal time spans, because the country is located near the equator. However, because of global warming, the summer season usually extends for almost 6 months a year. This is the reason I like winter the most. Winter starts in mid-November in India, and lasts till mid-February, which is about 3 months. I like winter because the climate remains pleasant, dry, energising, and soothing, throughout the entire duration of the season. . The skies remains sunny on most days, but, we don't feel any need to switch on the fan.
One more reason for favouring winter is the availability of fruits and vegetables. During winters, we get many seasonal fruits and vegetables that prove to be healthy and tasty additions to our diets. It is also said that such a diet, rich in a variety of fresh, seasonal

fruits and vegetables, keeps our bodies fit and healthy, throughout the year. I also like to wear woollen clothes, and winter is the only time of the year I can indulge myself. People in my city often wake up early in the morning and go for walks, or to the gym to exercise. Winter season also enhances work efficiency, because of two good reasons. The first reason being that we don't perspire much, so we can work for longer periods of time; and the second reason being, our appetites remain high throughout the season, so our higher food intake makes it possible for us to devote more energy to work.

I often go to the beautiful lake near my home for a morning walk, and then I drink fresh fruit juices to keep myself fit and healthy. I can say that just these three months of winter are capable of energizing us for the rest of the year.

Follow-up Questions & Answers:
1. How do seasonal changes affect children/senior citizens?
Seasonal changes affect everyone, but they have a higher impact on senior citizens and children, because they tend to have weaker immune systems than the rest of the population. They may suffer from seasonal colds, fevers, or epidemics, which spread quicker when seasons are changing. What's more, seasonal changes also bring some emotional changes in humans. Such changes can be felt more by children and old people because they are often more sensitive. Hence, I think we should make some arrangements in advance to keep up people's spirits, and ensure their wellbeing, when seasons are changing.

2. What types of facilities are required to face seasonal changes at home?
The house should be equipped to face both, regular seasonal changes, and extreme seasonal conditions. The house should have proper air circulation and sun exposure, so that it remains fresh, safe, and germ free. There should also be some machines fitted in the house like air conditioners for the summer months, dehumidifiers for monsoons, and room heaters for winters, based on individual requirements.

3. Why do people celebrate the starting of each season?
Historically, we used to survive on farming, and hence we used to either harvest crops, or sow seeds in the farms when seasons changed. Both these events had great importance, as farming was the main source of food and wealth that brought economic prosperity to India. Thus, it became a pattern for people to celebrate the beginning of every season with festivities and cheer, as a way to remain in touch with nature and show gratitude to the changing seasons for sustaining life on earth.

72. Describe your favourite time of the day.
  You should say
- **What time of the day you like most**
- **What you do at that time**
- **What your observations about that time of the day are**
Why is that your favourite time of the day?

Sample Answer:
It is really difficult to talk about my favourite time of the day, because every moment of our life is important. However, the time I enjoy the most on any given day is the early morning, from 6 to 6:30. I consider this my favourite time because I wake up at 6 o'clock every morning, feeling completely fresh, energetic, and prepared to take on a new day. I step out for a short walk, during which I energize myself with the fresh, soothing, and pollution free morning air. I also soothe my eyes by looking at the grass, flowers, and trees in the morning. These sights help me a lot in staying fresh, full of energy, and enthusiastic throughout the day. On the way back, I also prepare my day's schedule in my mind. I have selected this time for the preparation of my daily schedule, because at this hour the mind is completely unoccupied, and better suited to planning tasks efficiently. Early in the morning, I find that I can also give the desired priority to tasks on hand, without getting too attached to them. Finally, this morning time acts as a blue print for the rest of the day. This makes it a very important time, and so, also my favourite.

Practice Questions
1. What do your friends and family members do during your favourite time?
2. How do you plan your day?
3. Do you write your plan in a diary? Why?
4. Why don't some people change their routine life?
5. What activities do you suggest to a retired person?
6. Are habits and hobbies dependent on the routine of a person?

73. Describe your last visit to a lake, riverbank, or a seashore.
   You should say
- **The location**
- **What types of people go there, and why**
- **What you do there**

Why do you like this place?

Sample Answer:
I would like to speak about my visit to the Sabarmati Riverfront located along the banks of the Sabarmati River, in my city. I visited the riverfront last month with my family, and two of my friends who came with their families. The history of Ahmedabad is linked strongly with the Sabarmati, along whose banks the city was developed in the 15th century. Over time, the river started becoming polluted, as slums started to develop along its banks. A few years ago, the state government decided to allocate funds towards cleaning up the river and its banks, and towards constructing a clean, modern riverfront, which would transform the riverbank into a pleasant hangout place for citizens.

A large part of the riverfront has been allocated to recreational parks, sports facilities, gardens, food joints, and open grounds to host private and public events. Every now and then, the riverfront hosts sophisticated flea markets, kite festivals, yoga events, and open air horticulture and gardening exhibits. Apart from this, in the evenings, families can enjoy motorboat rides in the river at very affordable rates. The riverfront is lined with ample seating for people to spend their time enjoying the cool, moist breezes of the river as they meditate, or sit and chat with family members and friends.

Because of the very large area that the riverfront covers, the government has developed a two-level promenade stretching over 11 km along both banks of the river. This makes the Sabarmati Riverfront an ideal place for morning and evening walks, for people of all ages. Many youngsters also choose to jog by the river, while some use adjoining areas to play cricket late at night.

I go to the riverfront with friends, sometimes, when we step out for late night drives. We enjoy driving by the riverbank, and stopping at the ice cream parlour there for a scoop or two of their special creamy vanilla, especially in the summers. Occasionally, I visit the riverfront by myself, when I am craving moments of solitude to disconnect from the humdrum of my daily routine.

Follow-up Questions & Answers:

1. What should governments do to protect such places from getting polluted?

Governments must impose strict rules at such places for the prevention of pollution, such as a ban on plastic bags, a prohibition on the disposal of rubbish in the open, or in the water body itself. Governments should also appoint security guards, to monitor the activities of locals and visitors, to keep the place clean and safe.

2. What are the advantages and disadvantages of water sports?

Water sports are highly adventurous activities. They help us in building our confidence and familiarity with water, while also satisfying our desire to do something exciting and different. Moreover, water sorts offer career opportunities for those who establish a good grip on them. On the flipside, water sports are risky. People may drown and risk losing their lives. In addition, some people have very sensitive skin that reacts adversely to open waters.

3. Should children learn water sports? If yes, which ones?

Children should learn water sports. It has now been proven by science that children learn to swim, faster than adults. However, the selection of water sports depends a lot on their individual likings. But, I think all children must learn to swim, as this is a good exercise, a good relaxation activity, and an essential life skill, too.

4. Should water sports be taught in schools?

It depends on the discretion of the school management, and the resources available within the school premises to introduce water sports. According to me, it is not convenient or practical to teach water sports during school hours, because it is an outdoor activity where children cannot wear their school uniforms. Thus, as of now, in my opinion, it appears that introducing water sports on campus may prove troublesome for schools.

Practice Questions

1. Do you suggest any changes be made to that place?
2. What precautions should we take before stepping into a water body?
3. How often do you visit that place?

4. Name some water sports.
5. What facilities are available in your city to carry out water sports?
6. Should the government develop water sports facilities?
7. Would you like to learn water sports in future? Which ones, and why?

74. Describe your last visit to a zoo.

You should say
- **When you visited the zoo**
- **How that zoo was**
- **What you liked there**

Is this zoo an interesting place to take children to?

Sample Answer:

I would like to speak about the Kankaria zoo, which is one of the biggest zoos in my state. It houses a variety of national and international species of birds and animals. I often visit this zoo with my friends and their families, because it is very close to my home. It has also developed in such a way that it offers visitors the option of going there for a half-day family picnic. It is very big in size, with different sections where we can see a variety of species of domestic and wild animals like monkeys, elephants, cows, deer, zebra, cats, lions, tigers, leopards, bears, hippopotamuses, snakes, and crocodiles. Some of the birds there are pigeons, ostriches, peacocks, ducks, sparrows, and parrots.

This zoo is a well-maintained place, where animals are being taken care of, well. The flow of visitors has been managed sensitively, so that animals don't feel much interference from human visitors. The local Municipal Corporation governs this zoo. Their staff members are also co-operative and helpful. Each cage has a nameplate that carries information about the animals it houses, including their common and biological names, their natural habitats, and their life spans, in both English and vernacular languages. Strewn across the entire area, there are different signboards with instructions, rules, and regulations to be followed inside the zoo premises by all visitors.

Children love this place, because they can see lots of different animals, right in front of their eyes. Usually children have only seen such animals in books and on TV. So, when they see these magnificent creatures up close, they feel overwhelmed and awestruck. Overall, the place is very good, not only for children, but also for the rest of the family.

75. Describe your visit to a bank.

You should say
- **When and where you visited the bank**
- **Why you visited it**
- **What it looks like**

Do you have any suggestions for the bank?

Sample Answer:

Bank visits are a routine activity in the life of a working professional. I would like to talk about the State Bank of India's local branch that is very close to my home. I visited this branch just a few days back, one afternoon. I went there because I wanted to open a savings bank account. The main doors of the bank open into its reception area; to the left is a passage lined with manned counters for cash deposits and withdrawals, while to the right there is the loans section along with the manager's office. The interiors of the bank are attractive and spacious. The receptionist was welcoming, and gave me all the information I needed, to open a savings account. I then filled up the application form to open my account there, and waited for some time to get my cheque book, and other related documents.

While waiting there, I saw that the receptionist was handling multiple enquires at the same time, including phone calls. She was working to the best of her abilities, but I found that she was overworked. SO, I think if the bank management hires another employee to attend calls, the processes may become more efficient, because the reception is the first point of contact for customers, and if their calls go unanswered, or are not attended properly, they are likely to feel dissatisfied. However, I am quite satisfied with the bank and its services as a whole.

Follow-up Questions & Answers:

1. What is the role of a bank in our society?

Banks are the financial centre of our society. It is a place where we deposit our money for safekeeping. We also execute various financial transactions through banks. Thus, a bank promotes a sense of financial safety and stability that is essential for good economic growth of any society.

2. What is the role of a bank in the economy of a country?

Banks are an essential part of the economy of any country. All public and private sector businesses carry out their financial transactions through banks, only. Banks support the economy by helping it grow steadily. Banks are institutes through which governments can conduct transactions with the corporate companies of the nation. It is said that the banking system of any country is a mirror of its financial strength. Governments can collect taxes and deposits through banks. In addition, governments can also release currency into the market through banks.

3. Name some services offered by banks.

Banks offer numerous services. This includes opening savings accounts, current accounts, NRI accounts, and personalised accounts, and maintaining them. Banks also issue chequebooks, credit cards, and debit cards, accept cash deposits and facilitate withdrawals, and offer investment plans in the form of fixed deposits, to customers. Apart from this, banks provide their customers with facilities like Automated Teller Machines (ATMs), phone banking, internet banking, loans, overdrafts, safe deposit vaults, and other relationship oriented services.

4. Is it a good idea to deposit your money with the bank?

Yes, it is not only a good idea, but it is also a safe and lucrative notion to deposit money with the bank, because banks keep our money safe, and, in return, give us interest on our money. What's more, financial dealings and transfers can be done very easily and securely through banks, helping us avoid the risk of carrying a lot of cash with us.

Practice Questions
1. What did you like and dislike about that place?
2. How often do you visit that bank?

◆ ◆ ◆

76. Describe your visit to a garden.
OR
77. Describe a garden you enjoyed visiting.
   You should say
-   **The location of the garden**
-   **When you visited it**
-   **What facilities are available there**
What did you like about the garden?

Sample Answer:
The most amazing garden I have visited so far, is in fact a set of many gardens in one location, called 'Gardens by the Bay'. These gardens are located in Singapore, and are major tourist attractions. These gardens have an expert team of horticulturists, landscapers, and engineers who work in tandem with the high tech Research and Development facility, there. They have, together, managed to bring in thousands of species of flowering and non-flowering, terrestrial and aquatic plants, and trees from all locations and climes across the globe, to the Gardens by the Bay. All these different species of flora bloom and thrive simultaneously in one location, irrespective of their individual climatic requirements. This state of the art utilisation of science is nothing short of magic to the layman. Gardens by the Bay has three waterfront gardens called Bay East, Bay South, and Bay Central. Bay South has a flower dome with floral displays that they keep changing all year around, while Bay East gives a breath-taking view of the Singapore skyline in the peaceful backdrop of greenery.

These gardens also host festivals, movie screenings, musical concerts, educational workshops, and other community events from time to time. Millions of visitors have already been to the Gardens by the Bay, and many tourists make it a point to visit the gardens every time they go to Singapore. Anyone who visits these gardens gets dumbfounded by the sheer expanse of the gardens, its marvellous art installations, and the variety of flora on display.

Gardens by the Bay also offer guided tours to visitors throughout the day, either on foot or in golf carts. This is an especially good facility in my opinion, because most people are likely to get confused as regards where to start exploring and how to continue. The other great facility provided by these gardens is their display of maps all over the property, so that visitors may locate their positions and plan where to go next.

Follow-up Questions & Answers:

1. Do you think the number of gardens in your city should be increased?

It is necessary to increase the number of gardens in my city, for two good reasons. Firstly, a garden offers natural scenery that is most essential for the fast moving and polluted environment of my city. Secondly, it offers an opportunity to the city dwellers to pursue various recreational and health oriented activities like walks, physical exercise, laughing clubs, and games.

2. Should there be any entry charges for visiting gardens? Why?

I think authorities should take a token charge from people who want to visit gardens. This is because when we pay money, we act more responsibly towards a place. Further, the money can be used for the maintenance and development of the garden, so that it can serve people better. However, garden authorities should allow free entry for senior citizens and children.

3. What care should be taken while visiting a garden?

We should check the opening and closing timings of the garden, before visiting. Apart from that, we must read all the rules and instructions for visitors, before entering the garden, so that we may not break any rules or damage anything out of ignorance.

4. Do gardens need security? Why?

A garden is a public place. It needs security for many reasons, such as the protection of plants and trees from children and domestic animals, the safekeeping of playing equipment from getting damaged or stolen, guarding visitors from pick pockets and other antisocial elements, and the prevention of pollution in the form of rubbish thrown by visitors.

Practice Question

1. How often do you visit that garden?
2. Are similar gardens available in your city?
3. Who looks after the gardens in your city?
4. According to you, what is an ideal garden?
5. Is it a good idea to invite private companies to maintain public gardens?

78. Describe your visit to a railway station/bus station/an airport.

  You should say
- **When and where you visited it**
- **What the place is like**
- **Why you went there**

What other facilities does the place offer?

Sample Answer:

I would like to talk about my visit to the Kalupur Railway Station, It is located in my city, and I visited it last month, as I wanted to go to a nearby city in my state, with my family. It is located in the heart of Ahmedabad, and is very big, with a total of 12 platforms. It is connected to all the railway stations in my state, as well as all tier-I and tier-II railway stations in my country. It has a huge building for administration, a large parking lot, and a wide entry passage. A large printed train timetable is displayed along with a digital ticker at the entry gate, to update travellers regarding the train schedules and estimated arrival times. The station is a busy place, and is always crowded. It has more than 15 ticket counters, and a queue of 10–15 people can perpetually be seen at each counter. This situation reflects the number of people using the station on a daily basis.

This station is well maintained, and travellers get regular updates at all enquiry counters, as well as on the platforms. All the platforms are connected with three pedestrian over bridges, so people can easily move between platforms. A list of trains arriving and departing from a particular platforms is displayed near the staircase of each over bridge. Moreover, there are television displays on all platforms, at regular distances, that keep the passengers updated regarding their train schedules. In addition, we can buy medicines, refreshments, books, and other daily requirement goods from any platform. The station has a separate air-conditioned building for computer reservations, where we can book our train tickets in advance. I appreciate this place because it serves the people of my city and state quite well.

Follow-up Questions & Answers:
1. What facilities should be provided at such places?
There are a number of facilities required at such places. For example, a large parking area for visitors, enquiry counters, displayed timetables with real time updates, ample waiting area for passengers, free water, clean toilets, canteens for refreshments, cloakrooms, and good security systems to protect passengers and their luggage from thieves and miscreants.
2. Which type of travel do you prefer — air or rail? Why?
I prefer air travel to rail travel, because air travel is faster, more convenient, and more luxurious compared to rail travel. In addition, air travel is getting cheaper because of stiff competition among airline companies in many countries of the world.
3. What are the advantages and disadvantages of rail travel, compared to air travel?
Rail travel is cheaper, safer, and more enjoyable compared to air travel. However it is slower than air travel. This is the reason why I prefer rail travel for short distances. Railway stations are located in the downtown areas of most cities in my country, whereas airports are located in the peripheries of cities. So, when it comes to travelling short distances, the overall time taken from most people's homes to the airport, coupled with the flight duration, proves longer than the entire duration of rail travel.
4. Are you satisfied with the air travel/rail travel system of your country?
Well, both systems are quite competent in my country. However, I do have a few concerns about both. Firstly, railway stations are not very clean or tidy; at some points there are bad odours, too. Next, the security system is not so efficient at most railway stations, which allows criminals and terrorists to commute and execute their activities easily. For air travel, I would like to say that the number of airports is far lesser than what is required in the country, especially because the existing airports are not big enough to handle the increasing number of flights. Often, aircrafts waste valuable aviation fuel while waiting for their turn to land and take off, because of this.
5. Do you support strict security measures at such places?
I strongly favour strict security measures at bus stations, railway stations, and airports.

Security systems at such places serve manifold purposes. Firstly, they protect tourists and their luggage from thieves and miscreants. Secondly, they prevent the movement of antisocial elements and illegal goods. Lastly, they help in protecting people and property from terrorists, which, to me is the most important reason for having strict security measures at these places.

6. What are the disadvantages of imposing strict security at such places?

There are no disadvantages of imposing security measures at such places. However, some people feel disturbed and harassed because of excessive checking. At times, such security checks may cause delays at airports that might irritate the passengers and delay the schedules of flights, also.

7. How helpful is air travel in dissolving cultural differences?

Air travel is really helpful in dissolving cultural, regional, and continental differences. We can visit other countries, spend time with the people of other cultures, and understand them during air travel. This exposure to people of different cultures and nationalities inculcates a sense of tolerance in air travellers. Consequently, they become more compassionate and considerate towards people of other countries and cultures.

Practice Questions
1. What did you like and dislike about that place?
2. Do you frequently go to a bus station/railway station/an airport?

79. Speak about a person you met while travelling by bus, train, or aeroplane.

    You should say
- **How you met this person**
- **What topics you discussed with them**
- **What qualities you liked/disliked in that person**

Overall, how would you describe your experience of meeting this new person?

Sample Answer:

Last year, I met an interesting person while travelling from Ahmedabad to Mumbai. I was going to Mumbai for two days to attend a social function, and my wife and daughter had accompanied me. We had a confirmed booking on our seats, and on the berth opposite ours, were two men. Initially, we didn't talk to each other, as I observed they were busy attending calls. After almost an hour, my daughter started playing in the coach, and she started talking to one of the men. After a while, I came to know that his name was Vishal, and he lived in the same city as us. Based on his discussions, and reasons for visiting Mumbai, I was able to infer that he was a passionate dog trainer and breeder. I started discussing his hobby with him, and was really surprised at the numerous things I learnt about dog-breeding, various species of dogs, and their typical traits. He had won an award for being the youngest dog breeder, and what was even more amazing was that he had 22 dogs of different breeds. He showed us pictures of his 'pug' (the famous Vodafone ad dog), German shepherd, and Pomeranian, among others.

During our discussion, I noticed that the amount of care and special treatment that he gave to his dogs was as good as one would give to their family members. In today's world, where we see people betray each other for silly reasons, this young man proved to be a very good example of compassion. He told me that he woke up at 6 am each day, and spent at least 3 hours in the morning with all his pets, so that the loving bond between him and his pets remained intact. He also gave me his contact details and invited me to visit his house to see the dogs. He also promised my daughter that he would get her a puppy. Apart from this, we exchanged information about our families and businesses, too. Finally, our station came, and we departed with pleasant memories, as well as a commitment to stay in touch with each other.

Follow-up Questions & Answers:
1. What type of person do you like to talk to — an introvert or an extrovert? Why?
Well, quite obviously, it is difficult to talk at length with introverts because they have a tendency to remain silent and mind their own business, without talking unnecessarily. However, there are some people who may be introverted and hesitate in initiating a conversation, but then once they feel comfortable, they open up slowly, and turn out to be surprisingly interesting conversationalists, who can have fruitful discussions even with strangers. So, it depends on how different people responds to different conversations. As for me, I don't label people as introverts or extroverts, and I don't frame my discussions accordingly, either.
2. How do you initiate conversations when you meet strangers?
It depends a lot on the place where we meet, the occasion, and the personality of the stranger in question. If we meet someone in a public transport vehicle during transit, or at a party, or concert or similar crowded public place, I prefer initiating the conversation with a greeting, and then I continue by briefly introducing myself to them. Once these formalities are taken care of, I start my discussion based on what feels suitable to the occasion and venue we are at.
3. How safe is it in your country to talk to strangers in public transport?
Again, it depends on the mode of transport we have chosen to travel by. Talking to a stranger can be safer in a plane or in a first class air conditioned railway coach. However, if we are travelling in a bus or a general coach in a train, we are likely to find people from various socio economic classes, with different mentalities travelling together. Talking to strangers in such situations can be risky.
4. How important is it to learn communication skills in life?
Communication skills are an essential part of our day to day life. I think the phrase 'communication skills' is not understood properly by most people. We think that learning communication skills is important for executives and corporate employees, only. However, according to me, any interaction at any level, by any means, with another person qualifies as communication, and those who have good skills of communication often come out as winners in most life situations.
5. Do you think we should give our contact details to someone we meet while travelling?
I personally don't agree with sharing contact details with strangers, because unless one is very sure of the identity of the other person, sharing contact details can be detrimental to us.
6. Is it safe to share our food or snacks with co-passengers in public transport?

The Ultimate Guide to IELTS Speaking by Parthesh Thakkar

This, too, depends on the mode of travel we have taken. We do not need to share our food with someone if we are travelling by plane or in a first class air conditioned railway coach, as food is provided by the crew. But, in case we do share food with co-passengers on airlines, it is likely to be safe. However, sharing food with others in local public transports can be risky. I feel this way because we often read in newspapers about people being given sedatives mixed with food by their co-passengers, and then robbed.

7. What precautions should we take before travelling by public transport?

We should get the confirmed tickets in our hands, first. Then, we should reach the station or airport a little before time to avoid last minute hassles. Next, we should organise our luggage properly, we should pack suitcases and hand bags in such a way that we do not need to open big bags in public. In addition, when we get our seat, we should organise our luggage near our seats, and lock our bags if necessary, to avoid any possibility of theft. Finally, we should be aware of the route we are going by, and the expected time of arrival at our destination. This can ensure that we travel happily and safely.

8. What precautions should we take while travelling and interacting with co-passengers in public transport?

We should keep our luggage in the assigned space, so that there is enough room left for others to sit. We should not keep our luggage on the seats meant for other passengers. In addition, we should not open those bags which have expensive articles, or even our wallets if there is a lot of money in them, to avoid being targeted by thieves. We should also behave properly, should not speak very loudly, should not play songs on mobiles, and we must avoid smoking or consuming alcohol in public transport vehicles.

9. Does the government provide any security in public transport vehicles?

Yes, the government provides a special security force in all the trains that run in my country. There are two railway police armed guards per coach, and in some places where stealing in trains is more common, more guards may also be assigned to protect the luggage of passengers, and to make their journey safer and more enjoyable.

13. Have you seen/met foreigners in public transport vehicles in your country?

Yes, meeting foreigners while travelling by public transport is becoming more common these days. This is because India is booming economically, thereby attracting people from all over the world. Foreign nationals visit India for business, leisure, and other purposes, and they also travel freely by public transport, here.

14. Do they also interact with other people freely?

Yes, I have seen many foreigners interacting with local people without hesitation. However, they might face some problems in communicating if the other person doesn't know English. But, English speaking people are increasing in India with each passing day, so foreigners these days don't face too many issues caused by language barriers.

Practice Questions

1. Are you still in touch with that person?
2. How do you meet him?
3. How do people greet each other when they meet strangers in such places?
4. What is the difference between communicating with a foreigner, and a local individual?
5. What do you wish to know about a person when you meet him for the first time?
6. Are there some issues or topics that you feel uncomfortable about, when you discuss

them with someone for the first time?

◆ ◆ ◆

80. If you receive lot of money…

You should say

- **What you will do with it**
- **Who you will share it with**
- **How you will spend the spare money**

Will you place yourself before others, or vice versa?

Sample Answer:

It is indeed fascinating to imagine such a situation unfold in real life! I think almost everyone dreams of such a miracle happening in their lives, at some point. Most people have some ready plans for when such a fortunate turn of events takes place. If I receive a lot of money, I will use it in different proportions for different purposes. As we all know — charity begins at home. I will allocate a large sum of money to my family members, so that they can fulfil their dreams and ambitions, too. After that, I would help needy friends, relatives, and neighbours, so that they may live better, and grow in life. I would also like to set some money aside to invest in different segments like stock markets, mutual funds, real estate, bank deposits, and bullion. This will ensure that I have a sustainable source of income for the rest of my life. After that, I would like to establish a resort for people who want to live a stress free and spiritual life. There would be lodging, boarding, and recreation facilities for those who want to come to take a break, as well as for those who want to stay there for a few years of their life. This resort will have a focus on meditation and yoga, and lay emphasis on satisfying the spiritual cravings of people. It will also provide employment options for those who want to live there, so that they can sustain themselves, and live a beautiful life. This will be a calm zone devoid of greed, stress, competition, politics, and jealousy. Rather, visitors and residents will find peace, harmony, and cooperation, in the energetic and spiritual vibes of the resort. Lastly, I would spare some money for the maintenance and future development of the resort. I hope I can develop such a place, where life is given priority and respect over materialistic desires and wealth.

Follow-up Questions & Answers:

1. What is the importance of money in our life?

Money is an important part of our life. We need money to survive, grow, and to give stability of life to our family members, and ourselves. Money gives a sense of security to most people in their lives.

2. Should people select their career according to the remuneration, or based on self-satisfaction?

I think both aspects are important. We should consider both, money and satisfaction, before selecting a job. However, we can give a higher priority to remuneration in the beginning phases of our career, and to job satisfaction in the later stages of our career.

3. Should parents give more money to their children?

There is no harm in giving more money to children, provided they are also explained the importance of money. To make children aware of the importance of money is a time consuming and diligent task. Most people tend to be reluctant in giving more money to their children, because they worry that if they give too much money to their children, they may turn to destructive activities owing to their immaturity.

4. If a child has spare money, what should he spend it on?

I think a child should save money, or even invest it, rather than spending it immediately, so that the child can fund his future requirements with his own money, and feel independent and confident.

5. Do you think that we are losing our culture and traditional values in the rush to earn money?

Unfortunately, it appears to be true that we are sacrificing our cultural and moral values to earn money, because globalisation has increased the importance of wealth, and a materialistic lifestyle, across the globe. Owing to this, everyone wants to be rich in a short span of time, which is not possible. Thus, to attain this, people often adopt illegal or unethical ways to earn money. This is nothing but a loss of moral and cultural values.

Practice Questions

1. Do you agree with the statement that children these days spend more money compared to those in the past?
2. What are the effects of overspending on children who spend more money?
3. Is it important for children to learn financial planning, or should it be taught at a later age?

81. Speak about a club you are a member of, or have visited.

   You should say

- **The name and location of the club**
- **What facilities the club provides**
- **What activities you do there**

Do you have suggestions for the club?

Sample Answer:

My city has become a cosmopolitan in the last few years. Because of this, recreational facilities in the city, and the standard of living have gone up substantially. This change has created some space for an emerging club culture. Here, I would like to talk about Rajpath Club. This is not a new club; rather it is one of the oldest and the best clubs of my city. It is located on Sarkhej Gandhinagar highway. I am not a member of this club because the distance between the club and my house is too much. I cannot access this club on a regular basis. However, I have visited this club many times. It is spread over a very large area. It has ample parking place, a big clubhouse, three conference halls, an air-conditioned banquet hall, a party plot, and a big swimming pool. The interiors of the club are quite modern, and every part of the club is very calming. The club offers annual and lifetime memberships at premium rates; but, if we compare the services offered by this club with other clubs, the rates at Rajpath are very reasonable. It offers attractive discounts on the organisation of parties, conferences, and other functions to its members. The club management also organises various cultural and sport events for its members. It has a good restaurant, too, that serves Indian, Chinese, Italian, and Mexican food. I feel the club is a complete package of recreation, luxury, and convenience. Hence, I don't have any suggestions for the improvement of the club.

Follow-up Questions & Answers:
1. Why do you think people go to clubs?
People go to clubs for a variety of reasons. Most people visit clubs to enjoy the club's recreational facilities like the swimming pool, the gym, and areas for playing other games, as clubs are the only places that offer all these facilities under one roof.
2. What activities do youngsters/children/women/aged people do there?
Youngsters prefer playing indoor and outdoor games like cricket, tennis, and chess. They also like working out in the gym. Children visit clubs for swimming and other amusement rides. Women go to clubs to socialise. They often organise kitty parties at clubs. Old people go there for walks, to meet others, and to pass their time.
3. What facilities should be provided by an ideal club?
The list of services and facilities provided by a good club can be endless. Still, I will try to name some. An ideal club should have a garden, a swimming pool, a basketball court, a tennis court, a walking track, a party plot, a banquet hall, a restaurant and cafeteria, a parking lot, good accommodations with round-the-clock room service, lockers, and a functional 24 hour customer care help line.

Practice Questions
1. Why have you taken a membership of this club? OR Why do you want to take a membership of this club?
2. People these days join clubs to show their status. Do you agree with this statement?

82. Speak about a family member you resemble.
OR
83. Speak about a family member who has a great influence on you.
   You should say
-   **How you are related to this family member**
-   **How you resemble him/her**
-   **How you benefit from this resemblance**
How else has this resemblance impacted you?
Sample Answer:
In my family, I resemble my father. I resemble him in terms of overall appearance, especially my height, and hair. I resemble him so much that whenever any of my father's acquaintances see me, they recognise me as his son. I have come across this situation

---

The Ultimate Guide to IELTS Speaking by Parthesh Thakkar

many times in my life. Initially, I could not believe how someone could recognise me immediately as his son, but ever since I have seen photographs of my dad from when he was younger, things have become quite clear to me. I do in fact have a similar hair style, height, and skin complexion that helps my father's friends and acquaintances to identify me instantly.

I have received plentiful benefits from this resemblance. The first amongst them is acceptance in society, as my father is a well-known man in my community and area. Many people know him, and respect him. That is why, whenever I meet either my relatives, or his friends and business associates, I get similar acceptance and respect from them. This enables me to get recognition in society quite easily. People offer me the same welcome and warmth that they do to my father.

In addition to this, such acceptance has brought on early maturity and a sense of responsibility in my life. As others started respecting me, I had to start behaving maturely enough to live up to their respect. So, I developed myself as a responsible member of my community, who is as good as his father.

84. Describe a family you know (other than your own family).

You should say

- **How you know them**
- **How many members they have, and what each of them do**
- **With whom you spend more time, and why**

How would you describe your family's relations with this family?

Sample Answer:

I am going to talk about a joint family that lives in my neighbourhood. We have been living in the same apartment for more than 15 years, and I know them for the same period of time. There are eight members in their family. An elderly man and his wife, their two sons, two daughters-in-law, and two grandchildren, all live together under one roof. The elder of the two sons is my age; he is married, and has 2 kids — a boy, and a girl. His younger brother has got married recently, and thus he has no kids as of now. Their father, who is the eldest member of the family, runs a business of his own in my city. His younger son accompanies him, and helps with the business. The elder son — the one who is my friend — started his own business a while ago, and is doing well now.

We often visit each other's houses. We have helped, and taken assistance from each other many times over the last 15 years. I respect them a lot, because they are very humble, down to earth, and cooperative in their approach to all the neighbours and their relatives. As I said earlier, the elder son of the family is of my age, and I spend maximum time with him. We have studied together, and our interests match in many areas of life. We also worked in the same company for a while, immediately after completing college. The women in their family are very supportive, nurturing homemakers, too. I think our families are quite homogenised with each other, in terms of social beliefs and cultural set up. And according to me, it is for this reason, that we have been sharing a very good relationship with each other for over a decade. I hope we continue to do the same in future, as well.

Follow-up Questions & Answers:
1. How different is that family from your family?
Well, that family is not very different from mine. It mainly differs in the number of family members. Apart from that, we follow the same religion, we belong to same caste, and we have similar thoughts regarding the social set up of our families. This is the reason why we feel like we are united, and have a strong bond between ourselves.
2. Are similar kinds of families seen in other parts of our country, as well?
Finding families similar to the one I described is not difficult. We can find such families easily in almost all cities of India. This is because people of my community have settled in various parts of the country.

Practice Questions
1. When do you meet them?
2. How do you spend time with them?
3. Do your family members also interact with them?
4. Have you learned anything from that family?
5. Do you celebrate any events like festivals or birthdays, together?

85. Speak about a famous personality/celebrity of your city/country.
OR
86. Speak about a famous person of your country that you are interested in.
    You should say
-    **The name of the person**
-    **What he/she does for a living**
-    **What you like about him/her**
What is your overall opinion of this celebrity?
Suggestions:
Candidates can speak about a social worker, politician, police officer, sports person, industrialist, or film star.
Sample Answer:
There are many famous personalities in my city, in various fields and specialisations. Here, I would like to speak about Mr. Narendra Modi who is the Prime Minister of India. Before becoming PM, he used to be an MLA (member of legislative assembly) from my area of residence, and the CM (Chief Minister) of my state, Gujarat. I have known about him for over 15 years, because he has been a prominent strategic advisor in his political party since long. I also have some faith in the political agenda of this party, for the country.
During his term as Chief Minister, he changed the face of my state by introducing

economic reforms here. He holds the credit for completing the Narmada Dam project that provides irrigation facilities to the whole state. This project has brought about an agricultural revolution in my state. The farmers who were once dependant solely on rainfall in this semi-arid region, started getting very good product yields with the advent of irrigation facilities, instead of making huge losses when the rainfall in their region was scarce.

Mr. Narendra Modi is also focused on the overall development of the state, including small towns and remote villages, during his term as CM.

Because of his non-corrupt, energetic, hardworking nature, and his visionary approach towards the development of India, the people of the country elected him as Prime Minister in 2014. He took on this post with patriotic fervour and started working day and night for the betterment of the nation. He has taken many measures to improve the economic standing of the country on various international platforms, demonetised some old currency and brought in new notes in a bid to reduce the circulation of black money in the market, and he has taken it upon himself to ensure that the holy Ganges River is cleaned completely. Further, he has started a major 'Make in India' campaign to encourage citizens to produce more goods within the country, than importing or outsourcing production. Apart from this, his 'Swachh Bharat Abhiyaan' encourages the people of the country to keep their streets and areas clean and hygienic.

I am influenced by Mr. Modi because he works hard like a youngster, in spite of being so senior in age. He is always active and alert. I have never heard him making any controversial statements anywhere, and he is a great orator, which is an important quality in a leader. According to me, he is a decent politician who believes that actions speak louder than words.

Follow-up Questions & Answers:
1. **Do famous personalities have any influence on the society?**
Famous personalities do have a great influence on the society. They are successful in their fields, and so they have many followers in the society, who believe in what these celebrities say and do. These followers are also often ready to adopt everything that famous personalities endorse or follow. That's why they can have a strong influence on the society.

2. **What are the advantages and disadvantages of being a famous personality?**
Famous personalities get respect, recognition, fame, and followership in society. While this is an advantage, on the other hand, they always experience a lack of privacy, because the very people who make them famous and popular, tend to always be interested in their personal lives. It is rightly said that celebrities have to sacrifice their personal lives if they can't hide them well.

3. **Why are people interested in the personal lives of famous personalities?**
When people see a celebrity getting name and fame in society, they become inspired to live a life like his. In keeping with these aspirations, they keep a watch on the lifestyles of famous personalities. This includes observing their clothes, accessories, gadgets, vehicles, and even their eating habits. All this is done in a bid to emulate these celebrities, to induce feelings of being equal to, or similar to them. Those who try and yet fail to emulate celebrities, often criticise them by weighing every action of theirs on scales of morality.

However, even to do this, critics need to pry into the personal lives of famous personalities. Be it for adulation or criticism, in both cases, people take an active interest in the lives of celebrities.

4. What are the effects of their parents' fame on the children of famous personalities?

Children of famous personalities often live their lives under pressure. They are always compared with their parents, and expected to match up or do better in life. This pressure often starts at the outset of their careers. These comparisons, and society's expectations from them to outperform their parents, puts them under a lot of stress.

Practice Questions

1. Why does everyone want to become famous?
2. What are the differences between the famous people of the past and the present?

87. Describe an incident where you met a celebrity.

You should say

- **Who that celebrity was**
- **When and where you met them**
- **What your conversation was about**

How did you feel after meeting that person?

Sample Answer:

Life is full of pleasant surprises, and I have received many such surprises in my life. Meeting Mr. Sachin Tendulkar was one of them. I had booked an Indian Airlines ticket to Delhi from Ahmedabad one time, for a 3 day visit to meet some business associates. I was well prepared for the meetings, with my bags all packed, and my presentation ready. However, when I reached the airport, because of some technical reasons, my flight was cancelled, and we were given the option of boarding a flight that was coming from Mumbai, and would go to Delhi. However, on that flight, all the economy class seats were occupied. Owing to this, I had to book a first class seat. I got my confirmation, and was waiting for the flight to come in. After some time, the flight landed from Mumbai, and we boarded it. When I took my seat, I was surprised to see Mr. Sachin Tendulkar sitting next to me! When I saw him, I couldn't utter a word for the first few minutes. My favourite sportsman was sitting next to me in the same flight. I was thinking of starting a conversation with him, but he appeared busy in reading his magazine. After a few minutes, he looked at me and smiled. I was overwhelmed seeing his humble demeanour and politeness. Once he had broken the ice, we spoke to each other for the rest of the flight. He was going to Delhi for personal reasons, and was not on an official cricket tour. He had recently completed a successful tour of Australia, where he had scored his maiden one-day century against Australia. He was given 'man of the match' and 'man of the series' awards for his scintillating performance. I asked him a lot of questions about his liking for cricket, his attachment to the game, his reactions to criticism, and his way of handling tough times in his career. I must say, I had read a lot about him in newspapers, on the internet, and had also seen his interviews. But, he was even better in person, than I had perceived him to be. According to me, he is not only a legendary cricketer, but also a great person; someone who we would like to befriend in life, a great motivator, and a caring large-hearted human. I also came to know many things about his life and his nature from our chance meeting. He was honest, comfortable in talking to me, and willing to answer me even though I was neither a famous journalist, nor a professional cricketer. When our flight landed, he thanked me for being a fan, and asked me to pray for the Indian cricket team, and to keep supporting the team, in future, also. I must admit, it seemed like my time with him on that flight passed exceptionally fast, and I wished I could have spent some more time with him. He also invited me to visit him at home, whenever I went to Mumbai. I thanked him for the invite, and wished him all the very best for his future endeavours.

Follow-up Questions & Answers:
1. What are the reasons some celebrities behave rudely with people in public places?
It is tough for me to predict why celebrities behave rudely with people, because their reactions often depend on their mood, and the way they are approached by their fans. Some people pass cheap comments about their career, their work, their appearance, and many other personal things, which may irritate them. In turn they may respond rudely. I think such comments would irritate any one in their place. I believe we should behave with others how we would like them to behave with us. There is one more reason why some celebrities behave rudely; some young celebrities get egoistic when they become successful early in life, and at times, they are unable to handle and digest their overwhelming popularity. However, this doesn't happen nowadays, because most celebrities are well trained in handling extreme popularity. They seldom behave rudely in public.

2. Should celebrities keep security guards alongside, when they move in public?
Yes, unfortunately, it is important that celebrities keep security guards alongside, to protect themselves from many seen and unseen dangers. Sometimes, fans may harm them in public unintentionally. At times, they may also be harmed by people who don't like them, or people who are fans of their rivals. To top it, they have to protect themselves from criminals and terrorists, also.

3. Who was there with you when you met that celebrity?
Unfortunately, I was alone when I met him. I wish I had my family along, but I was travelling alone for work. There were other people also on the flight, who came and took his autographs as mementos, and asked him a question or two.

4. Why do some people show/display photographs of their meetings with celebrities in their homes/offices?
There are two reasons for this. Some people are genuine fans of some celebrities, and so they like to keep reliving their meetings with those celebrities. Secondly, some people display their pictures with celebrities, as a social status symbol, to gain more respect and acceptance in society.

Practice Questions
1. Was it a planned meeting?

---

2. What did you ask that celebrity?

3. How did that celebrity respond to you?

4. What type of questions do people ask, when they meet celebrities in person?

5. How can one meet a celebrity in your country?

88. Speak about a peaceful place you visit regularly.

You should say

- **The name and location of the place**

- **When and how you go there**

- **What the place is like**

What do you do there?

Suggestions:

Candidates can speak about temples, churches, gardens, farmhouses, their native village, the seashore, etc.

Sample Answer:

It is really difficult to find a truly peaceful place in big cities. People have to move away from cities, to small towns or villages to look for such places. I found a truly peaceful place near my city. It is a small village named 'Dholeshwar', located approximately 25 kilometres away from my home. This village is situated on the banks of the river, Sabarmati. There is a big Lord Shiva temple surrounded by a natural landscape, rich in a variety of trees and plants. The temple is located on the bank of the river, and on a big plateau. This place is amazingly peaceful and soothing. Because of the river, the air stays a little humid and cool throughout the year. The flow of the river is shallow and slow here. That makes this place ideal for people who like to swim, and play other games in the water.

I visit this place at least once in two months with my family members. I first go to the temple to offer a prayer to Lord Shiva, and then walk to the bank bare feet to feel the softness of the sand. We enjoy playing in the water for some time, and then we sit in the opening on the bank, between old trees and plants. The feel of the cool air, the sound of water flowing by, and the chirping of birds make this place truly alive, and refreshing. I just sit and try to enjoy the weather and absorb the vibes of this place. At times, I go there with my friends and we play games like cricket and volleyball. According to me, it is one of the most peaceful places I have ever seen in my life. I feel fresh, charged, ecstatic, joyous, and energised, there.

Follow-up Questions & Answers:

1. Under what circumstances do people go to such places?

People go to such places when they are exhausted, tired, or even frustrated. Some also use such places as stress busters. In short, those who are disconnected from peace and inner harmony in their routine lives, or those who want to strengthen their connection with peace, visit such places. When they go to such places, their mental disturbance gets reduced, and they feel calm and peaceful again. It is also seen that people often get new insights into their existing difficulties when they develop a harmony with their souls, at such places.

2. Should people spend some time alone regularly, as a part of their routine?

I think it is essential to spend some time by ourselves as a part of our routine, because when we are with others, our mind keeps receiving feedback from our surroundings. This constant input of emotions and reactions disturbs our mind, and reduces its efficiency. When we are alone, such disturbances settle and we can have a better, clearer look at our lives. Hence, I recommend that everyone spend at least twenty to thirty minutes a day all by themselves. Here, I would like to clear one more point. There is a big difference in being alone and being lonely. If we keep focusing our energies on others and on external situations when we are alone, we are bound to feel lonely, which can weaken our mind. But, if we stay connected with our feelings and emotions, we can enjoy being alone, and can also strengthen our mind with such exercises.

3. What should the government do to reduce noise pollution?

The government must impose strict rules to curb noise pollution. They should declare clear and strict guidelines for noise levels at various places. Those who breach these rules should be penalized in order to keep noise levels under control.

4. What is the future of meditation according to you?

I believe that meditation is the future of all mankind. Since the first day of human existence, we have been continuously evolving to achieve spiritual enlightenment in our lives, and meditation is the only tool to enhance our spiritual evolution. This is the reason why, I think, there will be a time when everyone will be practicing meditation to enhance their own spiritual evolution, as well as the collective spiritual evolution of humanity.

Practice Questions

1. Do you recommend that others visit that place?
2. What do people do at such places?
3. Which other peaceful places are there in your city?
4. Do you go there alone? Why?
5. Do you practice meditation?
6. What benefits do you get from meditation?
7. Should we practice meditation alone, or under the guidance of someone?

89. Speak about a person who has influenced you.

    You should say

- **The name of the person**
- **How you know them**
- **What their qualities are**

How have they influenced you?

Suggestions:
Candidates can speak about their friend, family member, neighbour, teacher, doctor, or their religious mentor (guru).

Sample Answer:
We meet many people in our life. Everyone we meet or come across has some influence on us. One person who has influenced me a lot is the former president of my country, the Late Dr APJ Abdul Kalam. I haven't met him in real life, but, I have seen him many times on TV, and I have attended some of his public speeches. I have also read his books, 'Ignited Minds' and 'Wings of Fire'. In his books, he has written a lot about his childhood, his family, his village, and his studies. I have learned a lot by reading incidents of his life. He has inspired me to work hard, and to believe in the dreams that I have for my future, and my society. I am influenced by the fact that he was sober, polite, compassionate, and inspiring in his approach even at the post of the President of India. He was a scientist, and was also well known for his invaluable contribution to our country's nuclear research program. Even in his old age, he used to walk, give speeches, and talk to others with the energy and drive of a young man. Even after his death, he serves as an ideal example for many people who are struggling to become successful in life. He was born in a poor family, in a small village in southern India, and he went on to become the 'First Man' of India. I became an admirer after reading his books. He has inspired me to do something useful for my country and its people, in the course of my life.

90. Speak about an article you read regularly in the newspaper/magazine.

  You should say
- **The title, and the name of the writer**
- **When you read it**
- **The topic of the article**

Why do you like it?

Suggestions:
Candidates can speak about any article of their interest, be it regarding politics, sports, social life, religion, films, music, management, or cooking. (Remember, don't bother if you are unable to recall the writer's name correctly, you can make a guess, also, and use any name while you are speaking.)

Sample Answer:
Reading the newspaper is one of the most important things that we do to become aware of our surroundings. A newspaper covers many articles that are helpful to its readers. I would like to talk about an article which is published every Wednesday in The Times of India in its supplement — Ascent. I would prefer to call this a feature with an article every week. I read this article the same afternoon, because I don't get enough time in the morning to read it in detail. It is largely related to topics concerning the corporate world, and management skills. This article is written by different people who are prominent in their field, every week. This is also why there is no specific title given to this article. The

articles focus on time management, interview skills, marketing skills, management case studies, investment strategies, emerging industries, and their present and future. There are a few industries that are doing well now, but I have read about them when they were in their beginning phases, in this newspaper. I believe such articles help youngsters a lot in selecting their career, or in selecting their subject for tertiary education. At times, we can also read real life experiences and challenges faced by top-notch industrialists in their life. This inspires young entrepreneurs to lead their business to success.

I have learned a lot about time management and office management, from this feature, apart from tips for recruiting people for my business. According to me, it is a must read article for every literate person.

Follow-up Questions & Answers:
1. How is this article useful to you?
It gives me detailed information regarding the practical application of management skills, so that I can also apply them in my profession. In the past, I read an article about time management. I found that implementation of the tips from that article actually improved my efficiency.

2. Should we read a newspaper every day?
Yes, if we want to stay abreast of the latest developments in our city, country, and the world, we should read newspapers every day.

3. What type of articles do youngsters prefer to read? Why?
Youngsters prefer reading articles on sports, fashion, lifestyle, and topics from the entertainment industry, such as music and cinema, because these are the common interests and discussion topics at this age.

4. What type of articles do old people prefer to read? Why?
Old people prefer to read articles on politics, business, stock markets, and on religion, because their interests evolve with age and settle on more abstract and social issues related to the country, the economy, and the community.

Practice Question
1. How is this article useful to society?
2. What other articles do you read?
3. Where do you read these articles?
4. Are there any negative impacts of such articles?
5. Is there a difference in the preference of articles, between men and women? Why?

91. Speak about your favourite author/columnist.
    You should say
- **The name**
- **What he/she writes or has written**
- **How his/her writing is useful to you**

How does his work inspire you?

Sample Answer:
I have read numerous books on various subjects like spirituality, philosophy, management, religion, fiction, self-development, and new age. Thus, it is indeed tough for me to narrow in on any one favourite author. However, here, I would like to talk about Mr Amish Tripathi, who became famous for his Shiva Trilogy, the first book of which, titled 'The Immortals of Meluha' became a No.1 National Bestseller. The other two books in the trilogy — 'The Secret of the Nagas', and 'The Oath of the Vayuputras' — also sold exceedingly well. While we can classify his books broadly under the banner of fiction, they are largely based on Indian mythology. Amish has a knack for taking a very old story and relaying it in the most contemporary manner possible. In his stories, he gives scientific explanations for what we would otherwise label as miracles of the Gods. In fact, he manages to do so without taking away from the flow of the story, or the relevance of the plot. He writes his books in such a way that a reader immediately visualises the entire story as if it is happening in front of his eyes, or better still, like he is watching a movie on the screen of his mind. What's more, he builds a lot of anticipation in readers' minds through his vivid descriptions of settings and scenes. While Amish's genre is such that his stories are far removed from our reality, there's not a page in his books that seems too farfetched. Apart from the Shiva Trilogy, Amish has also written 'Scion of Ikshvaku', which is part of The Ram Chandra Series. This book tells the saga of Lord Ram and his many adventures in Amish's classic style.

His writing is useful to me because it serves as an escape from the routine of my day. It makes me sit and wonder if in fact those we call Gods, were simply super humans with immense strength, knowledge, and leadership skills. His way of humanising deities, without removing the pedestal from under their feet, has helped me understand that maybe 'human is divine'. Having read his books, I now have one more lens through which I can view the world around me. Further, as a writer, I have learned many new writing techniques from him. Even though I have neither written fiction, nor plan to, I get inspired to write better and more useful material for IELTS students, when I read his books, and feel like they have contributed to my personal development.

Follow-up Questions & Answers:
1. Is that person popular in your city/country?
Yes, Mr Amish Tripathi is extremely popular in my city and country. He has lots of fans who adore his writing. You can find his fan pages on social networking sites, and there are many threads in literary forums, discussing his works in minute detail.
2. Do writers/columnists play any social role?
Writers do play a social role. Writers can work as motivators, educators, trainers, and as teachers, also. They can guide their readers by spreading awareness regarding the evil rituals society follows, harmful beliefs, and other unnecessary things that we carry in our minds. These things are in fact hindrances in the path of our growth. Good writers can show us the right way to deal with these hindrances, and guide us towards developing the right attitude and the requisite mind-set, in order to create and carry the legacy of a better, more developed society.
3. What age group in your city appreciates that writer/columnist more, as compared to other age groups?

If I talk about Mr. Amish Tripathi, he is appreciated by all age groups, because his topic of writing has tremendous mass appeal. His stories are as popular with twenty year olds, as they are with fifty year olds.

Practice Questions
1. Do your friends/family members also like him/her?
2. Did you ever want to become a writer/columnist?

92. Describe any important scientific invention (other than computers).

You should say
- **Its name, and when it was invented**
- **How it has changed the lives of people**
- **What kind of people use it more**

How do people use it?

Science and technology has been growing at an immense pace since the last few decades. We have seen newer inventions influencing all aspects of life. Health and fitness, communications, entertainment, education, and many others areas of life have been benefited by innovations in the field of science and technology. Here, I would like to talk about mobile phones. Mobiles were first introduced in the beginning of the 1990s. Since their introduction, they have been welcomed by people all over the world. Mobiles have changed our lives in many direct and indirect ways. They have completely changed the way we communicate with each other. Now, we can talk, send messages, store data, and perform many other business and entertainment oriented functions, with just a mobile phone in hand. Mobile phones have given us mobility, thus smoothening the way we work and socialise. Mobiles have brought radical changes in our lives. Mobiles have inbuilt phone books, which store phone numbers, email addresses, and postal addresses of hundreds of people. They can also store pictures, songs, games, data, software, and other media to facilitate our work and leisure. Mobiles are extremely useful in emergencies. They help us in finding the nearest available assistance, or in contacting someone who can arrange instant assistance for us remotely. What's more, mobiles come with fascinating features like inbuilt Bluetooth, wireless connectivity, QR code scanners, biometric security measures, voice recorders, Cameras, and Video recorders. Moreover, many mobile phone companies provide inbuilt GPS (Global Positioning System) software, too. This helps us in finding our way in any country or city of the world. This wonderful facility helps us a lot in unknown cities or foreign countries. Indeed, mobiles have become a necessity in almost everyone's life, today.

Follow-up Questions & Answers:
1. Does it have any drawbacks?
Yes, this is something that we must be aware of. Mobiles work on electromagnetic radiation. When we use a mobile phone, its transmitter and receiver work simultaneously.

This can cause harm to the cells of our body, especially of the brain. It has also been proven that excessive exposure to electromagnetic radiation can damage the cells of our brain permanently and also increase the risk of brain tumour. Even when we are not using our phone, its receiver stays on, and it also harms our body cells. So, we should use our mobile only when it is needed, and we should not keep it near our heart. We should keep it in a separate pocket near our waist or knee, instead. There are some bio magnetic products available these days, with which we can protect ourselves from the harmful effects of mobile phones, also.

(Note: To enquire further about bio magnetic products, readers can contact the numbers given in the book, or can send us an email)

2. Has it been modified ever since it was invented?

There have been immense changes in mobiles since they were launched. Mobiles used to be very big and heavy, contained only monophonic ringtones, and had black and white display screens. Now, mobiles come with MP3 ringtones, TFT colour screens or LCD touch screens, and they are very light and sleek. Moreover, they come with inbuilt software applications, and they can work as our personal computers, also.

3. Which country is leading in introducing such inventions?

It depends on the country where these inventions are being used most. However, if we see globally, Nokia, a well-established mobile brand in India and in the world, belongs to Finland. Samsung and LG are from South Korea, and Motorola and Apple are based out of America. However, I think, research is being done better in the USA. One such great invention that shook the world is Apple Inc.'s I-phone, whose research and development was done in the USA.

4. Are similar products invented in your country/other countries as well?

Yes, research for better and more user friendly mobiles is an ongoing process in India, China, Japan, and many other countries. We also host research centres of all big mobile companies.

Practice Questions

1. How do you use that invention in your daily life?
2. Is research given enough importance and support in your country at college level?
3. Would you like to invent something in the future? What, and why?
4. Do you think governments should encourage researchers by giving them awards and prizes?

93. Speak about the best gift you have received so far.

    You should say

- **What that gift was**
- **Who gave it to you**
- **When you received the gift**

Why do you like that gift?

           The Ultimate Guide to IELTS Speaking by Parthesh Thakkar

Sample Answer:

I have received many gifts in my life, but the gift that I would like to talk about today is very special to me, and the best that I have ever received in my life. I am talking about the year 1999, when I was assisting my father in his business, in which we had to move from one place to another in a very big market, and yet we had to stay connected to our clients. I was facing great difficulties, as I had to attend constant phone calls, and move about with my clients in the market. This task of handling both, the phone calls and the clients, was really tough for me. At that time, a mobile company had just started its services in my city. The moment I found out, I felt like buying a mobile. However, I put off the purchase for later, as it was a very new thing in the market, and I didn't know much about it. However, my father had been observing my difficulties, and he gifted me a mobile phone on my birthday, at home. It was a precious phone from Samsung with flip cover, and excellent contemporary features. I was very happy to receive such a precious gift on my birthday. The phone had excellent memory and display features. Mobile phones were very uncommon at that time in my city. Hence, the gift had elevated me to a privileged class of mobile phone users at that time. When he gave the wrapped gift pack to me, I had no idea what was in it. It was a surprise, and the moment I saw the mobile phone I jumped with joy. I thanked him and took his blessings that day. Then I showed the phone to all my family members, friends, and relatives, and the next day I started using it with pride and joy. I have preserved that phone with me as a memento of oldtimes.

Follow-up Questions & Answers:

1.Why do people give gifts?

People give gifts as a memento to others, to enhance the enjoyment and remembrance of an occasion. People also give gifts to express their feelings towards each other.

2.What are the best gifts for children? Why?

The best gifts for children are toys, games, comic books, educational and religious books, musical instruments, garments, and chocolates, because children like gifts that they can use or play with, in their everyday life.

3.What are the best gifts for men/women? Why?

The best gifts for men are accessories like wallets, wristwatches, cufflinks, pens, diaries, and leather belts. Moreover, they also like music CDs, photo frames, and garments as gifts. On the other hand, the best gifts for women are jewellery, make up kits, showpieces, cards, flowers, and garments.

4.With whom do you prefer to go to buy gifts?

I prefer buying gifts with my wife, because she has a better understanding of gift articles that suit the personality of the person to whom I want to give the gift. She also knows various outlets in my city where innovative gift articles are sold.

5.Should we select a gift of our choice, or should we select a gift of the receiver's choice?

I think a gift is an expression of our feelings towards another person. So I would buy gifts as per my choice. However, I do consider the likes and dislikes of the receiver of the gift, so that I may not end up giving a gift that the receiver wouldn't appreciate at all.

Practice Questions
1.Why is that gift so precious to you?
2.Do you still use that gift?

94. Speak about an important thing you lost in the past.

    You should say

- **What that thing was**
- **How you lost it**
- **What your reaction was, when you lost it**

Sample Answer:

It happened to me when I was in my first year of college. I had a large group of friends, and I used to enjoy a lot with them. We also exchanged our belongings like accessories, vehicles, and clothes, with each other. One day, I wanted to attend a function and I found that my blazer was not ironed. I immediately called a friend of mine, as our height and body measurements were quite similar. I knew he had a blazer of the same colour as mine, so I requested him to lend me it to me for that function. He instantly came over to my house and gave his blazer to me. I thanked him, wore that blazer, and went to the function. After attending the function, I came back to my home and decided to get the blazer dry cleaned before returning it to my friend. I went to a dry cleaner near my home. He took the blazer and committed to give it back to me, dry cleaned in two days. After two days, I got the blazer back from him, and started off towards home on my bike. When I reached my house, I was shocked to find that the bag in which I had kept the blazer was missing from my bike. It had probably fallen on the road. I panicked and made an about turn immediately, checking the entire route from my house all the way up to the dry cleaner's shop. I even asked passers-by if they had seen it anywhere in the vicinity. I went inside the dry cleaner's shop and enquired about the blazer, too but he had no idea about it. I was worried, as I lost an expensive blazer that belonged to my friend, because of my negligence. I was confused about what to do next, as I was supposed to return it to him soon. Finally, I spoke to my father about what had happened, and he advised me to buy a new blazer of the same colour, from the same shop for my friend. I liked the idea, so I thanked him and decided to buy a new blazer for my friend. However, the next day, as I was getting ready to visit the shop, I got a call from my dry cleaner, saying that someone had found the blazer on the road and returned it to him as the address written on the carry bag was of his shop. I was very happy to hear that, and I quickly reached his shop. I found that it was the same blazer that I had lost. I thanked the man who had returned the blazer to the dry cleaner, and then took it along, taking utmost care to not drop it again. I then gave it back to my friend and informed him about the entire incident. We both laughed it off, and started our work for the day.

Follow-up Questions & Answers:
1. What lesson did you learn after the loss of that thing?
The first thing I learned is that I should always carry my belongings with utmost care,

while I am riding a two wheeler. If possible, I should take someone along, who can hold whatever we are carrying, and sit behind me. Secondly, I learned that when we borrow something from someone, it is our responsibility to take good care of that article.

2. How should we take care of our important things in daily life?
We should keep our important daily life things in their proper places. For example, mobile phones, gold rings, necklaces, bracelets, and wallets should be kept in a drawer, and the drawer can be kept locked, so that they are safe from being stolen or damaged.

3. What measures should we take to protect valuable items from getting lost or stolen?
We should keep our valuables in a safe place; preferably in a cupboard or a separate safety case which is fixed to a wall and locked. Moreover, it is also possible to rent a locker in a bank, where we can store our valuables.

4. Do incidents of stealing or theft occur in your area?
Yes, unfortunately, instances of robbery, snatching, stealing, and pick pocketing do happen in my city. The problem of unbalanced financial growth can be one of the reasons behind this. My state is proliferating economically, every year. Compared to my state, other states are not advancing well, economically. This is the reason why criminals from other underdeveloped states come to my city to find 'soft' targets for their criminal activities.

5. How effective is the government in stopping crimes like theft and stealing?
The government is doing a great job in catching criminals. Every day, local newspapers contain information of a gang or a criminal seized by the local police, which actually reduces such acts of crime, and further deters other criminals from carrying out their illegal activities in my city. I am reasonably satisfied with the work of the government in preventing crime in my state.

Practice Questions
1. How did you manage without that thing?
2. Did you buy another thing to replace the thing you had lost?
3. What precautions can we take to prevent theft or break in?
4. How useful is technology in preventing crimes of theft and stealing?

95. Speak about the exercise people in your area do regularly.

OR

96. Describe an activity you do to keep fit.
    You should say
- **The name of the exercise**
- **Where, and when they/you do it**
- **Why they do this exercise**

How good is this exercise, according to you?

Sample Answer:
There are many options available in my city for people to do various exercises to stay fit

and healthy. There are gardens, heath clubs, aerobics centres, laughing clubs, and jogging tracks. However, the most common exercise that people in my area do is walking. There is a famous lake in my area that is surrounded by a special track where people go for walks every morning, evening, and night. The circumference of the lake is about 1.8 km, which is ideal for people who want to go for a long walk as part of a good workout. Apart from this, we now have a large riverfront with outstanding infrastructure for those who want to exercise or go for long walks.

Walking has enormous benefits. It improves blood circulation throughout the body. Secondly, it gives exercise to our legs and thighs, burning the unused, deposited fat from those spots, thereby helping us control our weight and obesity. It also helps to regulate the digestive system, so we can protect our body against diseases related to indigestion. Further, it is an easy exercise that requires no equipment or trainer, and can be done anywhere. Finally, it also helps our respiratory system to work efficiently, because we have to breathe fast while doing any exercise.

I don't get time to go for walks on weekdays, so I always go for long walks on weekends. I suggest that everyone take advantage of this exercise. Here I would like to cite the opinion of Mahatma Gandhi who used to say that walking is the best exercise.

◆ ◆ ◆

97. Describe a change that will improve your local area.

OR

98. Talk about a problem in your local area that you noticed.

   You should say
- **What this change should be** – Power supply.
- **How the change would work**
- **What kinds of problems the change will solve**

How would you feel if this change actually happened?

There are many civic problems in my local area, because like the rest of the country, my city is also still developing. Because we are not yet a fully developed city, the local corporation body and civilians are still working towards solving day-to-day issues. One major problem in my area is that of traffic congestion. This problem is not caused so much because of low quality infrastructure, as it is caused because of disorganised traffic. The infrastructure in my area is in fact quite good. However, the traffic management can be improved to a large extent. Improving traffic management will greatly help my local area by reducing the number of accidents and mishaps. This change would work if traffic police officers and civilians come together and strive to improve conditions. Civilians must take utmost care to follow all traffic rules, and traffic police must do their duties even more diligently. Rule breakers should be fined heftily by the traffic police, so as to deter them in future. This will solve the main problem of very long commuting hours. We spend way too much time covering very small distances in my area, only because of poor traffic management. This reduces our productivity, wastes a lot of time, tires us out, and in turn also makes us very irritable. Over time, people may resort to road rage, making the atmosphere on roads very unsafe. Many commuters already feel afraid to drive because of the unruly traffic. People are also scared to face the outbursts of frustrated drivers on streets. There are many who speed irrationally in response to delays caused by traffic congestions, as well. Such behaviour endangers others, and good traffic management can help resolve these issues. If this change actually happened, I would feel very happy and relieved. I would start enjoying the process of commuting from home to work and back on a daily basis. Further, I would start feeling like going out on long drives with my family and friends. The overall quality of life of people in my city would improve, too.

Follow ups:
1. Do changes always lead to a positive result?
Changes do not always lead to positive results. Most changes that are made with the right intent lead to good results, but, if changes are made with a negative intent, they will do more harm than good. At times, changes are made with very good intentions but with poor planning, and sometimes in spite of the best efforts of everyone involved in making changes, unforeseen circumstances may cause failures. However, in many cases, if executed well, then changes can lead to positive results.
2. How has your hometown changed in the past ten years?
The infrastructure in my hometown has had a major facelift in the past ten years. This is the most noticeable change in my locale. Further, more people have started pursuing primary and higher education, people have begun taking an interest in the arts, and many have started travelling more than before in the past ten years. This has brought in lots of new cuisines to my hometown from around the world, and many new business avenues have opened up here, too.
3. Why is it difficult for some people to make a change in their lives?
Some people are averse to change. They find comfort in permanence, and changes unsettle them. They are often set in their ways, and don't like meddling with methods and techniques for living life, until absolutely necessary. Some people also lack the skills required to cope with changes, and are unsure of whether they will be able to acquire new skills. They fear redundancy, and hence remain opposed to making changes in their lives.
4. Are there any changes you want to make this year?
This year I would like to pay more attention to my health, would like to travel a bit more than last year, and acquire a new skill such as learning to play a new musical instrument, or picking up a new language. I would also like to take out more spare time to spend with my friends and relatives this year.
5. Do you think governments should spend more money in making a city more beautiful?
If a city is otherwise well developed, then it makes sense for the government to spend more money in its beautification, by installing fountains and artwork, and repainting public structures. However, if the city is not yet fully developed in terms of infrastructure, sanitation, hygiene, cleanliness, education and healthcare facilities, and public transport systems, then the government should not bother much about beautification, and should instead divert funds to other more pressing matters.
6. What are the disadvantages of people knowing each other in a small village?

When people know each other well in small villages, there are many advantages; but, there are many disadvantages, too. People tend to take the liberty to interfere in the personal lives of those they know. They land up uninvited and unannounced at each other's homes, thereby disrupting routines every now and then. They expect unreasonable favours from those that they know, on and off, which may prove to be inconvenient from those who have to give favours. Further, idle minds of people from small villages may cook up rumours about those that they know, gossip about them, and spread slander just for the sake of it.

◆　◆　◆

99. Describe a situation you waited for something.

OR

100. Describe an incident where you were waiting for something or someone.

   You should say

-   **When and where you waited**
-   **What you waited for**
-   **Who you were with**

What did you do while you were waiting?

This is an incident that took place a few years ago, when I was slated to travel from my hometown, Ahmedabad, to New Delhi for work. I had booked my flight tickets well in advance, and reached the airport on time, as I usually do. But, when I reached the check in desk to hand over my luggage, the attendant there informed me that my flight had been delayed by three hours. I felt a little irritated, but such things happen often, and so I simply brushed it off. I decided to spend my extra hour browsing through the shops inside the airport premises. The only glitch was, the attendant at the desk had refused to check in my luggage then, because of the delay. He had politely told me to return to the desk after a while to hand over my bags. So, there I was, all by myself at the Ahmedabad airport, lugging my bags around as I looked for an empty seat to settle down. I wanted to visit the book store, check out the food stalls, and even felt like checking out the tie store and perfume shop at the other end from where I was. However, with all my luggage it was bound to be very inconvenient, so I continued to look for an empty seat. I noticed then, that people in general were quite ill mannered. Most of them had used up the vacant seats for keeping their bags, and in spite of requesting them to vacate those seats, they refused to budge. Finally, after a while a polite man who had been observing my plight waved to me from the distance and pointed out an empty seat next to him that I had overlooked. I took the seat, thanking him, and then we introduced ourselves to each other. He was more or less my age, and was also travelling for work on the same flight as mine. For a while we spoke to each other about work and other random things, but soon we both got hungry. However, it was necessary that one of us remain seated right there, to watch out for our seats, lest someone else decide to occupy them. So, my new acquaintance went and bought us both sandwiches and coffee. We sleepily sipped our coffees, checking our watches every few minutes. The wait was becoming unbearable as boredom fatigue took over. Just then, to my surprise, loud music started playing in the airport! As the popular movie song blared in the background, shaking us out of our stupor, some people got up from their seats and started dancing in perfectly synchronised steps. This group must have had about twenty people of varying ages, both men and women. It was a flash mob! As they continued dancing adeptly, other onlookers joined them and danced to their own beats. Before we knew it, half an hour had passed, and people kept dancing as songs changed. It was like having a small party with strangers, in an unexpected place. By the time I boarded my flight, I was grinning from ear to ear, and almost thankful for the delay.

◆ ◆ ◆

Follow-ups
1. Do you think patience is important?
Yes, I think patience is very important. Patience is a virtue we must all cultivate, because it helps us overcome even the toughest of situations with grace and dignity. Impatience does not accelerate processes in life. It only creates agitation and frustration, which lead to wrong decisions. Instead, if we can remain patient while waiting for the tables to turn in our favour, we may learn some important lessons along the journey of life, without sacrificing our health or taking bad decisions.
2. Why is it difficult for children to be patient?
Childhood is that stage of life where a human grows rapidly, both physically and mentally. They have much to learn, and a lot of curiosity to learn it all quickly; to absorb the world around them in every way possible. To add to this, children also have a lot of energy. This leads to a certain deep-seated restlessness in them, constantly urging them to expend their extra energies and explore their surroundings. So, it is very difficult for children to be patient.
3. How to teach children patience?
Patience can be taught to children by relaying stories and anecdotes that highlight the benefit of patience as a virtue, to them. When this is done on a regular basis, followed up by showing them real life incidents where impatience and haste have led to mishaps, the importance of being patient can be taught to children. Children also learn from seeing adults that they trust. So, displaying patience at an individual level can also encourage them to be patient themselves.
4. Do you easily feel angry when you wait for a long time?
I am usually very patient, so I don't feel angry when I wait for a long time for something. However, if in the bargain, the delay is going to cost me something important in life, I may get a little frustrated. Other than that, waiting for flights, waiting in queues at restaurants and banks, and waiting for my turn in general in different situations does not make me angry.
5. Have you ever been late for meeting someone?
I am usually very punctual, but on one occasion, a good friend of mine was counting on me to deliver some important documents to him at the airport, and I reached much later than he had expected. Although, this delay was caused by a series of unforeseen events that transpired as I tried to make my journey to the airport.

101. Describe a place (not your home) where you can read and write.

OR

102. Describe a place where you go to read and write, that is not your home.

You should say

- **Where this place is**
- **How you know this place**
- **What you do there**

Why do you think it is a good place for reading and writing?

To me, my home is the most comfortable place to read and write, but a close second would be the British Library in my city. Till the first year of my college, when one of my friends told me about this library, I did not even know that it existed. There were other libraries in my city, which were small but well stocked, and I used to visit them from time to time. But, once I visited the British Library with my friend, I realised how much better it was than the others. Located in the city centre, in a stately building, the library housed its collection of books in a large hall in the basement. The hall was air conditioned, and the books were well organised, sorted by genre and language. None of the books were dusty or torn, and there was ample seating for people to work comfortably. That very day, I bought a membership to the library, and started frequenting it. Now, the library has moved to another area, and it is even better. The comfortable tables and chairs, and the quiet, well-lit atmosphere are perfect for me to write chapters of my books, to read reference books, novels, self-help, and even browse through encyclopaedias, while simultaneously taking notes. I often even sit there and browse through international newspapers, once my other work is done. It is one of those places that take you away from the hustle bustle of the city, in spite of being located in a very noisy area. The British Library in my city is truly a sanctuary for the mind. It also hosts book club gatherings every week, organises book readings by famous authors, allows members to interact with authors, and holds great workshops for storytelling, creative writing, and other intellectually enriching activities. All these activities are held in a separate section from the reading area, so that no one gets disturbed. The librarians there are very helpful, well read, and well trained. They know exactly where to find which book, and are also great at suggesting good books to those who need help selecting. Because of all these facilities, I think it is a good place to read and write.

Follow ups:

1. Who likes to read more — young people or old people?

I think old people like to read more, these days, while youngsters have moved to other pastimes. Youngsters have a shorter span of attention today, and so they prefer activities that seek lesser involvement of time, and higher sensory involvement. They get this from their hi-tech gadgets with ease, making them less inclined to read. The older people still have good attention spans, and are also more patient. So, they enjoy reading more

2. Why do some people dislike reading books these days?

People in recent years have got used to activities such as watching movies, and playing digital games. These activities provide higher engagement of senses, and most people

---

have hi-tech gadgets to facilitate these interests of theirs. In comparison, reading books is more time consuming, and has no audio input. Further, there are no moving visuals, and a lot is left to imagination in books. So, people dislike reading books these days.

3. Are there many libraries in India?
Yes there are many libraries in India. While most of the libraries are run by the national government and local corporation bodies, there are some libraries that are founded and managed by private trusts and benevolent individuals who understand the importance of reading and wish to promote and propagate it in society.

4. What kinds of books should children read?
Children should read engaging books with interesting storylines and gripping plots. Picture books are a great choice for children, and books that tell fantasy-based or magical stories are just as good. Other than these, books that tell historical anecdotes in a child friendly manner are also great in order to help children learn morals and ethics in life, and to facilitate the development of their own sense of right and wrong.

103. Describe a person who does well at work.

You should say
- **Who this person is**
- **How you know this person**
- **What kinds of roles this person handles**

Why do you think this person works well?

I happen to have an employee who has been working with me for over ten years. He came to me when I was first hiring people for my business, and appeared to have a lot of potential to grow, learn, and help my business in the coming years. He is a highly skilled man with a very strong educational background. Not only is he well versed with communicating in English, Hindi, and Gujarati, he also knows a little bit of French, and has the most refined convincing skills I have ever seen. Having studied abroad himself, he knows what it takes to apply to foreign universities, crack entrance tests, secure admissions, acquire a visa, and to adjust to a new country. He is very skilled at handling queries of foreign education aspirants, and guiding them. This employee is well versed with the different procedures one needs to follow in order to get admissions and visas of different countries. When prospective students are unsure of which country they want to study in, he shows them the pros and cons of studying in various different places. He counsels them in a friendly manner, and understands what each student expects from his foreign education experience. In keeping with students' expectations, he suggests the right kinds of universities and informs them about the various entrance tests, language tests, and interviews they would need to appear for, in order to secure admissions. Further, he communicates well with universities and their admissions departments, in order to manage our business relationships, and to stay abreast with the latest eligibility requirements and fee structures of institutes and courses. When it comes to preparing visa files for students, I can count on him to never miss out on a single document. Everything he does is absolutely up to date with the industry requirements, and thanks to him, we have managed to build a very strong track record in helping people with foreign education and immigration. In fact, because of his own skills, and the amazing training he has given to my newer employees, we are also able to handle cases where students' visa applications and university applications have been rejected previously. Many such dejected applicants come to us seeking guidance, and we facilitate them with reapplication, quite successfully. The credit for this achievement goes entirely to this most loyal employee of mine.

Follow ups:
1. Why do young people keep changing jobs?
Young people get restless in desk jobs, and are often unsure about their career paths. They have many confusions regarding what they want to achieve in life, and are not confident about whether they are walking on the right path or not, when they are in a certain job. These confusions lead to fickleness, and the chase for something better, coupled with the fear of missing out on good opportunities makes young people change jobs frequently.
2. What kinds of work do you prefer to do in the future?
I quite like what I am doing right now, and I would prefer to continue doing the same thing. I might consider expanding my business geographically, and extending my services to more number of people, but I would still continue in the same line, because I know that the services my business offers are of a lot of value to society.
3. What kinds of work skills are important in India?
Skills such as team work, leadership, companionability and amicability, communications, convincing, and adaptability are very important in India. One must also have a certain doggedness and drive to succeed, in order to maintain an edge over competitors, here.
4. Why do some young people prefer to be unemployed?
There are very few young people who prefer to be unemployed. Many who appear unemployed, are in fact self-employed. However, there are some who do not work at all. A lot of times they are still exploring their likes and dislikes, and figuring out what they want to do with their lives. So, they remain on extended breaks after completing their education. In rare cases, parents of youngsters may be very affluent, making it unnecessary for youngsters to go out and earn money. Such youngsters may prefer to remain unemployed to enjoy a leisurely life.
5. Is teamwork important in the workplace?
Teamwork is very important in the workplace. Organisations these days have many employees, and they all need to work in coordination with each other to ensure the successful functioning of the business. They need to feel comfortable in each other's company, be supportive, and be willing to fill in for each other from time to time. This creates a feel-good factor in the office, and enhances productivity in the long run.
6. Is it easy to find a well-paying job in India?
It is not very easy to find a well-paying job in India, because the youth population is very high here, and there are many very qualified youngsters vying for good jobs. While there are nearly enough jobs to employ most of these educated youngsters, not all these jobs are well paying. Often, very good candidates miss out on well-paying job opportunities simply on account of not being in the right place at the right time. However, if one keeps

The Ultimate Guide to IELTS Speaking by Parthesh Thakkar

networking, updating one's knowledge base, and looking out for good opportunities, he is likely to find a well-paying job.

7. How should good employees be rewarded?

Good employees should be rewarded by acknowledgement and appreciation, recognition in the form of bestowing honours or small awards for good performance, promotions in the company, and monetary bonuses.

104. Describe an educational TV program that you have seen.

> **You should say**
> - **What the program is about/What the program is**
> - **How often you watch this program**
> - **Which segments of people enjoy this program**

Why is this program educational in your opinion?

I enjoy watching informative programs on TV from time to time. My family members are also interested in such shows, so often after dinner we tune into History Channel, Discovery Network channels, or National Geographic shows. We have seen many documentaries on wild animals in their natural habitats all over the world, we have seen videos of rare and endangered species, and learnt a lot about them, and have also seen travel programs that show viewers hill stations, sea shores, deserts, and forests across the world from the comfort of their homes. One of my favourite educational TV programs is Brain Games. This program is being aired in my country for quite a while now, and I have seen many episodes after work. Essentially the program explores the intricacies of human cognition, psychology, and brain functioning. The anchor poses interesting questions and riddles in each episode, and viewers can try and solve those within a given time frame. Once the time is up, the anchor reveals the correct answers to TV viewers, and explains the logic and science behind them with the help of psychiatrists, psychotherapists, and neuroscientists. Sometimes the anchor is shown addressing groups of people, giving them a chance to try and solve mind boggling interactive puzzles in different settings. These puzzles are very challenging, and they make me sit at the edge of my sofa, as I diligently try to work them out.

I record these episodes on my TV, and make it a point to watch a few every week, after dinner. I think people of all ages are likely to enjoy Brain Games, and even benefit from the show. However, one needs to be in the right frame of mind to absorb large amounts of information, to truly enjoy the show. It is not possible to put your brain aside and watch this program, like any other sci-fi movie or music channel.

In my opinion, this program is educational because it attempts to unravel the functioning of the human brain, which is a super computer in itself. The highest form of knowledge according to me is self-knowledge, and learning more about how my brain works allows me to look at myself more objectively. It also teaches me way to overcome common cognitive biases, thereby facilitating me in living my life more productively on a day to day basis.

Follow ups:

1. Please compare TV and radio programs. State the differences and similarities, and advantages and disadvantages of both.

TV programs provide audio-visual input simultaneously, while radio programs only provide audio input. Each radio program can last a few hours, while TV programs generally tend to be shorter. TV programs are more engaging because they appeal to two senses at the same time, while radio programs only engage the ears. Radio programs require more attention and focus than TV programs, because the lack of visual input can make it easy for listeners to feel distracted. TVs take up more space, and watching programs requires electricity and a cable or satellite connection, which can be expensive. Radios can run on batteries, and are quite affordable.

2. What types of TV programs are most popular in India? Why?

Soap operas, talent scouting programs, and reality shows with a lot of drama are very popular in India. There are many such programs constantly being aired on TV, so the easy accessibility to these shows attracts idle and bored people towards them. The element of drama, along with the extravagant costumes and sets makes these shows appear very entertaining and engaging to the masses. Majority of people, not only in India, but everywhere, watch TV to set their brains aside for a while and relax. Such programs don't require much thought or effort from the viewer; this makes them popular.

3. How are TV programs in India today different from those that were aired 20–40 years ago?

About 20 years ago, many TV shows used to be more progressive than they are now. Programs generally used to be lighter on the mind, and serials did not completely revolve around scheming, manipulative family members. Stories were more realistic, touched upon more real life issues, and had much lesser drama. There was lesser humbug, and more intelligent comedy. Even slapstick comedy shows were more tasteful. Content was safe for family viewing, and children did not need to be supervised when they were flipping channels. However, we had fewer channels and TV shows to select from, those days, thereby limiting our choices.

4. Do you have 24 hours television in India?

Yes, we have 24 hours television in India since many years, now. Indians are very fond of TV and there are takers for different kinds of television programs at all hours of the day. To cater to all these viewers' needs, it is absolutely necessary to have 24 hours television.

5. In the future, what changes do you think we will see concerning television?

In the future, television programs will be very easily accessible on our smart phones and tablets. Already, it has become possible to view certain TV programs such as matches, live, on our handheld gadgets. Soon, our smartphones and tablets will double up miniature TVs where we can subscribe to and view various channels real time. Further, all television sets will be made compatible for 3D viewing, and more 3D movies and serials will start being aired on a large scale.

6. In general, how does TV affect or influence people?

TV is highly accessible to people these days, even in the remotest parts of the world. Even the illiterate who cannot read newspapers, can understand television content. There are shows that appeal to various demographics across the world, on TV. Many people use these as an escape from reality, and watch shows without sufficient analysis. TV

The Ultimate Guide to IELTS Speaking by Parthesh Thakkar

influences these people to buy things they don't need, attempt risky antics, play dangerous pranks on others, and sometimes even indulge in violence. Sometimes, though, TV can even influence people to embark on positive campaigns to propagate important social causes, by bringing them in touch with world news.

7. Do you think there is anything negative about some TV programs?

News channels show many disturbing graphics on and off; and films and serials with dark, twisted storylines are often aired on TV. Some programs encourage rash driving, risky living, and violence in youth. Often, lifestyle shows create delusional fantasies and aspirations in the minds of impressionable viewers, too. These shows can lead to desensitisation of masses, mental disturbance and anxiety, and a misplaced sense of entitlement in people. Crimes are often offshoots of such mind-sets; so in that sense, there are negative aspects to some TV programs.

8. Do you think violent cartoons can have an adverse effect on young children?

Young children are the most impressionable section of society. Their minds are like wet cement, and they constantly absorb information from their surroundings. Seeing violent cartoons too often without good parental guidance can make children think that it is alright to be violent, to breach others' personal boundaries, and to manipulate or force others to bend to their will by employing violent intimidation tactics. Such children may turn into bullies, and later even resort to crime, if left unchecked.

105. Describe a time a child did something that made you laugh.

   You should say

- **When this happened**
- **Who this child was**
- **What the child did**

Why was it funny?

This is an event that transpired about ten years ago, with a very close friend of mine. One weekend, he was sitting with his wife and his four year old daughter, browsing through old photo albums, reminiscing old times and sharing interesting anecdotes related to various pictures. After an hour or so of browsing through family photos of festival celebrations and travels, they happened to dig a little deeper and came across a travel album from when their daughter was not born. It contained pictures of my friend and his wife on their trip to Himachal Pradesh. There were beautiful green meadows, snow-capped mountains, and pristine blue lakes in the pictures, and the young child was left gaping at them for a while, mesmerised by the beautiful landscapes. My friend went on to tell his curious daughter more about the hill station, and the various sights they had seen on that trip. In the course of the conversation, he flipped another page of the album. Staring back was a beautiful enlarged picture of him with his wife, against the backdrop of a river. Before he could start saying anything about the photograph, a stream of tears started flowing down his little daughter's cheeks; within minutes she was crying profusely, and her parents got worried sick!

No one could understand what had gone wrong; and then, accusingly she asked them —
"Why didn't you take me along on this holiday?!"
The parents heaved a sigh of relief, and broke into peals of laughter, as they tried to explain to the toddler that she wasn't even born when they went on the trip. Nothing would pacify the child, although, and she kept demanding an answer regarding why she had not been included on that trip!
When my friend told me about this incident, I could not help but burst out with laughter. What was he to say or do, to pacify his daughter's anger and sadness? While it's never nice to see a child cry, even now, I cannot contain my laughter when I think of the reason behind her tears. It was funny that she expected to be part of a family trip from a time when she didn't even exist. The fact that she had no concept of birth and time, made things all the more entertaining.

Follow ups:
1. Why do some adults miss their childhood?
Childhood is a jolly time full of innocent wonders, and ideas. In childhood, there are no worries, and nothing seems out of reach or impossible. One's imagination is at its peak in the early years of life, and big disappointments rarely touch children. In childhood, we are shielded from harsh realities of the practical world, and we have no responsibilities towards others. Adulthood does not offer these liberties, so, some adults miss their uncomplicated childhood.
2. Why do children feel happy easily?
Children do not overthink, they do not play politics and mind games, nor indulge in hypocrisy. They don't look too far into the future, or try to control the flow of their life. They are happy in the present moment, and simply absorb life as it is. They allow their imagination to run wild, and keep their little bodies busy with playtime and exploration of their surroundings. Their sense of wonder is alive, and they feel surprised at the smallest of things. This is why children feel happy easily.
3. In general, do children in India enjoy their childhoods?
In India, children from educated, functional, and understanding families enjoy their childhoods to the fullest. However, because of widespread illiteracy and poverty, some children are forced into illegal child labour, while others have to deal with oppressive, uneducated families on a regular basis. Further, there are children whose parents pressurise them into fitting into various ideals of right and wrong, completely ignoring the child's free will. Such children do not enjoy their childhoods.
4. Do you like to watch comedy?
I like to watch comedy a lot. Who doesn't like to enjoy a good laugh? After a long day at work, there is nothing better to refresh the mind than a healthy dose of comedy enjoyed with family and friends. It lightens me up and puts me in a very good mood.
5. What is the best stage in life in your opinion?
In my opinion, childhood is the best stage of life, because one can remain carefree and explore the world with an open mind during these years. However, every stage of life can be made beautiful with the right attitude and mind-set. If one can remain positive irrespective of external circumstances and situations, and stay in control of his thoughts and reactions, he can derive value from everything, and live every stage of life to the fullest.

106. Describe something that you want to learn more.

You should say
- What it is
- How you would learn it
- Where you can learn it

Why do you want to learn more of it?

A few years ago, while planning a family Euro-trip, I had bought myself a French phrase book. The idea behind this purchase was to facilitate our trip and ease our travel experience. Back when we went around Europe, it was not very easy to find English speakers, so this little pocket book proved helpful in navigating through the streets of French cities and towns. We were able to work our way around buying the kind of food we wanted, exploring museums and art galleries scattered across France, and shopping for high fashion shoes and clothes. The locals who are known to be rude to tourists, in fact behaved in a very friendly and helpful manner with us, when they saw us trying to speak their language.

By the end of the trip, I realised that the language was growing on to me, and I had begun to enjoy using its unique sounding words and phrases.

I would learn French at one of the foreign language coaching institutes in my city, by enrolling into their weekend or evening batches. One good institute where I can learn it is Alliance Française. I want to learn more of it because I think it would help my business, as French is gradually becoming a widely used international language. Although it is not at par with English in terms of popularity, many countries use it as one of their official languages. Also, something about French makes it sound very polished and elegant. It is probably for this reason that linguists across the world consider French a feminine tongue, unlike German. The soft sounds of spoken French are soothing to the ears, and the language effectively mirrors the nation's culture.

Follow ups:

1. Can you suggest a way by which people can study together?

People can study together online, in virtual peer groups. They can also study together in libraries or in classrooms inside institutions. Another alternative is to form a group and find a personal tutor who would be willing to come home and teach the group inside one of the members' houses.

2. Do you think governments should pay for old people to learn some things?

Governments need not pay for old people to learn things. Expecting the government to pay for uplifting the poor and the marginalised in society is a sensible idea. Further, if the government funds high achievers from various fields to help them learn new skills, it should be encouraged. However, old age is neither an achievement, nor a problem. It is simply a phase of life that everyone goes through. If old people wish to learn new skills, they must rely on their life savings, or on earning family members.

3. Why do people give up their hobbies?

People give up their hobbies because of unavailability of leisure time, lack of motivation, discouragement from family members, or lack of funds. Some people simply get bored of their hobbies, and are of a more changeable nature. They give up their old hobbies and find new ones from time to time, so as to maintain an element of fun and variety in their lives.

4. What are the difficulties that people may have to face in their pursuit of continued education courses?

People may not always find sufficient time to pursue continued education courses if they are working simultaneously. Many people who opt for such courses are either busy managing households, or doing jobs in offices with long hours. Then, there are some whose families are not very supportive, and they may face issues in the form of discouragement and conflicts at home, when they try to pursue continued education courses.

5. What do you think of online learning?

Online learning is a big boon to those of us who never want to stop learning new skills in life. The pursuit of knowledge is a very noble activity in my opinion, and anything that facilitates this pursuit is always welcome. Online learning makes it possible for people of all ages, irrespective of their locations, to acquire new skills and expand their horizons at low costs. I think it is the future of education.

6. Do you think learning material available on the internet is reliable?

The reliability of learning material does not depend much on the medium through which it is being made available. I think it depends more on who the authors and publishers are, and which universities or institutions are behind providing the learning material online. If one applies to a reputed body for continued learning, the learning material provided online is usually very reliable and of very good quality.

107. Describe a time when you felt surprised to meet someone after a long time.

   You should say
- **When this happened**
- **Who this person was**
- **What you did together on that day**

Why were you surprised to meet this person?

The first and most prominent incident that comes to mind when faced with this question is the time I went to New York with my family. My wife, my daughter, and I had been roaming around the city all morning, sight-seeing and shopping. We were ravenous and had begun scanning the streets for Indian restaurants. After a few minutes of looking, my daughter excitedly pointed at a colourful banner with mouth-watering pictures of Punjabi and South Indian food. We walked straight in and ordered a few curries, breads, some rice, and lentils. As we waited for our food impatiently, I noticed that the restaurant's interiors were decorated very tastefully, to give diners the feel of an Indian village. Soft music played in the background, and the air-conditioned room was lit with traditional Indian kerosene lanterns. The fragrances of Indian spices made us hungrier, and when the food arrived sizzling hot on our tables, we pounced on it and quickly made our way through the rice and breads. Until we were halfway through, we didn't even speak to each other; that's how engrossed we were in our plates. Then once I was a little satiated, I realised how delicious the food was. The lip-smacking curries were extraordinary, and the rice was steamed to perfection. The lentils were fragrant and creamy, and the assorted breads were nothing short of outstanding! I decided I needed to meet the owner and personally appreciate his restaurant; so I requested the waiter to please call him. A few minutes later, a familiar looking man emerged from a cabin in the corner. He appeared to be my age, too. Lo and behold! — It was my childhood friend from school! He recognised me immediately, and we hugged each other in utter surprise and elation! As he took a seat next to us and ordered a few more of his special delicacies, I introduced him to my family. We spent the next 2 hours there, laughing about old times and catching up with each other. As a child, I had shared the same bench with him in school, and we'd had many a laugh together. After the 10th grade he had changed schools and I had lost touch with him. So, I was surprised to see him there, and happy for him, because he was successfully running a great restaurant.

Follow ups:
1. Who do you like to be friends with?
I like to be friends with laid back, relaxed people, who are honest and kind hearted. I like people who are good to converse with and also value relationships. Further, I like being friends with people who have some shared interests with me, so we can enjoy spending time together.
2. Do you think it's necessary to hang out with friends regularly?
It's necessary to hang out with friends from time to time, so as to keep in touch with them, and to support or help them in life, if they so require. It is also necessary to keep them in the loop as regards the new developments in our lives, and to stay abreast with the goings on of their lives. For this, even though we may not meet them very frequently, it is important to hang out with them at regular intervals.
3. Is it safe to make friends on the internet?
In my opinion, it is absolutely unsafe to make friends on the internet. The first issue with this is that we can never know who is giving out their true identity, and who is roaming the internet with a fake account and identity. In the garb of an innocent friend could be a hacker, a criminal, a kidnapper, or even a trafficker, who may extract sensitive information from us on the pretext of casual chit chat. This can endanger our lives, and the lives of our family members.
4. Do parents in your country teach their children how to make friends?
Some parents in my country teach their children how to make friends, while others do not interfere in this process much. Most children manage to learn how to make friends on their own, once they get enrolled in school. Further, they learn the dynamics of hanging out in groups by themselves. This is a skill that cannot be taught. Parents can teach children to be good friends, but 'how to make friends' usually has to be self-taught.
5. Why do some people get distant from their friends?
In the course of life, people grow, change, and evolve. They want different things from life at different stages, and these things usually only become constant once a person grows beyond his teens. Most friends on the other hand are made during or before our teenage years. So, as our priorities, likes, and dislikes change with age, we outgrow some

friends, and hence get distanced from them. At times, some people have a habit of creating conflicts, and so they may get distanced from friends due to misunderstandings and ego issues. In some cases, friends may change cities or countries, and the physical distance may create an emotional and mental distance as well, over time.

6. What's the most important thing people can learn from their friendships?

People can learn about sharing, caring, concern, consideration, selflessness, and unity, from their friendships. They can learn to take responsibility of their actions when they hurt a friend, they can learn to stand by each other in tough times, through thick and thin, thereby helping them develop a strong character, and an even stronger sense of personal integrity. Friendships teach people to prioritise others above themselves at times when needed, and also to balance work with leisure.

◆ ◆ ◆

108. Describe an occasion when you got up extremely early.

   You should say
-   **When this happened**
-   **What you needed to do that day**
-   **Who were you with**

How did you feel about getting up early that day?

A few years ago, I was supposed to catch an early morning flight to the UK, from my city. I was slated to go out on a week long holiday with my family, and we were involved in a lot of last minute packing the previous afternoon. Just as we got done with everything, a friend of mine called and invited us to his house for a casual get-together. I tried to politely decline the invitation, stating that we needed to be fresh for our travels the next morning. But, my friend would have nothing of it, and he kept insisting, overriding every excuse I came up with, with his signature brand of goodhearted emotional blackmail. Finally, I discussed it with my wife and yielded. We drove down to his house at 7pm, and as we entered the driveway, we noticed there were a lot of cars parked there. It was not a small get together; instead, there were a lot of people. Right away, my wife and I knew that this party was going to go on till late. That's how it usually is with large groups of people; once the conversations start, and the wine begins to flow, no one wants to go home, because it is too much fun.

So, we entered, exchanged pleasantries, and made ourselves comfortable. Soon we started getting involved in different conversations, and began to enjoy the delicious starters that kept coming. The night went on, and after dinner my friend put on some music and got everyone to dance. I must admit, it was a lot of fun, but by the time we got in our car to drive back home, it was already past 2am. Tired from partying, but grinning ear to ear, we reached home. There was no point sleeping now, because we had to reach the airport at 5am, but we slept anyways. Our alarms rang in what seemed like just a few minutes. We freshened up and quickly headed to the airport, heaving a sigh of relief that we had managed to open our eyes so early in the morning, after such a late night. I did not feel very enthusiastic about waking up early that day, but after a few cups of coffee at the airport, I was alert once again, and excited about the trip.

Follow ups:

1. Who usually gets up early — young people or old people?

Old people usually get up earlier than young people, because with age it is noticed that people's requirement for sleep reduces. They also watch much less of TV, and spend less time online, or partying till late. So old people tend to wake up early, while young people often prefer to sleep in till a little late.

2. Will working till late at night influence the next day's work?

Working till late at night is likely to influence the next day's work. Working till late exhausts the body and mind, and reduces the efficiency of a person, the next morning. He has a tough time waking up itself, and from then on, he tends to work slowly, with lesser focus, and lesser enthusiasm.

3. Do young Indians stay up till late in the night?

Young Indians, like young people everywhere else, tend to stay up till late in the night very frequently. Most young Indians have long working hours, after which they go home, relax, and have their dinner with their family. Only after this do they find the time and energy to go and hang out with friends. Since they meet up with friends late, they also tend to stay out till late. Those who do not go out, find their relaxation by surfing the net or watching TV till way past midnight.

4. Is it easy for you to get up early?

It is easy for me to get up early because I am not a very late sleeper. I tend to have quite a disciplined routine, and I usually start feeling sleepy by 11pm. This ensures that I wake up fresh in time for my morning walk. Because sleeping early has been a habit of mine since many years, I do not find it tough to wake up early, as well.

5. What do you do to guarantee a good sleep?

I have a light dinner, enjoy good conversations with my family, watch relaxing shows on TV as opposed to action movies that could fire up my mind, and then I retire in bed with a good book. I make sure not to drink coffee or other stimulants after 6pm. These things guarantee a good sleep for me.

6. Can you sleep well if there is noise around?

I can usually sleep well irrespective of noises around me. Having been brought up in a highly populous country where every now and then someone in the vicinity wants to celebrate something loudly, I have trained my mind to be able to block out external noises. However, sometimes, if the decibel goes up too high, I cannot sleep soundly.

109. Describe a change that you always wanted to be done in your local area.

You should say
- What it is
- Whose responsibility it is
- How it can be done

Who all would this change help?

One change I have always wanted implemented in my local area is the development of a big park. When I went to New York, I had a lot of fun at the Central Park, and its sheer scale astonishes me even now, after having spent time there so many years ago. My locale has many small gardens, but pale in comparison to the Central Park. We pride ourselves at being residents of a developed city, but we are only more developed than some other cities within India. Most developed cities abroad have big parks for people to enjoy. The true sign of a developed area is the ease with which its residents can enjoy in public spaces. It is the responsibility of the local municipal corporation and the garden authorities to clear out a large area in the centre of the city, and dedicate it completely to developing a huge green park with many sections, for different people of different age groups to enjoy. It can be done by removing illegal structures from the streets, and buying out many adjacent plots of land from commercial buildings in the city centre. Once this is done, the buildings can be razed, and in their place a beautiful public park with ponds, or a large central lake can be built. This garden can have different kinds of grasses, lush lawns, flowering plants, leafy hedges, fruit trees, and other even a herb garden. The park can have a cobbled walkway or promenade surrounding its perimeter, and beyond this can be authorised sellers of popular snacks and drinks. The park can have a children's area with a huge sandpit, swings, slides, and see-saws. A forest-like enclosure with huge banyan trees can be created to facilitate picnics and dates. The park can have a Zen inspired area with white sands, fine gravel, bamboo trees, and an artificial waterfall, to support Yoga, meditation and other similar pursuits.

This would help the old who currently do not have any good place to hang out at, or spend evenings at. It would help children by giving them a large area to play in, and make new friends at. It would help youngsters and middle aged people to exercise, walk, and stay fit. It would help families by giving them a place to come to for outings and picnics. Creative people would be able to find inspiration in this park, and analytical stressed out people would find calm and peace of mind. Its development would generate employment, and tourists visiting the city would also have some place to relax at.

Follow-up Questions & Answers
1. Where do you and your friends usually meet?
My friends and I usually meet either at one of our homes, or at local cafes in the vicinity. Sometimes we simply get into a car and go out on a long drive, halting only to grab take-away snacks and drinks.
2. Do you like staying among people that you know?
Yes, I like staying among people I know. It gives me the comfort of familiarity, thereby creating a sense of security in my mind. Community living is engrained in human DNA since millennia, and I am no exception to the rule. Staying among people I know makes me feel relaxed and at ease.
3. What are the advantages and disadvantages of it?
The advantages of staying among people that one knows are plenty. One feels safe, secure, loved, and at ease. One has the liberty to be oneself, and express feelings and emotions unhesitatingly. The disadvantages of staying among people you know are a lack of privacy, excessive interference from others in one's personal matters, the risk of becoming constrained a small space, and losing the confidence and courage to step out of one's comfort zone.

4. Do people find it difficult to get used to new places? Why?

People find it difficult to get used to new places sometimes; but his largely depends on the nature of the person. Extroverts make friends easily, are very confident, and like trying new things in new places. For them, fitting in is not a challenge, and if they don't fit in, they do not mind standing out, either. For introverts, things are a little more difficult. Since they find it tough to relate to new people, and often remain reserved, they are not able to make new friends quickly. This leads to a feeling of loneliness, and the lack of a support group makes it tougher to face the challenges of settling into a new place.

5. What suggestion would you have for those people?

I would tell them to try and reach out to their new neighbours, and to make friends in cafes or other places that they frequent, in the new area or city. My suggestion to such people would be to make friends like themselves, who would be less likely to intrude on their privacy, but would still be available should the need arise.

110. Describe an interesting thing that you learned from the internet.

   You should say

- **What it is**
- **How you found out about it**
- **Which website you used**

How was your experience studying online?

A few years ago, websites such as Coursera and EdX were launched online, with the aim to make good quality education accessible to everyone. These websites got affiliated with various universities and institutes across the world, and started offering subjects from different fields of study to students, for studying online, remotely. The main benefit of this was that people could continue their education in a subject they had left halfway, or they could pick up a new subject they were interested in learning more about. For online studies, most universities did not require students to have studied a subject up to a certain level before enrolling. Institutes provided subject knowledge online at different levels, starting from the foundation level and going up to very advanced levels. So, one needed to gauge one's own proficiency in the subject of their choice when selecting the level of study to enrol in. Students could study from the comfort of their home or office, and the only thing they needed was a functional computer or smartphone, and an internet connection. I first found out about these web portals from a friend of mine, whose son had enrolled in a Physics course. I went online and explored the site EdX, just out of curiosity. While scrolling and browsing, I came across a foundation level photography course that was about to begin in a week. I took a close look at the course modules and syllabus, as well as the description of what I could hope to take back from the course. It seemed quite interesting, and I'd wanted to learn some photography since a while. The enrolment was absolutely free of cost, and the course was in affiliation with a very good university from the US. Divided into 8 weeks and 8 modules, I started right away, and diligently followed the study plan suggested by the university. There was scope to discuss course material with peers on the online forum designed for their course, and I had the liberty to pose questions to the tutors who taught us through recorded course videos. We also had to make submissions of our works from time to time, to meet the assignment submission requirements. These submissions were then reviewed by the professors, as well as by peers. These assessments provided constructive critical feedback on students' work, and helped each of us grow as photographers. When the course ended, I had qualified for certification and could order the certificate for a very small fee. I decided to go ahead and make the payment in order to get the certificate. My experience studying online was absolutely novel, enriching, and interesting. I learnt a lot at my own convenience, with flexible timings, without compromising on my work or other activities. I enjoyed the learning experience so much, that I immediately decided to enrol in the subsequent levels of the same course as and when they were launched.

Follow-up Questions & Answers:
1. What other things did you learn from the internet?
Apart from the foundational photography course, I have learned two subsequent levels of photography, I have studied a course in teaching English as a second language, and am currently in the process of studying a course titled — 'French Level 2'.
2. Can you always trust the source of information on the internet?
No, you cannot always trust the source of information on the internet. Not all sources are credible. Many are invalid when it comes to referencing because they lack a good reputation, there are some that share redundant information, and there are yet others that can be edited by anyone. So, only those sources of information that carry a good reputation can be trusted online.
3. Do you think that society depends on the use of internet nowadays?
Society is largely dependent on the use of internet nowadays. Businesses are conducted online, information is exchanged through emails and internet based text messaging services. People even share important data on the cloud. Buying and selling of goods and services happens online on a very large scale these days. Furthermore, people have started using the internet for dating, for finding a suitable spouse, for sharing art and music, and even for watching movies. Society has integrated video conferencing and online social networking in its day to day routine, too. Almost all our information these days comes from the internet.
4. Does the extensive use of the internet have an effect on business structures?
Yes, the extensive use of the internet has a noticeable effect on business structures today. Most businesses are completely dependent on the internet. E-commerce websites, for example, sell all their goods and services online, and many of these do not even have physical showrooms, offices, or warehouses. A lot of brokering happens online. Almost all business communications in developed nations, as well as most communications in urban developing regions happen online these days. Due to this, businesses have reduced investment in inventory, labour costs have come down, paper work has reduced and efficiency and speed of work have increased manifold.
5. How useful is the Internet to you?
The internet is a source of entertainment and information for me. I browse the web to read the daily news, to find out more about topics of my interest, to read articles, and

even to study online courses from time to time. I use it to communicate with my business collaborators and associates. Further, I use the internet to watch movies and videos, to download music, and to stay in touch with friends and relatives who live in different cities or countries.

6. How do social networking sites affect our society today?
Social networking sites have brought us back in touch with long lost friends and relatives. They have made it easy to stay connected with those that matter to us. We can now share videos, photos, audio clips, and news with them real time, and on a regular basis. However, social networking sites have created a few big issues as well. People have reduced socialising physically, with some choosing to live their entire social lives online. Many are addicted to sharing details of their lives online, and a lot of people have developed inferiority complexes. Introverts have started using social networking as a mask to hide behind, and many people have resorted to cyber-crimes and cyber bullying, as a pastime.

111. Speak about the happiest or funniest person you have met in your life.
   You should say
-   **When and where you met**
-   **Describe his/her nature**
-   **How helpful that person was to you**
What other peculiarities did he have?

Sample Answer:
The funniest person I have ever met is an old friend of mine, Mr. Ashish Shah. I met him in 1995, when I was in college. He was my classmate at that time. I can confidently say that he is a gifted person. His presence of mind, sense of humour, creativity, and spontaneity in giving replies to any comment are his most outstanding virtues. What was most peculiar about him was that he was short and a little obese, and always wore thick glasses. His appearance gave an impression of a reserved and introverted person, but when anyone heard him, all their judgments based on his appearance were shattered. He was able to find humour in everything, from the simplest to the most complex situations of life. Once, he made the strictest professor laugh out loud in our classroom. He was a favourite among all the students of our college. He used to handle the anchoring of many events that took place in our college. The most astonishing thing was that all his pranks were enjoyable, and his sense of humour had grace. Once, just before our college final exams. I suffered from a bout of typhoid, because of which I could not prepare thoroughly enough for the papers. I was tensed, frustrated, and depressed on the day of exam. When he saw me in that gloomy state at the college gate, he came to me and somehow managed to make me laugh even in such a serious situation. Because of him, I felt fresh and a little confident. After that, I took my exam and surprisingly, I scored better than my expectations. Actually, I just needed some lightness, and a fresh state of mind, both of which my funny friend provided, when I needed it most. I can never forget

his support. He is currently in the US, but we still keep in touch via emails and phone calls. He is still just as humorous as he was when we studied together.

Follow-up Questions & Answers:
1. How does a man/woman express happiness?
Men generally express their happiness by throwing a punch in the air, or even jumping in the air. Their reactions are very animated. We can immediately make out when a male is happy. However, women generally laugh or flash a smile to express happiness. They use their eyes and facial expressions more, when they are happy. Sometimes they even cry if they are overjoyed.
2. How does a child express happiness?
A child expresses happiness by becoming hyperactive. He starts running around, or laughing aloud, or even shouting into the air. A child also speaks more than usual and tries to share the happiness with all his family members and friends. What's more, children are able to extend their happiness for longer time spans than adults.
3. Do the feelings of a person change with age?
It is true that our feelings change with age, because our perceptions about life and other people change with time. We learn from our experiences in life, which in turn changes our reactions to various situations in life.
4. Describe the way people express their feelings at different ages.
We have already discussed how children and youngsters express their feelings. Middle aged and old people express their emotions when they are happy. They often express their happiness by giving gifts or small treats to their close ones.
5. How useful are the comedy programs on TV, when it comes to making us happy?
Television programs cannot make us happy. But, they can make us laugh, and that is definitely helpful in making us feel better, light, and refreshed. However, I don't think they can make us happy, because the joy we get from television programs is very short lived.
6. Has the level of happiness among the people of your country increased in the last few years? Why?
It is indeed difficult to say so confidently, but looking at the economic and industrial growth in my country, I think people don't suffer as much from a lack of basic services, unemployment, and insufficient income, as they used to, till a few years back. In this context, it seems that happiness has increased among the people of my country.

112. Speak about a communication device you use regularly.
    You should say
- **What it is**
- **Since when you have been using it**
- **What features it has**
How is it useful to you?

Suggestions:
Candidates can speak about their mobile or landline phones, computers, and laptops, where they use the email facility.

Sample Answer:
The communication sector has shown a tremendous revolution in the last decade. Now, we can communicate with any person at any time, and anywhere in the world. Here, I would like to speak about my mobile phone, which I use regularly. This mobile is compatible with all the latest communication features. A mobile phone gives us three-way connectivity in the form of calling, short message services, and emailing, respectively. I use all these facilities as per the requirement.

I use my phone to talk to my family, my friends, my relatives, my students, and my colleagues. In case of emergency, when I am not in the office, my mobile phone is a boon to me, because it stores large amounts of data including call logs and phone numbers of more than a thousand people. My phone's enhanced memory has relieved me from memorizing important contact numbers and maintaining a pocket telephone diary. Moreover, the messaging applications in my phone, and its short message service is useful to me when I want to send text messages or media to my contacts. I also check my emails using my mobile and, if there is something urgent, I even reply to emails from my mobile. In addition, my mobile gives me utility facilities like an alarm clock, a daily planner, a currency converter, a world clock, and some inbuilt games. All these facilities are really helpful in managing my day. So, in today's busy and commercial life, the mobile has become an essential instrument for everyone.

Follow-up Questions & Answers:
1.Do you want any additional feature in the device you use?
Mobile phones have become so smart, these days that they already offer more services than ever. A few years back, I could not even have imagined in my wildest dreams that such a small machine would offer so much to humans, one day. I cannot think of any additional features for the device I use, at this point.

2.Do you send text messages?
I do send text messages to my friends. When I receive a meaningful or funny message from someone, I forward it to others, too. Apart from this, I send messages on festivals and special occasions like Diwali, Holi, Independence Day, and Valentine's Day.

3.The use of greeting cards has declined because of text messages. Do you agree to this?
I agree to this statement. People now prefer using messaging applications over greeting cards, for three good reasons. First, they don't have to visit a card shop when they use text messages, so it saves their time. Second, text messaging is cheaper than greeting cards, and often even free of cost. And lastly, digital text messages reach people faster than hard copy greeting cards. A text message can reach recipients in seconds, whereas a greeting card takes a few days to reach its destination.

4.Is it a good or bad development?
It is indeed a good development because it is cheap, fast, and convenient. To top it, greeting cards are made up of paper that comes from trees. So, by avoiding the use of greeting cards, we can save trees, and help our environment.

5.What are the advantages and disadvantages of mobile phones?

Mobile phones offer many benefits like fast and easy communication with anyone at any time, storing, sending, and receiving data like phone numbers, music, photos, and videos. However, it has some drawbacks too. It can be misused in a number of ways such as for sending spam messages and emails, graphic multimedia messages, and viruses. Also mobile phones interfere with our privacy, because anyone can trace us easily if we are using a mobile phone. Finally, scientific research tells us that mobile phones emit waves that are harmful to our heart and brain, upon extensive use.

◆ ◆ ◆

113. Speak about a room of your house that is special to you.

You should say
- What the purpose of that room is
- What facilities are available there
- How much time you spend there

Why do you like that room?

Sample Answer:

I have an affinity towards every room in my house, but the room I have a special attachment for is our drawing room. It is a big room with seating arrangements for more than 20 people. It has a television, a music system, and a telephone table. The carpet area of the room is approximately 300 square feet. It has two windows, an attractive Plaster of Paris ceiling, and optimum lighting. I like this room because it is the face of our house. We receive and welcome our neighbours, guests, and relatives in this room. We pass our time with them, and share our warmth with them in the same room. This room connects us to the rest of the world, because here we watch TV, listen to the radio, read the newspapers, and even attend phone calls. All my family members sit together every night after dinner, share our day-to-day experiences with each other, and nurture our strong family bonds in the drawing room. To me, my family is like a team. In today's era, when every member is an important part of the family, this is the place where we constantly enhance our warmth and feelings towards each other, and enjoy life as a family, in the true sense of the word. We have been living in the same house for many years, now. I have shared all the ups and downs of my life with my family members and sought guidance and support from them when required, sitting in our drawing room. This room has been witness to all the events of my life, and my family members' lives. I can say that this room is not only a part of my house, but also an important part of my life. This room has been witness to my graduation party, my grandfather's condolence meeting, my daughter's first steps and first words, and many other memorable events that have happened in my family. This room is indeed very special to me.

Practice Questions
1. What do you do in that room?
2. What do others do in that room?
3. What changes do you want in that room?

114. Talk about a new skill that you would like to learn.

You should say *dancing*
- What it is — *master* *dancing class / instru*
- How you would learn it — *near my locatio*
- How it would help you — *not so helpful* *but build a skill which can locha eye*

Self defence

Do you think it would be easy to learn it?

There are a few new skills that I have been wanting to acquire for a long time now. My work requires me to delegate a lot of tasks to different people. Often these people need to work in teams to accomplish the tasks. However, when many different minds come together, there is a high likelihood of differences of opinion and conflicts, which slow down efficacy and prove counterproductive. To counteract this issue when working with teams, I would like to learn team management and team leading skills. Secondly, I want to learn some motivation skills, as I think these will help me motivate my employees, my family members, and myself. I have personally experienced the power of a well-timed motivational pep talk. I have seen that motivation encourages people to do their best and achieve their highest potential. If I am able to motivate people, it will enhance the quality of everyone's life and work. Finally, my work involves a fair bit of addressing small crowds and large groups of people. While I do a good job at oration, I feel that improved public speaking skills will further enhance my confidence and ensure better content delivery. So I would like to polish my public speaking skills, too. I would learn these things from online self-help videos, self-help books, and by attending workshops and seminars that teach these management skills.

I think these skills will be fairly easy for me to learn, because I do have a basic knowledge of all of these. I am a quick learner, I'm attentive when learning something, and am also good at implementing theoretical concepts in practical life. My habit of monitoring my progress will keep me aware of how much each of my skills have improved, and I will take continuous feedbacks from my family members to better myself where required.

Discussion
- What skills are necessary to be a good employee? Why?
- Do you think everyone is able to communicate well?
- Is communication a skill that one can learn?

◆ ◆ ◆

115. Talk about a difficult choice that you had to make, and realised later that it was the right decision.

You should say
- When and where you made this decision
- How you knew it was the right decision
- What made the choice difficult

Why was this decision important to you?

Here, I would like to talk about a difficult choice that I made many years ago. Back when I had started my business, we used to work out of a small but comfortable office close to my house. Work was going well, but five years down the line I realised that we'd need more space to accommodate the increasing number of clients and staff. I had searched for a new office space in my budget all across the city, along with my real estate broker, and had narrowed in on a few good ones. With help from my family members, I managed to pick the best one, too, in a few days. I knew this new place was perfect for my office. The office area was larger, the building management provided better services to office owners, and the building also had better amenities. It was a good looking commercial complex with a very classy façade, and the location was also very good. It was in the city centre and hence, more visible to passers-by. It was also easier to locate than the old office I was in. However, I was concerned about losing out on existing clients, and also about losing the brand identity that was associated with my original location. It had taken my team and me a lot of hard work and patience to develop our identity and become well known in the locality. Were we prepared to lose out on a few clients? Did we have what it took to retain clients in spite of a change in location? These thoughts kept clouding my mind, making it a very difficult choice.

But, the choice had to be taken, and a move had to be made. The original building was quite dilapidated from the outside. Because it had become old, it needed constant maintenance for which charges were levied to office owners every now and then. My clients were often inconvenienced when the elevators did not work, and the area was not exactly a prime location of the city. This decision of moving my office was important for expanding my scope for growth in business. Eventually it proved to be a good decision I did not lose a single existing client, and in the bargain I gained many new clients. A good office was also able to attract better staff and retain them.

Discussion
- What kind of choices do we make in our daily life?
- What kind of choices do children make in their daily lives?
- Is it important to go for a walk in the park these days?
- What do you do in a park?
- Do you think people these days prefer free time or money, more?
- When people work long hours, does it affect their family life? Why?

116. Describe the house or apartment you live in now.

You should say
- What the place looks like
- How many rooms it has
- What its highlights and special features are

What do you like/dislike about it? Why?

The house I currently live in is a big, spacious flat in an elegant looking apartment. The apartment's exterior is very modern, and the theme is quite urbane. The exterior walls are painted a classy shade of cream, and the large balconies of all the flats are visible from the bustling street below. Each floor has two flats. Mine is on the ninth floor, and has 3 bedrooms. The master bedroom is the largest, with a small balcony of its own, which overlooks the quiet society street and offers a decent amount of privacy. There is a second bedroom which is slightly smaller, but still very spacious. It can easily accommodate a couple, because it has space for a king size bed and then some small furniture. The third room is a children's bedroom. This is the smallest bedroom in the house, but its size is what makes it very cosy and comfortable. Perfect for a child or a single grown up, this room has large windows with ledges to place potted plants on. Each room has an attached bathroom, and we have all done up the interiors of our bedrooms and bathrooms differently, based on our own tastes. However the special feature here is that in spite of being different and reflecting individual personalities, each of the rooms blends in well with the overall theme of the house. Another attractive highlight of my house is the living area. The drawing and dining rooms are connected without any visual barriers, thereby making the home very open and airy. The ventilation in the house is amazing, and because our main balcony faces the north, beautiful soft sunrays keep the dining room well lit without increasing the temperature.

The only thing I dislike about the house is the noise we have to constantly live with. Our windows are sound proof to cut out the sound of traffic, but even with sound proof windows, a lot of noise manages to make its way in. So, we cannot even think of keeping the balcony doors and windows ajar, except early in the morning or late at night. This defeats the purpose of living in a flat which has scope for good air ventilation.

Discussion
- What kind of home would you prefer to have in the future? Why?
- Where would you like to live? Why?

117. Speak about your favourite advertisement.

OR

118. Describe an advertisement you recently saw.

    You should say
- **What the product is**
- **What the advertisement is like**
- **When you first saw it**

Why do you like it, and do you have any suggestions to make it better?

Sample Answer:
I have seen many unique and innovative advertisements in my life. But Vodafone India's Zoo Zoo advertisements are my favourites. I first saw them a while ago on television, at

---

home. Zoo Zoos are white humanoid creatures with ballooned heads and bodies, who express human feelings and emotions with their minimalistic facial features. Vodafone conceptualised and introduced Zoo Zoos as their bran ambassadors, and in these ads, they showed Zoo Zoos sing and talk to each other in an incomprehensible, yet funny sounding language, complete with exaggerated tones and pitches. In some ads, Zoo Zoos were shown dancing and jumping, too, and these ads grabbed the most eyeballs during the IPL matches. Zoo Zoos of both genders were shown in the ad, to make the ads more inclusive, and relatable.

Ogilvy & Mather, the ad agency behind the brilliant Zoo Zoo ads, made sure that Zoo Zoos looked cute, friendly, and likable to everyone. Further, they removed the possibility of regional and age-related associations with the brand, by introducing such characters.

Zoo Zoos featured in Vodafone ads to introduce new features or facilities that the company was offering its customers. They personified the brand name and gave it a unique, playful, feisty character. In the ads, Zoo Zoos were shown using different Vodafone services for different purposes. I like how these friendly looking characters manage to deliver such clear messages to viewers, without using any known language, and with the help of very few colours. I appreciate the creativity of the makers of this ad series from the bottom of my heart. I don't have any suggestions for their improvement because they are a complete series.

Follow-up Questions & Answers:
1. What types of products are advertised on TV/radio/in newspaper these days?
There are numerous products being promoted on television, radio, and in newspapers these days. We can commonly see, hear, and read advertisements of soaps, shampoos, hair oils, electronic goods, mobile instruments and services, soft drinks, packaged food, garments, and commodities.

2. Which advertisement according to you has a better impact — a TV ad or a newspaper ad? Why?
It depends a lot on the targeted class of consumers. If we want to target a local or regional mass of people, newspaper ads are more effective. But, if we want to promote the product on a national level, television ads bear better fruits, because they reach all corners of the country.

3. Do advertisements influence the buying behaviour of consumers?
Adverts can influence our buying behaviour by showing the utility and superiority of their products over other products. According to me, children can be influenced by adverts to a greater extent compared to adults, because they are easily attracted to new and different things that are shown on TV or on billboards.

4. Should companies hire celebrities for advertisements? Why?
Yes, companies can hire celebrities for brand endorsements. Actually, celebrities have their own fan club. When they endorse any product, their fans get inspired to acquire it, and are more likely to use that product. Here, companies should take one precaution. They should match their product's targeted consumers with the class of fans of celebrities that they hire. If these categories match, the campaign will bring about a boost in product sales, but if there is a mismatch, the company may lose money on their campaigns.

5. Do you think the government should restrict the advertisements telecast on TV?

In general, there is no need for the government to interfere in the number of advertisements shown on television, because companies keep doing market research regarding such issues. If viewers do not see ads on television, the frequency of the ads will reduce automatically. However, in case of a live telecast of an event like a cricket match, the government must limit the time and number of ads shown, so that the viewers can enjoy the event on television, better.

6. What is the difference between advertisements in your country and in foreign countries?

The main difference between the adverts in foreign countries, and in my country is in the theme, and the concept. Ads in my country often promote their products using themes of culture, religion, family values, and patriotism whereas ads in foreign countries show themes such as lifestyle, technology, and luxury to promote their products.

7. Do adverts of other countries impress people of your country?

Well, sometimes they do, but, not always. However, people living in urban areas are more impressed by foreign ads, because they can easily relate to them, and use those products in their life. This is also the reason why products from foreign countries are sold more in urban areas.

8. Do you buy products marketed by foreign adverts?

I do buy products marketed by foreign adverts, but I don't buy them just because their ads are good. I buy those products only if I am satisfied with their offering in terms of both, the price and the quality.

9. Do you think foreign advertisements should be banned in our country?

I don't think we should ban ads from foreign countries, except the ads selling alcohol, tobacco, and other addictive substances. In addition, ads which are disrespectful to the cultural and social values of our country should also be banned.

Practice Questions

1. Do you find similar advertisements in different media like on TV, radio, and in newspapers?
2. Did that advertisement inspire you to buy that product?
3. What changes have you seen in the world of advertising in recent years?
4. What are the latest methods used by companies to market their products?
5. What type of advertisements will be popular in the future?
6. What factors should companies consider before advertising their products?
7. Should the advertisements of alcohol and tobacco be banned? Why?
8. To which aspect should companies give more attention — marketing, or quality of the products? Why?

119. Speak about your favourite animal. | **120. Speak about an animal that is found**
OR **in your country.**

OR

121. Speak about your favourite wild animal/domestic animal.

  You should say

- **What the animal looks like**
- **Where and when you get to see it**
- **What you like about it**

What can you learn from this animal?

Sample Answer:

My favourite animal is the tiger. It is our national animal. It is found in many states of my country. It belongs to the cat family, and so it behaves like a large, but dangerous cat. I have seen tigers in zoos in my city, and in the forests of Gir, Ranthambhor, and Uttarakhand. It is the most beautiful wild animal found on earth, according to me. It has a golden coat, and some species have black stripes and spots on their body. These features contribute a lot to the gorgeous appearance of a tiger. We can find white tigers also, in some parts of eastern India. Tigers have sharp teeth and nails. They also possess a powerful sense of smell and sharp eyesight, which can be used in targeting and hunting their prey in the forest. The tiger is a highly dangerous animal that eventually kills anyone who comes in its way. It is a multi-skilled wild cat that can run as fast as 70 kilometres an hour, climb trees, and swim in rivers and lakes. It prefers to live in groups where it can procreate; the baby tiger is known as cub. However, humans have always killed tigers to use their skins to decorate their houses and to make various products from their teeth and skin. Because of excessive poaching and hunting, tigers are now an endangered species. But, the government these days is taking a lot of steps to help increase the population of one of the most beautiful and gorgeous animals of our country, by taking action against hunters, and making situations in forests conducive for tigers to survive and grow.

◆ ◆ ◆

122. Speak about your favourite book.

OR

123. Speak about something that you enjoy reading.

  You should say

- **The title, and the name of the author of the book**
- **What the book is about**
- **The message given by the book**

Why is that your favourite book?

Sample Answer:

I have read a lot of books in my life on various subjects like philosophy, spirituality, religion, personal development, psychology, and management. But, here I would like to speak about my most favourite book, 'Bhagavad Geeta'. The Bhagavad Geeta is actually a conversation between Lord Krishna and Arjuna, on the battlefield of Kurukshetra, where the Mahabharata war was waged. It was written by the great Rishi Ved Vyas about 3000 years ago. This book is actually a collection of verses spoken by Lord Krishna in Sanskrit, in different chapters. I have read its translation, and have also read different interpretations and explanations by various renowned writers of my country. This book is about the principles of life, and the laws of action (Karma). This book explains an eternal principle of life — we should do our duty while living in the present, and leave all expectations regarding the results or rewards of our actions to nature. I read this book in my childhood for the first time, but I couldn't understand anything in it, then. The second time I read it was just a few years ago, and I tried to understand it better, the second time around. It is spiritual, psychologically profound, and mysterious, also. I would describe having to speak about the great omnipotence of this book in two minutes, as pouring an ocean into a teapot.

I like this book, because it is not just an ordinary book, but a guideline for every human being. It is not just meant for those who are seeking spiritual enlightenment, but for one and all, as its principles are applicable to us in all walks of our life even today. In fact they are also likely to be applicable to human life in future. I also believe that this book is better read slowly over a length of time, to ensure a deeper understanding of its message.

Follow-up Questions & Answers:

1. How have you preserved your favourite book?
I have preserved that book by getting it hardbound, and by adding an extra cover to it. As I have mentioned earlier, I still read the book at regular intervals, so I have kept it in my cupboard from where I can take it whenever I want to read it.

2. Are there some books you don't like to read? Why?
I don't like to read history books, novels, and books based on social themes because I am not interested in history. In case of novels and social books, I have observed that some novelists often use extremely farfetched imaginations to make their books interesting and spicy. In this process, the writing gets removed from the social context of the plot, and enters into the category of fantasy. This combination only soothes our imaginations, but it cannot make any creative contribution to our life.

3. What is the difference in the preferences of books between youngsters and old people?
Youngsters like books based on fiction, management, self-improvement, humour, and autobiographies. Old people, on the other hand, like books based on religion, philosophy, spirituality, health, and financial planning. These preferences are based on general observations. They may differ as per the reader's interest.

4. What do you prefer more, reading a book as it is, or reading a book on the computer? Why?
I prefer reading a book as it is. Reading a hardcopy book is more convenient, and healthier, too. Reading books on computers requires electricity, and it has other drawbacks like eyestrain and backache.

5. Are books essential tools for study, or not? Are they the only tools for study?
Yes, I think books are essential tools for study, because books are an integral part of the way we have been studying for hundreds of years. Second, it is the most effective,

convenient, and economical way of studying compared to other digital media.

6. What material other than books is useful in studying?

There are many types of digital equipment, which are helpful in studying, like computers and television. They offer audio-visual learning output, enabling us to see, as well as hear them. This enhances our understanding of the subject of study to a large extent. However, digital tools are not complete and effective alternatives to books, because books have their own benefits in terms of studying, which cannot be replaced by any other medium of study.

124. Speak about your favourite colour.

    You should say

- **The name of the colour**
- **Why you like it**
- **How you use this colour**

What is this colour associated with most often?

Sample Answer:

I like many colours, and I use different colours in my everyday life. But, white is my favourite colour. I like this colour because it suits me a lot. Other reasons for appreciating the colour white are that it is a holy colour, and that it is associated with many religions. In addition, it is also used as a symbol of purity; we can sense a divine presence when we enter a structure that is made up of white marble. White clothes are useful in hot countries like India, because white reflects heat, and protects people from direct sunlight in summer. It is also associated with the beginning and end of life; we normally use white clothes to cover a new born baby, and also to cover dead bodies.

Apart from this, white is the symbol of peace and beauty. It is a part of our national flag, and it reflects that India is a peace loving country. What's more, whenever we see any white animal of any species, it looks even more gorgeous, compared to its coloured counterparts. For example, white elephants, pigeons, tigers, and peacocks, all look more beautiful white, than in their more commonly seen colours. These creatures look stunning, when they are white. It is also said that white is a combination of seven colours. Because of all these reasons, my favourite colour is white.

125. Speak about your favourite festival.

    You should say

- **The name of the festival**
- **The time of the year when it is celebrated**
- **How you celebrate it**

Why do you like it?

The Ultimate Guide to IELTS Speaking by Parthesh Thakkar

Sample Answer:
I live in a land of diverse, widespread cultures, where we give a lot of importance to many historical events, which also have religious associations. So, we celebrate many festivals. But, here I would like to speak about the biggest and the most important festival of the Hindus, 'Diwali'. Diwali comes in October or November months of the English calendar year, but as per the Hindu lunar calendar, it arrives in the last month of the year. It is part of a five-day festival where we follow different rituals on each day. We worship the goddess of wealth (Goddess Laxmi) on the first day of the festival, two days before the new moon day. We follow it up by bursting fire crackers and eating sweets with our close ones. On the next day, we arrange a special worship to our family deity, both, at home and in a nearby temple. On the third day (the new moon day), we celebrate Diwali in honour of Lord Rama's return to Ayodhya, his kingdom, after his fourteen year exile — an event that took place thousands of years ago. Because it was a new moon night, the people of Lord Rama's kingdom lit lots of lamps to illuminate the route to his palace, making it easier to find. We still commemorate the night by lighting lots of lamps and placing them on the peripheries of our homes. The fourth day is the New Year day. We wake up early, go to a temple, and pray to God to make the coming year better. We also take the blessings of our family members and elders. Then, we wish all our friends, relatives, and neighbours a happy new year. On the last day, brothers in the family go to their sisters' houses, eat meals prepared lovingly by their sisters, and give them gifts in return. I also follow all the rituals that I have described. I like this festival because the sweets, crackers, and new clothes are all very enjoyable, and praying with family also feels very good. The atmosphere of the whole country changes beautifully, making everyone feel ecstatic. Moreover, I also like to use this festival as an excuse to catch up with my friends and relatives, so I can keep in touch with them by exchanging wishes and greetings. No doubt, it is the best festival in my country.

126. Speak about your favourite motorbike.

    You should say
-    **The name of the bike**
-    **When and where you saw it for the first time**
-    **What it looks like**

Why is that bike your favourite?

Sample Answer:
My favourite bike is the Harley Davidson Iron 883. I first saw this bike at a road show in my city during its launch campaign, some time back. Later, I looked it up online and realised that as opposed to the Street 750 model from Harley that is made in India, the Iron 883 is more authentically American. This bike has some stunningly attractive features. It is a cruiser with a low ride silhouette, high mounted circular headlights and striking orange indicators. These features give the bike a striking front-view. Its black rear view mirrors and engine, and chrome-edged alloy wheels add to its classic Harley

appeal. While this bike originally has a single-seat, the company offers to fit a pillion seat, if required. The most outstanding feature of this bike is its strong and masculine frame, and the shape of its body. Because of its classic, masculine appearance, it garners second looks from all those who don't own it. This bike is designed to appeal to men who are trendy and young. It has achieved tremendous success in wooing the youth of my country. It is a masterpiece in the two-wheeler category. A close friend of mine bought this bike at the time of its launch and gave me a test ride. I was amazed by its sheer power, and the growl of its engine. I immediately wanted to acquire this 883 cc beauty! While all its colours are wonderful, its Charcoal Denim shade is just out of the world!

Follow-up Questions & Answers:
1. What factors should we consider before buying a motorbike?
We should consider many factors before buying a bike, like the price, fuel efficiency, shape, and frame of the bike. We should also consider the strength of the engine in 'cc' and 'bhp', take references from other users, check the reputation of the manufacturing company, and also ascertain the availability of service centres in our area.
2. What are the advantages or disadvantages of riding motorbikes?
Motorbikes offer better ride control because of their bigger wheels and frames. In addition, they have been a preferred choice of males for decades. Also, they pose lesser maintenance costs compared to other two wheelers, and give better mileage. However, extensive bike riding may cause back troubles to some users. Moreover, bikes don't have storage cabinets like most scooters do.
3. Are there any places that you prefer to go walking?
I prefer visiting places that are near my home on foot. There is a supermarket, a temple, and a chemist shop near my home, to which I always go walking.
4. Should there be any speed limit in the cities for motorbikes?
Yes, certainly, setting a speed limit is essential in cities and towns, because it is often seen that youngsters ride their bikes very fast to get the thrill of speed. But, most of them are amateur riders and hence, there exists an increased risk of accidents. So, to prevent such mishaps, the government must fix a speed limit in cities and towns, and make sure that these limits are obeyed by all bike riders.
5. Should helmets be compulsory for motorbike riders? Why?
A helmet is an important protection tool for all two-wheeler riders. It protects the riders from head injury, which can be fatal sometimes. So, helmets should be made compulsory not only for bike riders, but for all two-wheeler riders.

Practice Questions
1. Do you suggest any changes for your favourite motorbike?
2. Do you use the same bike?
3. Would you like to have that bike in the future?
4. When do you think you can buy that bike?
5. Are the driving habits of the people of your city good or bad?
6. Are the roads of your city good for riding bikes?
7. Why is bike racing more popular these days?
8. Should the government encourage/ban motorbike racing?

The Ultimate Guide to IELTS Speaking by Parthesh Thakkar

9. What type of motorbikes will be popular in future?

127. **Speak about your favourite newspaper/magazine.**

   You should say

- **The name, and how it is published**
- **When you read it**
- **What you like in it**

Do you have any suggestions for it?

Sample Answer:

There are many newspapers published in my city in different languages like Hindi, Gujarati, and English. There are papers that cater to different requirements of the readers like finance, tenders, shipping, chemicals, industries, and shopping. I read newspapers in both, English and Gujarati, and I also read newspapers on financial markets. However, my favourite newspaper is 'Times of India'. Times of India is a complete newspaper, according to me. It is a national newspaper published from many cities of my country. It has many pages that cover important headlines, international and national news, news from my state, and also, news from my city. It has separate pages for satellite channel program schedules, and movie schedules. It also has separate pages on stock markets and sports that cover all the information necessary to update reader's knowledge bases. It also has an editor's page where scholars from relevant fields discuss different social, political, or international issues. I never forget to read this page, because it always enhances my intellect in some way.

Moreover, everyday they give two supplements. One of them is based on our city, and it covers some news and articles related to the lifestyle related and social developments happening in our city. The other supplement that they give covers different topics every day, like stock markets, fashion and lifestyle, education, jobs and placements, the film industry, and entertainment.

I have been reading this newspaper for many years, and I am thoroughly satisfied with it. However, I believe they should give one supplement on science and technology where they can present articles about the latest developments in medicine, healthcare, information technology, mobile phones, and the holiday industry, so that we can get information on such fields as well.

Follow-up Questions & Answers:
1. Can English be improved by reading newspapers?
Reading an English newspaper certainly helps readers in enhancing their knowledge of the language, its various functions, and vocabulary related to different fields and contexts. But, it is also suggested by many prominent English trainers that English learners should start reading English newspapers only after they reach an intermediate level in language. Otherwise, initial difficulties in understanding the language while reading an English paper may frustrate the candidate.

2. What are the advantages of newspapers over other media like radio and TV?
Newspapers are cheap, easily available, convenient, and informative media, where we can get both, news and information about various aspects of life. It doesn't require electricity and it costs much less compared to radio and television.

Practice Questions
1. Name some newspapers/magazines available in your city?
2. Should a person read regional, or national newspapers?

◆　◆　◆

128. Speak about your favourite song.
　　You should say
-　　**The name of the song**
-　　**When you heard it for the first time**
-　　**What your reaction was**
Why do you like that song?

Sample Answer:
My favourite song is 'My heart will go on...' from the movie Titanic. Celine Dion, who is a famous playback singer and pop star in Canada and the US, has sung this song. I had first seen a video of this song on a music channel, before the movie was released in my country many years ago. I remember being highly impressed by the way the song was pictured. I liked the song, itself, too and immediately bought its audio CD from the market. For a while after that, I kept listening to the song on repeat. Its lyrics are wonderful and touching. The song talks about true love that is eternal, and it has been associated with the character of the heroine of the film in a wonderful way. Listeners feel like the song is her message as she falls in love with an artist on board the Titanic. In the movie, the ship sinks, she loses her love, and yet, she remembers him at 80, as she relays their story. Her memories of her love are as fresh as a newly bloomed flower, even after so many years.
While the lyrics are amazing, Celine Dion's melancholy voice has also done absolute justice to the song. She has made it sound melodious and impactful with her beautiful voice. In addition, the tune of the song and the music are so soothing that listeners feel like playing it again, and again. I like the song so much that when it had just been launched, I had set it as my mobile's ring tone, for a very long time. I still listen to it on my computer and mobile, sometimes. I think, apart from being my favourite, this is also Celine Dion's best song, ever.

◆　◆　◆

| **129. Speak about a scientific subject you studied in school/college.** | OR | **130. Speak about a commerce/management subject you studied in school/college.** |

131. Speak about your favourite subject that you studied in school/college.

   You should say
-    **The name of the subject**
-    **When and where you studied**
-    **With whom you studied it**

Why did you like it?

Suggestions:

Candidates can speak about the subject of their specialisation, so that they may be more comfortable while speaking.

Sample Answer:

My favourite subject during my school years was English. I have had an innate affinity towards English, right from my school days. I studied English as a subject at school for 7 years. In those seven years, I learnt the fundamentals of the language, and a reasonable amount of vocabulary for effective day-to-day communication. I always completed the English syllabus before all my other subjects, during my school years. I studied English with many teachers during my school years. This has given me an opportunity to learn English from different points of view, and to acquire proficiency in the language faster. I always enjoyed my English lessons, because, since childhood, I had observed the people of my city facing difficulties in communicating in English. Even in my school days, I used to read out stock market related letters from various companies to my relatives and neighbours, because they were not very comfortable with the language. I also wrote replies to those letters when required.

However, apart from the studies at school, my hobby of reading English books helped me a lot in developing my language skills. I used to read storybooks, religious books, and comics in English when I was in school. One more reason I liked English is that I always performed better in English tests, as compared to other subjects.

132. Describe an academic/educational course you did in the past?

   You should say
-    **The name of the course**
-    **Why you took it up**
-    **When and where you studied it**

What did you like and dislike about it?

Sample Answer:

I would like to talk about a computer applications course that I did about 10 years ago. It was a one year certificate course that offered complete knowledge of the subject to those who wished to learn Computer Applications in order to get a job in relevant industries. It was actually a vocational course aimed at employment. I did that course because I was interested in computers and wanted to learn it in some depth. I did not want to pursue my career in that field at the, time but the possibilities of the usage of computers inspired me to learn it. I did this course at SSI, a company teaching computer applications and software development. It had opened up a new training centre in my area at that time. I went there to collect information for their training courses, and I found that the facilities, services, and the quality of teaching that they were offering was excellent. Moreover, their fees were also reasonable for the course that I wanted to do. I joined their institute and found that Computer Applications was not an easy subject, but, if trained properly, any student could excel at it. My trainer, Miss Avni, was very good at teaching. She taught all the components of the course in depth. I learnt MS Office which includes the knowledge of MS Word, MS Excel, MS Power Point, and MS Outlook. Windows, Networking on LAN and WAN, Internet Usage, Emailing, Chatting, and many other computer applications were also taught to us during the course. During that course, I opened my first Email account, which I am using even today. I also appreciate the efforts of the management in taking care of the students, by means of feedbacks and regular interactions. We also had regular exams for the modules that we had learned, and we were all awarded certificates of attendance for the course, from the institute. I was completely satisfied with that course, and hence I do not have any suggestions, or dislike any aspects of that course or training institute.

Practice Questions

1. Are such courses available in all parts of your country?
2. How do you think this course will help you in your career?
3. Do you think expenditure behind academic studies is increasing with time? Why?
4. Is it good or bad for the students of your country?

133. Talk about an interesting and impressive speech, or talk that you have heard.

OR

134. Speak about an inspiring talk or speech that you have heard.

> **You should say**

- **Who the speaker was**
- **Where you heard the speech**
- **What it was about**

Why do you like the speech, and what impressed you so much?

Sample Answer:

I would like to talk about Steve Jobs' Stanford Commencement Speech. In American academic tradition, commencement addresses are highly revered events, and Stanford of course, is a great institute in itself. I saw this speech on television, in 2005, where Steve Jobs addressed the students at Stanford soon after being diagnosed with cancer. Jobs, who was himself a college dropout, started off with a joke, saying that the commencement ceremony he was addressing was the closest he has been to a college graduation. He then went on to relay three stories from his life. In his words, the first one was about connecting the dots. Here, he spoke about why he dropped out of college, his family background, and how he survived after dropping out.

The second story was about love and loss. He described in this story, his beginnings with Steve Wozniak, and how they started Apple in his parents' garage. The company had grown by leaps and bounds in just ten years, and at thirty, in spite of being one of the founders, Jobs was thrown out. Very candidly, he told all those present for his speech, that he was devastated by the turn of events. Jobs then detailed in his address how he rose up from the rubble and restarted his life, building new business avenues from scratch.

In his third story, Jobs spoke about death, and how he felt when he first came to know that he just had a few more months to live. He then went on to talk about the miraculous surgery that saved him, and further emphasised on the need to live each day to its fullest, on one's own terms. He spoke about the importance of listening to one's own heart and intuition, because they always have the answer.

I found this speech inspiring and touching, and it made me realise the importance of being true to myself, and living each day to its fullest. I also learned plenty of things from that speech in the form of useful content to improve my own understanding and attitude towards various aspects of my life. As a trainer, I grasped many skills necessary for delivering an impressive and useful lecture to a large mass of people. I was impressed at Steve Jobs' candour, his confidence, and his willingness to lay his life out bare for the world to witness. It takes a lot of faith in oneself to be able to open up to so many people about such personal life events.

Practice Questions
1. Why are some people good speakers, and some not?
2. How can you develop or improve your speaking skills?
3. What makes a speech interesting?
4. What skills must a successful orator have?
5. Are visual aids helpful in delivering a speech?
6. Are conferences related to integrating different cultures helpful?
7. Which is more useful — a discussion, or listening to a speech?

135. Speak about your favourite theatre/cinema hall.
   You should say
-    **The name and location**
-    **How often you visit it**
-    **What you like about it**
What suggestions do you have for the theatre/cinema hall?

Sample Answer:

Going to cinemas is one of my favourite recreational activities. I have visited all the cinema halls in my city, but I like Cinepolis the most. This multiplex is part of a large mall in the city centre that attracts enormous footfall daily, and even more so on weekends. The cinema is located on the topmost floor of the mall, and has 6 air conditioned auditoriums with HD surround sound technology. These auditoriums open onto a common floor which has washrooms for men and women, a café, and a large stall that sells flavoured popcorn, nachos, and soda, to movie-goers. A small part of this floor is also dedicated to a box office, from where visitors can purchase movie-tickets and borrow 3D glasses when required. The cinema has ample, well-trained staff, and even servers who willingly bring snacks into the auditoriums halfway through movie screenings, if requested. On the same floor as the cinema, there is a food court. Although it is not part of the cinema, it is easily accessible, and offers a huge array of cuisines and dishes. This makes it very convenient for those who are visiting the cinema around mealtimes. I have seen many movies in this multiplex with my friends, family, and colleagues. In addition, they also offer online booking of tickets for their customers. I think this cinema's product offerings are amazing. However, they should offer some more activities for children, such as arcade games and rides, so that they may enjoy their visit more. This will ultimately increase their business, too.

136. Talk about a library you are a member of, or have visited recently.

   You should say
- **The name and location of the library**
- **What the library is like**
- **Why you visited the library**

What are your suggestions for the library?

Sample Answer:

I have visited almost all public libraries of my area, and some big ones of my city, too, because of my hobby of reading books on various subjects. Here, I would like to talk about the biggest library in my state, M.J. Library. The city municipal corporation governs this library, and I am a lifetime member there. The library is actually a two storeyed building with a big parking lot. It is located on Ashram Road in my city. This library is very old, but still, it has an excellent collection of old and new books. Near the entry, we can find a water cooler and a separate reading room for newspapers and periodicals. After that, there is a big reception area where we can exchange or return books, or get information about the library. To the right, there is a computer room where a vast collection of CDs and DVDs is maintained for the members to borrow. We find bookshelves behind the reception, where hundreds of books are stacked on different racks for the members. Here, books in our first language and national language are available. On the first floor, we can find the English books section. It is said that this library has more than half a million books in all, on all conceivable subjects. I visit this library once a month to get books of my interest. I like this library because no other library in my city is so big in terms of the area and number of books. However, I have one suggestion. This library has a card index where we have to find the book through cards. Some cards are torn or have turned pale, and hence they are unintelligible. I strongly suggest that the library put in place a computer index, so that we may find our books easily, and save time.

Practice Questions
1. Do you have any suggestions for the library?
2. What facilities does a good library offer?
3. Do you think the internet is more useful than a library?

137. Speak about a departmental store/supermarket you visit often.

You should say
- **Its name and location**
- **What you buy from there**
- **Why you like it**

What changes would you want in it?

Sample Answer:
The store I visit often is 'Big Bazaar'. It is actually a supermarket with many branches in my city, and more than 15 branches across the country. I usually visit the branch closest to my home. The supermarket is a three storeyed building offering almost everything that a family needs in its day-to-day life. It offers grocery, fruits, vegetables, snacks, garments, toys, utensils and crockery, stationery, sport accessories, jewellery, electronic goods, and so on.
Big Bazaar offers attractive discount schemes to encourage consumers to buy almost everything from there. The arrangement of items is so perfect that the consumers have a clear view of all the products. The staff is co-operative and polite. They also offer free home delivery to all the customers in all areas of the city. I visit this place twice a month with my family to buy garments, fruits, vegetables, and other household things that we require in our daily life. I like the ambience of the place. It is centrally air-conditioned, and the lighting arrangement is also good. Big Bazaar has converted shopping into a pleasant experience. However, I feel they should hire some more staff members so that they can look after their customers in a better and more effective way, to optimise sales and customer satisfaction.

Follow-up Questions & Answers:
1. Do you think the trend of big supermarkets and shopping malls is harmful to the existence of small markets?
There will be some definite impact on the business of small markets, because malls are wooing consumers with luxurious facilities and attractive offers. However, if small

markets get organised and improve their product mix with lower profit margins, I think they will be able to survive, and they may grow in future, because the competition in their segment will decrease owing to consolidation. In short, according to me, small markets have to be competent to survive.

2. What will the effects of this trend be, on small towns and villages?

People of small towns and villages also expect local stores to provide the facilities that big supermarkets offer. This shift will bring consumer awareness, which is the first step to organise the retail market. Hence, I think it is a welcome development in retail sector.

138. Describe a type of dress you wear/wore on special occasions.

   You should say
-   **What the dress looks like**
-   **What occasions you usually wear it on**
-   **What effects it has on other people**

What do you like about it?

Sample Answer:

There are many events in our life where we have to wear different kinds of clothes that suit the occasion and our personality. I often have to be present at various occasions like parties, marriage ceremonies, festivals, religious celebrations, and inaugurations. I choose from western formals, casuals, and traditional clothes, depending on the occasion. However, I like my traditional outfits more. This outfit is actually a fusion of tradition and style. It is a long 'kurta' with a 'pyjama', and a traditional decorative cloth known as 'dupatta', that can be draped around the shoulders and neck like a stole. The whole outfit is made out of silk, making the wearer look rich. The cream coloured kurta has attractive traditional embroidery with some decorative stones embedded in it. The dupatta also has a beautiful traditional print on it. It is dark in colour and stands out in perfect contrast to the colour and work of the kurta. A beautiful turban is also part of the outfit. I remember wearing the entire outfit in my brother-in-law's marriage ceremony. I like this dress because of many reasons. Firstly, I selected this dress after screening a lot of different varieties at various garment outlets in my city. Secondly, I like the colour combination and material of the outfit. And lastly, this dress suits my personality. I have received numerous complements on my traditional kurta pyjama and turban. People get pleasantly surprised when they see me in this outfit, and most of the time it impresses them. I wear it on different but important occasions like marriage ceremonies, religious rituals, and cultural events at my home.

139. Speak about a time you bought clothes for yourself.

   You should say

- When and from where you bought them
- Why you bought them
- Describe the clothes

How do you feel when you wear those clothes?

Sample Answer:
It was in December, 2005, when I wanted to buy a suit for myself, to wear at my brother-in-law's reception function. His marriage was lined up for the coming January. I wanted to buy a designer suit because the occasion was important to me. I started searching for the suit at various outlets of my city, but I couldn't find the type of design and fabric that I was looking for. I visited some reputed tailors of my area, and some well-known shops, too, but everything I found there was usual and common. In the meantime, I met an old friend of mine who suggested a shop named 'Male Design'. I visited that shop, and I was impressed by their window display. I felt like I would find what I was looking for, in that shop. I went there with my wife. We tried many varieties of designer outfits, but, eventually I liked one black suit. It was a three-piece suit with trendy buttons on the jacket. I liked the style of the suit as it could be worn either as a three-piece suit, or as a casual blazer. The fabric was wrinkle free, smooth, and attractive. I tried that suit and immediately selected it. It has attractive metal buttons on the cuff, and a Chinese collar. I bought the suit instantly. I received many compliments when I wore the suit at my brother-in-law's reception. I still wear it on appropriate occasions, and I feel comfortable and happy when I wear it.

Follow-up Questions & Answers:
1. What is the difference between the garment buying habits of men and women?
I have found that men are not always selective and precise when they buy clothes for themselves, except when they want to buy clothes for a particular occasion. Women, on the other hand, are often choosy in their garment buying process, and have predetermined requirements when they enter a shop.
2. What is the difference between the attitudes of youngsters and old people in buying clothes?
Youngsters lay more emphasis on style, design, colour, and fashion. They often buy trendy clothes that are in keeping with the latest styles. They are always ready to pay more just for style. However, old people give more weight to the comfort of an outfit, and its appropriateness, based on their family status and their occupation.
3. What is the difference between branded and ordinary clothes?
Branded clothes are sold in big shopping malls, and in well-known shops of the city. They also give guarantees of fabric quality and colour fastness. What's more, we always get a bill of purchase when buying branded clothes. On the other hand, ordinary clothes are sold in small shops, open markets, or even by vendors. They don't give any assurances for colour fastness and fabric quality. Moreover, they often don't give any bill of purchase. However, ordinary clothes are cheaper compared to branded clothes.

Practice Questions
1. Was it a branded garment?

2. Is a brand name necessary, when buying such type of clothes?

3. Why do people pay more for branded goods?

140. Speak about your favourite satellite channel.

    You should say

- **The name of the channel**
- **How many hours you view it for**
- **What popular programs are telecast on it**

Sample Answer:

I do not get much time to watch TV, because of my busy schedule. I watch TV for about half an hour a day on weekdays, and for about two to three hours during weekends. The channel I like watching the most is Star Plus. This channel was first introduced in my country as Star TV. At that time, this was the first foreign channel in my country. However, despite having the label of a foreign channel and foreign management, this channel has been successful in understanding the tastes of Indian viewers, and hence it is the most widely watched satellite channel in my country. I watch some of its evening programs when I go home from office. This channel offers a variety of programs that appeal to all classes of people. It holds the reputation of telecasting India's first money game show on TV, named KBC. This channel has also brought the cinema legend, Mr. Amitabh Bachchan, on small screen. Moreover, many social serials are also being telecast on it, now, that bind the majority of television viewers in front of the small screen. Nowadays, we can see many comedy shows, and some open stage chat shows and talk shows, also, where scholars from different fields come and share their experiences and give guidelines to viewers and participants, regarding their fields of expertise. In addition, we can see recent Hindi and English movies, also, on the same channel. Also, children can enjoy its animation movies and cartoon programs in the evenings. What's more, the management keeps introducing innovations in the variety of their programs, so as to offer a better program mix to maintain the viewers' interest. According to me, this channel offers a complete package of entertainment.

Practice Questions

1. Do you have any suggestions for the channel?

2. What are the advantages and disadvantages of watching foreign channels/programs?

141. Speak about your favourite TV show.

    You should say

- **The name of the show, and when it is telecast**
- **What the theme of the show is**
- **Why you like it**

Who are your favourite characters on the show?

Sample Answer:

My favourite TV show is 'The Kapil Sharma Show'. It is telecast on Sony, on Saturdays and Sundays, at 9pm. In this program, comedian Kapil Sharma teams up with other comedians Sunil Grover, Ali Asghar, Kiku Sharda, Chandan Prabhakar, and Sumona Chakravarti, to create a laughter racket on stage. This show is shot in front of a live studio audience, and each of the comedians essay different characters in different episodes. Some comedians, such as Sunil Grover, repeatedly play the same character if their character becomes endearing to the audience. Kapil and his team also invite celebrity guests to their show in every episode, and crack jokes with them, while interviewing them, simultaneously. While some guests come on Kapil's show to promote their upcoming music videos and movies, other celebrities visit his show just for fun. After interviewing the celebrities, Kapil gives the live studio audience a chance to interact with the stars, which is a very unique aspect of his show.

It is my most favourite program because I like the performances of all the comedians. Furthermore, Kapil is a good singer, and in almost every episode we get to hear him sing a few lines, which makes my day. The team comes up with original ideas, and there is a lot of creativity and uniqueness in their presentation. The Kapil Sharma Show makes me laugh a lot, and I have even recorded a few episodes of the program for repeat viewing. My favourite character on the show is Dr Mashoor Gulati, essayed brilliantly by Sunil Grover. According to me, this is one of the best programs on TV.

Follow-up Questions & Answers:

1. Is watching TV a healthy way to get relaxation?

No, watching TV is actually a passive activity. We should indulge in some interactive or creative activities if we want to get relaxed. Such activities are helpful in relaxing our minds. But, watching television can only give some rest to our bodies, which is incorrectly perceived as relaxation. True relaxation must work on both, the mind and the body, and this cannot be achieved by watching television.

2. How do TV programs influence our society?

TV programs do have an influence on our society. The plots shown in serials are often taken seriously by some people in their real lives. In this context, television program makers must prepare their content keeping moral, cultural, and social values in mind. Instead, if they show evil winning over good, the society may start reflecting this over time, because many impressionable viewers get attached to TV characters and often forget the difference between reality and imagination.

3. What are the benefits and drawbacks of watching TV?

TV is a useful tool to get entertainment, news, and knowledge. However, if we watch TV for longer periods of time, it affects our eyes and our body negatively. It is even more harmful for children, because they live in worlds of their own imagination, which is further fuelled by excessive viewing of animation or fantasy based programs. This keeps them too far removed from real life, and inhibits their mental growth.

4. It is said that TV has reduced communication levels among family members. Do you agree to this statement?

This statement seems true to a certain extent, because, at night, when all the family members get the chance to sit together and spend their time with each other, some families prefer to watch TV, as this time is considered the prime time, and most channels telecast their best programs during these hours. In this situation, family members interact less with each other, because they are engrossed in their TV shows at that time. This change in their attitude creates a lack of communication among family members.

Practice Questions

1. Do you suggest any changes to your favourite TV show?
2. What do you prefer to see on TV, a local cultural program, or an international cultural program, and why?
3. What types of programs are more popular in your country?
4. Do you think that TV can create troubles for children? If yes, what are they?
5. Does watching TV influence the reading behaviour of children? Why?
6. What will be more popular in the near future — TV, radio or the internet? Why?
7. Do you think satellite TV channels affect your culture negatively?
8. How many hours a day according to you, should we watch TV?
9. How many hours a day should a child watch TV?

142. Speak about your favourite website.

OR

143. Speak about a website you like to visit.

  You should say
- **The name of the website**
- **When you came to know about it**
- **How often you visit it**

What do you like about the website?

Sample Answer:

The website I visit almost every day is my own business' site. The name of my business is Angel EduNext, and I have a website with the same URL: www.angeledunext.com. We offer IELTS and TOEFL coaching to those aspiring to study abroad, we help them with immigration and University applications, and we even help those aspiring immigrants who plan to go abroad for reasons other than education. My website has a user friendly landing page with multiple tabs that lead visitors to areas of their interest and usefulness. Each of the tabs, when clicked, give detailed information regarding the services we provide and our standard operating procedures.

Our website has our company logo on the top let corner of the page, and also has our contact details mentioned very clearly. Because it is my own website, I played an important role in its conceptualisation and creation. I launched this website with a view to making my business noticeable and accessible to Universities from all over the globe, and to students and other prospective clients who wish to go abroad, and require assistance.

I visit my website a few times a day when I am on the move, but when I am in office, I always have it open in a tab on my browser. Every time someone contacts us through the website, we get a notification in the associated email accounts, so we can give prompt responses to queries and provide the best possible service to our clients.

What I like most about my website is its easy functionality, understandable, uncomplicated dashboard and landing page, and its aesthetically appealing user interface, which makes it stand out from interfaces of my competitors, which are very loud, crowded, and have too much going on.

Follow-up Questions & Answers:

1. Do you have suggestions for the website?

It is a perfect website according to me. However, the web site keeps changing its privacy settings every time they introduce updates to their interface. This sometimes exposes account holders' private photographs and posts to strangers, until the accountholder notices and manually changes the settings again.

2. How useful is this website to you?

It is an important part of my life. It keeps me connected to the whole world, especially my friends, relatives, and colleagues, through posts, and through its free messenger service. Moreover, it offers me access to various online communities with different interests and discussion topics. This helps me enhance my knowledge base from time to time.

Practice Questions

1. What other websites do you visit?
2. How many hours a day do you use the internet?

144. Speak about an online blog/forum/social networking website you visit or are a member of.

You should say

- **What it is about**
- **How to operate it**
- **How you came to know about it**

Why do you like it?

Sample Answer:

Facebook. Facebook is a social networking site, which is free to join. To use this site, one must create an account on their URL: www.facebook.com. This account is connected to their email address. After the account is created, the next step is to create a profile that shows a picture of themselves, known as their profile picture, and a timeline photograph that goes behind their profile picture as a banner. This timeline photo is usually anything that the account-holder holds dear in life. Some people upload photographs of family members and pets, while others upload famous quotes or movie banners. Once the photographs are in place, the accountholder needs to add information about himself such as his age, gender, educational background, career, relationship status, hobbies, and likes and dislikes. Then the website offers to find the accountholder's friends, who are already using the network, based on the address book from the attached email account. Once the website finds these friends, the account holder can send them friend requests and connect with them. With time one is likely to find more friends, relatives, and acquaintances, who he can keep adding to his 'Friends' list. The account holder can then share photos, songs, audio clips, videos, and written content with his friends on Facebook.

This website also allows people to start pages to publicise their businesses and service offerings, apart from networking with friends. What's more, they now offer their services in a host of different languages from across the world, to cater to the whole globe. As you might be aware, there is hardly anyone in the world today, who knows how to use the internet and still does not have a Facebook account.

I came to know about Facebook when a friend of mine sent me a 'Friend Request' on my email address. At first I did not understand the concept, but now I spend most of my time on this website.

What I like most about this website is that it helps me stay in touch with my readers, students, colleagues, friends, family members, and relatives. It also brings me interesting news from around the world on a regular basis. This portal has managed to remove the age-old human problem of losing touch with old contacts, with the passage of time.

Practice Questions
1. Are there other similar social networking sites available on the net?
2. Why do people visit blogs and social networking sites?
3. What are the social benefits of social networking and blogging?
4. Are there any negative effects of blogging and social networking?
5. What kinds of blogs are more popular amongst youngsters of your country?
6. Do you think people should have complete freedom of expression on blogs?
7. Why are blogs increasing on the net?
8. Many websites and newspapers carry online polls on various current affairs. Why do you think they do it?

145. Speak about a relaxation activity of your choosing.
You should say
- **What the activity is**
- **When and how you do it**
- **How often you do it**

How does it help you?

Sample Answer:
The word relaxation was only a vague concept for me, till a few years back. In the past, I had tried many activities, right from listening to music, playing games, and surfing the internet, to going for walks, and sipping a cup of tea or coffee. However, I never really

got any relaxation from these activities, in the true sense of the word. I would momentarily engage my mind in something leisurely, but immediately at the end of that activity, I would realise that I was once again unrelaxed. Over time, I stopped indulging in such leisure activities, as they were proving futile for me. Then I read a book on spirituality, from which I came to know the real meaning of relaxation. Since then, whenever I feel the need for relaxation, I just sit in a comfortable place and start focusing all my attention entirely on the stream of thoughts that is flowing in my mind at that time. I start viewing my thoughts objectively, and slowly I feel relaxed and calm. Initially, this task was difficult for me, as I observed that at any given point in time, many different streams of thoughts kept running in my mind, simultaneously. As I practiced, I realized that exhaustion of the mind was nothing but a result of its hyperactivity. Whenever I focused and observed my thoughts, I realised that they were disappearing from my mind when I became aware of them. With each hyperactive stream of thought that disappeared, my mind was coming to a relaxed state in its authentic sense. When the mind comes to such a state, we start perceiving our surroundings in an enhanced way; wherever we are, our mind becomes totally present in that moment, and we stop carrying the load of the past and worries for the future. Consequently, we feel relaxed, stress-free, light, and energetic. What's more, after following the guidelines of the book, I was able to solve difficult problems in a very short span of time and yet, I haven't felt stressed out at all. Now, this activity is imbibed in me in such a way that I hardly ever need to sit in isolation with my eyes closed, in order to relax. I can do it anywhere, and with open eyes. (Note: I personally recommend this activity to all readers. The title of the book is "The Power Of Now", by Eckhart Tolle.)

Follow-up Questions & Answers:
1. What are the causes of stress?
There are a number of factors responsible for stress in our life. Children get stressed because of the competitive environment in schools and the increasing expectations of their parents. Youngsters work for more hours to maintain an edge over competitors, keep up with increased workload, and to cope with changing work patterns. Older people also have stress because of their weak health. In short, stress is a universal, highly contagious, and destructive evil of our society.

2. What can we do to reduce stress in life?
We should learn to prioritise various aspects of our life, and to accept the reality of our existence. People often compare themselves to others and then strive to work even harder, to supersede them. In this rush, they often condemn themselves mentally for not being good enough, or they feel dissatisfied with themselves, and fall prey to bouts of depression. This unhappiness is the first source of stress in life. So, we must learn to accept ourselves for who we are, and set our goals based on our requirements and skills. Such changes in our attitude towards life can make us feel relaxed, after which we can grow faster and better in life, and can sustain the growth for longer, too. Apart from this, we can start doing activities like yoga, aerobics, and meditation, or we can take up a creative hobby such as painting or sketching.

3. What are the effects of stress on people?
Stress has some egregious effects on our life. It disturbs our mind, and the disturbed mind

affects other regular functions of our body, like eating and sleeping. Once such functions get disturbed, our body attracts various functional disorders in different parts like the heart, skin, digestive system, muscular system, and the nervous system. These disorders then have negative effects on our work efficiency. Consequently, we get more stressed because our decreased work efficiency inhibits financial growth. In short, it is a vicious cycle that can be prove dangerous for us.

4. Do you think stress management should be taught in colleges? Why?

Yes, I think college time is the best time for youngsters to learn stress management. This education will equip them to combat stress in their future work life, and help them come out of college as better professionals, to succeed in their careers.

5. What is the difference between the causes of stress in the past and in the present?

In the past, the causes of stress were regarding the basic needs for survival and education. Most people were engaged in earning to satisfy their basic needs like food, shelter, water, healthcare, and education for themselves and their families. Today, most people in the world have an easy access to these fundamental requirements, and hence the causes of stress have transformed from fulfilling basic needs to satisfying a craving for luxury. Now, the struggle for acquiring material possessions and wealth, and achieving financial security gives more stress to people.

Practice Questions

1. Do you prefer other activities as well, to get relaxed?
2. What do people in your area do for relaxation?
3. Is there a difference between relaxation activities of men and women? Why?
4. How can we balance our family life/personal life and professional life?

146. Describe a foreign country you have not visited, but would like to visit?

OR

147. Talk about a country that you would like to visit in the future.

> **You should say**
> - **Where this place is**
> - **What it is like**
> - **What you can do in this country**

Why do you want to visit this country?

While I have been to many foreign countries, there are still many that I have yet to visit. Each continent and each country has something different, something unique to offer to a hungry traveller like myself. Some have pristine lakes, some have lush green meadows, and then there are some places that have magnificent mountain ranges. However, there is one place that has all three! Today, I'm going to speak about Switzerland. This is one country I have yet to visit, but it is on top of my list. Being from a very warm place with a 6 month long summer, I constantly crave for cooler climes. We never get any snow where I live, so a place like Switzerland, where snow is a given, feels like a piece of heaven.

Nestled in northern Europe, Switzerland is rated one of the happiest places in the world on many indices. Thanks to the snow and its altitude, cold winds blow through its hamlets day and night, keeping the weather quite chilly. Once the body is acclimatised, such weather is ideal for going on long walks, treks, and on picnics when the sun comes out. Being the birthplace of skiing and other similar snow sports, Switzerland is very conducive to such activities. Hotels provide basic skiing workshops to tourists, so as to give them a true blue Swiss experience. I look forward to trying out this amazing sport, followed by a mug full of hot chocolate at one of the classic Swiss ski inns in Zurich, one can hire a pedalo, row boat, or speed boat and spend an enchanting afternoon in the still lake. Or, one can hire a bicycle and ride up the Alpine pass to enjoy the view of Zurich from an altitude. In Zermatt, tourists can enjoy nerve-wrecking cable car rides, and breath-taking views of the Matterhorn Glacier Paradise. In Geneva and Lausanne, travellers can explore the history of Switzerland by visiting its various museums, galleries, music festivals, and old buildings. There are numerous things to do in this Alpine paradise, but the main reason I want to visit this country is, that it is a melting pot of French, German, Italian, and Austrian cultures, because it shares its border with these glorious nations. For travellers this means that they can experience Switzerland's scenic beauty with a sublime blend of the art, culture, language, and cuisines of surrounding nations.

Follow-up Questions & Answers:
1. Why do Indian people like to travel abroad?
Indians like to travel abroad for many reasons. The first is to expand their horizons and see and learn about other cultures. The second is to enjoy scenic places with natural beauty that is different from what Indian tourist destinations can offer. Another reason why Indians like to travel abroad is that most foreign countries are more developed than India, thus offering a more luxurious experience to tourists. Finally, Indians often have a tendency to show off their socio-economic status among friends and relatives. What better way to prove that one has arrived in life, than to travel to expensive destinations abroad?
2. How can people benefit from international travel?
International travel acquaints us with newer, more different cultures. This teaches us to accept diversity in terms of thoughts, languages, dialects, food habits, cultures, and even dressing. Accepting such diversities makes us more tolerant, and also expands our world view. In this way, travelling can prove to be very educative. Having travelled abroad and learned such things, when we return to our own country, we can imbibe the good things we have learnt from other cultures, appreciate the plus points of our own culture and behaviour patterns, and also be more tolerant towards others. In the long run this makes a nation more peaceful, and hence more progressive.
3. What effects will tourism have on our environment?
Tourism can affect our environment both, positively and negatively. People from some cultures may resort to hunting and poaching, while some other cultures may not have as much respect for our natural heritage and may intentionally or unintentionally damage it. However, on a more optimistic note, when people from more developed countries come in as tourists, they may spread awareness about cleanliness and code of conduct through

example, by respecting our systems and laws more than our own citizens do. They may go back to their own countries and gather funds to help preserve our natural wonders, too, at times. Further, revenue from tourism can be used for the maintenance, preservation, and beautification of tourist areas, thereby improving the environment.

4. Why do people like to travel abroad?

People like to travel abroad to see newer natural wonders, scenic destinations, and world architecture. Further people enjoy learning about world history by travelling to various foreign countries. They also like to travel abroad to immerse themselves in diverse cultures and partake in their way of life for a while. Travelling abroad allows people to get a relaxing break, while also expanding their horizons and enriching their minds.

5. Would you travel around the world in the future?

If given a chance, I would love to embark on a world tour at least once in my life. In fact I think this is one activity that is on everyone's bucket list. Just the thought of a few months spent seeing various countries, their country sides and their metros, their architecture and their art, immersing in world music, walking around lush meadows, trekking across various mountain ranges, relaxing by different beaches, inhaling the salty sea breezes, browsing through unending street markets, and catching words and phrases from different languages, fills my mind with a sense of wonder and anticipation. I look forward to travelling around the world in the near future.

6. What's the difference between traveling abroad and studying abroad?

While travelling abroad, one's intent is to enjoy in leisure, and absorb as much of the culture and sights of the places one visits. One aims to try as many different things as possible, and visit as many monuments, art galleries, natural sites, and other tourist places, as possible. On the other hand, while studying abroad, one does not usually find much time to explore the country where they are studying. The university curriculum is usually quite intensive, and asks a lot from the students. When students are not busy attending classes, they are usually spending their time completing the reading requirements for consequent lectures, or they are busy completing assignments on time. In the midst of these responsibilities, students rarely find the time or frame of mind to actually go sightseeing like tourists.

148. Describe a useful thing that you once borrowed
   You should say
- **What you borrowed**
- **Who lent this thing to you**
- **What kinds of features this thing has**
Why do you think what you borrowed was useful?

Just a few years ago, I was travelling abroad for business. The trip was sort of a last minute plan, and as is the case with most such trips, just before leaving for the airport, I was busy making sure that things at my office were in order, that my packing was all done, and that I wasn't forgetting anything important. But, as destiny would have it, I forgot a very important thing — my power bank. When the plane took off, I switched off my mobile phone without as much as a second glance, and ran through the list of people I had to call and arrange meetings with as soon as I landed. Surprisingly on the same flight, I met a friend of mine who was headed to the same destination for his own business meetings. We spoke to each other for a while and nodded off sleep. When we landed, as is the norm, I pressed the power button on my phone to turn it on. But, the phone wouldn't oblige. There wasn't enough battery in the phone to start up! It was a moment of utter panic! How was I supposed to get in touch with the cab company who was sending me a chauffeur? How was I supposed to contact the client with whom I was going to have lunch? There was going to be absolutely no time to go to the hotel and charge my phone before heading out for my meetings. All the details of the places I was supposed to visit were on my email, and the only way to access it then, was my mobile phone! Breaking into a sweat I confided in my friend; I told him that I was in trouble, and that a few of my immediate business meetings may even get cancelled, because all the addresses and phone numbers of my clients were in my email inbox. To my surprise, he laughed and handed me his iPhone — the same model as mine! He let me borrow it, feed in my account details, access my email, and derive all the necessary contacts and addresses. Only after everything was in order, and I'd managed to contact everyone I was supposed to meet, was I able to heave a sigh of relief. This phone I borrowed was absolutely vital to the success of my business trip, and I'm thankful to my friend for making it available when I needed it.

Follow-up Questions & Answers:
1. What do Indian people usually borrow?
Indian people usually borrow mobile phone chargers, bottles of water for a few sips to quench their thirst on the go, and exquisite clothes from friends and relatives to wear for occasions and festive celebrations. At times, in large families, Indians tend to borrow jewellery from one another, from time to time. Many Indians borrow vehicles from their neighbours in emergencies. Often, in offices Indians borrow stationery from colleagues, and during winters it is very common for people to borrow each other's shawls and sweaters.

2. Does borrowing things make people uncomfortable?
In India, the culture of borrowing is widespread and has been going on since time immemorial. Indian culture is fundamentally based on the tenets of community living, and community living is all about caring for one another by sharing everything with friends, neighbours, and relatives, without as much as a second thought. This strengthens the bonds between people, and most people are comfortable with it. However, many youngsters today are slowly getting removed from this culture of community living, and it is seen at times that they get uncomfortable when others seek to borrow things from them.

3. What do you do if you don't want to lend something to someone?
I usually don't have issues lending things to others. However, if the demand is unreasonable, I politely decline, while also supplying my reasons for not lending the item in question. In most cases people do not get offended. In very rare cases, I am very sure

---

that the other person will get offended if I tell them the real reasons behind my unwillingness to lend something. In such cases, I come up with an intelligent excuse, and manage to keep my possessions to myself.

4. Why do people dislike lending valuable items?

Valuable items, as the name suggests are usually precious to the people who own them. Often they are expensive, and people have worked hard to procure and purchase them. At times they may even be rare, and irreplaceable. In some cases, a thing may be valuable not in terms of money, but because of the emotional value attached to it. Lending anything always carries with it the risk of the borrower unintentionally damaging or losing it. People don't want to run the risk of losing things that are valuable to them. So they dislike lending such things.

5. What would you do if your friends didn't give back what they borrowed from you?

If my friends have borrowed something that is not of much importance to me, I don't even bring up the topic. I let it go, and don't think about it again. However, if my friend has borrowed something of importance to me, I politely ask him to return it to me, saying that I need to use it myself. Even after repeatedly asking for it back, if my friend does not return something, I would keep a mental note to not lend things to him in future. But, I would not quarrel over a thing, because I think relationships are more important than materialistic possessions.

149. Describe something you would like to do if you were given a day off.

> **You should say**

- **What you would like to do**
- **Who you would like to be with**
- **Where you would like to do it**

How would you feel at the end of the day?

I am very fond of road trips. Since my childhood, I have always enjoyed travelling around the country by road. After I learnt how to drive a car, I started enjoying going on long drives by myself, as well as with friends. When we were all a little less busy in our jobs and businesses, we used to go on long drives very frequently. With time, the frequency of our long drives has noticeably reduced, but if I were given a day off, I would most definitely like to fuel up my car and hit the road once more. There are quite a few beautiful picnic spots around my city, which are ideal to visit on a day off. One such place is the Polo forest, about four hours' drive from my city. I would love to visit this forest with my group of friends and all our families. Polo forest has much to offer to everyone, and is usually not crowded. I would like for us to start off early in the morning, reach by mid-morning, and park our cars in a shaded place. We'd walk to the ancient Shiva temple in the forest, sit there for a while, and then trek through the lush hills behind it. From these hills we'd enjoy the view of the gushing stream below, and lie down on our picnic mats, enjoying the cool forest breezes. If the monsoons have brought in good rains, we might even be lucky enough to see waterfalls. In that case I would definitely like to make the most of them, by standing underneath for the longest time. Then, after drying up, we'd either dig into our picnic baskets for packed sandwiches and wafers, or we'd walk down to the nearby restaurant and eat steaming hot traditional Indian food. Stomachs filled up, and hearts happy, we'd all be homeward bound, already planning our next trip to Polo. At the end of the day I'm sure I'd feel satiated and relaxed, albeit a little exhausted.

Follow-up Questions & Answers:
1. Are people busy these days?
People are definitely a little busier these days, than they used to be before. Earlier, the population of the world, and of my country used to be much lesser than it is now. In the last century alone, our population has grown four-fold. With more mouths needing to be fed, and growing aspirations among the large youth base, naturally there is a lot of competition in the market, both in the job sphere, and in the business arena. To stay on top of the competition, it is necessary for people to work harder and faster than they did before. So, people are very busy these days.

2. What do people in your country like to do if they are not busy?
When people in my country are not busy, they enjoy visiting relatives, hanging out with friends, catching up on old times with people they have not been in touch with for long, and relaxing at home. People also like to go to the mall for shopping, sometimes people enjoy going to watch movies with their family members, and at other times people like stepping out for meals at good restaurants.

3. Do you like short holidays or long holidays?
I prefer many short holidays throughout the year, than just one long holiday once a year. Holidays serve as breaks from work, and I use them to help me rejuvenate myself. Just as we take Sundays off after six working days, to help us return to work refreshed on Monday mornings, similarly short holidays help us rid our minds and bodies of the built up exhaustion of work. When I take a long holiday I have a tough time convincing myself to get back to work, and then I feel guilty taking more short holidays. Instead, if I take short holidays every now and then, I have noticed that my productivity at work increases manifold.

4. Do you think today's lifestyles give people enough time for leisure?
I think people need more time for leisure than their lifestyles today allow them to take out. In earlier times, it is believed that people used to be happier, more relaxed, and rarely stressed out in general. This is because they had a lot of leisure time to themselves, which they often spent simply relaxing and watching the world go by. Even now, this can be seen in small villages. However, most of us in cities have forgotten how to make the most of our leisure time, because we hardly get any.

5. Do you think people today have more time to relax them in the past?
On the contrary, people today have less time to relax than they did in the past. Instead of reducing our workload, all our technological innovations have increased it. With faster communication, transport, and logistical planning, we are now able to get things done ten times faster than we used to, just twenty years ago. Taking advantage of this speed, instead of freeing up more time for ourselves, we have increased the quantity of work we do each day, leaving us with less time to relax than in the past.

---

6. Do you think it's important for people to have leisure time or time to relax?

It is absolutely vital for people to have leisure time to refresh and rejuvenate themselves. Time off to relax is all the more important today, as our lives have become very stressful, thanks to the increasing workload, and pressures brought on by the increasing competition around us. Everything today needs to be done faster; the need of the day is to constantly update oneself to work smart. These daily demands take a toll on our minds and bodies, making it important to find time to relax.

7. Do old people and young people spend their leisure time similarly, and relax in the same way?

Old people tend to spend their leisure time indulging in more laidback activities than youngsters. Old people are more comfortable sitting in solitude, contemplating life, meditating, taking a walk in the garden, or simply sitting with their family members. Youngsters on the other hand usually need music in order to relax. Most youngsters have portable MP3 players with long diverse playlists to suit different moods. A lot of times youngsters prefer intensive cardio or weightlifting to relieve their stress. Video gaming is another common activity for youth today to de-stress.

150. Describe an important conversation that influenced you.

   You should say
-   **When this happened**
-   **Who you were talking to**
-   **What you talked about**
How has this conversation influenced you?

I have had many important conversations with different people through the course of my life. A lot of my most enriching conversations have been with my nearest family members, because they have always been well-wishers, and they usually know my goals and ambitions in life. However, not all of these have been influencing in nature. An important conversation that influenced me, happened years ago, when I was looking to go abroad for higher studies. I had completed my undergraduate studies, and was considering applying to foreign universities for my post-graduation. After conducting much research, and seeking the opinions of acquaintances and relatives who had already been abroad, I had managed to narrow down to two countries — Canada and USA. But, for a long time, in spite of committing myself to listing down the pros and cons of various universities in both countries, I could not reach a conclusion. Then, one day in an international education fair organised by an education consultant in my city, I happened to meet a Canadian immigration officer. This friendly gentleman was understanding and knowledgeable. He was well versed with the things Indian students look for from universities, and also knew the struggles Indians faced when they went abroad. He sat down with me for a long time, and explained to me what Canada was like, as a country. He told me a little bit about various cities and universities, there. He showed me the plus points and minus points of each of the universities I had been considering, and even gave

The Ultimate Guide to IELTS Speaking by Parthesh Thakkar

me pointers regarding how I should write my essay, in order to secure admission in the places I had shortlisted. He further told me more about the immigration laws in Canada, and what my options for working there were, after post-graduation. This conversation influenced me to pick Canada over the USA for my further studies, and also helped me decide which universities to apply to. In hindsight, this conversation has probably shaped my career to a certain extent, so far.

Follow-up Questions & Answers:

1. How do friends communicate with each other?

Friends usually communicate with each other very causally, without manipulation or pretence. They hang out at cafes and at each other's homes, sit together, and discuss the goings on of their lives.

2. What's the difference between having a conversation with a man, and having a conversation with a woman?

In general, men tend to be less chatty than women, and some researches have even shown that men speak fewer words than women per day. Women are generally more animated in their discussions, their conversations tend to be more descriptive, and are sometimes also sprinkled with emotional or personal talk. Even among very close friends, women tend to be quite polite. Men on the other hand keep things concise when they talk, and rarely discuss personal or emotional issues. Further, with close friends, men don't pay much attention to politeness and formalities.

3. Do you think women like to chat more than men?

Women usually like to chat more than men, and are often more interested in each other's lives than men are. However, this is not writ in stone. There are many men who are exceptionally chatty, as there are lots of women who are quite silent and reserved.

4. When men chat with other men do they usually talk about the same things that women do when they chat with other women?

From what I have seen so far, men talk about absolutely different things with other men, than women do with other women. Men tend to discuss gadgets, new technology, automobiles, and politics amongst each other. Once all serious talk is out of the way, they move on to cracking jokes. Women on the other hand tend to discuss more feminine things such as their feelings, emotions, the impact of various events on them, their dealing strategies, and what's going on in their workplace.

5. What is the difference between chatting and gossiping?

Chatting is more casual in nature, and usually does not have an intent underlying it. Topics range from the weather to politics, when two or more people are chatting. The moment a conversation turns towards other people, their characteristics, personalities, behaviours, and the goings on in their lives, it can no longer be labelled as casual chatting. It becomes gossip. While a lot of gossip is quite harmless at least, to begin with, sometimes gossip may turn malicious and have a negative effect on the people who are being spoken of.

6. Who do you prefer chatting with — your parents, or your friends?

I enjoy chatting with both, my parents and my friends. The two, in my opinion, cannot be compared. When I talk to my parents we chat about different kinds of things than when I sit to talk with friends. The nature and tone of conversation is different with parents and friends, and at times the topics we discuss also differ. When I wasn't serious advice regarding my life path, I prefer to have a chat with my parents. But, if I want to chat casually, I prefer doing so with friends.

7. Do most people have just a small number of friends, or many friends?
This is a very individual thing. It differs from person to person. Some people prefer to keep their circles close, and like having a few close friends. Other like to hang out in large groups, with people who may or may not be very close friends. The first category is usually made up of introverts, while the second is made up of extroverts. There is a third category who are a bit of both. Sometimes they can be seen partying with big groups, while at other times they prefer staying in with just a couple of close friends.

8. How do most people make new friends in your country?
Most people in my country make friends in school or college, by introducing themselves in the course of their studies. After college, people in my country make friends in the workplace by breaking the ice with colleagues. Some people are involved in hobbies in their leisure time, and they make friends with similar hobbies if they happen to meet such people. A lot of elderly people tend to meet each other in gardens and parks when they go for walks. They make friends with each other there, over a period of time. Often friends of spouses also become friends.

9. Do you think people's abilities or intelligence is a factor, when they become friends?
I don't think people's abilities or intelligence is a factor when they become friends. Most people tend to be quite large hearted when it comes to selecting friends. They usually overlook each other's abilities, intelligence, or the lack thereof, and instead focus on how much fun it is to be with one another, or how true and genuine the other is, in the friendship. Abilities and intelligence are factors to check when hiring a person or partnering with them for work. A relationship as pure as friendship should not be tainted by such calculative assessments.

10. What qualities do you think a good friend should have?
A good friend should be honest, trustworthy, non-judgmental, encouraging, supportive, and good to talk to. He should be at a similar wavelength to ours, and we should enjoy doing some similar things together on and off. A good friend should be positive towards us, and should enrich our lives by his presence.

11. Do you think it's possible to determine how sincere a person is, the first time you meet him?
In my opinion, it is next to impossible to determine how sincere a person is, the first time we meet him. In some rare cases we may come to know if someone is an absolute crook, or is involved in underhand dealings and dishonest manipulations. But, this is rare. Most of the time, in order to gauge how sincere a person is, we need to know them closely, and also need to see them react to different situations in life. I've often heard people say that an entire lifetime is not enough to truly know a person. A first meeting would hardly suffice.

151. Describe a time someone or something made noise.
   You should say

- When this happened
- Who this person was/What this thing was
- What kind of noise you heard

What did you do when you heard the noise?

Here, I'm going to detail an incident that happened recently. I live in a multi-storeyed high rise apartment in a generally quiet locale, with my family. Because I work six days a week, the only day I get to really wind down and relax is Sunday. Just next to my apartment is a large empty plot that is often rented out for parties and celebrations. In India, as you may know already, decibel levels tend to go out of control when people celebrate. Celebrations in this adjoining plot, too, are as loud as they are colourful. They often involve the use of very loud firecrackers, and there is usually a DJ involved, trying to make his music heard to the entire block.

Very recently, someone decided to celebrate their wedding in that very plot, on a Sunday afternoon. The voices of people talking to each other, and little children playing had already begun to make their way up to my eighth floor flat. I decided to ignore the chatter and go to bed. Just as I had shut my eyes for a peaceful nap, the DJ came onto the scene, and loud music started blaring through mediocre quality speakers. Echoing against all the buildings in the vicinity, it made its way into my dreams and woke me up with a start! To say the least, the experience wasn't pleasant, and I felt quite irritated. However, from experience, I knew that going and fighting with the organisers was going to get me nowhere. I calmed myself down, and made a polite but stern phone call to the plot managers, requesting them to turn down the volume. Fortunately, they obliged, and in a few minutes, I was able to retire back to enjoy my afternoon siesta.

Follow ups:
1. Is noise pollution serious in India?
Yes, noise pollution is a serious issue in India. The population here is very high, and by consequence, in most areas the population density is also quite high. People here tend to talk at loud volumes, in general, and also frequently celebrate occasions and events with blaring music and loud fire crackers. Further, the number of vehicles are increasing each day, and everyone is quite horn happy here. This has led to noise pollution becoming a problem here.

2. Do you like to live in a noisy place?
I prefer to live in quiet, serene places that offer a lot of privacy and tranquillity. Noisy places disturb my peace of mind, and noises interfere with my thoughts. If I stay in a noisy place for long, I tend to become moody and irritable.

3. Do you like to go to noisy places?
I like to go to noisy places only if they are parties of people I am close to, concerts of bands and musicians that I like, or wedding of close relatives. Sometimes, I like visiting noisy festive celebrations, as well. However, on a regular basis, I stay away from noisy places.

4. Where can you hear loud noises?
Loud noises can be heard in many places. They can be heard when people blow loud horns on the streets of my city. They can be heard when there is a marriage procession, or

a political campaign procession going on. Loud noises can frequently be heard in public transport and in planes, when little children decide to howl and cry; in addition, they can be heard during festivals like Diwali, during thunderstorms, and during other natural calamities.

5. Do you think there is more noise in people's lives today than there was in the past?

Yes there is much more noise in people's lives today than there was in the past. First of all, in the past we did not have speakers that were able to sound music at such high decibels. Manually played acoustics in weddings were most definitely not capable of creating as much of a ruckus. Secondly, there were fewer vehicles on the streets, leading to lesser engine sounds, and lesser honking.

6. Do you think that cities will become noisier in the future?

Today people have slowly become desensitised to loud noises, and hence more tolerant. No one makes noise complaints, and hence the situation has gone from bad to worse, making our lives noisier than they used to be before.

If things continue to be this way, cities will very likely become noisier in the future.

7. Do you like to go to places where there are many people?

While I am more than comfortable in crowded places, or places where there are many people, it is certainly not a conscious choice that I would make. I prefer quieter, more tranquil places with fewer, but like-minded people. It would be even more preferable if I already know most of the people present anywhere. In general, I do not like frequenting places where there are many people, because such situations usually do not add anything of value to my life.

8. What would you do if your neighbours were noisy all the time?

If my neighbours were noisy all the time, I would politely request them to be mindful of the noise they were making. Hopefully, that would work. In case that doesn't work, each time they disturb me with their noise, I would either make a phone call to them to turn it down a few notches, or I would knock on their doors to request the same thing. This constant polite nagging on my part would eventually make them realise that they were truly disturbing me, and they'd lower their noise levels.

152. Describe a law about the environment you would like to see in the future.

   You should say
-   **What this law would be**
-   **How this law would take effect**
-   **What changes this law would bring about**

Why do you think this law is important?

There is a pressing need today, for each individual to do his bit to preserve the environment around him. While one person cannot make a major change all at once, if many individuals take small steps collectively, it can lead to a positive change in the condition of the environment. The need of the hour is to make sure that future generations have clean air to breathe. With the increasing number of vehicles all over the world, the carbon emissions on our streets have increased tremendously. The more fuel we consume, the more our carbon footprint increases. High carbon emissions cause the greenhouse effect, wherein the mean temperature of our surroundings keeps increasing, thanks to the capacity of carbon compounds to hold heat. In a country like India, which is already quite densely populated, and faces scorching heats for most part of the year, it is essential we do something drastic to lower the levels of air pollution. Many places in Europe have integrated electric cars into their transport system, with both, the government, as well as private citizens purchasing and using these vehicles. Electric cars do not consume petroleum products, thereby giving out close to zero emissions. The car runs entirely on battery, and the battery need only be charged by plugging the vehicle into an electric socket. What's more, these cars don't take too long to charge, and then they run for miles on end without their battery dying out. I think India should enforce a law which makes it compulsory for people to buy only electric cars after a certain date. Gradually gas stations can be replaced by charging booths, and over time we would completely get rid of fuel-operated cars. This would bring about a noticeable difference in the quality of air we breathe, thereby improving our health, and increasing the overall life expectancy of people. This law is very important because if we don't make a change in our fuel consumption patterns today, our future generations will be left with a polluted, unhealthy planet. As the Native American quote goes, 'We do not inherit the earth from our ancestors, we borrow it from our children'. Each generation owes it to the next to hand over the planet in a better state than they found it.

Follow-up Questions & Answers:
1. Why do schools make rules?
Schools make rules to instil a sense of responsibility and discipline in students. Some rules regarding codes of conduct, manners, and accountability for one's actions are necessary in order to shape children into good future citizens. In the long run, children who learn necessary codes of conduct through school rules become good adults, and shape the country well.
2. What's the importance of obeying laws?
Laws are kept in place in any region, to ensure the safety and security of all residents. Laws help maintain the physical, mental, and emotional wellbeing of citizens of an area. The purpose of laws is to ensure that neither the strong, nor the feeble face any injustice in any sphere of life. They are the foundation of civilised society; civilisation is what differentiates humans from animals. Obeying laws ensures that the structure of civilised society remains in place, and everyone gets to live life to their fullest potential without feeling threatened directly or indirectly.
3. What can parents and teachers do to help children follow rules?
Parents and teachers can explain to children the reasons behind why there are certain rules in place for certain things. Children are curious by nature, so if a set of rules is enforced on them without proper explanations, they are likely to feel the urge to go against the grain and explore the consequences of rule breaking. Parents and teachers can take the help of stories with morals, and anecdotes from life to explain the importance of following rules, and what happens when rules are broken.
4. Is it a good thing to break rules sometimes?

One must always use one's own inner compass when faced with any rule in life. No rule should be followed blindly without understanding why it has been put I place, and what the consequences of obeying it are. If a majority of any population starts following rules blindly, without questioning them, a nation can slowly end up encouraging dictatorship. There have been rules in the past in colonised nations, as well as in free ones, which were quite unfair to certain sects of society. Had these rules not been broken, we would not have progressed as a species. If rules begin to oppress people instead of uplifting them, then it may be a good thing to break those rules.

5. Why do some people say that rules are made to be broken?

Some people are rebels at heart. This is just another human personality trait. Such people tend to constantly want to go against the grain and do something different. They are always curious to explore the consequences of rule breaking. Some even enjoy the thrill of going against the law. Then again, there are many who genuinely feel unhappy about the rules that bind them, for various reasons. Over time they develop the mind-set that rules are meant to be broken. Most of the time, however, rebels say this statement simply to seek attention from others.

6. Do you think children should follow all kinds of rules?

Children should not follow all kinds of rules. If the rules set in place for children do not agree with their personal sense of righteousness or correctness, they must reject those rules fearlessly. If a certain rule is causing pain, harm, or injustice to anyone, and a child does not agree with the effects of the rule, he must not follow it.

7. Do you think it is necessary for children to wear school uniforms?

This is a debatable question. Wearing school uniforms is important in my opinion, because I think being dressed the same way fosters a strong bond of friendship, equality, and unity among students. When children are dressed the same way, comparisons based on socioeconomic differences do not start taking place in their minds at a young age. This keeps their innocence and sense of respect for each other alive, through the course of their academics, thereby helping them make genuine friends based on personality traits, and not on the basis of similarities in lifestyles.

◆ ◆ ◆

153. Describe a long walk you went on.

You should say
- **When this happened**
- **Where you walked**
- **Who you were with**

How do you feel when you remember the walk?

About four years ago, I was travelling through the United States with my family. It was essentially a leisure trip mixed with a little bit of business here and there. In the course of my month long trip through the US, I had decided to make a stop in Florida. A childhood friend of mine had moved to America when we were in college, and had eventually settled in Miami Beach. It had been many years since I had seen him, and even though we used to stay in touch through emails and social media exchanges, there was a lot we needed to catch up on. When I finally reached his home in the afternoon, both of us were ecstatic at the reunion. After some refreshments at his home, while our families spent time relaxing, we decided to head out for a long walk by the beach. By the time we reached the sandy sea shore, the sun had turned orange and begun to start its descent into the beautiful blue Atlantic. The sound of gentle waves caressing the shoreline was most relaxing to my tired mind. My friend and I kept walking, staring at the horizon, enjoying the salty sea breeze on our faces, as we spoke of everything under the sun, starting from the day he'd left my city to move to the US. It was indeed a nostalgic walk down memory lane, and in the course of just a few hours, we had told each other everything of importance that had happened in our lives till then. We laughed about how our appearances had changed over time, he asked me what our old city was like, and we reminisced about our old haunts in India. Both of us were so engrossed in our discussion, we didn't even realise when evening turned to night. Physically we had walked just a few miles that day, but mentally we had travelled back and forth in time. The journey took its toll on us, and smiling, we sat on the soft sands with chilled cans of soda in our hands. The silence between us was as comfortable as it used to be when we were back in college, and I when I look back on the walk now, I realise that no matter how far we go in life, or how many new people we meet, some things remain the same.

Follow-ups

1. What are the most popular outdoor sports in India?

The most popular outdoor sports in India are cricket, football, hockey, and kabaddi. Indians these days have once again started taking interest in horse riding, which used to be a sport of the royals in the medieval times. Youngsters in India have started taking high altitude trekking very seriously, too.

2. Why do some people dislike walking?

People have become very used to reaching from one point to another very fast, using cars, bikes, or public transport vehicles. Lifestyles have become faster, and in the race to constantly outdo others and reach their destinations, most people have forgotten the value of the journey. Walking is all about deriving joy from the journey, with or without a specific destination in sight. It requires a slightly meditative bent of mind to enjoy walking. Since some people lack this, they dislike walking.

3. Who is walking more suitable for?

Walking is a suitable activity for anyone who can walk unaided on his own two feet. Walking does not require any extra equipment, nor does it consume too much of the walker's energy. It is not very tiring, yet is a very good cardio exercise. Walking improves blood circulation, too. All these reasons make it universally suitable.

4. Do Indian people like to play indoor sports or outdoor sports?

India is a very large country with a very large population made up of diverse people of different castes, cultures, communities, ages, genders, and economic levels. Everyone has individual tastes and distastes, likes and dislikes. What is convenient to one, may be inconvenient to another. So, it cannot be specified whether Indians like to play indoor sports or outdoor sports. Different Indians like to play different kinds of sports, depending on their childhood conditioning, the availability of equipment, terrain, and guidance where they live, and their personal preferences.

5. What are the benefits of playing outdoor games, for children?

Childhood is the phase of highest physical and mental growth and development in humans. In these ages, if one plays outdoor games, they tend to provide the necessary exercise and movement to their bodies, thereby aiding their own growth and development. Playing outdoor games helps children stay fit and healthy, regulates their metabolism, increases their hand-eye coordination, teaches them the importance of team play, and enhances their concentration capacity by improving blood circulation to the brain.

6. Would you say your hometown is a suitable place for walking?

Unfortunately, my hometown is not very suitable for walking. There are hardly any footpaths and walkways in my city, and the ones that are there are either broken in parts, or are used by people to park their private vehicles. Furthermore, people drive quite rashly on the main roads, making it quite unsafe to walk there. However, there are a few specific places such as the Riverfront and gardens developed by the government, where people can go for walks.

7. Did you like walking when you were a child?

I always enjoyed walking, even when I was a child. Back then, the traffic in my city was much lesser, so it used to be quite safe for walkers to venture out. I used to often run errands for my mother, by walking to the nearby grocery and other stores to fetch things for the home. Often when I wanted to meet friends who lived just a few blocks away, I would walk down to their homes. A private tutor of mine also lived close to home, and I quite enjoyed my walk to his classes.

8. In the future do you think you'll continue to enjoy walking or would you prefer some form of transportation?

In future, unless the city's streets become highly conducive for walking, I don't think I can continue to enjoy walking on a regular basis. Further, my workplace is far from my home, so it would hardly be feasible to walk down there. Keeping these practical considerations in mind, I would prefer alternate forms of transportation to walking.

9. What do you think are the benefits of walking?

Walking improves blood circulation in the body, it increases our intake of oxygen, thereby enriching our cellular system, and it keeps us fit. Walking regularly ensures that we don't put on unwanted kilos. It keeps our minds active, helps rid us of lethargy and fatigue, and is also a very good way to prevent and cure depression. Walking in the morning is invigorating and energising, and walking in the evening is relaxing and rejuvenating.

◆ ◆ ◆

154. Describe a person whose job is important to the society.

OR

155. Describe a person who does an important job in your opinion.

156. Describe a person whose job is important to the society.

You should say

- Who this person is
- What job this person does
- How you know this person

Why is their job important to society?

Here, I would like to speak about not just one person, but many people of the same profession who have all played an important role in my life and helped shape me into the person I am today. These people are the teachers who have taught me different things through life, both in school, and in college. Teachers do the important job of teaching subjects of their expertise to students. At the primary level in school, one teacher manages to teach lots of different subjects to a large classroom full of children. This in itself is a difficult task, as each class has many different individuals with different personalities and unique learning requirements. Students also have very different levels of comprehension and attention. A teacher manages to teach different things to all these individuals simultaneously, making sure none of them is lagging behind or feeling left out. A teacher teaches manners and life skills to students, too. In higher levels of education, different teachers teach different subjects to students, in tandem with one another. They keep an eye on students' activities inside the classroom and outside, and where necessary they guide students to become better human beings. If they notice a student going the wrong way in life, or making the wrong decisions, they act as counsellors and gently bring the student back on the right track. They ensure that students get along with each other, in order to keep the classroom environment conducive to learning. They motivate students to excel at subjects they are already good at, and support them to try harder when it comes to subjects they are weak at. Teachers answer crucial questions that cloud the minds of students at various stages in their school and college lives.

Teachers lay the foundation for a successful, progressive, tolerant nation, by educating future generations to turn them into civic, caring, sensitive, considerate, and ambitious individuals. Teachers are responsible for instilling moral and ethical values in students, who then go on to grow up into law abiding citizens. Education is the basic requirement for a nation to become developed. Education nurtures creativity and encourages innovation. It emphasises the importance of peace and tolerance, thereby making a society safe for its residents. Because teachers provide education, their job is of much importance to society. Unfortunately, in India, teachers are often unappreciated and underpaid.

Follow ups:

1. What jobs are well paid in India?

Jobs in the field of medicine and management are well paid in India in general. Jobs involving front facing, like the ones available in the hospitality industry, also pay well.

2. What jobs are poorly paid in your country?

Skill based jobs, public service jobs, teaching jobs, engineering jobs, and clerical jobs are some examples of jobs that are poorly paid in my country.

3. Do people with different levels of income feel happy about how much they earn?

That depends on an individual's personal requirements with respect to his earnings. If one has fewer requirements in comparison to the income they earn they may be very happy. However, if someone earns a lot, but still his earnings aren't enough to meet his expenses, he may not be happy. Further, there are some people who are never satisfied, and keep trying to earn and accumulate more money. On the other hand, I have also come across saints and sages who hardly have enough to get by in life, and yet are completely satisfied.

4. Do you think students who have just graduated should have the same income as old people?

Income, in my opinion, should depend more on skill and contribution than on experience alone. Experience in a field is only of any value if that experience enables a person to offer more to his field of work than others who are less experienced. If experience is blindly rewarded, it encourages complacency in the older generations and discouragement to the newer generations. Instead people should earn based on their contributions, irrespective of how long they have been working somewhere.

5. What should schools do to help students survive well in society?

Instead of only concentrating on imparting bookish knowledge to students, schools should concentrate on teaching life skills to students. Most of us step out of schools with no knowledge of banking, taxation, manoeuvring a vehicle, growing our own food, lighting a fire, cooking, woodwork, plumbing, or electrical work. Funnily, many of us don't even know how to change a bulb or car tyre. Schools should ensure that students learn such life skills, and more, by the time they complete their school education. Further, schools should teach negotiation skills, public speaking and oration, networking, and convincing skills to students to help them survive well in society.

6. Why do people sometimes get bored of their job?

Some people tend to have lower boredom thresholds than other. Creative people often have changeable minds that constantly require new stimulation to remain interested in their job. At times, jobs do not offer employees scope for mental growth or any new learning. In such cases, those who are not of a clerical bent of mind sometimes get bored of their job.

7. What do you think employers are supervisors can do to help motivate their employees to perform better at work, besides giving them a pay raise?

Employers and supervisors can give incentives other than money and pay hikes to their employees, to motivate them. At times things like prepaid family holidays help to retain and encourage overworked employees to perform better at work. Appreciation and acknowledgement go a long way in motivating employees to work harder, as they feel important and necessary for the business when they are appreciated. Often a promotion in terms of job designation can motivate employees, as well.

8. If someone is bored of their job, is it easy for them to change to a different job?

If someone is bored of their job, it may or may not be easy for them to change jobs, depending on what their situation in life is, what their educational qualifications are, and what skill sets they possess. Highly skilled, well qualified people tend to be able to change jobs with ease. Those with sufficient life savings also feel more empowered to quit

---

a job and change workplaces, because they have a reserve fund to rely on, if the job change doesn't work out well for them. Willingness to adjust to different roles, and higher adaptability in general, also make job change easy.

9. Do you think it's good to change jobs frequently?

In my opinion it is not good to change jobs frequently, as every change of workplace causes temporary displacement and instability, until a person has settled down in the new job. A lot of times people tend to form part of their identity based on the work they do, and the company they belong to. Frequent job changes thus create an identity crisis, because those who do not stay in one place for long do not feel like they belong anywhere. When a person has changed too many jobs, employers feel wary of hiring them, because attrition is a big problem in organisations.

◆ ◆ ◆

157. Describe an article about healthy living that you read from a magazine or from the internet.

You should say

- In which magazine/on which website you read it
- Who the article was written by
- What the article was about

Why did you like the article?

I read a lot of articles online, as well as in magazines, in my free time. At office, when I want a small break from my routine tasks, I often resort to articles on healthy living, wellness, and self-help. Such articles inspire me to be more health conscious and to improve the quality of my life. One author whose articles I particularly enjoy is Paul McKenna. This international bestselling author is a renowned hypnotherapist, who has also been recognised as one of the world's most important modern self-help gurus by The Times of London. While I have read a lot of Paul McKenna's book excerpts, the one I remember most is his write up on becoming thin without consciously dieting. He said that often people's diets failed, not because of the things they ate, but because of the things they thought. In this particular write up, the author showed ways to reduce weight in a healthy manner, without resorting to calorie counting or low fat recipes. In fact he said nothing whatsoever about what to eat and what not to eat. Instead he detailed methods to lose weight through healthy self-talk, by encouraging readers to bring about a transformation in the way they think. Further, Paul McKenna mentioned various negative patterns that people followed in life, such as obsessive dieting, emotional eating, faulty mental programming, not eating when one is hungry, not eating what one wants to, not eating consciously, and not being sensitive to the limitations of one's appetite. He gave pointers to overcome these negative patterns, in order to bring oneself closer to one's ideal weight. I read this article in an online newspaper, whose name has slipped out of my mind. However, McKenna's articles are easy to find online, and his books are available in stores everywhere. I liked this article for many reasons, but mostly because

---

all the things mentioned in it resonate with my idea of health and wellbeing. I cannot help but notice that the article has no logical fallacies, even though the author does not detail anything quantitatively. Often such self-help articles run the risk of becoming too abstract, but this article does not fall into that trap. It is helpful, concise, and worth a read.

Follow ups:
1. Why do magazines have health related articles?
These days, people are becoming very conscious about their health, and with increasing life spans, everyone wants to ensure that they are able to make the most of their bodies till the end of their time. This has led many people to scout for articles, books, and other media that provide information on healthcare and wellness. To cater to this segment of health conscious readers, magazines have started publishing health related articles.

2. What do Indian people do to keep fit?
Indian people generally go on walks to stay fit. Many Indians cycle, jog, and even go on frequent hiking trips to achieve their fitness goals. The growing number of gyms in every corner of the city has urged many people to get gym memberships and to make physical exercise an integral part of their lives. Yoga, which has originated in India, of course, is very popular among Indians, as a method to keep fit. Furthermore, many Indians follow a vegetarian diet, which keeps levels of toxins in the body low.

3. Do you play any sports?
I like to play different sports in my leisure time. I am fond of cricket, football, volleyball, and even tennis. Usually I only get the time to play sports when I am travelling with friends and relatives during my holidays, or when I visit the local recreation club. However, during my school and college days I used to play these sports regularly.

4. Do you think children should learn how to live healthily?
Children should definitely learn how to live healthily, because when healthy habits are inculcated during the early years of life, they tend to become lifestyle patterns which prove to be quite rewarding in future. Children who learn how to live healthily can also encourage elders in their families to adopt healthier lifestyles, thereby creating wellbeing around them.

5. How do people in India get information about healthcare?
People in India read lots of magazines, and online articles all the time. With the advent of free messaging services, people these days send lots of tips and pointers on the latest trends in healthcare to their kith and kin. Further, word of mouth has always been a very effective communication tool in India. Elderly people who do not use gadgets and are not net savvy tend to derive their information regarding healthcare through this channel.

6. Are there any negative influences of health related information?
Usually health related information does not pose negative influences; on the contrary it raises awareness regarding healthcare and wellness among people. However, at times, because of easy access to free messaging services and the internet, many quacks and self-confessed health experts spread rumours regarding healthcare. Such false information can prove lethal at times. Another negative effect is that people resort to self-diagnosis and run the risk of medicating themselves incorrectly, or even overdosing.

7. Do you think sports can help people improve their health?
Sports can definitely help people improve their health, in my opinion. Sports provide

much needed cardio activity to players, improve their respiratory systems, increase lung strength, enhance heart health, and regulate metabolism, if played routinely.

8. How to maintain a healthy diet?
A healthy diet constitutes of a balanced intake of nutrients through the food we eat. Eating healthy involves reducing or completely cutting out the intake of over-processed food and junk food, while increasing the intake of good fats, complex carbohydrates, and leafy vegetables. Being conscious of what we put in our mouth every time we are hungry, and satisfying cravings with healthy meal options helps maintain a healthy diet pattern.

9. Do most young Indians have a healthy lifestyle?
I would not go so far as to say that most young Indians have a healthy lifestyle, because in my opinion a lot of youngsters are eating all the wrong kinds of food, very frequently. Eating out has increased manifold as compared to just a decade ago; and with eating out, come the negative effects of poor quality ingredients and unhealthy saturated fats. However, many youngsters today consciously get more physical exercise than those of previous generations, by frequenting gyms and exercising at home.

10. What kinds of things are unhealthy for people to eat?
Processed food, junk food, food that is low in fibre, high in simple carbohydrates, and food that is devoid of nutrients is unhealthy for people to eat. Further, food options with empty calories, such as sodas, candies, and packaged juices, are very unhealthy. These tend to be very high on sugar, which is a leading cause of obesity.

158. Describe a place you visited that has been affected by pollution.

   You should say
-   **Where it is**
-   **When you visited this place**
-   **What kind of pollution you saw there**
How has pollution affected this place?

While there are many highly polluted places all over the world, including in India, in my opinion, nothing causes as much pollution as a landfill. Landfills are especially common to find in the outskirts of large cities, which produce more waste than the environment within can decompose in a timely manner. In order to facilitate survival within the city, municipal corporations look for empty lands outside of city limits, to dump waste. Each day, landfills on the peripheries of large cities in India, gather thousands of tonnes or garbage, far exceeding their actual capacity. Here, I would like to talk about the Bhalswa landfill, which is very close to Delhi. On a business trip to the capital, I happened to pass by this massive mountain of a dump yard, when my taxi driver drove past it. A stench like none that I had ever smelled before filled my nostrils through the vents of my cars air conditioner, even though all the windows were turned up. A smoky haze was visible over the giant mountain of garbage, increasing the overall temperature of the area by a significant few degrees. These toxic gases were gradually making their way into the atmosphere of Delhi on a daily basis, and I couldn't help but think of the long term effects of inhaling such air. I visited the area a few years ago, but from what I hear, today the situation is much worse. The landfill is a constant inferno, and the smallest hint of a spark causes garbage to incinerate, releasing methane and similar compounds into the air. The government has not yet put in place a system to capture and use these biogases as fuel. So, those living nearby constantly have to inhale the toxic fumes from the landfill, reducing their lifespans considerably. This landfill is proving terribly hazardous for pregnant women and new born babies; residents cannot think of opening their doors and windows, and playing outside is not an option for school children in the vicinity.

Follow ups:
1. What kinds of pollution are serious in your country?
All kinds of pollution are equally harmful to human, animal, and plant life. My country suffers from high levels of soil, water, and noise pollution, but the most serious kind of pollution in my country, according to me is air pollution. While soil and water can still be treated in a somewhat timely manner, air pollution is almost impossible to treat. Unlike using some patches of land or drinking from some water bodies, breathing is not an optional activity, making air pollution the most serious kind of pollution in my country.
2. What can individuals do to protect the environment?
At an individual level, we can reduce our consumption of plastics, paper, and electricity. We can practice healthy recycling habits, and learn about the correct methods of dumping garbage. If each individual takes care of these factors, we can bring about a significant improvement in the environment.
3. Do you think individuals should take the responsibility for pollution prevention?
Individuals should be held accountable for the levels of pollution in their vicinity, be it where they live or where they work. Individuals should protest the disposal of untreated industrial waste, reduce the use of private transport, and switch to using alternate sources of energy wherever possible.
4. Why is there a need to involve the government in environmental protection?
While individuals can take small steps at their own level, and even protest against the disposal of untreated industrial waste in their areas, eventually it is up to government authorities such as pollution control boards of respective regions, to actually clamp down on activities that cause a lot of pollution and endanger various life forms. So, beyond a point, it becomes necessary to involve the government in activities regarding environmental protection.

159. Describe the first time that you used a foreign language to communicate.

OR

160. Describe the first time you spoke to someone in a foreign language.

OR

161. Talk about an instance when you spoke with someone in a foreign language for the first time.

You should say
- **Where it happened**
- **When it happened**
- **Who you talked to**

How did you feel about the conversation?

A few years ago, I went on a holiday with my family, to Europe. Seeing as it was a Euro trip, France was definitely one of our stops. Back in those days, it was a well-known fact that the French were not well-versed with English. The tour operator who had helped us plan our itinerary had explained this to us in detail, with elaborate anecdotes about people who went to France and had a tough time even asking for a cup of coffee. He knew that we were going to be travelling without a tour guide, and so we'd need to ask directions while walking around, we'd need to ask for vegetarian food options, and many other basics. He even warned us that the French were not a very patient lot. So, while I was quite excited about the trip, I realised that learning basic French before going there would be quite important. The next day I bought a Basic French phrase book, and started practicing from it.

When we finally went to France, I was waiting for an opportunity to put my new linguistic skills to use. While the airport staff was quite good at English, the moment we stepped out and decided to hire a taxi, I got my chance. The cabbie that we had hailed looked at us blankly for a while, and then mumbled something in French. I couldn't catch a word of what he said, but undeterred, I told him where we needed to go in slow but sure French. I could see he was quite impressed because he was half expecting me to stammer and stutter. Once he saw me try to speak in his language, he immediately shifted to English, and to my surprise he spoke it quite fluently. He turned out quite friendly, and informed us that the locals there usually didn't speak in English with tourists unless they saw tourists making an effort to speak in French, first. He taught me a few more French phrases to help me during my stay over there, and also showed us some good food joints near our hotel.

I felt quite proud of myself for having successfully communicated in a new language with a native speaker of that tongue. I also felt happy that it helped us, and my confidence remained high through the rest of our holidays.

Follow ups:
1. What is your opinion on the need for children to learn a foreign language?
I think it is important that children learn at least one foreign language. A language carries the values and norms of the culture it belongs to. So, in my opinion, learning a new language expands one's scope, increases one's potential to achieve success, and broadens one's horizons. Children who learn a foreign language become more accepting of different cultures and opinions, and they become less likely to discriminate and hold prejudices. Tolerant children make tolerant adults, and this in turn makes a more tolerant, open, and accepting society.

2. Why are some language classes boring?
Language learning is not always easy, because different languages have different rules. Some languages are based more on phonetics, while some less. Then there are some

---

languages that use the Latin script, and some which have scripts of their own. When a language class is teaching a language that has very new sounds, scripts, and grammar rules, it becomes too much for the learners' minds to take in all at once. In response to this overload, the learner often feels sleepy and bored.

3. Some students hate to learn foreign languages. What can teachers do to develop their interest?

Teachers can introduce lots of fun activities in the class as tools to teach new foreign languages. An effective way to create interest in a language is to go to its cultural roots, and make learning about them a part of the class. Teachers can regularly give information about the country of origin of the language while teaching it to the class, they can speak about the country's history, its highlights, its attractions, and its culture to generate interest in class. E.g. many French teachers talk about French wines and cheeses in class. They also teach vocabulary with the help of French comic books, which ensures that students remain interested.

4. Some people travel to learn a foreign language. Do you think this is a good reason to travel?

Yes, I think this is a good reason to travel. In fact, almost any reason to travel is good, because travelling enriches people's lives and brings the world closer together. Those who travel to learn a foreign language, travel with an open mind. This receptivity helps them learn many things from their touring and wandering, apart from the foreign language itself.

5. What's the best way to learn a foreign language?

The best way to learn a foreign language is to converse in it, listen to audio recordings of that language before sleeping, watch movies in that language, and attempt to think in that language. This approach ensures that our senses and mind remain engaged in the new language for a major portion of our day. Extended exposure to a foreign language helps to pick it up fast.

6. Why can some people learn languages fast, white others learn slowly?

Different people's brains are wired differently, and hence they have different aptitudes. Some people have a higher numerical aptitude, while others are savvier with spatial skills. Likewise, there is a category of people who have high linguistic aptitude. Those with linguistic leanings learn languages faster than others because they are hardwired to grasp new sounds and associate meanings with them. Language is instinctive to humans, so those who are more attentive in general, also tend to learn new languages faster than others.

7. Does age affect a person's language learning abilities?

In my opinion age does not affect a person's language learning abilities. But, age can affect a person's attention span. Primary school children tend to have longer attention spans than adults because they are accustomed to listening to teachers addressing them in class for prolonged spans of time. Adults, on the other hand tend to get bored of concentrating on one thing for long, because their minds are more preoccupied with other thoughts and tasks, and because they have become unused to paying attention to just one person or thing for long.

162. Describe a person you know that has made a contribution to society.

You should say

- **Who this person is**
- **How you know this person**
- **What kind of contribution this person has made**

How do you feel about this person's contributions to the society?

There are many people who have come and gone, walked this planet and left their mark behind, by the number of lives they have touched. One such person is Mother Teresa. Born in 1910 in modern day Republic of Macedonia as Anjeze, Mother Teresa lived in her birthplace for 18 years, before moving to Ireland and India. She spent most of her life in India and passed away in 1997, in Kolkata, West Bengal. Mother Teresa was a Roman Catholic nun, and is most famous for founding the Missionaries of Charity, a Catholic religious congregation. This organisation is active in more than a hundred countries, and is well known for establishing and running homes for those suffering from leprosy, tuberculosis, and AIDS. Further it runs many orphanages and schools for the poor. Mother Teresa touched many lives during her lifetime, and was much loved and revered by those she helped and those who had the privilege of seeing her work with fervour for the needy. She fearlessly ventured into places where people feared to tread, and mixed with people who were treated as outcastes by society in general. Her unconditional love for every living being urged her to improve the lives of the needy, and eventually after her death she was given sainthood. Many international governments honoured her for her work even while she was alive, and India, too, felicitated her with the Padma Shri. I came to know of Mother Teresa and her contribution to society during my school years, because excerpts of her life story were taught to us as part of our curriculum. Later, as I grew up, I kept reading about her from time to time in newspapers and online. I feel very humbled that a lady from another nation came and selflessly gave a major part of her life force and time, to the betterment of my countrymen. I feel inspired by her drive to help people even in the face of insurmountable odds, and her stories motivate me to never lose hope in life.

Follow ups:

1. How can one be a good member of the society?

There are many ways in which one can be a good member of the society. In my opinion, if we take care of the overall wellbeing of all the citizens in society, be mindful not to damage the shared property of society, respect the beliefs and values of all the members, and treat everyone the way we would like to be treated, we can be good members of the society.

2. What kinds of jobs are well paid in your country?

Jobs in the fields of medicine and healthcare, beauty and cosmetic services, BPOs and KPOs, computer programming and robotics, and the hospitality, as well as the entertainment industry are well paying in my country today.

3. How do university students make their career plans in your country?

In my country, university students research the various available career options in the regions they are willing to work in, based on their interests, qualification, and skill sets. After narrowing down some options, they consult trusted family members, relatives, and friends to decide on their career path. Often professors at college also guide students in career planning.

4. What kinds of jobs will deserve higher salaries in future?

In my opinion, jobs that require large amounts of travelling, and seek long work hours from employees will deserve higher salaries. Further, jobs that require highly specialised skills, such as arts, computer programming, robotics, microsurgery, and complex sciences, will deserve higher salaries in future.

5. Does university education help students to find good jobs in your country?

University education most definitely helps students to find good jobs in my country. These days a large number of students are opting to get their degrees from good universities, and after competing under-graduation, they are also pursuing specialised post-graduation courses, to increase their employability.

6. Do people like to talk about their salaries with their friends in your country?

Most people in India are open to the idea of discussing their salaries and income bands with their friends. While it is a private and sensitive topic in most cultures, it is quite normal to discuss such things with friends where I come from. However, with the influence of western culture and etiquette, many youngsters are averse to discussing salaries and earnings with their friends.

163. Describe one time when the weather changed your plan.

  You should say
- **When this happened**
- **What plans you had to cancel**
- **What kind of weather you experienced**

What did you do instead, after the weather made you change your plan?

There have been many instances in my life when I have had to change my plans because of the weather. Where I live, sudden weather changes don't usually happen, but in some months we randomly get a few days of clear skies and a few days of thunderstorms and rains. One such instance I would like to discuss here is a time from many years ago. It was the last day of college, before Diwali. During Diwali we used to get a long 10 day break from classes. So, most of us would usually go out of town with our families. However, my friends and I had planned to leave for our vacations after a day or two. So, on the day before Diwali breaks begun, we made plans to visit a nearby bird sanctuary, called Thol. This sanctuary is located about an hour away from the city by car. One of my friends had a jeep large enough to fit all seven of us. We had arrived at college that morning all prepped up to bunk the last lecture. Our picnic baskets were packed and waiting in the back of his jeep, and we were getting restless through the entire day. Early in the morning, the weather had seemed perfect for such an outing. However, by the time we decided to make a move, the skies became overcast. We ignored this slight alteration in weather and continued on our journey. About fifteen minutes after we had hit the road, however, it started drizzling, then raining a little fast, and then pouring cats and dogs. There was no point driving all the way to Thol in such weather. Further, it was not even safe.

But, instead of feeling upset, we simply parked the car, got off, and let the rains drench us to the bone. Such showers have always been welcomed by people in my city, even if they are unseasonal, because most of the year, the city stays very hot. We were no exception to the rule. In a few minutes hawkers selling freshly roasted corn and deep fried lentil fritters started crowding the sidewalks, as was the norm. My friend and I queued up and helped ourselves to the classic monsoon munchies, while still getting wet in the rains. After spending a few hours in the rains, my friend dropped us all home, and tired yet satisfied, we called it a day.

Follow ups:
1. Where can people get weather reports from?
People can get weather reports from daily newspapers, the television, and the internet. These days, people often get up to date weather reports from mobile weather apps, too.
2. How do weather reports affect people's lives?
Weather reports help people plan their outings and trips. They help people decide when to and when not to schedule important meetings. Further, weather reports help safeguard people by giving timely information regarding the possibility of extreme weather conditions. On rainy days, weather reports act as reminders to us, to carry our raincoats and umbrellas.
3. What do people do on rainy days and sunny days?
On rainy days, people get drenched in the rains, go for long drives, enjoy monsoon-specific street foods, and listen to melodious nostalgic music if they are stuck in traffic jams. Roads often get waterlogged so offices and schools remain shut, giving people surprise holidays at times. On sunny days, people wear reflective pastel coloured clothes in comfortable materials like cotton and linen, set out on picnics with their family members and friends, and go out window shopping. They also enjoy ice creams and ice lollies, which are very popular in my city.
4. Has climate change affected your country?
In my opinion, climate change has started to affect my country in the last decade very noticeably. Summers start later than usual, winters are either too cold or not cold at all, and rains instead of being intermittent like they used to, have become quite scattered. We frequently have flood like situations for a few days in the monsoons, followed by worryingly long dry spells. These are made up for, by unseasonal rains during the summers. This has affected the ecosystem at large, confusing the birds and animals as regards their migrating patterns and breeding times. Further, people find it difficult to make plans relying on seasonal patterns. Many open air functions have started getting cancelled or spoiled because of unseasonal rains.

164. Describe a sport you would like to try for the first time.

OR

165. Describe a sport you would like to learn.

166. Describe an adventure sport you would like to learn.

OR

167. Describe an adventure sport you would like to try for the first time.

168. Describe an outdoor sport you would like to learn.

OR

169. Describe a thrilling activity you would like to try.

You should say

- What this sport/adventurous activity/thrilling activity is
- How you would learn it
- What equipment you would need for this sport/adventurous activity/thrilling activity
- Why do you want to learn it/try it out? So and so

I am a big fan of adventurous activities and outdoor sports. When given the chance, I never miss out on an opportunity to go trekking, hiking, or mountain climbing. However, I have yet to try many adventurous activities. Once in my lifetime, if I get the chance, I want to try skydiving. Meant for adrenalin junkies, I have only had the privilege of seeing people go skydiving in movies and on TV so far. However, from what I have seen, it seems like one of the most thrilling sports out there. I would learn skydiving on a trip to New Zealand or any other similar holiday destination, It is important that my mind is receptive to instructions and free from routine worries, when I try this activity. So a holiday would be an ideal time to try it. I would join a small workshop with an experienced instructor who would guide me through the procedure and pep me up, before the actual jump. Skydiving essentially involves jumping down from a hovering helicopter many miles above the ground, and then opening up the parachute at the instructions of the mentor, when one has fallen to a considerably low altitude. It requires equipment such as a skydiving suit, strong harnesses, good quality skydiving eye gear, comfortable shoes, a parachute, and a helicopter. All these equipment are provided by companies that organise the activity in popular tourist destinations. What fascinates me about this activity is that it urges people to go against their basic survival instinct and jump from an unbelievably high altitude, into nothingness. The illusion of risk, wrapped in the blanket of security in the form of strong harnesses and experienced guides, makes this a perfect adventure sport to add to one's bucket list. I think skydiving will test my courage in the truest sense of the word. It will push me to the edge of my comfort zone, and then beyond. This is why I want to try it out at least once in my life.

Follow ups:
1. Do you play any sports at night?
I personally do not prefer to play sports at night. However, there are facilities in my city to play cricket and football on well-lit grounds even at night. Many people also play

squash, tennis, and billiards at night, in bright rooms and courts inside clubs.

2. What are the benefits of playing sports?
Playing sports keeps one healthy and fit. It improves the respiratory system and cardiac system of players. Further it improves blood circulation in the body, and helps with regulating metabolism. Playing sports relaxes the mind, and helps with weight management, too.

3. What is the difference between playing sports on your own, and playing sports in a group?
When playing sports in a group, we need to keep in mind things such as good team play, good sportsman spirit, and the concept of taking turns at different aspects of playing the sport. We need to have a sharing attitude, and must be friendly with the other players in the group. Group sports are often more entertaining than sports that are played alone. However, the advantage of playing a sport alone is that the players can have privacy while playing, and do not need to bother about giving others a chance to play. Solo sorts or two people sports are thus very de-stressing in nature, and well suited to working professionals in highly demanding jobs.

4. Do children need to exercise?
Children need to exercise regularly, for the same reasons as adults. Exercising from an early age is very beneficial as it forms a habit of physical activity a lifestyle pattern for later years. This ensures that childhood obesity stays at bay, and lifestyle diseases like diabetes and high blood pressure don't set in, in adult years.

5. Why do people need to play sports?
People need to play sports in order to refresh their minds and rejuvenate their bodies before or after work, so as to increase their productivity in life, keep stress at bay, and channelise frustrations in a healthy manner. People also need to play sports to keep their bodies active, their weight in control, and the reflexes strong.

6. Which is the most popular sport in your country?
Cricket is undoubtedly the most popular sport in my country. In fact, many people view it less as a sport or game, and more like a religion. When highly anticipated matches being played, cricket fans bunk schools, colleges, and even offices to see the game. Good cricket players are worshipped and people in my country take wins and losses in the game very personally.

7. Do you think the media plays an important role in popularising sports?
The media definitely plays an important role in popularising sports. Thanks to the media, sports other than cricket, such as hockey, football, tennis, badminton, and kabaddi have come in the spotlight in recent years. The media has also brought much needed attention to women's sports.

8. Why do people spend money on watching sports?
Watching sports is a very relaxing activity. The energy in the stadium or arena refreshes and revitalises sports fans, and many times sports also generate feelings of patriotism. This highly charged atmosphere during games is very thrilling to many people, and so they spend money on watching sports.

9. Do you think people should play sports alone, or in a team with others?
That depends entirely on the sport. Team sports are impossible to play alone, and often solo or duet sports are impossible to play in large groups. So, according to me there are

---

no set rules or guidelines regarding what kinds of sports people should play, and with how many people. As long as players enjoy the sport and play fair, any sporting activity is just as good as its counterparts.

◆ ◆ ◆

170. When was the first time you admired the sky?
   You should say
- **What you were doing**
- **Who was with you**
- **How old you were**
What did the sky look like, that day?

The first time I remember admiring the sky was when I was just a child of four years. It was a beautiful winter evening, and my parents had taken me to our farm house which was far removed from the hustle bustle and pollution of the main city. We had visited the farmhouse to spend a long weekend there, with a few of my parents' friends and their children. There were six others of my age, and we had spent all afternoon playing catch and hide and seek. Tired and hungry from the running around, I recall we had headed back to where our parents were picnicking on large rugs spread out on the lush green lawns. My mother handed me a sandwich, and I sat eating it, staring blankly into nothingness. Slowly, my tired gaze shifted to the sky, and to my surprise, it was a beautiful deep orange, interspersed with purple grey streaks of clouds. I had never seen the sky in such splendour, and was quite surprised that it could be any other colour but blue. I kept staring at God's masterpiece, and admired his artwork innocently. As time passed, the sun turned into a blood red orb that I could look at without wrinkling up my eyes! The beauty of the sun absorbed me completely, and it felt like something out of a picture book. The skies turned a deep pink as the orb started disappearing beyond the horizon. I could hear the faint sounds of people around me, but the sight of the beautiful winter sky had drowned out what they were saying. When my friends finished their sandwiches and called me back to play, I simply ignored them, and kept admiring the wonderful cloud formations. I remember, after that evening I stopped painting the sky blue in my sketchbook, and started using many different colours, instead.

Follow ups:
1. Why do people like to study the sky?
People like to study the sky because it is very beautiful, whether the day is sunny, cloudy, or a mix of both. Studying the sky gives people an idea of what kind of weather they can expect on a particular day. Further, studying the sky opens up the avenue of star gazing — a most delightful leisure activity.
2. Do you know any story related to the planets?
I know a few stories about planets based on Indian astrology and mythology. My grandmother used to tell me these stories when I was a child, and most of them had interesting characters, as well as good morals.

The Ultimate Guide to IELTS Speaking by Parthesh Thakkar

3. Do you think children should be told stories about stars and planets to improve their imagination?

Children should be told stories about stars and planets to improve their imagination. A good imagination makes way for creativity, and could shape a child into an artist or story teller, if such stories pique his interest at a young age.

4. Would children benefit from stargazing?

Children would benefit from tar gazing, in my opinion. Star gazing would teach them to be patient, to observe the beauty of the universe, and to enjoy nature in complete silence. It would engage their imagination and make them curious about the universe. Such curiosity is very healthy in children, as it prevents their minds from becoming dull and lazy. Further, children would learn to put things in perspective from a very young age, when they see how small human life is in comparison to the universe. This would make them more humble, compassionate, and sensitive.

5. Would you like to watch movies about other planets?

I would like to watch movies about other planets and other galaxies. I am an avid fan of science fiction movies, as they provide me with the perfect escape from my routine. They pique my curiosity, and their storyline are usually complicated, so they engross me completely. Most such movies have nail-biting twists in their plots, which I find very entertaining.

6. Did you like to watch the sky when you were young?

As mentioned before, I truly enjoyed watching the sky when I was young. Gazing at the sky was an intriguing activity for me. Pretty cloud formations always seemed to catch my eye, and I would often halt gameplay to just stare at the breath-taking view that the sky provided. To my innocent childlike mind, it was like an empty canvas on which the gods painted their masterpieces; each day a new one. I even used to enjoy painting the sky in my sketchbook, when I was young.

171. Describe an interesting animal.

   You should say
-   **What it looks like**
-   **When you first saw it**
-   **Where you first saw it**

Why do you find this animal interesting?

I have had the privilege of travelling a lot, and so, I have seen many interesting animals. Kangaroos grab my interest because of their high leaps and the pockets in which they keep their young ones, lions interest me because of their royal behaviour and appearance, tigers interest me because of their ferocity, leopards interest me because of their speed and agility, and monkeys interest me because of their intelligence. However, the animal I find most interesting is the Chihuahua. The Chihuahua is a very peculiar kind of dog, unlike any other I have ever seen. I love dogs and truly consider them man's best friends. But before I saw the Chihuahua, I had only seen larger breeds such as Labradors, Bull dogs, Boxers, and Alsatians. The smallest dogs I had seen were Lhasa dogs and Pomeranians.

The first time I saw a Chihuahua was when one of my friends who is a dog breeder and trainer, brought one home. One of his clients wanted to adopt a Chihuahua as a pet, and I got the opportunity to see it before it was handed over to them. The Chihuahua is very interesting because it is one of the tiniest dogs in the world, small enough to carry comfortably in one's arms. It has peculiar features such as a pointy snout and large round eyes. Its body is slim and proportionate, unlike that of a Dachshund, and it carries itself with surprising pride. Astonishingly, it is one of the most aggressive breeds of dogs, but is quite harmless because it is so tiny. Chihuahuas are popular with the wealthy, because they are quite expensive. May wealthy women are seen carrying Chihuahuas in comfortable open handbags, as status symbols.

Follow ups:
1. Why do people like to keep pets?
Pets keep people company, and animals have a unique quality of loving their companions and owners quite unconditionally. Pets are less demanding than humans, and playing with them is very therapeutic. They help many people overcome their loneliness, too. So, people like to keep pets.
2. What should we do to protect endangered animals?
We should spread awareness about endangered animals among school and college students, and among adults in society, too. We should inform people of the dangers faced by these animals on a daily basis, and organise campaigns to educate society about the necessity of protecting and preserving wildlife. Further, we should make appeals to the government to create safe habitats for endangered animals, and to clamp down on poaching and hunting of those species.
3. Do you support doing experiments on animals?
I am absolutely against doing experiments on animals. I believe that every creature on the planet has a free will that should be acknowledged and respected. Animals are often defenceless against the wiles and tactics of humans, so they cannot protect themselves when humans experiment on them. However, taking advantage of another species' weakness is cruel, and shows a lack of wisdom on our part. Like humans of all races, animals of all species have the right to live safely, unharmed.
4. Why do some people refuse to eat animals?
Some people believe in non-violence, and the free will of animals. They are animal lovers in the true sense, and their sensitive, compassionate nature does not allow them to hurt any creature. So, they refuse to eat animals. Many people also refuse to eat animals because their religion forbids them.
5. What would happen when some species disappear from the planet?
The earth is a self-regulating body. Frequently, old species of animals disappear, and new species appear, in keeping with the rhythms and cycles of nature. However, if some species of animals disappear from the planet because of human interference, and not naturally, then this can cause a break in the rhythms and cycles of nature, thereby disturbing many food chains and food webs. When the eco system is disturbed, human life also inevitably gets impacted negatively. When some species disappear from the

The Ultimate Guide to IELTS Speaking by Parthesh Thakkar

planet, the species that feed of them may either change their diets, or they may go extinct, themselves. If they change their diet, they will threaten the lives of another species of animals. Further, f some species of animals disappear from the planet, populations of animals that they feed on would increase manifold. Eventually this would disturb the balance of demand and supply of food on the planet.

172. Talk about something you bought that you are pleased to have.

OR

173. Talk about a recent purchase that you are pleased with.

OR

174. Describe an item you have recently bought that is useful to you.

You should say

- When, and from where you bought it

- What it is

- Why you bought it

Why are you pleased to have it?

In the recent past, I have purchased quite a few interesting things. I must add here, that all my purchases have proven quite pleasing. However, today I would like to talk about a new smart phone I purchased. Just a week ago I bought the new iPhone 7. It is Apple Inc.'s latest launch, and has only started becoming available here since some time. I am a huge Apple fan, so I am among the first few in the city to have purchased it. The moment I heard of its launch on TV, I decided that I would buy it as soon as it is available at a local Apple store. I had in fact even told the Apple dealer near my home to call and inform me when it became available at his outlet. As soon as I got his phone call, I went to the store and bought it. The entire journey back home, I was excited about unboxing it with my family. I bought the phone because I like all of Apple Inc.'s products, and I am deeply inspired by its founder, the late Mr Steve Jobs. More importantly, each new product from Apple has some brand new features that the R&D team at their headquarters has worked very hard to introduce. The operating system in iPhones, i.e. the iOS, is mind-blowing in my opinion. It facilitates high speed manoeuvring of the phone, and supports many functions all at once. I love the display of the phone, and the graphics keep improving with every new product that Apple launches.

I am pleased to have bought this phone because it allows me to enjoy the characteristic Apple graphics, lets me integrate all my favourite music from my ITunes into my new device in a matter of minutes, and also lets me transfer media very fast. This purchase has brought me a lot of positive attention from my colleagues and friends, and has elevated my status in society as iPhones are known to do. I also enjoy using the camera on this phone, because it lets me click high definition photographs, almost like a D-SLR camera. Apples cloud computing features have let me integrate all my existing data, apart from music, such as important documents, into the new phone, too. The battery life on this phone is also better than previous models. So, all in all, I'm quite pleased with my purchase.

Discussion
- Let's talk about shopping.
- What are the different ways to shop nowadays?
- Why do people like big shopping centres?
- Describe a person who is a shopaholic in your opinion.
- Do you know such a person?
- What is the difference between shopping centres in your home country, and in Canada?
- Do you like shopping?
- When do you go shopping?
- How do people buy things in your country?
- Nowadays people buy things they don't need. Why is that?
- Why are shopping centres crowded in your country?
- Do you think marketing is important? Why?
- What types of marketing are there?
- Do you think all products need marketing?
- How does marketing help?
- What do you think about marketing products?
- What do you think about brand value?
- Is there a direct correlation between a brand and its quality?

175. Describe a person you know who dresses well/who is fashionable.
OR
176. Talk about a person who likes to wear fashionable clothes.

    You should say
-   **Who the person is**
-   **What kinds of clothes the person likes to wear**
-   **How you know this person**

Why do you think this person dresses well?

I admire the fashion sensibilities of many of my friends, and a lot of celebrities these days. People are becoming more stylish in general, thanks to increased international exposure brought in by the internet. But, in my opinion, the best dressed person is Bollywood actor and humanitarian, Salman Khan. I do not know him personally, but I have seen many of his movies and appearances on TV. Whether he wears casual clothes like a pair of jeans and a round necked T-shirt, or he dresses up formally in trousers and a well fitted shirt, he looks fabulous. Salman even looks dashing in blazers and jackets. No matter what colours he wears, he can carry them well; and never have I seen him in anything garish up until now. That in itself, is saying a lot, because Salman has been around in the public eye since the nineties, when his first successful movie made him popular among the masses. Even when he was new to the industry, Salman used to dress very well, and was a trendsetter of sorts. Since then, his dressing and fashion sense has evolved a lot. He accessorises well, be it with the help of contrasting ties and cravats, or a tasteful pocket square. Salman knows how to pair the right kinds of shoes with different outfits, and his belts always go well with his shoes. I have often seen him wear interesting socks, too. Some years ago, Salman started his own clothing label by the name of Being Human. Now, we often get to see him wearing outfits from his own brand. These outfits are also very classy, in spite of being colourful and casual. Whether he attends press conferences or travels for promoting his films, he is always dressed impeccably. I even like his look when he hosts TV shows and makes appearances in comedy shows or celebrity interview segments. Salman's airport look is also quite cool, and he has been inspiring youngsters to dress better and emulate his style for generations, now. Salman's dressing is effortless, natural, and attractive, all at once, in keeping with his personality.

Follow ups:
1. What kinds of clothes are proper for work?
Formal or semi-formal clothes are ideal for work. Clothes for work must not be garish, jarring, or too colourful. They must not be wrinkled or crumpled, and they must not offend anyone's sensibilities. In many places, casual clothing is considered proper for work, depending on the role of the employee and the nature of the work. The key to proper dressing for work lies in comfort. If we are happy about our look and feel comfortable, it will reflect positively in our work.
2. Would you like to wear a uniform to work?
Personally I would not like to wear a uniform to work. While a uniform is good for floor staff in a factory setting, my kind of work does not require a uniform. Further, in childhood, a uniform increases feelings of unity and bonding among children, but as an adult, wearing a uniform stifles one's person style. My dressing reflects who I am, and wearing a uniform would compromise that.
3. Is it easy to buy cheap clothes in India?
It is very easy to buy cheap clothes in India. There are many small and medium retailers who sell local brands, as well as non-branded clothes in their stores, all across the country. Further, people can buy cheap clothes at discounted rates from the internet using online shopping apps, too. In India, people can even buy their clothes off the streets, very literally, from open street markets, at very cheap rates.
4. Do young Indians shop on the internet?
Young Indians shop on the internet very regularly. Online shopping and window shopping is a common pastime of many youngsters in India. People buy books, music, art, clothes, shoes, accessories, and even gadgets from the internet these days. Young Indians have in fact started purchasing costly jewellery online, too.
5. Do you like to go shopping on your own or with friends?
This depends largely on my mood and the purpose of my shopping trip. If I need to quickly shop for something, and I know exactly what I want, I prefer to go and shop for it on my own, as this saves a lot of time. However, if I want to go on a leisurely shopping spree with no fixed goal in mind, I like to go with friends, because that way we can help each other in deciding what to buy, and I can get opinions of others on my purchases, too.

6. Should parents buy their children expensive clothes?

Parents should buy their children the best kind of clothes that they can comfortably afford. If parents can afford expensive clothes without going out of their way or putting in extra efforts, there is no harm in buying expensive clothes for children. However, parents must be careful not to buy exorbitantly priced branded outfits for their children, as this may make the child mildly delusional as regards the reality of life, at a young age.

177. Talk about a crowded place you visited   *youngster, family*

    You should say

- **Where is it** – *Ahmedabad*
- **With whom you visited that place** – *around*
- **Why it is so crowded** – *food famous*

How you felt after being there – *Advantage disadvantage*

Practice Questions:

1. Do all people like to visit crowded places?
2. Which places do young people like to visit?
3. What are the advantageous and disadvantages of visiting crowded places?
4. Have you ever bought a product after watching an advertisement?
5. How do you feel when advertisements pop up on your computer screen?

178. A time when you heard about riots in another country

    You should say

- **What did you hear**
- **When did you hear it**
- **How did it make you feel to hear about it**

What suggestions can you make for reducing riots?

Practice Questions:

1. What are problems caused by riots?
2. Can there be any benefits/advantages of riots?
3. Are riots becoming more common all over the world?
4. How do riots affect society?

Cue Cards with Suggestions followed by Follow-up Questions with Sample Answers and Practice Questions

1. Talk about a leisure activity that you want to start.
   You should say
- When you are starting it
- Where it is going to take place
- How useful this activity is to you
What do you like about it?

2. Describe a situation in your life when you became successful.
   You should say
- When and where it happened
- What you did
- Why you think you were successful
What did you learn from your success?

Practice Questions:
1. Does success depend on the support of other people?
2. Have you ever changed your view of success? If yes, when and how? If no, why?

3. Describe an aquatic centre you visited recently.
   You should say
- Where it is
- When and with whom you visited it
- What you liked there
What was unique about this place?

Practice Questions:
1. What are the sources of water in your country?
2. What is the government doing in increasing/maintaining the water resources of your country?
3. What may happen if we do not take care of the water resources?

4. Talk about an important thing that you had forgotten about until recently.

   You should say
- **What it is**
- **Why you forgot about it**
- **What was your reaction was when you remembered**

What triggered your memory?

Practice Questions:
- Do you think most people forget things? Why?
- Do you think it is possible to hire a person to remember the things you need?
- How often do you forget things?
- Does technology play a role in making people forget things?
- What should be done to remember things better?

5. Describe a time you and your friend had a disagreement.

   You should say
- **When this happened**
- **Who you disagreed with**
- **What you and your friend argued about**

Did you solve the argument in the end?

Practice Questions:
1. How do you usually feel when others disagree with you?
2. Do you like to hear different opinions?
3. Do schools in India teach critical thinking?
4. How should young people communicate with old people?
5. Are you a person who often disagrees with others?
6. Why do we sometimes feel that a chat will be boring if there are only agreements?

6. Describe a small and successful company you know.

   You should say
- **What this company does**
- **How you know this company**
- **What kind of business this company does**

Why do you think this company is successful?

The Ultimate Guide to IELTS Speaking by Parthesh Thakkar

Practice Questions:
1.What factors can affect a company's development?
2.Would you work for a small but successful company if given a chance?
3.Is it hard to run a company in India?
4.Do you think online shopping will replace shopping malls in the near future?

7. Describe a time when you gave some good news to a person you know.
   You should say
- Who the person is
- What the good news was
- How you heard that news and describe what that person's reaction was the news.

Practice Questions:
- Do people tend to share more good news or bad news with other people? Why do you
  think this is?
- How has social media changed the sharing of news with other people?
- How you heard any good news from international media recently? What is it?
- How important you think it is to be up to date with world news why?

8. Talk about your first experience playing any sport as a child.
   You should say
- What your experience was, and when
- Who your coach was
- What the sport was
How did you feel about it?

Practice Questions:
- Are there any significant benefits of playing sports?
- Do you think children should be taught sports in schools?
- Which sports are the best for children — indoor sports, or outdoor sports?
- What sport would you like your kids to play?

9. Describe a person who has apologised to you.
   You should say
- Who this person is
- When they apologised to you
- What words they used, to apologise

How did you feel about receiving the apology?

Practice Questions:
1. Is it important to say sorry?
2. What situations do people say sorry in?
3. Why do some people hate to say sorry?
4. In what situations should we apologise immediately?
5. When do people say thank you?
6. When was the last time you found it hard to accept an apology?

10. Describe a family that is not your own, that you like.
   You should say
- Whose family this is
- Where this family lives
- How many members it has

Why do you like this family?

Practice Questions:
1. In a typical Indian family, who is the leader of the household?
2. In India what kinds of family members usually live together?
3. Do young and middle-aged people live with old people in your country?
4. Do grandparents educate their grandchildren in your country?

11. Does the weather affect your mood?
OR
12. Describe a situation when the weather affected your work plans or day plans.
   You should say
- What you originally intended to do
- How the weather affected your plans
- How you spent your time once your plans were impacted

Do weather changes impact your plans often?

Practice Questions:
1. How many seasons are there in your country?
2. Which are these seasons?
3. Describe the weather during these seasons.
4. What kind of weather is preferred by people in your country?
5. How does the weather affect people in your country?
6. What kind of activities do people do in different seasons?

13. Describe one of your best friends.

You should say

- **Who this person is**
- **How you became friends with this person**
- **What activities you like to do with this person**

Why is this person your best friend?

Practice Questions:
1. How do people in your country make friends these days?
2. Do you trust friends that you meet on the internet?
3. How do you get along with people you don't like?
4. Why is it hard for some people to maintain friendships?
5. Would you only make friends with people who are similar to you?
6. Do you like to have many friends?

14. Describe a piece of local news that was interesting to you.

You should say

- **What the news was about**
- **Where you saw or heard the news**
- **When you saw or heard the news**

Why was it interesting to you?

Practice Questions:
1. Why do local people like to read local news?
2. Why do people like local news more than international news?
3. How often do Indian people buy newspapers?
4. Is it convenient to read news on the internet, in your country?

15. Describe a special trip you would like to go on, in future.

You should say
- Where this place is
- Who would you like to go with
- What you would like to do there

Why would this trip be special?

For this topic, candidates should refer to the Cue Card: 'Describe a foreign country you have not visited, but would like to visit?'

16. Describe a time that you forgot something important.

OR

17. Talk about an important thing that you had forgotten about until recently.

You should say
- When this happened
- What you forgot to do
- Who you were with

What consequences did you have to face?

Practice Questions:
1. What do people do to remember things?
2. Why do old people forget things easily?
3. What tips do you use to remember things?
4. What kinds of things can people do to prevent the recall of bad memories?
5. Do you think memory is important for language learning?
6. What kinds of jobs require good memory?
7. How can technology help humans improve memory?

18. Describe a person who likes to travel by plane.

You should say
- Who this person is
- How you know this person
- Where this person travels to usually

Why does this person like to travel by plane?

Practice Questions:
1. What are the advantages and disadvantages of traveling by plane?

The Ultimate Guide to IELTS Speaking by Parthesh Thakkar

2. Is it good to live near an airport?
3. Do Indian people like to travel by plane?
4. What kinds of transportation do people choose when they go on long journeys?
5. Would you like to travel by your own car in the future?
6. What kinds of people travel by plane in India?
7. Are you happy with the service on planes in India?
8. Why do some people dislike air travel?

19. **Describe a village near your hometown.**

    You should say
-   **Which is it**
-   **Where is it**
-   **When you went there**

Describe your expression there

Practice Questions:
1. What is the difference between urban and rural life?
2. How are urbanites different from villages?
3. Will people move to the country side in future?
4. What can e done to improve life in rural area?
5. Does the government pay more attention to urban areas?

20. **Describe an art or craft activity/project that you did in school.**

    You should say
-   **When this happened**
-   **What you did in the activity**
-   **Who you did it with**

How did you feel about the final result?

Practice Questions:
1. What kinds off traditional handicrafts are there in your country?
2. Should children learn more about art?
3. Why do some people think it is difficult to understand art?
4. What can we do to make young people pay more attention to traditional art?
5. Do you think it's important to cultivate an appreciation of art in children?
6. Do you think it should be included in school curriculums? Why?

---

7. How do you imagine that art will be taught in the future?
8. Have you attended any lessons about art?
9. What have you learned from these lessons?

OR

21. **Describe a handicraft that you made at school.**
    You should say
-   **What it was**
-   **What it looked like**
-   **What materials you used**
Was it easy to make?

Practice Questions:
1. What handmade items do people give as gifts to each other?
2. Are there advantages to giving a handmade gift?
3. Do many people give handmade gifts nowadays? Why?

OR

22. **Describe an activity that you did in school such as sports, arts, or crafts.**
    You should say
-   **What it was**
-   **When, and how long you did it for**
-   **How you felt about it**
How good were you at it?

Practice Questions:
1. What is the importance of traditional clothes?
2. Do you think traditional arts and crafts are important for children?
3. Is it better to give handmade presents to our friends and relatives?
4. What is the role of traditional clothes and crafts in our life?
5. Should we pass the knowledge of our traditions and culture to our children?
6. Why do you think so?

23. **Talk about an interesting neighbour of yours.**
    You should say
-   **Who this neighbour is**

The Ultimate Guide to IELTS Speaking by Parthesh Thakkar

- What makes the neighbour interesting
- Are you on good terms with this neighbour

Do you often notice the quirks of people living around you?

Practice Questions:
1. Is it important to foster good relations with neighbours?
2. What are the qualities of a good neighbour?
3. What things should neighbours avoid doing?
4. How can one develop good relations with one's neighbours?

24. **Describe a popular place where you like to go swimming.**
    You should say
- **What that place is**
- **How far it is from your home**
- **How often you visit it**

What is special about that place?

Practice Questions:
1. Is there a need for more swimming pools in your city?
2. What time of the year is most favourable for swimming in your city?
3. In which season do people prefer to swim more, in your locality?
4. How hygienic are the swimming pools in your area?
5. What measures are taken by management authorities to ensure the health and safety of swimmers?

25. **Describe a bicycle, car, or motorcycle trip that was enjoyable?**
    You should say
- **Where you went on the trip**
- **With whom you went on the trip**
- **Why you decided to embark on that trip**

How did you feel about the journey?

Practice Questions:
1. Is it tiring to travel long distances on two wheelers?
2. Do you travel a lot using two wheelers
3. Are there any risks involved in travelling on motorcycles?

26. Speak about a song that you find interesting.

   You should say
- **Which song this is**
- **Where you first heard it**
- **Why you find it interesting**

Do you listen to it often?

Practice Questions:
1. Which are your favourite instruments?
2. Do you listen to music on a large music system or on an MP3 player?
3. What is your opinion on buying expensive high definition speakers?
4. Can you listen to the same song on repeat many times?

27. Speak about a person you have met before and want to know more about.

   You should say
- **Who the person is**
- **Where you met them**
- **Why you would like to meet them again**

When do you think it would be possible to meet him?

Suggested answer: Candidates can speak about a successful businessman or mentor they have met in the past. This can be followed up by a description of how this meeting impacted them positively.

28. Speak about a time when you were very busy.

   You should say
- **When you were very busy**
- **What kept you so busy**
- **How you managed your time**

Did you enjoy being very busy?

Practice Questions:
1. How do busy people manage their time?
2. Is it true that no matter how busy someone is, they always find time for things that are important?
3. Is a busy lifestyle good for health in the long run?

---

29. Speak about a place you often visit.

   You should say

- **Which place this is**
- **Who you visit it with**
- **How you discovered it**

What do you like about this place?

Practice Questions:

1. How far is it from your home?
2. Do you often explore new places?
3. Do you consider yourself adventurous?
4. Are you fond of visiting this place in solitude?

30. Speak about a place or MNC in a foreign country, where you would like to work
   for a short while.

   You should say

- **Which place/MNC you would like to work in**
- **The name of the country where you would like to work**
- **What kind of job you would like to do**

Why would you like to work there in particular?

Practice Questions:

1. Do MNCs offer a better work atmosphere than local companies?
2. Is the work culture in MNCs more professional than in other companies?
3. Do all MNCs have lots of employees?
4. Is there more scope for growth in MNCs?

31. Describe a tall building in your hometown that you like/dislike.

   You should say

- **What the building looks like**
- **Where it is located**
- **Which features of the building you like/dislike**

Why do you like/dislike the building?

Practice Questions:

1. Should the government put in place some guidelines for how buildings should be made?

2. Is it important to make aesthetically pleasing buildings?
3. Should there be restrictions on the use of certain colours and shapes in construction?

32. **Speak about a subject or an area of study that you are interested in.**
    You should say
- **What this subject/area of study is**
- **Where you first found out about it**
- **What you find interesting about it**
Why do you want to learn more about it?

Practice Questions:
1. Which subject did you hate studying in school?
2. What can schools do to help students study subjects that they dislike?
3. Which subjects are most commonly disliked by students?
4. Why do many students find Mathematics tough?

33. **Can you recall a time when you missed an important appointment?**
    You should say
- **When you missed the appointment**
- **What led you to miss it**
- **How you felt about missing the appointment**
Were you able to salvage the situation?

Practice Questions:
1. Has anyone missed an appointment with you?
2. What would you do if someone didn't turn up for a scheduled appointment?
3. Are you judgmental about people who cannot keep their word?

34. **Describe a paid job that you or someone you know, did.**
OR
35. **Talk about a paid job you and your friend did together.**
    You should say
- **What the job was**

- How you/this person found the job
- For how long you/this person kept this job

How did you/this person feel about this job?

Practice Questions:
1. Is it hard to find a good job in India?
2. What kinds of preparation should people do for a job interview?
3. Why do some people keep changing their jobs?
4. What should a good employer do?
5. Would you like to work on weekends?
6. How would you define "a good job"?

Discussion
- What kind of work do young people like doing?
- Do you think old people need to work?
- What kind of work should old people do?

36. Describe a team that you have been a part of.
- **When this team was formed?**
- **Who was on the team?**
- **What did you do together?**
- **Explain why you became a part of the team?**

Practice Questions:
1. Do you think group activity is good for children?
2. What kinds of children do not like teamwork?
3. How would you select a team leader?
4. What do you think of leadership?
5. Have you ever led a team?
6. If you were a leader and your teammates didn't respect you, what would you do?

37. Speak about a book that inspired you in your life.
   You should say
- **From where you bought it**
- **Who wrote it**
- **How it inspired you**

What is the book about?

Suggestions:
Candidates can speak about any religious book, personality development book, or autobiography that has given them motivation to do better things in their life.

38. **Talk about a piece of clothing that you received as a gift recently.**
    You should say
- **What it was and when you received it**
- **Who gave it to you**
- **Why it was important to you?**
Do you often receive clothes as gifts?

Practice Questions:
1. Do you think the internet influences the fashion industry today? Why?
2. Who should wear trendy clothes — the youth, or older people? Why?
3. What are the benefits of having a fashion industry, to a country?
4. Why do people wear different styles of clothing?
5. Why do some companies have uniforms for their employees?
6. Which segment of people usually purchases designer clothes?
7. Does taste in clothing depend on the age of people? Why?

39. **Talk about a happily married couple you know.**
    You should say
- **Who they are**
- **How you know them**
- **What they usually do together**
Explain how you feel about their marriage

Practice Questions:
1. At what age do people get married in your country?
2. Are weddings celebrated extravagantly in your country?
3. Is this a good or a bad trend?
4. What effect does this have on society?
5. How do you celebrate your birthday?
6. Did you celebrate your birthdays differently when you were a child?

40. Speak about a book you want to write.

You should say
- **What it will be about**
- **When you plan to write it**
- **Who you think will read it**

How long will your book be?

Suggestions:
Candidates can speak about a book on any technical subject, management, parenting, hobbies, projects, experiences of life, religion, their personal interests, cooking, lifestyle, etc.

Follow-up Questions & Answers:

1. Have you read similar books in the past?
Yes, I have read so many books on the same topic in the past. I implemented many things from those books in my life, and have got good success from it. Yet, I think there is a requirement for a book that covers all the latest topics and findings on this subject.

2. Why do people write about life?
People write about life because they want to share their experiences, knowledge, and findings about life with their readers, so that they, too, can learn from the book and avoid similar difficulties, or solve similar problems in their lives.

3. Why do you think people select writing as a profession?
Some people want to convey their message in the form of a book, only. They think they can spread information to a large number of people across the world, through their books. By doing so, they can quench their thirst to write and to spread their word.

4. What are the advantages and disadvantages of selecting writing as a profession?
Writing, as a profession, gives reputation and acceptance in society. Writers also earn well, provided readers appreciate their books. This income also helps them in living a comfortable and luxurious lifestyle. On top of it, the prime benefit of writing is self-actualization. Writers feel satisfied, contented, and fulfilled when they see others follow their books and help themselves. On the other hand, chances of failure in this profession are extremely high. And once a writer fails, it becomes very difficult for him to succeed in future. Moreover, writing a book requires a lot of effort, understanding of the language, and time. At times, because of a lack of time or financial resources, many writers fail to complete their books.

5. What skills are needed to be a good writer, according to you?
Writers require a number of skills in order to achieve success. First, they must have excellent knowledge of the subject they want to write on. Second, they must have outstanding command of the language in which they want to write their book. Last, they should understand the requirements of the readers so that their books appeal to the targeted class of readers.

6. What range of reading material is available on the internet?
The internet is an ocean of knowledge. We get reading material in the form of an e-book, an excerpt, a journal, or a forum on every conceivable subject like science, technology, politics, history, drama, arts, entertainment, fiction, management, religion, philosophy, poetry, essays, and research projects. In short, the internet can satisfy the reading

requirements of readers of all interests.

Practice Questions
1. Do you think people who write about life have suffered in their past?
2. What other books do you suggest to people to read? Why?

◆　◆　◆

41. Speak about a difficult thing/task you did well.
   You should say
- **What that thing/task was**   Rump cevalk
- **When you did it**
- **What preparations you did for it**
How did you feel when you completed it?
Suggestions:
Candidates can speak about their business project or presentation as part of a job, a deal or meeting where they performed well, the launch of a new product, branch, or business scheme, an exam, assignment, or study project, a difficult social situation, an illness, and even child rearing tasks that they succeeded at..

Follow-up Questions & Answers:
1. Does everyone have difficulties in life?
Yes, difficulties are a part of life. Actually, life itself never moves in a linear direction. It always moves in a different and unique pattern decided by nature, or the divine. This means we have to go through all types of experiences in life. It is a human tendency to label and define things in life, and so, we label some things as difficulties, but they are an essential part of our life that we should welcome if we want to grow and evolve, both spiritually and intellectually.
2. How should we face difficulties in life?
Difficulties should be faced with an open and welcoming attitude and mind. I think the main hurdle we meet is our own perception of difficulties. We should not develop any mental resistance or hype when faced with tough situations in life. Rather, we should try to learn as best as we can from those situations. We should use our tough times as our stepping stones in life, instead of road blocks. I believe in the title of Robert H. Schuler's famous book 'Tough Times Never Last but Tough People Do'.
3. What can we learn from the difficulties of life?
We can learn a lot from the difficulties of life. We can analyse our strategy for tackling such situations and sharpen our skills for the same. Moreover, we can also develop our psychological strength to withstand tough times in our life. In the words of Franklin D. Roosevelt, "A smooth sea never made a skilled sailor".

Practice Questions
1. If given a chance, would you do it again?

2. What have you learnt from that task?

3. Would you change your way of doing it in future?

4. Do you like to take on challenges in life?

5. Do challenges play any role in the development of a person in his life?

6. Who is more helpful in tough times according to you — friends, or relatives? Why?

42. Speak about a traffic jam you got into.

You should say

- **When and where it happened**

- **For how long you were stuck up in that jam**

- **What you felt about the situation**

Did the traffic jam cause you any inconvenience or disadvantage?

43. Speak about a gift you received in your childhood.

You should say

- **What that gift was**

- **Who you received it from**

- **When and where you received the gift**

How did you react to it?

Suggestions:
Candidates can speak about a toy like a teddy bear, a game, a musical instrument, or a video game they received as a gift.

Practice Question:
1.What should we pay more attention to while buying gifts — the price, or the quality? Why?

44. Describe a historical movie you have seen in the past.

You should say

- **When and where you saw it**

- **With whom you saw it**

- **What the story was**

What did you like about it?

Suggestions:
Candidates can speak about Mughal-e-Azam, Mahabharata, Ashoka, Mangal Pandey, and

other historical films. Candidates can also speak about English movies like The Gladiator, Titanic, Schindler's List, 300, Brave Heart, and Pearl Harbour.

45. Speak about a person who looked after you when you were a child.

You should say
- The name of the person
- How he/she is related to you
- How they took care of you

What are your fondest childhood memories with that person?

46. Speak about a person you know, who speaks different languages.

You should say
- The name of the person
- When and where you met them
- What you learned from them

Which languages can this person speak in?

Suggestions:
Candidates can speak about their IELTS or English teachers who speak their first language, and English. Apart from this, candidates can speak about anyone else, too, who speaks more than one language.

Practice Questions:
1. In what ways can you meet people who speak many languages?
2. What difficulties do you face when you meet someone who speaks many languages?

47. Describe a piece of art (painting, sculpture) you have seen.

You should say
- What it was
- Where it was displayed
- Why you like it

What did you feel on seeing it?

Suggestion:
Candidates can speak about sculptures or monuments like the Taj Mahal, Qutub Minar, and any historical or artistic temple or idol. They can also speak about a painting like the Mona Lisa by Leonardo Da Vinci, or The Persistence of Memory painted by Salvador Dali.

Follow-up Questions & Answers:

1. Why do you think some pieces of art are priceless?

It is true that some pieces are invaluable because it is almost impossible to create them again, e.g. the painting of Mona Lisa, which is a picture of a lady with a mysterious smile on her face. Thousands of painters have tried to recreate similar paintings but they all have been unsuccessful. This is the reason why some pieces of art are priceless and unique.

2. Why do children paint pictures?

I think children like to create things which are different and vibrant. They also like to do some creative work in their free time. Moreover, some children like to give an expression to their inner world of dreams and imaginations. All these reasons motivate them to paint pictures.

3. Why do old people paint pictures?

Elders paint pictures for a variety of reasons. One of them is to pass their time in a creative manner. Another is to give a message to the community, based on their experiences in life. At times, they may paint to sell some of their works to earn money and survive.

Practice Questions:

1. Is there any message given by that painting/sculpture?
2. How important is it for children to learn art?
3. If given a chance, would you pursue art as a hobby or a profession? Why?
4. Why do people pursue art as a profession?
5. What will the future trend in arts be?
6. Have you ever painted a picture in your childhood?

48. Describe an activity you do in the open air.

   You should say
- **What that activity is**
- **How often you do it**
- **Why it is important to you**

What equipment or tools do you need to perform that activity?

Suggestions:

Candidates can speak about any outdoor game they play, like cricket, or football. They can also speak about shopping, roaming around, visiting a garden, lake, or seashore, or going hiking.

Practice Questions:

1. What activities do youngsters do in open air?
2. What activities do children/old people like to do in open air?
3. What outdoor activities can you do in your city?
4. How beneficial are the outdoor activities to you/society/people?

49. An event that takes place regularly in your city.
   You should say
- The name of the event
- When and where it takes place
- What happens on that day

What do you do during that event?

Suggestions:
Candidates can speak about any religious celebrations, or New Year celebrations that happen in their city.

Follow-up Questions & Answers:
1. Should people support such events financially?
I think it is up to an individual whether or not he wants to donate some money for the organisation of the event. However, there should be no compulsion of any form on civilians, to provide financial support to such events.
2. Should government give financial support to public events?
The government should give financial support only to those events that are organised by them or other non-government bodies, provided the event has been organised for national interest, and not for any personal, communal, or political interest. Apart from this, governments should not provide any grants to private bodies or individuals to celebrate any events.

Practice Questions:
1. Who takes part in that event?
2. Do similar events take place in your city?

50. Speak about an unusual activity you did in your free time.
   You should say
- What it was
- When and where you did it
- With whom you did it

How did you feel after doing that activity?

Suggestions:
Candidates can speak about any different thing they have done in their free time, like preparing food at home if they don't usually cook, painting the house, learning a musical instrument, going for a theme party or a fancy dress party, or going for an adventure trip.

Practice Questions:
1. Do you do such activities often?
2. How are such unusual activities useful in life?
3. Is there any difference in the preferences of men and women in doing such activities?

51. Talk about a positive change in your teenage life or childhood.

You should say

- **What it was**
- **When it happened**
- **How it changed your life**

What did you learn from it?

Suggestions:

Candidates can speak about any event or incident that changed a negative habit of theirs into a positive one, during their childhood, such as a failure in an exam, consequences faced due to mischievous behaviour, or a lack of responsibility that they may have overcome with the guidance of their elders, or after an impactful incident. They can also speak about a bad habit such as telling lies or harassing others, which they changed in response to something.

Follow-up Questions & Answers:

1. What type of problems do teenagers face in your city/country/culture?

I don't think there are any specific problems for youngsters in my city or culture. However, there are some common conflicts, which can be labelled as a generation gap. This is because teenagers live with dreams in their eyes and they perceive the whole world based only on their whims and fancies. With this approach, they may deviate from their practical life's demands. At such times, parents can intervene in teenagers' lives, and inspire them to learn life skills. Some conflicts generally occur here, but, they can be resolved with the help of proper counselling and handling by parents.

2. How do youngsters and old people exchange knowledge?

The process of exchanging knowledge is carried out in different ways by different people. People generally share their ideas and thoughts about various aspects of life with each other, on a regular basis, in the form of casual chats or serious discussions, to exchange knowledge. This may be done at home while taking meals together, or in a family meeting at night, or over weekends. In this process, youngsters learn from the experiences and knowledge of elders, whereas elders learn the art of remaining positive, enthusiastic, and diligent, from the youngsters.

Practice Questions:

1. How is the relationship between teenagers and old people in your culture?
2. Do you think a generation gap exists between teenagers and old people in your culture?
3. How can we decrease this generation gap?

52. Describe your favourite hill station.

You should say

- **The name and location**
- **How often you go there**

- **What you do there**
Why do you like it?

◆ ◆ ◆

53. **Describe your own idea of a perfect public park.**
You should say
- **Where it should be located**
- **What facilities it should offer**
- **What it should look like**
Which age groups will like the park more?

Practice Questions:
1. What kind of activities can be carried out in that park?
2. What should the opening and closing timings of the park be?
3. Which rules do you think should be followed in the park?

◆ ◆ ◆

54. **Describe a company where friends and family members like to work together.**
You should say
- **Which company that is**
- **What type of work the company does**
- **How the company is useful to its members**
What makes it good for friends and family members to work there together?
Suggestions:
Candidates can speak about any family run enterprise, small-scale industry, business, or shop.

Follow-up Questions & Answers:
1. How can an employee support his parents or family?
An employee can serve as a financial backbone for his family. He can support his family by giving them money for their everyday requirements, healthcare needs, and for recreational activities.
2. Should employees form a union against the management?
This requirement is conditional. If the management is exploiting its employees for monetary gains, then it may be necessary for employees to form an active union against the management, to protest against the authorities when required, and stop them from becoming dictators. However, in case of a friendly and employee-oriented management, it is better if employees form a group that keeps an eye on the management, without disrupting day-to-day work, so that the organisation runs smoothly for the benefit of all.

Practice Questions:

1. What are the other important concerns in the mind of an employee about a job, except the salary?
2. What are the effects of long working hours on employees?
3. What can a union do to help the workers?

55. Speak about someone you know, who is a good employee.

   You should say

-    **Their name, and how you know them**
-    **What job they do**
-    **How good they are at the job**

Follow-up Questions & Answers:

1. Do you believe that good employees create a positive impact on other employees, also?

Yes, I believe that good employees always spread good vibes among other employees to boost their morale, which results in enhanced performance of the company. They do so in various ways. They motivate their colleagues and subordinates when needed, they help colleagues in solving their problems, and also give them opportunities to prove their skills to the management.

Practice Questions:

1. Why do you think this person is a better employee than others?
2. What have you learned from him?
3. Do you think excessive competition amongst employees of a company can be harmful? Justify your answer.
4. Why do some companies give more opportunities to younger people?

56. Speak about someone you know who is a good entrepreneur/businessman of your area or city.

   You should say

-    **The name of the entrepreneur, and how you know him**
-    **What work he does**
-    **How good he is at that work**

Follow-up Questions & Answers

1. Where can you find similar people in your country?

Such people can normally be found in metro and mega cities of my country, where bigger industrial development exists. They shift to those cities where they can find a suitable environment for the growth of their company. In India, we can find such people in

Mumbai, Kolkata, Delhi, Chennai, Bangalore, Pune, Chandigarh, Ahmedabad and many other cities of my country.

2. How do such people help the society?

Such people can prove to be positive examples for youngsters and those of newer generations, to emulate. We remember Mr J R D Tata, Mr Dhirubhai Ambani, and many more successful entrepreneurs, even today, and try to take some inspiration from their lives, to make our lives better. Such people also help in supporting the economy of their country by generating large revenues, giving employment to many people, and uplifting shareholders of their companies.

Practice Questions:

1. If given a chance, would you like to work under him?
2. Do you want to become a good entrepreneur/businessman?
3. Do you have any suggestions for that person?
4. Have you ever met him?
5. What qualities do you admire the most in him?

57. Describe an office (government or private) you visited.

    You should say

- **Where it is located**
- **What activities the office is engaged in**
- **Why you visited that office**

What was the office like?

Practice Questions:

1. Was there anything that you disliked in that office?
2. Did the staff of that office attend to you properly?
3. In future, would you like to have an office of your own?
4. Do you have any suggestions for that office?
5. Why are office complexes taller than residential complexes in some cities?
6. What facilities are necessary in an office complex?
7. Would you prefer living in a complex where offices and residences coexist?
8. What are the positive and negative aspects of living in such a complex?
9. Do you think the government should separate commercial and residential areas completely? Why?

58. Describe a happy event from your childhood/teenage years.

    You should say

- **When it happened**
- **What happened**
- **Why you remember it**

Did you learn anything special from it?

Suggestions:

Candidates can speak about a good exam result, birthday party, picnic, or winning a competition.

Follow-up Question & Answer:

1. What things do people like to keep, from their childhood?

People like to keep all those memorable things that they had enjoyed or received in their childhood. They like to preserve their toys, gifts, paintings, or other things that they may have prepared on their own. They also like to preserve storybooks, photographs, results of their school tests, uniforms, and all those things with which they have had an emotional attachment in their early years.

Practice Questions:

1. What are the differences between your childhood, and the childhood of children these days?
2. What are the factors that affect the happiness of a child?

59. Describe a memorable visit you made to your friend or relative.

You should say

- **When you went to them**
- **Where you went to see them**
- **How that visit was**

Why do you remember that visit?

Suggestions:

Candidates can speak about their visit to the home of a friend or relative, where they enjoyed each other's company.

Follow-up Questions & Answers:

1. What would you like more, to be a guest, or a host? Why?

I like being a host more than being a guest. That is because I like receiving and welcoming people at my home. This has been the tradition in my culture for ages. I like giving my guests all the facilities they require, so as to make them feel comfortable and ensure that they enjoy my hospitality.

2. What different preparations do people make when they expect guests?

That depends a lot on the relation between the host and the guest, and the time of their arrival. If the hosts expect an intimate relative, they prepare the guest's favourite food

---

dishes, because they know what their guest likes. They also order special foods like ice creams or pastries, which are their guests' favourites. However, if they expect a formal visitor, they may not make too many preparations for them, and may offer only tea or coffee with some light snacks.

3. Should one ask prior permission before becoming a guest?

Yes, I think it is an essential part of our social etiquette to take prior consent of the host, before we visit him. This is because we live in a world where everyone has many personal and social commitments, and we generally fall short of time when it comes to fulfilling them. In this scenario we should not land up as unwanted or unexpected guests at anyone's home. We ought to confirm the time and date of our visit, too, before going to see anyone.

4. Did people take permission from their hosts before visiting as guests, in the past? Why?

No, this practice was not so popular in the past, because people lived in small villages and towns, where almost all of them had a similar lifestyle, and so, people were usually aware of others' routines. What's more, the level of warmth and hospitality was very high in the past, compared to these days.

5. What kind of conversations do people have with their guests?

That depends on the type of relationship and the level of intimacy shared between the guest and the host. But, generally, they talk about their lives, families, jobs, society, culture, religion, business, the stock market, politics, and so on.

Practice Questions

1. Do you often visit that person?
2. Do you make similar visits to other friends/relatives?
3. Does that person often visit you?
4. What problems can people face when they receive guests?
5. How do children behave at others' places?
6. How do adults enjoy when they visit somebody's place?
7. Do you think children can create problems for adults when they receive/communicate with their guests?

60. Describe a party that you attended.

   You should say

-   **The location and date of the party**
-   **What the reason for the party was**
-   **What you did there**

Was it formal or informal?

OR

61. Describe a party you arranged.

   You should say

-   **The date and reason for giving the party**

- What preparations you had made
- How you felt after the party got over

How many people did you invite?

Follow-up Questions & Answers:
1. Why do you think people throw parties?
There are many reasons for organising parties. One good reason is to celebrate our success in business, studies, or in other aspects of our lives, and share it with others. Secondly, people often throw parties just to meet their relatives, friends, and colleagues. Next, some people also like to show their financial strength to others, so they use big parties as occasions to show their wealth off.
2. Where do youngsters like to give parties?
Youngsters like to give parties on dance floors, where they can enjoy dancing and good food. Some youngsters give parties only at restaurants, whereas some prefer only their homes for arranging parties. In short, the venue depends on the convenience and budget of the host.

Practice Questions:
1. Do you often attend/arrange such parties?
2. Do you think parties are important to maintain social contacts?
3. Have you ever had a good/bad experience at a party?
4. At which places do people give parties in your city? OR What are the popular party spots in your city?
5. Do you have any suggestions for the party you attended?

62. Describe a picnic you enjoyed.
   You should say
- **When and where you went**
- **With whom you went there**
- **What you enjoyed**

What was special about that picnic?

Follow-up Questions & Answers:
1. What time of the year do you prefer for picnics?
I opt for the winter season for picnics because I live in a city where the summer lasts for almost six months a year. I have experienced that it is very difficult to step out for picnics in the summer and monsoon. The impact of bad weather on our activities is so high, that it becomes impossible to really enjoy ourselves. I like winters, when the climate is cool and dry, making it conducive for us to arrange picnics in open places like gardens, riverbanks, or other popular spots in the state.
2. Do you prefer to take your own vehicle when you go for a picnic, or do you select public transport?

It depends a lot on the type of place we want to go to, the number of people accompanying us, and our budget. If only a few of us want to go someplace, I like to move about in my own car because it gives us the freedom of time and flexibility, which no public transport vehicle can provide. However, if a large number of people want to go together, then I think a bus or a train becomes a more suitable alternative, as it is economical and it allows all members to commute together.

3. Should schools organise picnics for their students?

Yes, it is important for schools to organise picnics at least once a year. This gives students an opportunity to spend good time with each other in an informal environment. Moreover, teachers can also enjoy with students and form a closer bond with them. In addition, picnics pave the way for great lifetime memories for school children. I think schools shouldn't miss any opportunity to give beautiful lifelong memories to their students.

Practice Questions:
1. Have you enjoyed similar picnics after that?
2. What are your favourite picnic spots?
3. What are the popular places around your city where people normally go for picnics?
4. Why do people go for picnics?
5. With whom do you prefer to go for a picnic — friends, family members, or colleagues?
6. What type of places do you suggest for schools to arrange picnics?

63. Describe a popular building of your city.
    You should say
- **The location of the building**
- **The purpose of the building**
- **The features of the building**
When did you visit the building?

Suggestions:
Candidates can speak about a shopping mall, multiplex, or even a government building like the parliament or legislative assembly.

Practice Questions:
1. Do you find similar buildings in other areas of your city?
2. How popular is the building?

64. Describe a session/lesson/seminar about English language that you attended in the past.
    You should say
-    **When and where you attended it**

The Ultimate Guide to IELTS Speaking by Parthesh Thakkar

- **What the topic was**
- **How helpful it was to you**

What were the speakers there like?

Suggestions:
Candidates can speak about any lecture or session on grammar, reading, speaking, listening, or writing skills that they have attended in their coaching institute, or somewhere else.

Practice Questions:
1. What is the importance of that session in your life?
2. Did others enjoy the session?
3. Do you think it is difficult to learn two or three languages at a time?
4. At what age should we start learning a foreign language according to you?

65. Describe the school or the college building where you have studied.

You should say
- **Its location**
- **What the building looks like**
- **What its special features are**

What are your fondest memories of that building?

Follow-up Questions & Answers:
1. When did you last visit your school/college?
I last visited my school in January, 2007. My school had completed one hundred years since its establishment on that day. A grand ceremony had been organised at school, where all the ex-students had been invited. I met many of my schoolmates, and refreshed memories from my school days.

2. Do you think there should be a separate school building for children below 5 years of age (pre-primary)?
Yes, a separate building is required for pre-primary students because they are small, playful, and vulnerable. They need a larger area to play, and to carry out other activities. If there is no separate area for them, at times they may collide with other older students and injure themselves. Moreover, pre-primary school children often learn through games and by singing songs. This may disturb secondary or higher secondary students if their classes are located in the same building.

3. Should the government provide accommodation to secondary and higher secondary school students?
No, there is no need to provide accommodation to all students. In fact, most schools in my country are day schools. In this case, most candidates belong to the same residential area or city as the school campus. Thus, providing accommodation to all students is neither necessary, nor a good idea. However, the government should provide hostel facilities to those students who come from other cities or villages to study.

4. Do you think school children in villages have different facilities than those in cities?
Usually, there is no major difference in the facilities offered by schools in villages and cities. The only difference is in the use of technology; the use of computers and overhead projectors is higher in cities compared to villages.

5. What types of buildings will the schools have in future?
Future schools will be more spacious and away from commercial areas. They will have energy efficient systems like solar panels or wind turbines. They may have bigger and separate sections for all levels of education. What's more, they will conform to very high safety standards.

◆ ◆ ◆

66. Speak about one of your classmates from school or college.

　　You should say

- **Their name**
- **How you spent time with them**
- **What you liked in them**

Are the two of you still in touch?

Practice Questions:
1. What activities did you do with your classmates?
2. Are you still in touch with him?
3. Why do some people remember their childhood or young age friends throughout their lifetime?
4. Was there any incident where he helped you?
5. Was there any incident where you helped him?
6. How different was he from your other classmates?
7. Do you think the company of scholarly classmates helps students in improving their grades?

◆ ◆ ◆

67. Describe a thing/an object that you had bought and were dissatisfied with.
You should say
- **When you bought it**
- **Where you bought it from**
- **What you disliked about it**
What did you do with it?

Suggestions:
Candidates can speak about defective garments, instrument like mobiles, computers, laptops, and music players that might have had a technical fault, or automobiles like

two-wheelers and cars that kept needing repair.

Follow-up Questions & Answers:
1. Is there any support available from the government to help consumers with such problems?
Yes, the government has set up special consumer courts which follow the laws and guidelines provided in the Consumer Protection Act to give justice to consumers. If any consumer is dissatisfied, he can lodge a complaint against the manufacturer or trader who has wronged him, and can seek compensation for the same.
2. What actions should be taken against traders/companies that make false claims about their products or services?
The government can organise a separate department which monitors the marketing activities of various companies and dealers. This department can keep an eye on all the offers and claims made on different products, and if its officers find that any claims or offers are fake or misleading, they can order the concerned companies to stop their campaigns. In addition, such people should be punished so that neither they, nor others repeat such gimmicks.

Practice Questions:
1. What is the difference between the services provided by a small shop and a supermarket/big shop?
2. What are your suggestions for the product you mentioned?
3. Which precautions do you think we should take before buying such products?
4. How effective is government support for consumer protection according to you?

68. Describe a thing you made, that was appreciated by all.
   You should say
- **What that thing was**
- **When you made it**
- **What difficulties you faced while making it**
How did you feel after making it?
Suggestions:
Candidates can speak about a study project, assignment, software, instrument, business deal, or a new food item that they prepared.
Practice Questions:
1. Did you make similar things after that?
2. Why did you make that thing?
3. How much time did it take for you to make it?
4. What is the importance of that thing in your life?
5. Did you get inspiration to do even better after receiving appreciation?
6. Were the skills required to make such things taught to you at your school or college?

69. Describe a thing/an object you possess.

You should say

- What that thing/object is
- When you got that thing/object
- How it is useful to you

What are its special features?

Suggestions:

Candidates can speak about computers, mobiles, vehicles, houses, music players, etc.

70. Describe a wedding you attended.

You should say

- Whose wedding it was
- Where and when it was organised
- What you did in that ceremony

Was there anything unique about the wedding arrangements?

Follow-up Questions & Answers:

1. In general, at what age do people get married in your culture/city/country?

It depends a lot on an individual's culture and city of origin. However, a majority of people get married between the ages of 23 and 27. But, in some cases, if someone wants to study more — for example medical students who need to study hard for more than 8 to 10 years, or someone wants to establish a business — they get married at around 30 years of age.

2. Do you think the minimum age limit for marriage should be increased/decreased? Why?

No, I don't think the minimum age limit should be increased or decreased. The minimum marriage age for boys and girls is 21 and 18, respectively, in my country. I think people become mature enough at this age to lead responsible married lives, and thus they can live happily and cooperatively with each other.

3. Why do people force their children into child marriage?

It is an age-old tradition in many cultures of my country for people to get married in their childhood, so some people still follow this tradition to uphold their cultural values. They fear that if they don't follow this tradition they will be going against their cultural norms. What's more, some people feel insecure about their children growing up and marrying partners of their own choosing, who may be from other communities or castes. So, they force their children to get married at a very young age.

4. What are the consequences of child marriage on the society/individuals?

Child marriage is indeed a curse for our society. Children aren't mentally mature or physically equipped to handle married life till they grow up. This situation creates conflicts, as generally males tend to dominate females in the family, thereby stunting the growth of female children who get married early. Moreover, many victims of child marriage may fall in love with other people when they become older and develop minds of their own. This may lead to a rise in extramarital affairs in the society, causing a breakdown in family structures.

5. Many individuals now use websites/marriage bureaus to select their life partners. Is this a good trend?

Yes, this emerging trend is quite good. Marriage bureaus and websites give us details of many prospective partners, so that we may meet likeminded people and select a bride/groom. They also have databases from all the cities within the country, and from foreign countries. However, there are some chances of getting fake information from people, or coming across frauds. We should enquire properly about anyone we meet on matrimonial websites or marriage bureaus before making a selection.

6. Do you think internet marriage is a good trend? Why?

Such incidents are happening nowadays wherein two people who belong to different cities or countries chat online with each other and fall in love. Some of them also take the bold step of getting married with their chatting partner. There is nothing wrong with this, because, to me, marriage is a meeting of two souls. If both people know each other well, and think they can live their lives together, they should be allowed to get married. It is however, too early to judge if this is a good or bad trend.

Practice Questions:

1. What rituals and traditions were followed in that wedding?
2. Are these rituals and traditions important in weddings?
3. Are such types of weddings arranged in most cultures in your city?
4. What is the difference in the way weddings were performed in the past, versus now?
5. What are the possible reasons for such changes?
6. What should the government do to stop child marriages?
7. Do you have any suggestions for the host of the wedding ceremony?
8. Should we spend more money on the celebration of weddings?
9. What factors should we consider before selecting someone as our life partner?

71. Describe an accident you have seen/witnessed.

　　You should say

- **When and where it happened**
- **What happened exactly**
- **What you did at that time**

Did the accident scare you?

Practice Questions:

1. What should the government do to prevent such accidents?
2. Is there any government/non-government organisation that helps the victims of accidents?
3. What precautions should we take while driving on highways?
4. What actions should an individual take if he sees an accident?
5. What safety measures should be provided in cars/buses?

72. Describe an equipment (mobile, computer, or television) that you largely use at your home or at work.

You should say
- What it is
- How you learned to operate it
- How it is useful to you

How long have you been using it for?

Follow-up Questions & Answers:

1.How are such equipment useful in leisure time?

These equipment can be great tools to pass time with. We can play games, listen to music, and watch movies and photographs on both, computers and mobiles. We can surf the internet and get news and information from it. Moreover, mobiles and computers have chatting facilities, so we can talk to people online in our leisure time. Thus, such equipment can provide us with creative and interactive options to indulge in, in our free time.

2.Is it true that unemployment increases with the increasing use of latest equipment at home and at work?

It seems to be a pessimistic view that unemployment increases because of such equipment. I think the opposite is true; employment increases because of such equipment. For example, we had never heard about a job profile such as a mobile call centre executive, or a computer programmer, a web developer, or a mobile repairer. All these jobs have come into existence only because of the increased use of such equipment.

73. Describe an important year/time of your life.

You should say
- What your age was
- What happened to you
- Why that year was important to you

What were your biggest learnings from that time?

Suggestions:

Candidates can speak about their final year of graduation or school, their first year in a job or marriage, or a time when they established something new, like a business.

74. Describe an old person you know very well.

You should say
- The name of the person, and your relation with them
- Describe the person's appearance and nature

- **What you do with them**

Do you spend a lot of time with this person?

Follow-up Questions & Answers:

1. What are the difficulties faced by today's old timers?

Today's old timers face a new type of problem regarding their health. Firstly, because of the rise in pollution levels, their respiratory health has suffered a great deal. Due to changing lifestyles, their food intake and other habits have changed, too and are not as healthy as they used to be in the past. To top it, improved medicines and healthcare standards have helped in extending our average life span to 80 years and beyond, as compared to the average 60 or 65 year life span of humans in the past. Now, because of such developments, old people need higher and more extensive healthcare treatments, which are often expensive. On the other hand, they cannot even enjoy the last years of their lives if they become victims of chronic diseases. To prevent such situations, I think old timers should divert themselves towards healthier lifestyles, so that they need the least healthcare support possible, and can live their lives well, with healthy bodies.

2. Should the government support old people? How?

The government should support old people in various ways. It can provide free healthcare for them in government hospitals. It can also give them discounts on accessing public services. In addition, the government can also make some employment arrangements for old people, so that they may also survive well, and live their lives with self-respect. Finally, I believe that the government must introduce a compulsory pension scheme for employees of all private and public companies.

Practice Questions:

1. How often do you meet this person?
2. What can you learn from them?
3. How can they be helpful to their family?
4. How can they be helpful to the society?
5. What common activities do old people in your area do?
6. Should old people do some paid work?
7. How are old people treated in your society?
8. What age is considered to be old age in your culture?

75. Describe any antique object that you have at your home, or have seen elsewhere.

   You should say

- **The name of the antique object**
- **What it looks like**
- **How old it is**

What is special about this antique?

Suggestions:

Candidates can speak about any idol of a god or goddess, a piece of jewellery or an ornament, an ancient weapon like a sword, a collection of antique coins, a sculpture, or a painting.

Practice Questions:
1. Is there any history linked to that antique object?
2. How have you preserved it? OR How is it preserved?
3. Should we keep antiques at our home, or in a museum?
4. People spend large sums of money for acquiring antiques. Do you support the practice?

76. Describe any one thing that was established by your friends or family.
   You should say
- **When and where it was established**
- **What it looks like**
- **What benefits you have received from it**
What is your overall opinion of it?
Suggestions:
Candidates can speak about a family run company, trust, or cooperative society. They can also speak about traditions set by their family.

Practice Questions:
1. How often do you visit that place?
2. What future benefits do you think you can get from it?

77. Describe different electronic gadgets that you use in your house.
   You should say
- **What they are**
- **How you use them**
- **Their benefits and drawbacks**
Do all your family members use these gadgets?
Suggestions:
Candidates can speak about their computer, laptop, television, or music system, among other things.

Practice Questions:
1. What difference have these gadgets made to your life?
2. Who uses these gadgets more in your house, and why?
3. How were people's lives without these gadgets?
4. Is there any gadget you want to buy in the future?

The Ultimate Guide to IELTS Speaking by Parthesh Thakkar

78. Describe the last meal you took.

   You should say
- **When and where you took it**
- **What you ate**
- **With whom you ate it**

What was the food like?

Follow-up Questions & Answers:
1. What should children take in their meals?
Children must consume a balanced diet which consists of all the required nutrients such as proteins, carbohydrates, fats, vitamins, and minerals. While I understand that children aren't usually aware of nutritious food sources, their parents should take care of their diets, and should ensure that they consume adequate quantities of milk, vegetables, cereals, and pulses in their meals, so that children may attain optimum physical and mental growth. In addition, parents can take guidance from their family doctors or paediatricians regarding the same.
2. How many meals should we take in a day, according to you?
Well, I think we should take a maximum of three meals a day; breakfast in the morning, one meal in the afternoon, and dinner or supper in the evening, so that our body can get a regular and consistent supply of nutrients.

Practice Questions:
1. What is the ideal time for taking lunch and dinner, according to you?
2. What should old people take more/less in their meals?
3. Do you think we should take dietary consultation to organise our meals? Why?
4. What do people normally eat in their meals in your culture/city?

79. Describe the most embarrassing moment of your life.

   You should say
- **When and where it happened**
- **What happened**
- **How you felt after that**

What did you do to salvage the situation?

Suggestions:
Candidates can speak about any experience that made them blush, feel ashamed, awkward, flustered, or uncomfortable. For example reaching late for a meeting or a conference, writing a letter or an email to the wrong person, making a mistake or creating a funny situation in public, like slipping or spilling things in a party, or soiling your own or someone else's clothes.

Practice Questions:
1. Did you learn anything from that experience?

---

2. Have your friends or family members gone through similar experiences in their lives?

3. Was their reaction to that situation similar to yours?

4. Why do different people react differently in any given situation?

80. **Describe a stage of your life in which you struggled the most.**

    OR

    Describe a critical/difficult stage of your life.

    You should say

- **How old you were**
- **What difficulties you faced**
- **What lessons you learned**

Did anyone guide you through that stage/situation?

Follow-up Question & Answer:

1. What is the role of friends/family in difficult periods of life?

The role of friends and family members becomes more vital in difficult stages of life. This is because difficult stages are those where things don't pan out in our favour, and instead, go wrong unexpectedly. We feel defeated, frustrated, and find ourselves suffering from low levels of self-confidence. Here, friends and family members can give us the support we need. They can remind us that whenever we need their presence, they will be there for us. This kind of unconditional support is essential to restore our confidence, and to bring our lives back on track.

Practice Questions:

1. Who supported you the most in that stage of life?

3. How should we manage our relations and economic conditions through tough times in life?

4. How is the internet/technology helpful in the difficult times in life?

81. **Describe a friend or a relative who lives in a foreign country.**

    You should say

- **The name of that person**
- **Where he lives, and what he does**
- **How you communicate with him**

Is he close to you?

Practice Questions:

1. When did you meet him for the last time?

2. Why has he gone to a foreign country?

3. What changes are seen in the social statuses of people who go abroad?

4. If given a chance, would you like to visit your friend who lives abroad?

82. Describe your ideal house.

    You should say

- **Where the house would be located**
- **How big it would be, and what facilities it would have**
- **What special features it would have**

With whom would you live in that house?

Practice Questions:

1. When will it be possible for you to have a house like that?
2. How different is your present house from your ideal house?

83. Describe your ideal job.

    You should say

- **The job designation**
- **The name of the company that can offer you that job**
- **What job responsibilities you expect**

How much do you expect to earn from the job?

Practice Questions:

1. Are such jobs available in your country?
2. What will you have to do to get this job?
3. When do you think you will be able to get that job?
4. Can women or men perform better in your ideal job?
5. Should a person take early retirement, or not?

84. Speak about a news story/event which became very popular in your city/country.

    You should say

- **What happened**
- **When and where it happened**

- Why it became popular
Do such events happen often where you live?

Practice Questions:
1. Do you think some stories/events are given more footage by the media than required?
2. What are the reasons behind this?
3. Is it good or bad, according to you?
4. Should there be some guidelines for the media, when it comes to covering events like bomb blasts, accidents, or calamities?
5. Are the news channels increasing/decreasing in your country? Why?
6. What are the benefits and drawbacks of increasing news channels in your country?

85. Describe your last visit to a museum.
   You should say
- **When and where you visited the museum**
- **With whom you visited**
- **What that museum was about**
What did you like there?

86. Speak about your visit to a jewellery show room/shop.
   You should say
- **The name and location of that shop/showroom**
- **When and why you visited it**
- **What you liked there**
Did you make any purchases there?

Practice Questions:
1. Do you visit such places often?
2. What changes have you seen in such places in the last few years?
3. Which metal is more preferred for jewellery in your culture/country, silver or gold and why?
4. Is there any specific time or occasion when people buy jewellery in your culture/city?
5. Why do people invest their money in gold?
6. Why do women like diamond jewellery more than other varieties?
7. Will this trend be seen in the future also?
8. What security measures are taken by jewellery merchants in your city?

The Ultimate Guide to IELTS Speaking by Parthesh Thakkar

87. Describe your last visit to a garment store/show room.

You should say
- The name and location of that shop/showroom
- When and why you visited it
- What you liked there

What was the most attractive garment that you saw there?

Practice Question:
1. Do you have any suggestions for that store?

88. Describe your last visit to an exhibition.

You should say
- When and where you visited it
- What the theme of the exhibition was
- What you liked there

How big was the exhibition?

Suggestions:
Candidates can speak about any exhibition they have visited, for example, a book fair an art and craft exhibit, a technology exhibit, or an exhibition related to large services sector industries such as education, healthcare, and tourism. They may also describe a religious or cultural exhibit that they may have come across.

Follow-up Questions & Answers:
1. Should we organise exhibitions of works done by children?
Yes, I think it is really helpful to children to exhibit their works, because they get a lot of motivation from the appreciation they receive from those who visit the exhibition. Moreover, they also get inspiration to do better, and to enhance their skills in that field.
2. How does an exhibition help in the education and development of children?
An exhibition can teach some important things very easily at times, as compared to conventional classroom training. Children can learn a lot from exhibitions based on culture, history, religion, and patriotism. I can say this from my own experience, because even though my own grandfather participated in India's fight for independence, I only understood the importance of his contribution when I saw an exhibition interactively depicting the fight for freedom, when I was in school. Before that, everything was only a theoretical concept for me. However, now I salute all those who fought for the nation.
3. Do you think children like to go to exhibitions?
Children like to go to an exhibition only if they like the theme of that exhibition. They prefer themes surrounding fun characters or super heroes, animals, paintings, toys, crafts, and so on. Children usually don't like exhibitions depicting sculpture, history, and books, because such subjects don't appeal to their age group.

Practice Questions:
1. Are you interested in museums/exhibitions/art galleries? Why?
2. What kind of people are interested in such places, according to you?
3. What is the role of technology in today's museums, exhibitions, and art galleries?
4. How can we encourage people to develop an interest in such places?
5. Have you visited other exhibitions as well?

89. Describe your siblings or cousins.
   You should say
-   **Their ages and what their personalities are like**
-   **The kind of relationship you have with them**
-   **What their peculiarities/specialities are**

Do you spend a lot of time with them?

Follow-up Questions & Answers:
1. How can siblings be helpful in life?
Siblings are really helpful to us in life. They can help us in both, good and bad times in our lives. They can stand by us in all walks of life, because they are a part of our family. What's more, generally, they are similar in age to us, so they can understand our problems much better than our parents, or other elders in the family. This is because, there is no generation gap between brothers and sisters who belong to the same age group. They can be our good friends, companions, support systems, and guides in life.

2. What problems do you think a child who doesn't have brothers/sisters may face?
Well, it is true that we live in a society where the single child concept prevails in most cultures. However, a single child may feel lonely at times if he doesn't get enough love and attention from his family, especially his parents. A single child often feels spending time outdoors with his friends to beat boredom, rather than staying at home. At times, a single child may start having one-way conversations with his toys or developing imaginary friends, to fill the gap of a sibling or playmate. In extreme cases, such a lonely child may suffer from strange phobias or psychotic disorders. All these can be taken care of if proper attention is given by parents, so that the child never feels lonely.

Practice Questions:
1. Do you enjoy a similar relationship with your cousins?
2. Do you share all your secrets with your siblings?
3. What is the role of parents in the development of a relationship between siblings?
4. Do you think siblings can be good friends? Why?
5. What activities do you do with your siblings?
6. Have they influenced you in any way?

90. Speak about the most successful member of your family.

   You should say
- **Who he is**
- **What he does**
- **How you interact with him**

Why is he more successful, according to you?

Practice Questions:
1. Do you think the success of family members also helps us socially and personally?
2. Should the successful members take more responsibility of the family?
3. What kind of support should we give to the family member who is more successful?
4. Do you believe that success is inherited, or that it comes in one's genes?
5. What is the role of education in this family member's success, according to you?

91. Speak about one of your cousins whom you admire the most.

   You should say
- **How you are related to him**
- **Why you admire him**
- **How he is different from you**

What negative qualities does this cousin have, according to you?

Practice Questions:
1. How do you spend time with him?
2. Do you think that cousins can be good friends, too?

92. Consider and talk about a scenario where you want to start your business.

   You should say
- **What type of business you will start**
- **What you will need for it**
- **How it will affect your life**

Whose guidance would you take in setting up the business?

Follow-up Questions & Answers:
1. Will you invite your family members/friends to join you in business?
It is indeed a good idea to share our business with our family members and friends, because sharing our work gives us flexibility and peace of mind. However, I believe that

we should invite them only if they have the required skills for the type of business we are involved in, or if they can make a creative contribution to the business.

2. Should we take loans from a bank if we want to start a business?

There is no harm in taking loans from a bank for business purposes. Here, some factors should be taken into consideration before taking finances from outside. Firstly, we should be confident enough about our business model, and its revenue generation potential, which should be enough to meet the maintenance expenses, salaries of employees, and the instalments of the loan. What's more, we should also envisage estimated returns from the business so that we can repay the loan as early as possible, and can reach the breakeven point.

Practice Questions:
1. Where will you start your business?
2. How much do you expect to earn out of it?
3. What do people in your city/area/culture normally prefer — doing a job, or doing a business? Why?
4. Would you help someone in your family or friends if they wants to start their business? How?

93. If you have to travel, which place you would like to travel to?
   You should say
- **When and where you will travel**
- **With whom you will travel**
- **Why you want to take a trip to that place**

Have you been there before?

94. Discuss an important hope for your future.
   You should say
- **What that hope is**
- **Why you have that hope**
- **How you will fulfil it**

How will its fulfilment affect your life?

Suggestions:
Candidates can speak about their ambitions, future goals and projects in hand, dreams of foreign settlement, or the completion of their studies in a foreign country.

Follow-up Questions & Answers:
1. What is the importance of setting goals in life?

Goal setting is an essential process for humans to evolve and grow in life. All our actions are based on our conscious and subconscious thoughts. Here, unless we have a clear direction or goal in our mind, we may waste the invaluable assets of our life like time, youth, and opportunities. I think a person without a goal is like a boat without a sailor. This boat can float on the water, but ultimately it sinks. Similarly, a goalless person may live his life and get by, but he can never lead in his life or be successful.

2. What, according to you, is an ideal age to set up goals in life?
It depends on the type of goal we want to set. We should set goals regarding our studies from high school onwards, so that we start working hard to secure admissions in a discipline of our choice. We should set career goals in the beginning phases of our professional life, so that we may put in proactive efforts to achieve them, right from the start. In short, early planning is the key to success.

Practice Questions:
1. What changes will you have to make in yourself to fulfil your hope?
2. Who do you think can support you in doing so?
3. How will you feel after you attain what you have hoped for?
4. What do you feel about those youngsters who do not have goals in their life?
5. What factors can affect the goal setting process in life?
6. Should we help others in setting up goals of their life?
7. Should we help others in fulfilling their life goals?
8. Do you think big companies should decide their goals in advance?

95. Speak about an important decision you took in the past.
   You should say
- **What the decision was**
- **When you took it**
- **What positive and negative factors you had to consider before taking that decision**
How has that decision affected your life?
Suggestions:
Candidates can speak about the selection of their fields of study, their school, or their college. They can also speak about starting a business, joining a job, getting married, buying a house, or joining any personality development training.

96. Speak about an award/prize, or an honour you received in life.
   You should say
- **When and where you won it**
- **Why it was given to you**

- How you reacted after getting it

What preparations did you make, to win the award?

Practice Questions:
1. How did you celebrate your success?
2. What are the benefits of such honours?
3. How do awards and prizes motivate children?
4. What do you think should be given as a prize — a trophy, or money in the form of a cheque or cash?

97. Speak about an adventurous person you know.
   You should say
- **How you know him**
- **When and where you met him**
- **What type of adventures he likes**
Why do you think he is adventurous?

Suggestions:
Candidates can speak about someone who is adventurous in nature, and likes going for exciting activities like trekking, paragliding, and river rafting. They can also speak about someone who is adventurous in their business or job sphere.

Practice Questions:
1. Are you adventurous by nature?
2. Could you describe an incident when your friend behaved adventurously?
3. Should society help adventurous people when they are in trouble?
4. Do you think children should be given the freedom to learn adventurous activities?

98. Speak about one interesting thing you would like to do in the future.
   You should say
- **What it will be**
- **How you will do it**
- **How easy it will be for you**
When do you think you will do it?

Suggestions:
Candidates can speak about any new activity that they may pursue in future, such as learning a new language, learning to sing or to play a musical instrument, acquiring new

qualifications, and learning new sports or games.

Practice Question:

1. Do you think that the government's strategic decisions are always helpful in the long run?

99. Describe an activity you do to remain healthy.

   You should say

- **What you do**

- **When and where you do it**

- **Why you do it**

Is this a popular activity in your vicinity?

Practice Questions:

1. Do you take anyone's guidance to do the activity?
2. Do you think the activity can be done better in the company of a friend or a family member?
3. Is there any equipment needed to do this activity?
4. What are the advantages of doing this activity?
5. Is there any possible disadvantage of such an activity?
6. Why do some people choose to live an unhealthy lifestyle?

100. Speak about a dream you had.

   You should say

- **When you had it**

- **What it was**

- **How you felt**

Do you usually remember your dreams after you wake up?

Follow-up Questions & Answers:

1. Do dreams have factual information? OR Should we believe in the dreams that we see, or not?

Dreams come from the subconscious part of our mind. This part of the mind is active even when we are asleep. This part reveals our past and present conditions, our problems, and our feelings and expectations about life. At times, it also contains information about the future. The only problem is that dreams have symbolic or metaphorical meanings. To top it, the meanings of symbols and metaphors differ from person to person, making it difficult to interpret our dreams. However, one branch of psychology, which is known as psychoanalysis is advancing in this field. This branch deals with the interpretation of dreams for humans, so that we can gather information about our past and future by tapping into our subconscious.

2. Is it possible to know the personality of a person by analysing his dreams or dream patterns?

Yes, it is now possible to learn about the nature and personality traits of a person by analysing his dreams. For example, if a person keeps having dreams that he doesn't remember much, then we can say that his level of conscious attention towards life is generally low. This person has a mind which is preoccupied with thoughts that are reflected in his dreams. On the other hand, if a person doesn't get many vivid dreams, we can infer that he is calm and happy, and doesn't get emotionally disturbed, often.

Practice Questions:
1. Do you get such dreams often?
2. Do dreams come true?
3. Have any of your dreams come true? How?

101. Speak about a person with whom you like to spend time.
   You should say
-   **The name of the person**
-   **How you know him**
-   **What you like to do with him**
How often do you meet him?

102. Speak about a pet animal or bird you have or your friend/relative has.
   You should say
-   **What that bird/animal is**
-   **How you interact with it**
-   **What you like about it**
Have you always been fond of pets?

Practice Questions:
1. What do people prefer more as a pet — a bird, or an animal? Why?
2. What care should we take of our pets?
3. Is the trend of keeping pets rising in your city? Justify your answer.
4. If you get the opportunity to keep a pet, which animal/bird would you keep, and why?
5. Is there any disadvantage of keeping pets in the house?

6. Do you think the media influences people to have pets?
7. Pets are not allowed at some places like hotels and restaurants. Do you think this is right, or wrong? Why?
8. Do you think the government should ban keeping pet animals or birds at home? Why?
9. Where can we find more pets in your country — in urban areas, or in rural areas? Why?

103. Speak about an argument/a conflict you had with someone in the past (at work, or at school/college).

   You should say
- What happened exactly
- Why the argument/conflict happened
- How you reacted to it

Could it have been avoided, if you had handled the situation differently?

Practice Questions:
1. Do you think your reaction to the conflict was good? Why?
2. Why do some people have more conflicts with others?
3. How do people settle conflicts with others in your culture/city?
4. What should we do to avoid conflicts with others?
5. What are the disadvantages of having conflicts at work, or in family, or with friends?
6. What are the common causes of conflicts between people in your city?
7. Do you think that the tolerance level of people is decreasing these days?
8. Why do you think so?
9. Is it good, or bad for the society?
10. Do you think the tolerance level of people also depends on their culture/religion?
11. What is the role of education in increasing the level of tolerance in a society?
12. Do movies/the media play any role in increasing/decreasing the tolerance levels of the people of your country?

104. Describe a course (other than academic), that you have done.

   You should say
- The name of the course, and why you did it
- When and where you did it
- What you liked and disliked about it

Would you recommend this course to others?

Suggestions: learning a musical instrument, painting, drawing, swimming, skating, and cricket, all qualify as non-academic skills, and can be spoken about in context of this question.

Practice Questions:
1. Was it easy for you to complete that course?
2. Did you have any suggestions about the course?
3. How will this course help you in life?
4. Do old people also take up such courses? Why?
5. How helpful is technology in learning/teaching such courses?

105. Speak about an environment-friendly activity you do.
　　You should say
-　**What that activity is**
-　**When and where you do it**
-　**How it helps the environment**
Does anyone else accompany you in performing this activity?

Practice Questions:
1. When did you start doing it, and why?
2. Do you inspire others to do the same activity?
3. What do you feel when you do it?
4. Do you think the awareness about environmental issues in your country is good/not good?
5. Should the government honour those who help in preserving the environment?

106. Speak about something you do to save energy.
　　You should say
-　**What it is**
-　**Where you learned it**
-　**How it is useful**
Is this something that many people around you do, in order to save energy?

Practice Questions:
1. Who inspired you to do it?
2. Are the people of your city aware of this activity?
3. How can one spread awareness about the benefits of this activity?
4. What should we do to motivate people to save more energy?
5. Why should we save energy?
6. Do you think there is a difference in energy usage between urban and rural people?

107. Describe an important tradition/custom you follow in your family/culture.
   You should say
- What it is
- When and where you follow it
- Why you follow it

Is this tradition/custom time consuming?

Practice Questions:
1. What is the importance of that tradition/custom in your family/culture?
2. How did you come to know about it?
3. Why do customs/traditions differ in different cultures/countries?
4. Do you think the importance and belief in traditions/customs has changed with time? Why?

108. Speak about your favourite sportsperson/ athlete.
   You should say
- The name of the sportsperson/athlete
- What sports he plays
- Why you like him

What are his best personality traits/virtues?

109. Speak about a health problem that you had in the past.
   You should say
- What the problem was
- Why the problem happened
- What you did to recover from it

What difficulties did you face because of that problem?

110. Tell me about a childhood group activity that you enjoyed the most.
   You should say
- What you did
- When and with whom you did it
- What you enjoyed about the activity

Do children these days also indulge in this activity?

◆ ◆ ◆

111. Speak about a change you want to bring in your daily routine, to improve your health.

You should say
- What it is
- How you will bring about this change
- How useful it will be to you

Will it be easy to bring about this change and sustain it?

◆ ◆ ◆

112. Speak about a place you visit often.

OR

113. Speak about your favourite place in your city.

You should say
- The name and location of the place
- When you visit it
- With whom you visit it

What do you do there, and why do you like that place so much?

Suggestions:
Candidates can speak about a shopping mall, garden, lake, river, zoo, amusement park, theatre, or a temple that they enjoy visiting.

Practice Questions:
1. Are there similar places available in your city?
2. How did you come to know about that place?
3. What do other people do at there?
4. Do you recommend that place to others? Why?
5. What is the importance of travelling?

◆ ◆ ◆

114. Describe a countryside/rural/forest area that you know, or visit often.

You should say
- Where it is located
- Why you like it

- What activities you and other people do there

How do you usually reach there?

115. Speak about a child who is dear to you.

You should say
- The name of the child, and your relation with him
- The peculiarities of that child/describe the appearance of the child
- Why you like that child

What activities do you do with that child?

Practice Questions:

1. How much time do you spend with that child?

2. What activities do you do with that child?

116. Describe a teenager you know well.

You should say
- How you know the teenager
- What his qualities are
- How you relate to him/spend time with him

Do you gain any insights into life by spending time with him?

Follow-up Questions & Answers:

1. What is the role of education in the condition of present day teenagers?

Education has played a vital role in improving the overall condition of present day teenagers. Today's teenagers have more up-to-date knowledge in terms of academic subjects, as the curriculum changes regularly, based on new developments across subjects. Teenagers today have access to more facilities when it comes to education, intellectual development, arts, entertainment, hobby, science and technology, and so on. This is the reason, present day teenagers get more respect and consideration in their family and society.

2. What changes do you think we should bring in our education system to improve the efficiency of today's teenagers?

We should try to increase the interaction between teachers and students in the education system. I believe that education should also bring about creative development in students, and not just academic excellence. We should try to impart more practical life skills to make them better equipped to handle the pressures of tertiary education, and also because these skills will lay the foundation for teenagers to be better, more competent, and more efficient civilians in future.

3. Should teenagers become aware of international news? Justify your answer.

According to me, it is desirable for today's teenagers to keep up with international news, because it can help them stay aware of the new trends in education, science and technology, arts, fashion, lifestyle, and sports. At times, such information also helps them in selecting or developing hobbies, life skills, intellectual resources, and also helps them in choosing their career.

4. What are the interests and hobbies seen in today's teenagers?

Today's teenagers seem to have more hobbies to pursue than ever. They like sports, art, such as drawing or painting, and skills like dancing. However, I have also noticed that they are quite gadget savvy. So, they often spend their time on computers, mobiles, and interactive video games on the Play Station and X Box.

Practice Questions:

1. What is the difference between today's teenagers, and teenagers a decade ago?
2. Who is living a better life according to you — the teenager of today, or the teenager of a decade ago?
3. How different is the teenager you know, from other teenagers?

117. Describe a decorative article/item you possess in your house, or have seen somewhere. (E.g. this could be a wall painting, an antique lamp, a show piece, a handicraft, or even an ornament.)

You should say

- **When and where you saw/got it**
- **What its features are**
- **Why you like it**

Is this article rare, or is it easily available?

Practice Questions:

1. What type of articles do people keep in their houses, in your culture/city?
2. Does culture/religion influence the selection of decorative articles that we keep in our homes?
3. Why do people keep some symbols in their houses?
4. Do you think such symbols have positive effects on the surroundings?
5. What can be judged about people, by observing the decorative articles they keep in their houses?
6. What type of things do children like to keep in their rooms?

118. Speak about the most difficult exam you have appeared for, in your life.

　　You should say

- **The date and subject of the exam**
- **How you had prepared**
- **How that exam was**

What result did you get in that exam?

Practice Questions:

1. How did you react when you received your results?
2. What did you learn from that experience?
3. What is the general attitude of youngsters towards exams?
4. Should we completely remove exams from schools and colleges? Why?
5. How should youngsters prepare for their exams?

119. Describe any reference material you use, or have used in the past, such as a book, journal, or CD.

　　You should say

- **What topic that material is/was on**
- **When and how you got it**
- **How it helped you**

Is/Was the material brief, or extensive and elaborate?

Practice Questions

1. Did you recommend that material to others?
2. Did you have any suggestions for that material?
3. Is any material on the same subject available on the internet?

120. Speak about a book that you read in your childhood.

　　You should say

- **The name of the book**
- **When and where you read it**
- **What message the book gave**

What was the theme of the book?

Suggestions:

Candidates can speak about any religious book or storybook that they have read in their childhood.

Practice Questions:

1.Is it still your favourite book?

2.Are there any benefits of reading funny or comic books?

3.If someone doesn't read during their childhood, can they read in the future?

121. Speak about your favourite childhood activity.

   You should say

-   **What that activity was**

-   **Where, and how you did it**

-   **With whom you did it**

Why do you remember that activity?

Suggestions:

Candidates can speak about any outdoor or indoor game, a hobby like painting, or singing, or about any social or religious activity.

Practice Questions:

1. What activities do children like to participate in at school, apart from studies?

2. Should children be taught that activity in school?

3. Do you do that activity or similar activities now?

4. With whom do children want to play more — older people, or people of their age group? Why?

122. Speak about your favourite food dish.

   You should say

-   **The name of the dish**

-   **How it is prepared**

-   **What you like about it**

What are the benefits and drawbacks of the dish?

Practice Question:

1. Is there any special food available in your area?

123. Speak about your favourite motorcar.

   You should say

-   **The brand name of the car**

The Ultimate Guide to IELTS Speaking by Parthesh Thakkar

- When and where you saw it for the first time
- Why that car is your favourite

What are its special features?

Follow-up Questions & Answers:
1. Should seat belts be made compulsory for car drivers and passengers?
Yes, I think seat belts are essential for those who travel in cars, because if they meet with an accident, the seat belt prevents them from colliding immediately with the body of the car, by holding them back and resisting the brutal force of the accident. Such belts have proved to be life-saving in many dangerous accidents. This is the reason why most governments of the world have made the use of seat belts compulsory for all car passengers.

Practice Questions:
1. Should the government restrict cars in downtown (central) areas of the city?
2. What facilities should be provided in cars?

124. Speak about your favourite photograph.
   You should say
- What the photograph depicts
- By whom, and when the photograph was taken
- How memorable that photograph is to you

Do you have other similar photographs that you cherish?
Suggestions:
Candidates can speak about any family photo taken at a function, or a group photo with friends or colleagues.

125. Speak about the importance of explorers in today's society.
   You should say
- How they get motivation to explore new places
- Who should finance them
- If you would like to go on an exploratory trip

Have you ever felt inspired by the tales of any explorer?
Suggestions:
Candidates can speak about the exploration of a new land or a new planet. Columbus and Hillary are good examples of explorers.

126. Talk about a trip you went on, that did not live up to your expectations.

   You should say
-   **When and where you went**
-   **What went wrong**
-   **How you felt about the trip**

What could have been done differently to make the trip better?

◆ ◆ ◆

127. Describe an educational trip you went on, when you were in school/college.

   You should say
-   **When and where you went**
-   **With whom you went**
-   **What you learned there**

Have you visited that place again, afterwards?

Practice Questions:

1. What is your opinion of learning at home?
2. Should educational trips be made compulsory in schools/colleges?
3. How does a picnic differ from an educational trip?
4. Do all candidates enjoy educational trips?
5. Will the trend of organising educational trips increase or decrease in future?

◆ ◆ ◆

128. Describe a historical personality you have read about.

OR

129. Speak about a historical character/hero (national or international) you studied about in school/college.

   You should say
-   **The name of that character**
-   **How you came to know about him**
-   **What he did**

Are there any qualities in him that you would like to emulate?

Follow-up Questions & Answers

1. Do you think studying about such people helps us in our present day life?

Yes, studying about the lives of such people always helps us in our present day life. First, we can understand the lifestyles, mind sets, and cultures of the past. This helps us in understanding our present day lives better. To top it, we can learn from the mistakes they committed in their life, the virtues present behind their success, their strengths, and their strategies for achieving success. All these can eventually help us in our present day life also.

2. What are the advantages and disadvantages of keeping statues of national leaders at public places?

Statues of national leaders help people in remembering them easily. Here, I am not talking about remembering them as individuals. Instead, I think, the main motive behind installing their statues is to remind people about their morals, their commitment to the betterment of society, their patriotism, their virtues, and the other principles and messages given by those leaders, so that we can implement them in our everyday lives.

Practice Questions:
1. How has he influenced you in your life?
2. Does the government of your country honour them with awards?
3. Do you think celebrities related to entertainment and sports should also be given similar respect and honour?

130. Speak about your favourite political leader.
   You should say
-   **The name of the leader**
-   **How you know about him**
-   **The qualities of the leader**
How has he influenced you?

Follow-up Questions & Answers:
1. What are the qualities of a good political leader?
A political leader must have all the necessary leadership traits like courage, hard work, and the ability to lead and address large groups of people at any time. Apart from this, I think they must have compassion and dedication towards their work, towards their objectives, and towards their followers. Moreover, leaders must be good visionaries, and have decision-making abilities that can help the nation. Unfortunately, it is often seen that leaders become self-centred once they reach a powerful position in their career.

2. What is the role of a politician in the development of his country?
Politicians have the power to shape their country in a good or bad way. They can help to create opinions among people, which can be the driving force behind many strategic and policy related decisions regarding the country. These decisions hold the foundations of the country for the future.

3. Do you think there should be an upper age restriction for politicians?
I think we should make some restrictions for those who work in the parliament. I don't agree with implementing and age bar, because, while some people can work efficiently at 80, there are others who cannot even walk properly at 60. Thus, rather than setting an age

limit, we should put in place physical fitness related restrictions for those who want to work as politicians.

4. Why do you think youngsters do not prefer to go in politics?

There are many reasons behind this. One of them is the overall perception of politics as a career. Politics is not considered a good and reputable career in society. Rather, some perceive it as a filthy and corrupt occupation. Moreover, in politics, it takes decades for beginners to reach a respectable position, where they can get job satisfaction. Further, there are plenty of job opportunities available in existing and emerging fields, other than politics, where youngsters can get good jobs with growth prospects. All these factors prevent youngsters from pursuing politics as a career.

5. Does media play any role in increasing/decreasing the popularity of politicians?

Media does play a significant role in increasing or decreasing the popularity of a politician. The press has the freedom to write for or against any politician in their publications. This is the reason why these days we can observe an understanding between some politicians and media personnel, in most countries of the world.

6. Are politicians respected in your country?

Honestly speaking, politicians are not given enough respect in my country. My country has seen many corrupt ministers and leaders, who have exploited their positions to fulfil their own greed for money. However, because of the wide spread reach of the media, and the improved quality of education accessible to the public, more promising leaders are coming up. They are gradually changing the perception of politicians in the minds of the people.

7. Are leaders born or made?

We all have, to a more or less extent, a raw potential to become leaders. However, personalities like Sardar Patel and Lal Bahadur Shastri were born leaders, i.e. they had leadership qualities since their childhood and they further developed them in order to lead the nation in the struggle for independence. On the other hand, leaders like Mahatma Gandhi are made leaders. Despite having good leadership abilities, Gandhi didn't start his career as a leader. But, situations in his life motivated him to take up leadership to help others, and to uphold values such as freedom, nonviolence, and truth.

Practice Questions:

1. Do you have any suggestion for your favourite leader?
2. What will you do if you meet him?
3. Are there similar leaders in your country?
4. Should media focus more on political issues?
5. If a politician is found guilty of a criminal activity, do you think he should be more severely punished compared to an ordinary civilian?

◆ ◆ ◆

131. Speak about your favourite teacher.

  You should say
- **The name of the teacher**

- What subject he taught you
- Why he is your favourite teacher

What good personality traits and virtues did your favourite teacher have?

132. Describe one of your neighbours/relatives whom you know well.
     You should say
- The name of the neighbour/relative, and how you first met them
- What qualities you like in the neighbour/relative
- How you spend time with this person

Have you ever travelled with this neighbour/relative?

Practice Questions:
1. Have you ever had any memorable incident with your neighbour?
2. How different is that person from other neighbours?

133. Speak about your first day at college.
     You should say
- How old you were
- How you reached there
- What happened on that day

How did you feel at the end of the day?

Follow-up Questions & Answers:
1. Do you think senior students should welcome fresh students?
Yes, it is really helpful for freshmen if their seniors welcome them on their first day at college, because new students often feel nervous during their first few days. They are unaware of the college system and campus initially, and if their seniors behave in a friendly way with them, they can get acquainted easily, and adjust themselves to the college environment.
2. Do you think the government should completely ban ragging in colleges?
Ragging is an evil of college campuses. Students have no right to humiliate their juniors for fun. Ragging leaves a deep psychological impact on freshmen. Sometimes, they drop out of college, or become violent and attack others. All these consequences are not conducive to academic growth. Thus, ragging must be banned in all colleges and universities, and if someone tries to rag juniors, that student should be punished severely to set an example for others.

3. Should colleges organise orientation lectures before a new term starts?
Yes, it is necessary for students to have an orientation session that is organised by college authorities, so that fresh students get a quick know-how of the functioning of the college, and get acquainted with its rules. Students also learn about who to approach for various problems that they may face during their time at college. Further, a well organised orientation session can make students feel comfortable and ready to start their studies without any difficulty.

4. Is it essential for a college to have a canteen — yes, or no? Why?
It is essential for a college to have a canteen, for many reasons. Firstly, college studies are a full time activity, where students come from different parts of the city, or even from nearby cities and towns. This means that they may not necessarily have access to healthy home cooked meals during the day. So, it is important for them to get economical and hygienic food, which can be best offered by a college canteen. What's more, college canteens also prevent students from stepping out of the college campus just to eat. This can help improve their attendance in lectures, because when students go out to eat, they often bunk some lectures in the bargain, too.

Practice Questions:
1. Some students say that there should be no academic lectures on the first day of the college. Do you agree with this statement?
2. Why do you think students bunk lectures?
3. Should college authorities make attendance compulsory? Why?

134. Speak about a hectic/busy day at your work/college/home.
   You should say
-   **What that day was**
-   **What happened on that day**
-   **How you handled the workload**
Do you often have such busy days?

Follow-up Questions & Answers:
1. How different is the modern time management system from that of the olden days?
There is a vast difference in present day time management, compared to the past. Present day time management techniques lay major emphasis on multi-tasking. Multi-tasking is a skill that involves performing more than one task at a time, effectively. This is the mantra of many successful management gurus today. In the past, we focused on scheduling things as per the time available to us, and completed them one by one. Now, we start many tasks all at once, and work at completing them simultaneously.

2. Do you think the importance given to time management is different in different countries/cultures?
I think the basic concept of time management remains uniform everywhere. However,

the difference lies in prioritising the tasks on hand. The perception of tasks and patterns of scheduling depend a lot on cultural conditioning. This is the reason why we feel that the importance given to time management is different across cultures.

Practice Questions:
1. How different was that day from other days?
2. Did you take support from someone on that day?
3. How did you feel at the end of the day?
4. Should we teach time management skills in schools and colleges, also?
5. What skills are needed to manage time effectively, according to you?
6. How can time management help children/housewives?
7. How is technology useful in time management?
8. What, according to you, are the possible reasons behind a lack of time management in some people?
9. Do the people of your culture/city/country manage their time well?
10. Do you know anyone who is not punctual?
11. What kind of troubles one can face if he is not punctual?
12. Do you take special precautions when you deal with someone who is not punctual?

◆ ◆ ◆

135. Speak about something which you are good at doing.
You should say
- **How you do it**
- **How you learned it**
- **What feelings you get when you do it**

Do you know others who are also good at the same thing?

Suggestions:
Candidates can speak about their special skills, like painting, dancing, singing, sports, language, cooking, studies, anchoring, or accounting.

Follow-up Questions & Answers:
1. What facilities are available in your area for the development of skills and abilities of children?
Apart from schools, where children get a good platform to sharpen their skills, there are some private and government centres that run special classes that teach vocal and instrumental music, dance, drawing, painting, various sports, sewing, cooking, and other extracurricular activities. Children can learn and develop new skills at these centres. What's more, some classes organise big public events where their students can display their skills before the public.
2. What is the role of parents and teachers in the life of a child who is differently abled?
The role of parents and teachers becomes more important in the life of a child who is differently abled, because such children have to rely a lot on their parents and teachers

for their learning and development. Such children are more vulnerable and sensitive compared to other children of their age, and so, I assert that we should be more compassionate in our approach to them. I believe that they only need support, and not mercy from the society.

Practice Questions:
1. Should a person develop new skills in their middle ages?
2. If given a chance, what skill would you like to develop in yourself, and why?
3. What facilities do you think you will need to pursue your hobbies/skills?

136. Speak about something that was important for you, which you forgot to do.
   You should say
-   **What that thing was**
-   **When you realised that you had forgotten to do it**
-   **What happened after that**
Were you able to salvage the situation?

Practice Questions:
1. What did you learn from that incident?
2. What should we do to remember our tasks?
3. How did you react when you came to know that you had forgotten to do it?

137. Speak about a bad habit/an addiction that you gave up in the past.
   You should say
-   **What it was**
-   **How you gave it up**
-   **How it benefited you**
What would you recommend to others who are looking to give up an addiction?

Practice Questions:
1. Who motivated you to give it up?
2. Did you take anyone's help in giving it up?
3. What is the role of family/culture in developing a person's habits?
4. What bad habits or addictions can be found in today's teenagers?
5. Do bad habits of people also change from generation to generation?
6. How should we help others in giving up bad habits?
7. Do you think one's inclination towards bad habits also depends on their friends?

8. What support does the government provide to those people who want to give up addictions?
9. Does the media play a positive/negative role in the spread of addictions in the society?
10. What should we do to keep children away from bad habits and addictions?

138. Talk about your level of proficiency in English.

You should say

- **How you rate your proficiency**
- **What difficulties you faced while learning English**
- **How useful English language is, in your life**

Do you use English more for writing, or for speaking?

Practice Questions:
1. What is the general level of English proficiency of the people of your city?
2. What factors are important in learning English?

139. Talk about your favourite month.

You should say

- **The name of the month**
- **How the weather is, during that month**
- **What you do during that month**

Why do you like that month?

Practice Questions:
1. What do your family members do during that month?
2. How important is that month for you?

140. Talk about your school/college life.

You should say

- **What kinds of friends and teachers you had in school/college**
- **What activities you performed or excelled at**
- **What special memories you have**

Was your school/college located near your home?

Practice Questions:
1. Did you study in the same school/college throughout?
2. What problems do children face when they have to change their schools frequently?
3. Would you recommend your school/college to others?

141. Describe your favourite music album.

   You should say
-    The name of that album
-    When you heard it for the first time
-    What you like about it

Which musicians are responsible for creating that album?

Follow-up Questions & Answers:
1. What is a better way to listen to music according to you — audio cassettes, CDs, or MP3 players?
It depends on the choice of the listeners. However, I feel that a CD player is the best option. This is because cassette players are quite out of date these days. Cassettes have a shorter life compared to Compact Discs. Also, cassettes and their players cannot give as high definition audio output, as CDs and CD players can, because CDs are digitally recorded. Apart from CDs, MP3 players are also good and convenient options for listening to music, because we can simply use head phones and listen to our songs anywhere without disturbing others. But, prolonged use of head phones may damage our hearing. So, I prefer listening to a CD on a music system, rather than using an Mp3 player where I have to use head phones.
2. Many people listen to music while they drive or travel; is this practice good or bad?
This is a good way to provide entertainment to ourselves and our co-passengers, but if we tune our car audio system too loud, it can be disadvantageous. Firstly, it creates lots of noise pollution. Secondly, at times we become so involved in listening to music that we may not concentrate properly on driving. This can be hazardous to us, and to others.
3. How do websites that facilitate free music downloads affect the business of music albums?
There are some websites that allow its users to download music absolutely for free. This is a form of piracy that hurts the profit margins of the music industry badly, because the end user doesn't pay for the music he downloads. Further, when word of such websites spreads, more and more people get attracted to using this mode of downloading music, instead of going to the market to legally buy music CDs. Hence, the business of music industry is adversely affected by websites that promote piracy.
4. What are the negative effects of piracy?
Piracy affects the business in an egregious way. It damages the business of the industry by preventing the sale of original copies. This reduces profit margins of businesses and subsequently, artists or writers engaged with the product do not get the rewards due to

them for their work. In addition, pirated copies are sold on the streets without any bill or invoice. This harms the tax collection and affects the total tax revenue of the government. On a more dangerous note, the money earned from sales of pirated CDs goes to the pockets of mafias and other antisocial elements. Now, we all know how dangerous such people can be to the society if they get stronger financially.

5. What should we do at an individual level to stop piracy?

As individuals, we must not buy any pirated book or CD, to reduce piracy, one product at a time. We must understand that our greed to save a few rupees translates into huge profits for the antisocial elements that are involved in piracy. We should also inform the concerned publisher or artist, and the local police, about any piracy being carried out in our area.

Practice Questions:
1. How different is that album from other albums of the same category?
2. Are there similar music albums created in other languages or other countries?
3. Why do youngsters watch music channels?
5. Are there any drawbacks of watching music channels, for the youngsters of your country?
6. What challenges are faced by the music industry in your country?
7. What are your suggestions for overcoming these challenges?
8. How can the government help in stopping music piracy?

142. Describe your favourite musical band/group.

You should say
- **The name of the band**
- **What kind of music they play**
- **Why you like that band**

Have you ever been to a live concert of that musical band/group?

Practice Questions
1. Did you ever want to be a part of that band?
2. Who do you like the most in that music band?
3. Do your friends also like that music band?
7. How can young music artistes and bands showcase their talent in your country?
8. What qualities are required to become a good musical artiste according to you?
9. Did you ever want to learn music?
10. If given a chance, will you learn music in future?
11. What types of music albums become more popular in your city/country?
12. Are independent music albums given more importance than film music in your country?
13. Are international pop stars popular in your country — yes, or no? Why?

14. What are the different types of music albums released in your country?

15. Does local or folk music get affected because of pop albums?

16. Are these effects positive or negative?

143. Speak about a live performance (event) you watched/enjoyed, e.g. a drama, a music concert, a sports match, or a dance show.

   You should say

- **When and where that event was held**

- **With whom you watched it**

- **Who performed in that event**

What did you enjoy the most about the performance/event?

Practice Questions:

1. How did you reach there?

2. People of what ages like such events more?

3. Do you watch such events often?

4. What are the ideal places in your city to host such events?

5. How do event management companies help in organising such events?

6. Is the popularity of event management companies increasing or decreasing in your country/city?

7. Do you think event management can be learned better with proper education, or with experience?

8. Are there any institutes which teach event management skills?

9. What are the benefits and drawbacks of selecting event management as a career?

144. Describe the most exciting/adventurous experience you have had in your life.

   You should say

- **What it was**

- **When and where it happened**

- **What you did**

Would you like to have such an experience again?

Practice Questions:

1. Have you had similar exciting activities after that?

2. Did you learn anything from it?

3. Should today's parents give enough freedom to their children to indulge in adventurous activities?

4. What exciting activities do people prefer?

The Ultimate Guide to IELTS Speaking by Parthesh Thakkar

5. What is the difference between the exciting activities that people from urban and rural areas enjoy?
6. Should the government ban some exciting but life-threatening activities?
7. Should society have to bear the cost of such activities?

145. Speak about the type of clothes, and ornaments you normally wear.
  You should say
- **What the clothes and ornaments look like**
- **When you wear them**
- **Why you wear them**

How do you feel when you wear them?

146. Describe an incident which made you emotional.
  You should say
- **What happened**
- **Where, and with whom you were, when it happened**
- **How you reacted to it**

Do you usually get emotional quickly?

Practice Questions:
1. Did that incident give any message or inspiration to you?
2. How does a child express emotions?
3. Do you believe that women are more emotional than men?
4. Why is it so?
5. How does a woman express her emotions?
6. What kind of support should we give to those who are emotionally disturbed?
7. Is emotional disturbance harmful to our health?
8. How should we handle situations when we get emotional?
9. Do people in your culture express their emotions in public?
10. Do you think we should express our emotions clearly when needed?
11. What are the possible disadvantages if we don't express our emotions properly or clearly?
12. What are the advantages of expressing our emotions clearly and properly?
13. Do you think we should learn to admit to/confess our mistakes?
14. Do you believe there should be a confession box system in every religion?
15. Why do we need to confess to our mistakes? OR What are the advantages of making a confession?
16. Should we forgive the people who confess their mistakes to us?

147. Speak about something which annoys/irritates you.
    You should say
-   What it is
-   Why it annoys you
-   What you do about it
Are you easily irritated, or do you consider yourself quite patient?

148. Speak about an incident/event which benefited you/your family/your city/your country.
    You should say
-   What happened
-   When and where it happened
-   Why you consider it beneficial to yourself/your family/your city/your country
Were you actively involved in the occurrence of that event/incident?

Practice Questions:
1. Do you think authorities should take public opinions before implementing important changes in the city/country?
2. In what ways are public opinions taken?
3. Are these reliable ways of taking public polls? Why?
4. What are the benefits of taking public opinions, to the government and to the society?

149. Speak about a volunteering activity you did in the past.
    You should say
-   When and where you did it
-   How you felt about that activity
-   How your family members and friends reacted to it
Do you volunteer often?

Practice Questions:
1. Did you do similar things after that?
2. Do you suggest that activity to others, also?
3. What did you learn from it?
4. Do you think working people should also engage in volunteering for causes?
5. What are the advantages of doing volunteering activities?

150. Speak about what you do to get success in life.

You should say

- Why you have chosen this way to get success
- What benefits you get through adopting this way
- What drawbacks you think you may face with this method

Do you feel you are on the right path to success?

Suggestions:

Candidates can speak about their strategy for studying, doing jobs, or solving problems in life. They can also describe those positive traits and skills that they have, which are helpful in becoming successful. This includes positive thinking, persistence, financial planning, the ability to work hard, and time management.

Follow-up Questions & Answers:

1. If an employee works harder, should he be paid more, or not?

Certainly, if any employee works hard and achieves better output, he should be paid more than the others. This is because, the prime motive behind hard work in the work sphere is money, and if the management deprives the employee of his deserved rewards and incentives, the employee may feel dissatisfied and leave the job. What's more, the management sets a bad example for other workers by showing a lack of appreciation for hard work.

2. Do you think people these days adopt unethical ways to achieve success in business?

Yes, I think the extent to which people are adopting unethical means to become successful is increasing in today's world. This is because there is tremendous competition in both, jobs and businesses. In this situation, if someone wants to survive, he has to either earn a lot of money, or show phenomenal achievements in his work. These things generally come from a combination of hard work, intelligence, and patience. Unfortunately, most people don't have much patience, and so, to achieve quick success, they adopt illegal or unethical ways. Such success is often short lived; therefore, they have to keep resorting to such gimmicks to sustain their so-called performance record. Soon, they get caught in the trap of unethical means to achieve success, and usually cannot extricate themselves until it is too late.

Practice Questions:

1. What should workers do to achieve success in their jobs?
2. What is the difference between the ways people adopted to achieve success in the past, and the ways people adopt now?
3. What is the difference between the goals people keep these days compared to those they kept in the past? Why?
4. Is there any difference between the life goals of men and women? Why?
5. What are the goals of today's youngsters? Or what do today's youngsters expect from their lives?

---

151. Describe an organisation (government or non-government), which helps the needy/disabled/poor/women/old people in your city/state/country.

You should say
- The name of the organisation
- What they do
- How you came to know about them

Is this organisation popular, and does it receive a lot of funding?

Practice Questions:
1. Do you contribute to that organisation? How?
2. Do you think the existence of such organisations will help in improving the social condition of the people it supports?
3. Should the government help such organisations in their activities? How?
4. How can the media be helpful in expanding the base of such organisations?
5. What is the need for such organisations in your country/the world?
6. How can people be motivated to support such organisations?

152. Describe your visit to a hospital/doctor's clinic.

You should say
- When and where you went
- Why you visited
- What you liked about that place

Did the visit serve your purpose?

Practice Questions:
1. Do you think we should take some precautions when we visit a hospital?
2. Do you think there should be a specific time to meet patients? Why?
3. What facilities should good hospitals offer to indoor patients and their relatives?
4. What facilities should good hospitals offer to patients who come only for consultation?
5. What types of hospitals can be found in your city?
6. How have hospitals changed in the last few years?
7. How useful are emergency medical services in today's era?
8. Are emergency medical services good in your city?
9. What are the differences between government and private hospitals?
10. Should the government ban private hospitals or not?
11. How are big hospitals helpful to the country?
12. Do all the people in your country get health insurance?
13. Do you think the overall health expenses are increasing in your country? Why?
14. It is said that doctors and nurses are in less numbers in many countries. What is the scenario in your country?

The Ultimate Guide to IELTS Speaking by Parthesh Thakkar

15. Is there any difference between the hospitals and health system in your country, and those in the country you want to go to?
16. Do you think the government should give free medical facilities to poor people or senior citizens?
17. What kind of diseases are common in your city/country?
18. What do most people do when they don't feel well?
19. What do you do when you realize that you are not feeling well?
20. Are more diseases related to age or lifestyle?

153. Speak about a time when you helped someone.
   You should say
-   **Who you helped**
-   **How you helped them**
-   **What you felt after helping that person**
Do you consider yourself generally helpful?
Suggestions:
Candidates can speak about any kind of help that they rendered to their friends, relatives, neighbours or even strangers, e.g. financial help, study related help, or help in an emergency.

Practice Questions:
1. Do you often help others?
2. Do people feel jealous of someone who receives/provides help? Why?
3. When do you think people need help?
4. What type of people need help?
5. Is there any government/non-government organisation that helps people in your country?
6. Should society create some organisations that can help the needy people?
7. Why do people help each other?
8. Do you think we should help strangers?
9. What should the government do to support poor people/beggars?

154. Speak about a time when you received help from someone.
   You should say
-   **When and where you received the help**
-   **How you received the help**
-   **How helpful it was to you**
Do you accept help from people without hesitation?

Practice Questions:
1. How did you feel after getting that help?
2. Have you reciprocated the help? How?

155. Describe any calamity/disaster (natural) that you have seen or heard about, such as a hurricane, storm, flood, tsunami, or earthquake.

You should say
- **What happened**
- **When and where it happened**
- **How it damaged the area and affected the local people**

Have you ever faced negative consequences of a calamity personally?

Practice Questions:
1. Did you come to know that the calamity was about to happen, in advance?
2. Did your city authorities receive international aid and support after the calamity?
3. Do you think international support should come to the aid of every country when it suffers from a natural disaster?
4. What support can be offered by domestic corporate bodies when such natural disasters happen?

156. Describe any calamity/disaster (manmade) that you have seen or heard about (e.g. an act of terrorism or mass destruction).

You should say
- **What happened**
- **When and where it happened**
- **How it affected you/the area**

Do such things happen often in your country?

Practice Questions:
1. What actions did the local police or authorities take to save the people?
2. How did the local people support the government in handling the situation?
3. What were the reasons behind that disaster according to you?
4. What precautionary actions did the government take after that incident?
5. Is there any action that you can suggest to prevent such incidents from happening again?
6. What actions can be taken against terrorists?
7. How can other countries help in the fight against terrorism?
8. Is war the final choice for curbing terrorism?

The Ultimate Guide to IELTS Speaking by Parthesh Thakkar

9. Do you think other countries of the world also participate in the fight against terrorism?

157. Talk about your ambition in life.
   You should say
-   **What it is**
-   **How you can achieve it**
-   **Why you have this ambition**
Since when have you wanted to accomplish this?

Practice Questions:
1. What qualifications will you need to achieve your ambition?
2. Do you think your present qualifications will be of any help to you?
3. Are there any additional skills you need to attain your ambition?
4. Will you need the help of other individuals in achieving your ambition? If no, why?
   And If yes, why, and what kind of help?
5. Should we have ambitions in life? OR Is it good to be ambitious in life?

158. Speak about your favourite radio program.
   You should say
-   **The name of the program**
-   **When it is broadcast**
-   **What the program is about**
Do you listen to this program regularly?

Red fm thappa

Suggestions:
Candidates can speak about programs that declare the positions of songs on the charts on a weekly basis, interactive programs that are aired every morning, or other interview based programs where various celebrities share their views with listeners on the radio.

Follow-up Questions & Answers:
1.Is the popularity of radio increasing or decreasing these days? Why?
The popularity of radio has increased a lot in the last few years in my country because of the entry of private companies with FM (Frequency Modulation) channels. These channels offer excellent quality of sound, and many interactive, interesting programs that most listeners enjoy.
2.What are the advantages offered by radio over TV?
Radio offers some benefits over television. It is an audio-only medium, so it can be carried along anywhere and enjoyed. What's more, people now have radios in their mobiles which provides them entertainment at their fingertips. All these facilities are not offered

by television sets because they require big screens and are bulky, so cannot be carried around.

Practice Questions:
1. When do you listen to that radio program?
2. What do you like about it?
3. Do you have any suggestions for the improvement of that program?
4. What is the importance of radio?
5. What is the future of radio?
6. What is the future of your favourite radio program?
7. What should the government do to increase the popularity of radio?
8. What type of programs should be broadcasted more on radio according to you?

159. Describe your leisure time activities.

    You should say
- **What they are**
- **Where, and how you do them**
- **What benefits you get from them**

Do you get a lot of leisure time in your routine?

Suggestions:
Candidates can speak about their free time activities like listening to music, reading books, window-shopping, playing games, surfing the internet, or painting.

160. Speak about how you spent your last weekend.

    You should say
- **Where you spent it**
- **What you did**
- **With whom you spent your time**

Do you often spend your weekends in a similar manner?

161. Speak about something you did to pass/kill time in the past.

    You should say
- **What that activity was**
- **When you did it**

- How it helped you in passing your time

Do you think it was a productive activity?

Follow-up Questions & Answers:

1. What activities do people of your generation do to pass/kill time?

To me, pastime activities are different from leisure activities. However, it is up to us to convert our spare time towards creative pursuits. Most people of my generation usually don't waste their time when they are free. They try to engage themselves in their next priority task, check their emails, reorganise their schedule, complete pending office work, and so on. However, some people listen to music and play games on their mobiles or laptops if their mood doesn't permit them to work in their free time.

2. What activities do children/old people/housewives do to pass/kill time?

Children are highly diligent in nature. They often try to play with something or the other when they are free. They also try to draw or paint in their sketchbooks, and can often be spotted creating things using their craft skills. Sometimes they watch television or talk to their friends or family members. I have also seen children taking naps when they have nothing to do. Old people often engage themselves in religious, social, or other welfare activities where they can spend their time and also feel satisfied about contributing to their society.

Practice Questions:

1. What activities do you suggest to those who have too much free time?
2. What are the disadvantages of such pastime activities to individuals?
3. What are the disadvantages of such pastime activities to the society/country?
4. What should be done to remove people's laziness?
5. Is laziness in the people of your country increasing/decreasing. Why?
6. Should we make some changes in our education system to make people capable of better time management? If yes, what changes can be made?

162. Speak about a person who you think is intelligent.

You should say

- **The name of the person, and what he does**
- **Where you met that person**
- **Why you think he is intelligent**

What are his other good qualities?

Practice Questions:

1. How important is intelligence in life, in your view?
2. Is intelligence the most important thing in life?
3. Do you think the need of intelligence is higher these days compared to the past?
4. Are there sources available to enhance our intelligence?

5. What is intelligence according to you?
6. Do you think intelligent people live happy lives?
7. In your view, where do we need more intelligence — in our job or in our studies?

163. Describe a future plan that you made.

    You should say

- **What it is**
- **When you will follow it**
- **Who will help you with the plan**

Do you often make future plans in advance?

164. Speak about your role model.

    You should say

- **The name of your role model**
- **How you know that person**
- **Why he is your role model**

Do you think our role models change as we grow?

Suggestions:

Candidates can speak about a person like whom they want to become (emulate). If someone wants to be a cricketer, Sachin Tendulkar or Ricky Pointing might be their role model. There is a difference between an idealistic person and a role model. Mahatma Gandhi or Swami Vivekanand can be your role models only if you agree with most of their ideologies, and wish to implement something from their lives in your life. In context of this cue-card topic, generally, a friend, family member, colleague, boss, or a teacher could be described as your role model.

Section III

Questions and Answers about Various Topics for Part 3 of the IELTS Speaking Test Followed by Practice Questions.

Questions and Answers about Various Topics for Part 3 of the IELTS Speaking Test Followed by Practice Questions.

ANIMALS, ZOO, WILDLIFE

1. Which is the better place for animals — a zoo, or a forests? Why?

I think a forest is better than a zoo for animals. Forests are natural habitats for animals, where they live in freedom, whereas zoos are manmade structures where animals live in captivity.

2. What are the advantages and disadvantages of keeping animals in zoos?

As stated above, zoos take away the freedom of animals from them. Moreover, visitors often disturb animals in zoos. Animals cannot live their lives naturally in zoos. However, zoos offer some benefits to some animals, like protection from predators, and from natural calamities like floods, droughts, and forest fires etc. In addition, animals also get treatment from veterinary doctors when they fall sick.

3. Why do you think people keep pets?

People keep pets for a variety of reasons. Some people keep pets because they feel lonely. Some keep pets to nurture them, because of their sympathy towards animals. At times, people also keep pets for personal protection; and some people have a hobby of taming animals.

4. How should we save animals that are facing a danger of extinction?

The species that face a danger of extinction should be declared 'endangered species'. Their natural habitats should be converted into sanctuaries and there should be severe punishment for those who kill or harm them. What's more, some animals of the endangered species should be taken to breeding centres where they can increase their numbers. After those baby animals mature, they should be introduced to their natural habitats.

5. Do you think we should use animal products? Justify your answer.

We may use animal products provided they are made from the dead bodies of animals. However, we should never kill animals to make products out of their body parts.

6. What should governments/people do to protect animals?

Governments should create laws to protect animals from hunters. They should also declare certain areas as wild life sanctuaries if required. In addition, governments should ban animal products and their trade in the country. On the other hand, not only should we never kill animals for our benefit, we should also prevent others from doing it.

7. What is the role of a zoo in our society?

Zoos play an important role in our society. They serve as recreational centres for the society, as education centres for children, and as research and development centres for various vaccines that can protect animals from various diseases.

8. Why do you think children like to visit zoos?

Children like animals a lot, but they usually get to see them only in books, and on television. Because of this they develop a curiosity for seeing live animals at a close range. Now, it is not possible for every child to go to a forest to see animals. So, zoos satisfy their curiosity.

9. What facilities should be provided to the animals in zoos?

The enclosures of animals should be wide and big enough to offer free movement. In addition, the enclosures should be designed like their natural habitat as far as possible so that they don't feel captive. Moreover, they should be given regular food and medical check-ups. Lastly, they should be given protection from seasonal changes, accidents, and human interference.

10. Should the authorities charge entry fees to visit zoos?
Yes, there should be a token entry charge for all visitors to the zoo. This money can be used on the maintenance expenses of zoos such as food, water, electricity, and medicines for animals, as well as facilities for zoo staff.

11. What is the future of zoos?
In future, the role of zoos will transform from being recreational places, to research and development centres. In such centres, we will be able to breed endangered species (i.e. species that are facing danger of extinction), and increase their numbers. We will also be able to conduct medical research to protect animals from various diseases.

Practice Questions:
1. How are animals useful to mankind?
2. Should we tame animals, or not?
3. What is the role of animals in maintaining the environment?
4. What is the role of forests in maintaining the environment?
5. Should we kill animals to feed people? OR Should we encourage the consumption of non-vegetarian food?
6. Describe the wildlife of your country.
7. Who is responsible for the protection of wildlife?
8. Why are wild animals important?
9. What facilities should be provided to people who visit the zoo?

AREA

1. How has your area changed in recent years?
The area in which I live has undergone dramatic transformation in the last few years. Earlier, there were old houses, plots, and small shopping complexes around my house. Now, there are plenty of new apartments, latest shopping and commercial complexes, restaurants, hotels, and high-rise buildings. The roads in my area are now wider. The number of people living in my area has gone up substantially. In short, it is developing into a posh, cosmopolitan area.

2. Describe the transportation system in your area.
Most people in my area use their own vehicles to commute, but, some of them have now started using buses because the bus system in the city has improved a lot. In addition, people use auto rickshaws, too, for their day-to-day travel. Lastly, a railway station is also easily accessible to people in my area, for long distance travel.

3. Describe the health/education facilities in your area.

There are two big government hospitals in my area. Apart from them, there are many private super specialty hospitals in my area. There are both, public and private schools available offering education in Gujarati, Hindi, and English.

4. What are the advantages and disadvantages of changing one's area/residence frequently?

Frequent changes of area prevent us from developing strong relationships with our neighbours. It is also difficult at times, to commute in new areas, as we may not be familiar with the different parts, roads, and transport systems of those areas. Moreover, children suffer a lot from frequent residence changes, because either they have to change schools, or they have to change their usual travel routes every now and then. On the other hand, frequent changes in our area of residence give us the opportunity to meet different types of people.

Practice Questions:
1. Describe the area in which you live.
2. What are the popular sites/landmarks of your area?
3. What are the positive and negative points of living in your area?
4. Do you want any change to be introduced in your area?
5. If given a chance, would you change your area, or not? Why?
6. What kind of recreation facilities are available in your area?

ARTS AND CRAFTS, ARTISTS, MUSEUMS, ART GALLERIES

1. Should art, or basic knowledge of arts be made compulsory in schools?

A basic knowledge of art should be provided in schools. For example, drawing, painting, and craft work on paper, wood, and cloth can be taught to children as part of their curriculum. This knowledge makes children aware of arts and crafts, and more importantly, children with extraordinary skills can be identified at an early age and encouraged to pursue their talents.

2. Do you think creativity is given enough importance in schools these days?

Unfortunately, most schools do not focus on creativity. This is because the curriculum is often already too long for the school management to be completed during the term. In this situation, if they shift their focus from the syllabus to extra-curricular activities, they may have to sacrifice academic subjects, which will not be appreciated by students, or parents.

3. What do you understand by handicrafts?

Handicrafts are articles prepared by hand, using skills like sewing, weaving, and carving on materials like cloth, paper, and wood.

4. What is the importance of art in our lives?

Art is an expression of our creativity, imagination, and skills. Art can help us in living a balanced life because it gives a passage or channel for our hidden energies and skills. Art is an essential part of our lives.

5. Should artists be given the freedom to express whatever they want?

Yes, I think artists should be given freedom of expression because creativity sees no boundaries. If we restrict the content of art, then it loses its charm. However, there should be one condition, the creation should not hurt or harm anybody's personal, social, or religious emotions.

6. What is more important — arts, commerce, or the sciences? Why?

Each field has its own importance. Commerce is vital for our economy and business operations. Sciences are essential for the betterment of the quality of our lives, our comforts, and our safety. Art is important for creativity, leisure, and self-expression. It is difficult to say which is more important, because each of them affects different aspects of our life.

7. Should the government support artists? Why?

The government should support artists by giving them awards and certificates of honour. This kind of encouragement will help retain artists' interest in their art, and will inspire them to keep excelling at it. Such honours from the government help artists to achieve great heights of creativity, which can improve the reputation of the country in the world.

8. What skills are required in making crafts?

Crafts require some age-old skills such as carving, sewing, weaving, and knitting, along with an understanding of different types of raw materials that can be used in the preparation of various articles. Apart from these, good knowledge of culture, religion, and the history of the nation is also required so as to be able to incorporate these things in crafts.

10. Why do you think the handicraft industry is facing survival problems?

Handicrafts are a set of traditional skills possessed by few rural cultures in our country. Because of industrial and economic development, many rural artisans shifted to big cities over time, and accepted new professions to earn their living. Moreover, the production of handicrafts is slower than machines and takes long, thus making the process of earning very slow. In the process of shifting to urban areas and picking up new professions, skilled artisans lost touch with their craft, and also stopped passing it down to future generations. Consequently, handicrafts are showing signs of extinction in some regions.

11. How can we preserve our handicrafts, and what should the government do for them?

The government should take an active interest in promoting handicrafts and helping artists by giving them platforms to showcase their talents. The government should give subsidies to those who want to start commercial production of handicrafts. Concerned authorities should also organise handicraft exhibition in urban areas of the country to help artisans get recognised and earn money. In addition, the government should honour extraordinary artisans and their workmanship with awards and recognition. Such incentives will attract more people towards pursuing handicraft, and help the industry grow.

12. Should we promote our handicrafts and arts to foreigners? Justify your answer.

Yes, we must promote our arts and handicrafts to foreigners. This gives two major benefits. Firstly, foreigners buy product that they like, which increases the earnings of the artists, and also brings foreign revenue to the country. Secondly, foreigners promote our arts and crafts among their countrymen, when they return. This improves the reputation of our country, and also attracts more foreign visitors, thus increasing tourism.

13. Should Indian artistes perform in other countries?

Indian artistes should perform in other countries, because by doing so, they can generate global recognition for our art and culture. In addition, they can earn more money from their shows.

14. What is a museum?

A museum is a place where historical and antique articles are preserved and displayed for people to see. Museum collections can be as old as a few hundred years to a few thousand years.

15. What is the importance of museums?

A museum is a link between the past and the present. Museums hold relics of the past in them, for the people of the present to remain in touch with their history, and learn from it.

16. Should there be any entry fee for museum visitors?

Yes, entry fees should be taken from museum visitors. This gives two benefits. Firstly, it supports the maintenance of the museum, including the security and expansion of the place. Secondly, people who pay fees to enter behave responsibly, as opposed to free visitors, who often underestimate the importance of the museum experience, because it has come free of cost. In turn, they behave carelessly.

17. What is the future of museums?

I believe that museums will be given even more importance in the future. The reason for this is the current trend of globalisation. Because of globalisation, the whole world is moving towards an identical culture. This may lead to the loss of many vernacular cultures and languages. So, people in future will be even more intrigued by ancient artefacts and tales of extinct cultures, which will only be found in museums. Thus, in future, we may require more museums to preserve rare articles.

18. What is the difference between an art gallery and a museum?

An art gallery is an exhibition hall where the works of artists are showcased. They can include paintings, sculptures, carvings, and other artwork. Art galleries host exhibits of works of those artists who are alive, and wish to show or sell their art to people. On the other hand, in museums we can find only historical or antique items.

Practice Questions:

1. How does art contribute to the progress of a country?
2. What do you prefer — machine made products, or handicrafts? Why?
3. Which handicraft products do you use?
4. What is the importance of handicrafts?
5. Who should spend money for the development of museums — the government, or the society? Why?
6. How should we preserve/maintain our historical monuments?

BOOKS, READING HABITS

1. What are the benefits of reading books?

It is said that books are man's best friends. Reading books increases our knowledge and understanding of various subjects. Reading also helps by giving us better direction in life and in business. What's more, reading increases our language proficiency, concentration, and comprehension skills, too. To me, it is one of the best habits one can develop in life.

2. Do you think the reading habits of people have changed over the time?
Reading habits of people have certainly changed over time because of various reasons. Now, we have more recreational and leisure activity options available, like the TV, radio, computer, and internet. People prefer spending their time doing such activities, rather than reading books. Moreover, work patterns have undergone big changes. People these days work longer hours under more stressful conditions. This exhausts them and motivates them to seek lighter entertainment options that require more passive engagement than reading, which is an active process that requires people to fully apply their minds to the act.

3. What is the difference between books sold in the past, and those being sold nowadays?
In the past, books about religion, philosophy, history, and poetry were sold more, but now books on technology, management, self-improvement, fiction, lifestyle, and psychology are being sold more. This change reflects a shift in the interests of readers.

4. What type of books do children prefer to read?
Children like reading pictorial books on subjects such as fantasy, animation, or fiction. They like such themes because their minds are full of imagination. Such picture books help children in visualizing the characters of the book better.

5. How does reading help a child?
Children are playful and mischievous in nature. Because of this, they might not concentrate much on their studies, and underperform at school. If they read books, they can improve their concentration, because reading demands focused attention on the subject. What's more, apart from improving their general knowledge and language, they can also satisfy their curiosity about various subjects.

6. What topics/subjects do you suggest to children for reading?
Children should read books that offer easy understanding and clear illustration with pictures. They can read any subject as per their interest, but, I suggest that they include science and technology magazines, autobiographies, religious books, and historical texts in their reading list.

7. How much should a child read every day?
It depends on the school timings and the study demands of the child. But, I think children should read for at least 30–60 minutes a day, apart from their regular school studies. During vacations, they can read more depending on their convenience.

8. Where, and when do youngsters prefer to read?
Youngsters prefer to read in their rooms, or in private reading libraries. Sometimes they also go to their friends' houses to read together. However, they do not like to read at public places.

9. Where, and when do old people prefer to read?
Old people read at their homes, in public libraries, and in gardens or parks. They often go to such places to pass their time, so they select these places for reading, too.

10. Are there any disadvantages of reading books?
If we read only extreme or non-consensual material, it may leave a negative impact on our mind, because the human mind is susceptible to being influenced by written content.

This is why people often try to commit crimes based on plots of the books they have read.

11. What should we do to improve reading and writing abilities of illiterate people?

We should develop a team of volunteers who can go to illiterate people and teach them. They may arrange night or evening classes and provide them free education, with some free study material. To support this, the government should start campaigns which illustrate the benefits of literacy. The government should also provide free education up to higher-secondary level to children who belong to illiterate families.

12. What can be done to motivate people to read more?

Unfortunately, there isn't much that can be done for this. Still, the government can open more public libraries and can fund some campaigns that inspire people to read more. They should also make some subjects compulsory, which require reading outside the syllabus in schools and colleges.

13. Why are self-help/personality development related books being sold in large numbers in the market nowadays?

In today's era of globalization, everyone wants fast growth. This desire may find some resistance if we have negative points or blocks in our personality. To remove them, people often read books on subjects of self-help or personality development. With the help of these books, they can also enhance their efficiency and output at their work places.

Practice Questions:
1. Which are the popular newspapers and magazines in your city?
2. What types of books does today's young generation read more?
3. What are the advantages and disadvantages of reading e-books?
4. How do religious books help us in life?
5. Where and when do you prefer to read books?
6. How many hours a day should we read books according to you?
7. Should we read historical books?
8. Who is your favourite writer/author?

BUILDING

1. In your view how will future buildings be constructed?

In the future, buildings will be energy efficient, techno savvy, and flexible. They will consume less electricity by using solar energy and other features. They will be operated by technology so that we can have remote access to systems installed in them. Moreover, they will offer flexible roofs or partitions, enabling us to make adjustments as per our requirements.

2. How should we monitor the activity of private construction companies in order to assure optimum quality of construction?

This is a function of the government. They should appoint civil engineers who can go to the sites of construction, observe the structures, test the construction material when needed, and give their suggestions where required. All these functions can make the buildings better and safer for people. In addition, the government should take punitive action against those builders who use inferior material for construction, or do not follow structural rules for their personal benefits, so that an example can be set in the society for others who are thinking of indulging in similar malpractices.

3. Speak about the different types of buildings of your city?
There is a large variety of buildings in my city. We can see low-rise and high-rise flats, bungalows, tenements, row houses, shopping complexes, high-rise commercial and office complexes, multiplexes, old houses, and religious buildings like temples, churches, and mosques.

4. Which type of building do you prefer to live in — a bungalow or a flat? Why?
I prefer living in a bungalow, because a bungalow gives privacy and space. We can live without interference from neighbours, which is very common in flats. A bungalow also gives us more comforts and luxury, compared to a flat.

5. What things do you look for before purchasing a new house?
There are numerous factors that we should consider before buying a house. These factors include location, area of residence, price, net carpet area offered, elevators in case of flats, reputation of the builder, time of giving possession, payment conditions, basic connections like water, drainage, electricity, telephone, and air and light distribution. We may repent in future if we overlook any of these factors when buying a house.

Practice Questions:
1. Which building do you like to visit often?
2. Which types of buildings are preferred nowadays?
3. What do you prefer more while studying away from home — a hostel, a rented apartment, or a paying guest accommodation? Why?
4. What are the advantages and disadvantages in developing the cities of our country?

CHILDHOOD, CHILDREN

1. Why are childhood days important in our life?
Childhood days are the beginning days of our life. These are the days in which we develop into individuals. In other words, childhood is the mould that gives shape to our personality. To me childhood days are as important to developing individuality, as the foundation is to a building.

2. What things can a child learn during childhood?
A child can learn a lot during its childhood. Along with education, the child gets knowledge of the language, culture, tradition, and religion. Apart from this, a child develops various skills such as playing games, and dealing with friends, teachers and other members of society. These learnings develop his understanding and attitude towards life.

3. Describe any memorable experience from your childhood.
When I was in grade four, my class teacher announced that the school wanted some

students to participate in an inter-school story telling competition. He invited some students to tell a story with a message. I went up and told my story and he selected me as the representative of my class, for the competition. It was my first experience speaking on stage, but I followed my class teacher's guidelines, and I told the story to a large audience. At the end, to my surprise, I was awarded the 1st prize for my story. This was one of the most memorable events of my childhood.

4. What is the difference between grown up life and childhood?
There is a lot of difference between the life of a grown up person, and that of a child. Children live an innocent and playful life in which they have no responsibilities to fulfil. Children can do whatever they want to. The only job they have is to study well at school, whereas in adulthood we have to play many roles like that of a professional, a spouse, and a parent, among others. In addition, we have to fulfil plenty of duties and responsibilities. This is the reason why adults find that their lives actually pull them away from themselves. To summarize, children can live life on their own terms for as long as they want, but adults have to take holidays to do so.

5. What is the proper age according to you for a child to attend school?
I think the proper age for a child to go to school is five years, for they need the warmth of their parents up to 4–5 years, so that they can be mentally and physically fit to handle the demands of school education.

6. Some people say that the government should ban pre–primary schools (nursery and kindergarten). Do you agree with them? Why?
I don't completely agree with this, but it is true that most schools use pre-school education as a means to earn extra money from parents. This attitude is harmful to both, the society and the children, because parents line up to enrol their children in pre-school, just to secure the child's admission. Schools charge heavy fees for pre-school education, which places an added financial burden on parents. Here, I think, government should intervene and stop such schools from this practice.

7. Do you think today's children are overburdened by education?
Yes, this sentence is true to a large extent. Now, children study more subjects than they did at any given time in the past. What's more, some skill-based subjects like computer, art, crafts, and new languages are also included in the curriculum in most schools. These were not compulsory in the past. To top it, parents have to hire private tutors to improve their children's academic performance. These tuitions keep the child engaged in studies even after school hours. I feel, as a society, we should do something to stop this increasing burden on children.

8. Do today's children have any bad habits? If yes, what are they?
Today's children have some common unhealthy habits like eating junk food and chocolates, watching TV, especially cartoon channels, for long hours, and playing games on computer or online. These habits actually inhibit their physical and mental growth, because they eat high calorie food, and then they do not go out to play games which can burn those unhealthy calories.

Practice Questions:
1. Describe your childhood days.
2. What developments have you seen in your personality since childhood?

3. Do you think today's children are lazy / watch more cartoon channels?
4. Do you think children should live with their grandparents?

CHOCOLATES

1. Are you fond of eating chocolates?
I am very fond of eating chocolates. Since my childhood, chocolates have always made me very happy. Every time I did a good deed as a child, my parents would give me some chocolates as reward and appreciation. Even now, from time to time I reward myself with chocolates of different brands and types.

2. Have you tried many different types of chocolates?
Yes, I have tried chocolates with different concentrations of cocoa in them. Those with higher percentage of cocoa tend to be bitterer, while the ones with lower percentage of cocoa tend to be sweeter. Bitter chocolates are also known as dark chocolates, while regular sweet chocolates are known as milk chocolates. Then, there are white chocolates, too, and they have no cocoa in them at all.

3. What foods taste good in chocolate flavour/with chocolate?
I think pretty much any dessert tastes good with some chocolate in it. Chocolate ice creams and chocolate cakes are universally liked by people. Sugar coated candies also have chocolate inside them. Fudges, brownies, and cupcakes, are all elevated by chocolate. Even ice lollies and fruit plates taste good when topped with chocolate syrup.

4. Do you think eating too much chocolate is bad for the body?
I think eating too much of anything could prove harmful for the body. Most foods are good for the body when eaten in moderation. The same applies for chocolate. If overdone, it can lead to weight gain, imbalance in blood sugar, and cavities in the teeth. However, in moderate quantities, chocolate can be good for lowering cholesterol, and for elevating one's mood.

CLIMATE, ENVIRONMENT, SEASONS, POLLUTION, NATURAL CALAMITIES

1. How many seasons do you experience in your country?
In my country we experience three seasons, i.e. summer, monsoon, and winter. However, summer lasts a little longer than the other seasons in the western and central regions of my country.

2. Would you prefer if any one season continued throughout the year, or are you happy that seasons keep changing?
It is impossible to expect a season to remain the same throughout the year, because each season has its own function in the environment. If any season remains for the whole year,

---

then, I think life will soon disappear from our planet.

3. Does the climate affect a person's mood?

Yes, our body reacts to the climate we're in. For instance, if the climate is hot, our body loses water and electrolytes in the form of perspiration. When these elements are in short supply, the brain can't work efficiently. Consequently, our emotions change, and are reflected in our mood in the form of irritability.

4. What are the threats to our climate, and what are their consequences?

Pollution is the greatest threat to climate. Pollution leads to global warming, which is responsible for causing disturbances in the weather cycle in most countries. In addition, the rising temperature of earth raises sea levels, which is dangerous for coastal areas, as they can get submerged under water.

5. Do you wear different clothes in different seasons?

Yes, I prefer cotton clothes during summer, because cotton helps in maintaining the body temperature. I wear woollen clothes in winter, so that I can protect my body from the cold. Lastly, I prefer wearing raincoats in the monsoon, so that I don't get drenched in the rains when I'm out.

6. Give one major environmental problem of your area/city/country, and give solutions for it.

The most disturbing problem of my city is the air pollution caused by smoke from vehicles and industries. The smoke creates a thick smog in the evening, which irritates the eyes and the respiratory system. I think, in my city the authorities should take steps to reduce the number of petrol and diesel vehicles on road. This can be done by making people aware of the benefits of using public transport. They should also introduce better traffic management systems, so that congestion on streets can be reduced. The government should also regulate the emissions from industries, so that people in my city get clean and healthy air to breathe.

7. What are the major sources of pollution?

The major sources of pollution are the emissions from automobiles, and from heavy industries such as those manufacturing cement, steel, and chemicals. The smoke from the burning of plants in forests and other rural areas also adds to air pollution. Next, dumping of garbage and chemical waste in the sea and on land also increases the level of soil and water pollution.

8. What should governments do to protect people from natural calamities?

Governments should take a two-stage approach for this. First, it should take precautionary measures, such as the implementation of efficient systems to predict calamities like floods tsunamis, thunderstorms, and hurricanes, in advance. In addition, it should train people to protect themselves in the face of such calamities. What's more, it should also evacuate people from dangerous areas. The second approach is rescue. If an unpredictable calamity occurs, there should be trained disaster management teams that can take charge of the affected areas. Moreover, the government should open relief camps to provide food and shelter to the affected people.

Practice Questions:

1. Speak about the climate of your country/city.
2. How does the climate of your country differ from that of the country you are planning

to go to?

3. How can we preserve/protect our environment?
4. Have you ever experienced bad/extreme weather?
5. What should individuals do to control pollution?
6. How can we protect the earth from global warming/the greenhouse effect?
7. How should we protect ourselves from calamities like fire, storms, and floods?

COLOUR

1. How do colours affect our mood?
Each colour absorbs various frequencies from the spectrum of light, and reflects back some frequencies. When we see any colour, we receive these reflected colour vibrations in the form of light energy, which can change our emotional patterns for a while. As a result, we can feel changes in our mood, when exposed to certain colours. For example, when we go to a place with natural greenery and flowers, we feel soothed and fresh. In contrast, if we go to a room full of dull colours, such as a factory floor, we feel down and fatigued.

2. Do colours have religious importance?
Yes, colours do have religious importance. In the past, some religions and races associated their identities with particular colours, by extensive use of those colours. For example, more often than not, white is associated with Christianity, green is associated with Islam, and saffron is associated with Hindus.

3. Do colours reveal the personality of a person — yes or no? Why?
The attitude of a person, his nature, and his likes and dislikes can be understood to a greater extent on the basis of his selection of colours. For example, if a person always wears vibrant and fluorescent colours, he might be showing youthfulness, whereas someone who wears pastel coloured clothes may reflect sobriety, responsibility, and maturity. These are superficial assumptions, but they are helpful in certain situations in life.

Practice Questions:
1. Which colours do youngsters prefer nowadays?
2. Can colours be used to express particular feelings?

COMPUTERS, INTERNET

1. What are the applications of a computer?
Computers have numerous applications in our life. They are used to store, transfer, and analyse data. They are also highly useful in communication, preparation of documents, programming, taking printouts, playing games, listening, storing and creating music, watching movies, and so on. Computers have become an essential part of our life.

---

2. What are the negative effects of using a computer?

Prolonged use of computer can cause strain and harm to our eyes. Its extensive use also causes back and neck pain, medically known as RSI (Repetitive Strain Injury). In addition, excessive use of computers makes us so dependent on them that when they fail to work, our work comes to a standstill.

3. What precautions should we take before and while using computers?

We should check the system configurations properly, before starting to use any computer. We should also install an anti-glare screen on the computer monitor to protect our eyes. Lastly, we should ensure that the seating arrangement doesn't harm the muscles of our back, neck and forearms.

4. How are computers helpful in education?

Computers are a blessing to the field of education. We can provide animated learning software to children, so that they can easily visualize academic concepts while studying. It is also a useful tool to prepare assignments and project reports. Also, distance learning can be best supported with the help of computers.

5. Should the study of computers be made compulsory in school education?

Yes, computer education must be included in the school curriculum, because looking at the present spread of computer usage in society, it is easy to envisage how difficult it will be for people to progress in life without computer education. So, to make our future generations competent and to ensure their growth in life, we should start imparting the knowledge of computers at the school level itself.

6. What are the advantages and disadvantages of imparting education via computers?

Computers are of great assistance in audio-visual teaching for boring subjects like history, or for complex subjects like science. College students can also gain a lot by using computers in their assignments. However, computers are costly, and hence can't be afforded by all students and institutes. Moreover, they also make youngsters dependent on machines, and might inhibit their independent skill development.

7. What are the advantages and disadvantages of e-learning?

E-learning opens the doors of education across the globe. It makes studying possible for those who cannot physically attend classes, or for those who cannot attend classes because they are otherwise occupied during class hours. In addition, it also provides a platform for individual development, because students cannot get everyday support from their tutors, making it necessary for them to adopt independent learning strategies. However, the same reason can be a drawback for some candidates who can't cope with the study requirements without the constant guidance of a tutor. This is because, when it comes to e-learning, student-teacher interaction is not always possible.

8. What do you think will be the future of computers?

I think our life will become impossible without computers. Over time, computers will be serving humans in every home and office. We will access computers at every step of our lives. In my opinion, it would not be an exaggeration to say that computers will be the future of mankind.

9. What are the good and bad effects of the internet?

Internet is one of the most astonishing inventions of technology. It is an ocean of information. We have access to the whole world if we are connected to the internet. In addition, we can communicate with anyone at any time, across the globe. Moreover, we can send large amounts of data to any computer within seconds via the internet. On the darker side, some people use the internet to spread viruses. It is also used to hack other websites to disturb their network or to sabotage competition. On top of it, some illegal websites misuse the internet to spread evils like pornography in the world.

10. Why are old people reluctant in accepting and using computers?
This happens with some old, uneducated, and conservative people only, because they are accustomed to their existing setup and work patterns. The introduction of computers can bring radical changes in that setup, which also pushes those elders to change according to the times. In this case, those who cannot change themselves resist the use of computers.

Practice Questions:
1. Do you use a computer?
2. How have you learnt to use the computer?
3. Which subjects cannot be taught with the help of computers?
4. Can computers replace teachers in the classroom?
5. Some people say that computers affect students' analytical and calculation abilities negatively. Do you agree with them? Why?
6. How have computers changed in recent years?
7. Can a computer ever replace the human brain?
8. Should the government support research to develop new technology? If yes, how?

CULTURE, SUPERSTITIONS

1. What is the importance of culture in our life?
Culture is the identity of an individual. It is a set of rituals, traditions, and belief systems that we follow. Culture gives our community a presence in the society, which also works as a tool to identify others, and their cultures. Just as our name is our individual identity, and our region is our national identity, our culture is our social and religious identity.

2. Describe your culture.
This answer will vary with each candidate. Candidates can include their surname, traditions and rituals they follow routinely, festivals and occasions they celebrate, and gods they believe in.

3. Is there any important number in your culture?
Every culture has given some importance to numbers. In India, the Hindu culture gives importance to the number 11. People fast on the eleventh day of every month as per the lunar calendar. We also start anything new at home or at work on this day of the month. Moreover, when we give cash gifts to others on festivals or ceremonies, we add Rs. 11 to any sum we gift, e.g. Rs. 111, Rs. 211, and Rs. 511.

4. What do you remember faster — a number or a name? Why?
Generally, we tend to remember names faster than numbers, because when we hear a name, our mind also stores characteristics of that person whose name we have heard, such as their face, voice, nature, and personality. These associations with the person strengthen and reinforce the recall of their name. When we come across a person we

have been introduced to, again, we perceive these traits and retrieve the associated name from our memory. On the other hand, it is not so easy to make qualitative associations with numbers, because numbers are the same everywhere, irrespective of the context in which they are used.

5. Do you think today's people are inclined more towards superstitions?

This is a debatable question. But, it is true that the craving to achieve rapid success in a fast and competitive world encourages people to adopt certain illogical, mystical sounding beliefs and habits, better known as superstitions. For example, people change the spellings of their names and home addresses, they wear clothes of particular colours, and adopt gemstones in the form of finger rings; they keep carved metallic symbols and images in their wallets or pockets, too. What's more, such beliefs are quite commonly seen among celebrities like film stars, and sports stars. Considering this, I can say that superstitions are on the rise in the world.

6. What are the bad effects of superstitions?

Superstitions are an evil in today's society. They change the focus of the people from hard work, to short cuts like worshiping symbols. People get distracted from the fundamental rules of life like honesty, simplicity, hard work, and self-confidence, and they become jealous and manipulative, because they feel that if one short cut works for someone, it should work for them, too. On top of it, the most depressing fact is that the more these superstitions fail to deliver, the harder people try to adhere to them, to make them work. In such situations, both, the followers and their family members suffer.

7. How can we eradicate superstitions?

Superstitions can be eradicated by bringing awareness and education among people. The government should hire specialists who can go to communities and educate people about the reality of superstitions. Whenever necessary, these officers should expose those who spread superstitions among people for their personal benefits. Apart from this, the government should include myths and facts about superstitions in the school curriculum. When school children study it, they can educate their families, too.

8. Do you think that we are losing our culture — yes, or no? Why?

I don't think we are losing our culture. I accept that present shifts in our lifestyles don't allow many of us to follow all the customs of our culture. However, it is only a change in our methods of adhering to our culture. To me, culture is a flowing phenomenon. We don't follow all the customs that our ancestors did, and we cannot expect our offspring to follow all the customs that we do.

9. How can we promote our culture?

The best way to promote a culture is to follow it. Next, we can impart its values to the younger generations of our society, by organizing cultural events during festivals and public holidays. What's more, we can also spread the specialities of our culture among others, so that they may also understand and adopt our cultural values in their lives.

10. What is the role of an individual in maintaining his culture?

I believe that an individual is an ideal representative of his culture. We must follow our culture first, if we want to maintain it. When others see us following the customs of our culture and getting the benefits from them, they, too, will feel encouraged to adopt the same in their lives.

11. Should the government take any action in preventing the erosion of culture?

The Ultimate Guide to IELTS Speaking by Parthesh Thakkar

The government should not interfere in such issues. However, the government must take some steps to stop those groups which try to manipulate others' beliefs or hurt the feelings of people of other cultures by disrespecting their beliefs.

12. What do you understand by the term global culture?
People these days migrate to different countries of the world. When they settle there, they take their culture with them. However, they also adopt some part of the host culture. This fusion of cultures is emerging across the globe, and that is what I call global culture.

13. What are the good and bad effects of global culture?
Global culture offers flexibility to people. We don't feel guilty if we don't follow certain parts of it. In addition, global culture supports people who migrate and settle abroad, to fit in without much of a cultural shock. This is a welcome development in bringing universal harmony and peace across nations. On the other hand, global culture may cause vernacular cultures and languages to disappear. Moreover, the variety and uniqueness of different cultures may also be lost in future in the wake of a growing global culture.

Practice Questions:
1. What are the specialties of Indian/your culture?
2. What different traditions/customs do you follow?
3. How do you remember numbers?
4. Which factors are responsible for the deterioration of our culture?
5. What are the differences between your culture, and the culture of the country you want to go to?
6. Will you adopt that culture completely?
7. How can we keep our culture alive when we are living in another country?
8. What are the positive and negative aspects of your culture?

EDUCATION

1. What is the importance of education in our life?
Education is the foundation of our life that supports our career path in future. Education gives us the skills and knowledge necessary to survive, grow, and support our family and society. According to me, it is the fuel for the growth engine that is this world.

2. What is your opinion — can the government or private institutes impart education in a better way?
It depends on the level and branch of education. We can see that up to the higher secondary level, government schools are not as good as private ones. However, at tertiary or vocational levels (polytechnic, ITI, IIM etc.) private institutes cannot provide as good quality education as public institutes, such as polytechnics, it is, and IIMs. This is partly because the government gives funding to public universities to improve their standards of education, on top of the fees they receive, whereas private educational institutions have to depend on fee collection only.

3. Why do people prefer private schools to government schools?

The first consideration is the quality of teaching offered by private schools. They constantly compete among themselves and with government schools to excel in their quality, thereby paying attention to their service quality. Thus, teachers of such schools have to perform at their optimum levels. The second factor is facilities. Private schools offer higher and better facilities like better infrastructure, support for co-curricular activities, school buses, and computers. The last factor is teaching English as the first language; government schools offer English as a second or third language, and not as the main medium of education. Most parents today want to enrol their children in English medium schools, only. These are the reasons parents opt for private schools over government schools.

4. What is the education system of your country like?

My country offers a three-tier education system. The first level is known as primary education, and covers standards 1—7. The second level is known as secondary education, which is divided into two parts — the secondary, that is from standards 8—10 and higher secondary, which covers standards 11 and 12. The last level is tertiary education. At this level, candidates complete their graduation and post-graduation from a university-affiliated college.

5. What changes have you seen in the field of education in the last few years?

The education system has remained unchanged for many decades, but the way of imparting education has undergone a huge transformation. In recent years many corporate groups have developed their own schools and colleges. This has brought innovation in teaching methods and an improvement in standards of education. In addition, introduction of technology in education at all levels has also supported the rise in teaching quality. Apart from this, a number of new disciplines have emerged at the tertiary level, to offer better, more career options to today's graduates.

6. Is it important to have practical training at the college level? Why?

Yes, it is essential to give practical training to students. This is the only way to eliminate the disparity between practical applications and theoretical concepts. Without practical training, students acquire only bookish knowledge, which may not be useful to them when they try to apply their learnings practically.

7. Why do you think people prefer foreign countries to get higher education?

There are many reasons behind why people prefer to go abroad for higher studies. Some study overseas to get a degree from a reputed university. Some study in foreign countries to gain increased exposure to international environment, other languages, and different cultures. Many candidates go abroad because the host country offers opportunities to settle down after the completion of studies.

8. In what ways can education be imparted?

Education can be imparted mainly in three ways. The first method is conventional classroom training. The second is with the help of technology, where a large number of students can study by watching lessons on a computer screen, or with the help of an overhead projector. The last is known as distance learning, where students don't come physically to the university to study.

9. Should the government provide free education?

I think the government should provide free education up to the higher secondary level only. This facility encourages those parents who cannot afford school fees, to send their children to school free of cost. This step can be an important development in reducing illiteracy.

10. Do you think that the government should provide free education to all the people of the country?
No, I don't agree to this statement. The government should provide free education to children up to higher secondary level only, and specifically, only to those who cannot afford school fees. Moreover, the government can offer scholarships at tertiary level to help needy students. But, there is no need to provide free education for all, at all levels.

11. What is the difference between school and college education?
There is a lot of difference between school education and college education. Teacher parent interaction is very high in schools with regular monitoring of students, both at school, and at home. At college level, students are treated as mature learners, i.e. they have to take the responsibility of independent learning, and get support from their tutor only when required. In short, the dependence of students on teachers is far less in colleges, compared to schools.

12. What is the role of extra-curricular activities in education?
Extra-curricular activities help students to develop various skills that are required to grow in life. These skills include physical exercises, social interactions, teamwork, public speaking, dance, music, painting, and drawing, among others. Moreover, we can identify gifted children at an early stage and support them to hone their skills by encouraging extra-curricular activities.

13. Do you prefer co-education, why?
Yes, I believe in co-education. As we live together in society, we must study together in schools, also. Co-education develops an understanding of the differences and commonalities between genders in children, so that they can work and live with each other without any hesitation in practical life.

14. Do you think that a teacher's job should be limited to teaching his subject only?
Not at all. I firmly believe that teachers must teach other practical aspects of life, too. They must teach students what is good and bad, how to behave with different people at home and outside home, the importance of education in real life, and study skills and techniques. I believe that teachers should not train students only for academic subjects, but should also take care of the other aspects of their development.

Practice Questions:
1. What are the positive and negative aspects of the education system of your country?
2. Does your education help you in any way in your present life?
3. What changes can be introduced in our education system according to you?
4. What is the role of the government in imparting education?
5. What should we do to eradicate illiteracy from India?
6. What is the role of our parents in our education?
7. Do youngsters face problems when they go abroad for studies? If yes, what problems do they face?
8. What changes do/did you want in your school/college?
9. Which type of learning method suits you best?
10. Do you think today's parents can't give enough attention to their children?

EXERCISE

1. What are the benefits of doing exercise?
Exercise offers a bunch of benefits. It works on both, the physical and the mental level. At the physical level, it improves blood circulation throughout the body, stretches the muscles to maintain their flexibility, and improves the rate of respiration (breathing). It also burns excessive calories and makes our body fit and healthy. At the mental level, it relaxes the mind by increased blood and oxygen supply to the brain. It also makes us feel fresh and energetic throughout the day.

2. What equipment can we use for exercise?
There are a number of equipment we can use to carry out our exercise routine at home, and at gym. We can use a bicycle, a treadmill, ropes, dumb-bells, barbells, the bull-worker, etc.

3. Are there any exercises where we do not need to use any equipment?
Yes, exercises like walking, jogging, sit-ups, stretching, yoga, and aerobics do not require any equipment.

4. Are there any harmful effects of doing exercise?
Exercise should be done in a regular regime and/or under the guidance of a physical trainer. If we don't follow the regime or instructions of the trainer, we may harm our muscles, and in extreme cases there can be a permanent damage to our body.

5. Which type of exercises are becoming more popular nowadays?
There are a few exercises that are becoming highly popular these days. They are aerobics (especially dance aerobics), yoga, and laughing club routines. Generally, these exercises have been perceived to be for middle aged people, but, nowadays we can see youngsters also actively participating in such activities to keep themselves fit and healthy.

6. In future, which type of exercises do you think will be popular?
Exercises that provide energy to both, the body and mind will be more popular in future, because these exercises are completely harmless to our body. What's more, they can help in activating our mind, from the spiritual perspective. Even now we can see this trend emerging. People have turned towards active meditation, where some active body movements are required in the meditation process, dance aerobics, yoga, and so on.

Practice Question
1. What types of exercise can a person do in your city/country?
2. How many minutes a day should a person spend on exercising?
3. Many people say that they do not get enough time for physical exercise. What are your suggestions for them?

FAMILY

1. When do you talk with your family members?
I talk with my family members when I reach home, late in the evening. This is because all the members of my family are at home at that time, so, we have our dinner together, and

---

The Ultimate Guide to IELTS Speaking by Parthesh Thakkar

simultaneously, we discuss our day with each other, share new or present events, tasks at hand, social functions, and the problems in our lives.

2. What changes have you seen in the family system in the last decade?
Nuclear families and small families are emerging in large proportions in the society. This is because people prefer to have only one child, and in urban areas people live in small flats where they cannot live in joint families. However, a reverse trend is also visible in some countryside areas of my nation, where all members of the family have started to live together under one roof.

3. What are the positive and negative points of living in a joint family?
A joint family offers warmth and unity. We can have each other's support in a joint family, and that can be a boon in difficult phases of life. Moreover, cultural legacy can be easily passed on to the next generations in joint families. On the other hand, there is a lack of privacy in joint families at times. In addition, some self-centred people cannot share their materials with others, which may lead to conflicts in joint families.

4. What are the positive and negative points of living in a nuclear family?
A nuclear family gives us command over our life. People can enjoy higher freedom and privacy in their life. In addition, the financial responsibilities are also reduced in nuclear families. However, social and family responsibilities increase in nuclear families. In addition, people may feel lonely and helpless at difficult times in life.

5. What is the importance of family in your life?
Family is our first world. This is the world where we develop ourselves in various aspects of life, so that we can survive in the outer world and society at large. A family is a setup where we can live a natural life, i.e. without playing any psychological games with each other that we normally play with outsiders. In other words, it is a base of our life where we can lay the foundation for our future.

6. Do you think there should be a separate room in the house for every family member?
Yes, if possible, there should be a separate room for each member of the family. This arrangement gives the desired privacy in order to maintain feelings for each other. Otherwise, there are chances that some family members may feel intimidated by others' interference in their personal matters, which can cause conflicts in the future.

7. Do you think today's family members show less warmth and feelings compared to the past?
I don't agree to this. I do accept that the changes in lifestyle don't allow family members to give enough time to each other, but it doesn't mean that they have less respect and feelings for each other. I think blood relations don't need time to strengthen. They are inherently strong, and are beyond such requirements.

8. How do you solve the problems in your family?
We always discuss any problem with all the family members and get opinions from them. After that, we discuss possible consequences of following through with each suggestion. Finally, we come to the conclusion that sounds most suitable for the whole family.

9. How do you greet older people of your family, and relatives?
We greet elders of our family and relatives by either joining our hands before them, or by touching their feet. We also say the name of our god (Jai Shree Krishna or Jai Shree Ram; this differs from culture to culture) as a greeting. This method of greeting elders is an integral part of Hindu tradition.

10. What are the reasons behind the breaking down of joint families into nuclear families?

The prime reason for this is the economic development of the country. Because of this, people started shifting to bigger, industrial cities from small towns and villages. It is obvious that when we migrate, we cannot shift as a joint family in the beginning. So, families broke and members started living in different places of the country. Secondly, in the past, most families lived in houses which were big enough to accommodate all the members, whereas these days most people live in flats. These flats are usually not spacious enough for a joint family.

11. What things can we learn from our grandparents?

We can learn virtues like patience, faith, compassion, cooperation, and problem solving strategies from our grandparents. Moreover, we can gain knowledge about our family's history, culture, rituals, and traditions from them.

12. What can grandparents learn from youngsters?

Grandparents can learn enthusiasm, persistence, and optimism from the younger generation, because grandparents have entered a late phase of their lives, where they may feel exhausted. Therefore, when they see youngsters they get energised, and become zealous again.

Practice Questions:
1. Describe your family.
2. Who is closest to you in your family, and why?
3. How much time do you spend with your family?
4. What activities do you do with your family?
5. What according to you is an ideal family?
6. Which type of family do you prefer to live in — joint or nuclear? Why?
7. Describe the qualities of a good father/mother/son/daughter.
8. How important is it to know the history of our family?
9. How can we keep the history of our family alive?
10. Who takes important decisions in your family?
11. Do all family members obey that decision?
12. How are relatives/neighbours/friends treated in your family?
13. What things have you learnt from your family?
14. What is the role of your parents/family in your development?
15. What are our duties towards our parents?
16. Are you close to your grandparents?

FASHION, COSMETICS, CLOTHES

1. Why do you think people follow fashion?

People follow fashion because most of them like to feel youthful, and to look different, because being fashionable is perceived as being young and innovative. So, by following fashion, people can actually satisfy their desire to feel and look youthful. This encourages them to keep following fashion trends.

2. Who is more inclined to follow fashion — men or women? Why?

I think women are more inclined towards fashion. Traditionally, they have been the symbols of beauty in our society, and the society has always associated them with enhancements and innovations in terms of their appearance, clothes, jewellery, and so on. This is the reason why we can see that most fashion products are prepared keeping feminine customers in focus. Also, to look fashionable and beautiful is perceived as a feminine characteristic. However, the trend is changing these days, and we can find men also actively participating in buying fashion and related products. Still, the women who follow fashion trends outnumber the men.

3. Which type of clothes do today's young people prefer?

Today's young generation prefers a variety of clothes and styles. Men prefer T-shirts, shorts shirts, caps, cargos, denim trousers, and so on. Women prefer T-shirts, cotton or synthetic tops, skirts, denim or cotton trousers, and salwar kameez among other trendy outfits.

4. Why does fashion change with time?

Fashion keeps changing because innovation is its inherent nature. Any innovation is called so, for a short period of time. When a new fashion gets popular, it spreads like wildfire, and those who stick to older fashion trends cease to find novelty in them after a few uses. So, something new is introduced to the market every now and then, and the masses adopt these new fashion trends eagerly. This has become an ongoing process, which ensures that fashion keeps changing regularly.

5. Do you wear different clothes on different occasions?

Yes, I wear formal clothes at my work place, and casual clothes on weekends or holidays. I also prefer to put on different clothes when I attend parties. Lastly, I wear traditional clothes for festivals and marriage ceremonies. I believe that different clothes give us different feelings. When we wear clothes suitable to an occasion, we feel that we are an active and important part of the event. This feeling multiplies our involvement and enjoyment.

6. Why do you think old people in your country don't wear westernized clothes?

Old people identify with their traditional style of dressing, because they have been wearing their traditional clothes for decades. This prolonged use has made them associate their personality with their dressing style. Moreover, they often feel uncomfortable when they wear different fabrics and clothes. So, they resist changes in their clothing style. However, these days we can see elders in western clothes in most urban areas.

7. What are the reasons why people these days have become more conscious of their appearance?

Marketing, publicity, and impressive presentation are given great importance in the present era. In such an environment, one has to be aware of his appearance in order to get better acceptance at work. Moreover, fashion as an industry is spreading its wings to all classes of people. Thus, there is an inclination in the minds of people towards fashion and their looks. Therefore, we find that many people pay a lot of attention to their appearance.

8. How important are clothes for us?

The basic function of clothes is to protect our body from heat, cold, and rain. But, these days, clothes are used for a variety of functions, i.e. as uniforms, as a way to express different emotions, as symbols of religious and cultural identity, for exhibiting fashion, to display social and financial status, and so on.

9. Many people spend more on clothes to look different. Do you agree with them?

It is necessary for people like film stars, models, television actors, and anchors to look different, because they have to remain the centre of attention in the eyes of the media and society. This justifies their spending heavily on clothes, so as to wear different clothes even in their daily life, to keep changing their looks. However, I personally don't believe in spending a lot on clothes. To me, it is a waste of time and money.

10. What is your preference — fashionable clothes or comfortable clothes? Why?

I choose comfortable clothes over fashionable clothes. I believe in wearing clothes that are convenient. If I wear fashionable but inconvenient outfits, I will not look comfortable. In such cases my discomfort will ruin my enjoyment of fashionable clothes. Thus, I give priority to comfort over fashion.

11. Do clothes reveal the personality of a person?

Yes, at times, if we look at the clothes of a person, we can understand many things about his personality. For example, if we see a young man in a trendy t-shirt and casual trousers, we can assume that he's a college student. However, this assessment is done better by psychologists who use their knowledge to understand the different characteristics of human personality.

12. How much do you rely on the impression given by the clothes of a person?

At times, I use the impression given by the clothes to understand others' present stage in life, i.e. whether he is a student, employee, or businessman. But, I don't rely much on the impression of clothes, because firstly, I don't like to judge people so superficially, and secondly, such impressions can be misleading in certain situations.

13. Are there any harmful effects of cosmetics? If yes, what are they?

Prolonged use of cosmetics can damage our skin complexion. Some cosmetics may have toxic materials that can cause irritation to our eyes, skin, and other parts of our body. For example, lipsticks often touch our tongue and go to our stomach. If they contain harmful chemicals, they can show some adverse effects on our digestive system.

14. Many organisations have introduced a uniform for their employees. Do you think it is a good idea?

It is important for companies to maintain a sense of identity in the minds of their customers and employees. For this, they use specific coloured uniforms with certain styles as rank signs for employees to identify each other's positions and roles, as well as for customers to identify the roles of employees. Moreover, uniforms also bring a sense of equality among the employees of a company.

15. What type of clothes do you wear when you go out with your friends?

It depends on the particular situation. I wear casual clothes when I go out with my friends for shopping, movies, picnics, or informal events. But, if I have to attend a ceremony, a meeting, or a party, I wear formal clothes that suit the occasion.

Practice Questions:
1. How do people in your city/area/country follow fashion?
2. What changes have you seen in the way people follow fashion during the last decade?

3. Is there a difference in the preferences in modern fashion, between men and women?
4. Should we wear traditional clothes on festivals or ceremonies?
5. Do you think that we spend too much time and money on clothes? Yes, or no, and why?
6. Which types of clothes suit your personality?
7. Is there any difference between weekend dressing and weekday dressing?
8. Describe your traditional wear choices.
9. What is the importance of traditional dressing?
10. When and where can you wear traditional clothes in a foreign country?
11. What type of fashion will be popular in future, according to you?

FESTIVALS

1. What is the importance of festivals? OR Why are festivals celebrated?
Festivals are vehicles that carry our culture, religion, and history for new generations. They help us in remembering, following, and celebrating the importance of our cultural or religious history. Moreover, they give us a good break from work. They also provide an opportunity to meet our relatives and friends to strengthen our social bonds.

2. What is the difference between the way festivals were celebrated in the past and the way they are celebrated in the present?
In the past, people celebrated their festivals with their families at home, and in temples. Their celebrations included special prayers or worship. Now, people prefer to celebrate festivals with both, their family members, and their friends. These days they go out on holidays more, instead of visiting temples.

3. How can festivals be used to promote tourism?
Festivals can be used to attract international visitors and investors. Governments can promote special features of celebrations along with art that is associated with those festivals, in various countries. These promotions attract people from all over the world to visit our nation to be a part of our celebrations.

4. Do all the people in your country celebrate all the festivals actively?
No, those who do not belong to the religion in which the festival is celebrated don't take an active part in the celebrations. However, we all greet revellers with good wishes on their festivals.

5. Do you celebrate Christmas/festivals of other cultures? Why?
I do celebrate festivals of other religions or cultures like Christmas, Ganesh Chaturthi, and Eid, because I have friends who belong to different religions. I believe in being an active part of their festival celebrations also, because fosters feelings of closeness and warmth between other families and my family. In addition, I can learn many things about their festivals and religions by participating in them actively.

6. What happens in your city during festivals like Christmas and Diwali?
We have public holidays on most festivals in my country. Because of this, people of my city go out for shopping, for watching movies, to restaurants, for holidays, and so on. On the other hand, shopping malls and big companies introduce festive sales to woo consumers of my city, because most people buy clothes, gifts, sweets, and even consumer

durables during festive seasons.

Practice Questions:
1. How do you celebrate festivals?
2. Do you think we waste money on the celebration of festivals?
3. Are seasons and festivals interconnected?
4. Compare the festivals of your country with the festivals of the country you are planning to migrate to, or study in.

FOOD, RESTAURANT, ORGANIC FOOD, VEG AND NON-VEG FOOD

1. What are the main ingredients of the food that you eat daily?
The main ingredients of my daily food are carbohydrates, proteins, and lipids that we get from wheat and rice, cereals and milk, and oils, respectively. Apart from these, we get vitamins and minerals from fruits and vegetables, from our regular diet.

2. What do you prefer more — homemade food or restaurant food? Why?
I prefer homemade food, because it is not feasible for me to go to restaurants every day. Next, my tastes and likings are taken care of with homemade food, which is not always the case with restaurant food.

3. What is the difference between homemade food and restaurant food?
Homemade food is healthy, hygienic, economical, and nutritious, whereas restaurant food is spicy, expensive, and, at times, unhygienic. However, it is true that restaurants offer variety in both, food items and tastes. But, their food tastes good only if we eat it occasionally.

4. What is the difference between the food of the past, and that of the present?
In the past, people used to eat traditional food specific to their culture and region. But, now we have fast food and continental food available across the globe. So, people have included pizzas, sandwiches, burgers, pastas, noodles, etc. in their regular diet.

5. What is hygienic food, and what is nutritious food?
Food that is clean, safe, and free from contaminants and germs is known as hygienic food, while food that contains a balance of nutrients like vitamins, minerals, proteins, fats, and carbohydrates is known as nutritious food.

6. Does seasonal change affect our food intake?
Yes, seasonal changes do affect our food intake in terms of both, quantity and variety. Firstly, the availability of vegetables and fruits varies with the seasons. For example, we can eat more green vegetables in winter, and more citrus fruits in summer. Secondly, seasonal changes also affect our appetite. In winter our appetite is much larger than in summer.

7. Does food reflect our culture?
Food is an integral part of our culture. People across the world make food choices based on their cultures, only. For example, in China people eat noodles and other Chinese food. Within India also people eat different foods, varying based on their culture and region.

The Ultimate Guide to IELTS Speaking by Parthesh Thakkar

E.g. People in southern India eat dosa and idli, Punjabi people eat their special blend of vegetables and flatbreads like 'sarso da saag' and 'makke di roti', and Gujarati people often eat chapatti, rice, and lentil curry.

8. What changes have you observed in the eating habits of people of your city?

These days our eating habits are changing at a great pace. Firstly, the time of our meals is changing. A major change has come in, in terms of our dinner time. Most working people in my city sit for dinner at 10 pm or later, compared to the past, when people used to have dinner between 8 and 9 pm. In addition, fast food like pizza, sandwiches, and burgers, and other international food items from Chinese, Italian, Mexican, and Thai cuisines are also becoming a part of our regular diet. This shift in eating patterns is visible across the globe, which is a sign of an emerging global culture.

9. What factors do you consider before selecting a restaurant for eating in?

There are many factors which we should consider before selecting a restaurant. The restaurant should offer pleasant ambience, attractive interiors, proper lighting, hygienic and tasty food, prompt table service, cooperative and expert service staff, comfortable tables and chairs, and a variety of food items on offer, to cater to the different tastes of people.

10. What are the reasons why people frequently go to restaurants nowadays?

It is obvious that we cannot eat new food items on a regular basis at home. Still, most people want a variety in their diet from time to time. Hence, to satisfy their need for novelty, they visit restaurants. In addition, a visit to a restaurant turns out to be a good break for the women of the house, as they don't have to cook meal at home and all the members of the family can enjoy a good time with each other.

11. What are the advantages of eating with the family members?

It is essential to eat at least one meal a day with family members. This gives lots of benefits. We can discuss our everyday developments, difficulties, and problems with each other. We can also seek each other's suggestions and support. Such interaction is vital in strengthening family bonds, which is one of the most important factors behind the success of all family members.

12. Is there any food which you don't like? Why?

I don't like to eat too much spicy food, and non-vegetarian food. I have never tasted non-vegetarian food in my life, because the very thought of eating a cooked body part of an animal makes me uncomfortable. I also don't like my food too spicy, because it is harmful to our digestive system.

13. Do you think the concept of organic food will be popular in the future? Why?

Organic food will certainly gain popularity in future. These days we can see that the overall approach of medical science is shifting from treatment to prevention. As organic food is the healthiest food, it is getting favour over chemically grown food and GM food, across the globe. According to me this trend will pick up pace in future. (Organic food is that food which is derived from crops that are grown without using any chemical fertilisers and GM (Genetically Modified) seeds).

14. Are there any people for whom consumption of non-vegetarian food is a must? Who are they, and why is it necessary for them?

Some people live in regions where natural food sources like fruits and vegetables are not available. Non-vegetarian food is the only option for them to survive. E.g. For people who

---

live in deserts or polar ice regions like Greenland, and Antarctica where farming is almost impossible, non-vegetarian food is the only alternative for them.

15. Which type of food do you prefer — vegetarian, or non-vegetarian? Why?
I prefer vegetarian food for many reasons. Vegetarian food is healthy, nutritious, easily available, and easily cooked, and it is light on our stomach. On the other hand, non-vegetarian food is very heavy and stiff; so, we usually have to add spices in large quantities to make it palatable. Consequently, the overall dish can become very heavy for our stomach to digest. In addition, non-vegetarian food is not always healthy and hygienic. If a diseased animal is cooked and served, the consumer may get infected. We all are well aware of bird flu and mad cow disease, which can harm those who eat infected meat.

Practice Questions:
1. Which type of food is used/popular in various parts of your country?
2. Which type of Indian food would you offer to a foreign visitor?
3. What advantages are offered by your traditional food?
4. What are the differences between the food of your country, and the country you are planning to go to?
5. Which type of food will be more popular in the future?
6. Should we completely ban non-vegetarian food? Why?

FRIEND, FRIENDSHIP

1. Can you define a true friend?
I think a true friend is one who knows all our negative points and still loves us. It is indeed rare to find such a friend. However, those who have true friends are really lucky people, because in this materialistic world, they have someone with whom they can share everything.

2. What is the importance of a friend in our life?
A friend is a source of continuing support in life. A friend is someone with whom we can share everything that goes on in our life; someone we can expect to stand by us through all walks of our life. I believe that the importance of a friend can only be experienced, it cannot be described.

3. Who is more important to you — friends or family members?
Both are important in our life. It is true that we have blood relations with our family members, but we are also attached emotionally to our friends. Thus, both are equally important to me.

4. What things do you consider before making someone your friend?
I see only genuine commitment towards the relationship, before considering someone my friend. I think that much is enough for me. Some people see the other person's qualifications, nature, financial status, and religion. But, I believe that a person can prove to be a true friend in life if he is honestly dedicated to the relationship.

5. What is the difference between a school friend and a college friend?

School friends are innocent, altruistic, and cooperative in nature. They have only one thing in common, that is to enjoy life to its fullest. College friends are mature and selective in their relationships. It is often seen that college friends are more calculative and forge reciprocal relationships, unlike school friends, who are unconditional in their friendships.

6. Do you think friendships depend on destiny? OR Do you think making friends is a matter of luck?

We select friends as per our nature and status, which is a part of our destiny. In this context, we can say that the friends we make is determined by our fate, because it often happens that we study with many students in school or college, but we forge strong friendships only with some of them, even after years of knowing each other. On the other hand, we make friends with some people from the first meeting itself. For those who believe in luck, friendship might as well be considered dependent on luck.

7. When and where do you meet your friends?

We meet on weekends and holidays, because this is the preferred time for working people to meet. We often meet at our homes, restaurants, shopping malls, and multiplexes. Most youngsters, especially teenagers and college students frequent various popular hangout joints in the city. They also meet at discotheques, game parlours, cyber cafés, and coffee or snacks parlours.

8. How do you maintain your friendships?

I believe true friendship doesn't require maintenance. Still, we should stay in regular touch through phone calls, text messages, or emails when we cannot meet each other personally, so that we may update each other about the developments in our lives.

9. Do you think we should keep some expectations from our friends?

We should not keep any expectations from our friends. I won't call it friendship if we have expectations from people. I call such relationships give-and-take contacts. Such relationships are only purpose oriented and temporary. Friendship is a relationship where you get help from your friends even before you expect it from them.

10. How do you manage disputes in your friendship?

True friendship is beyond disputes. However, if my friends and I have any misunderstanding or face a communication gap, we first meet each other and clarify everything. In spite of this, if we reach an irreconcilable situation, we always act keeping in mind each other's interests.

11. Why do you think friends keep on changing in some people's life?

Some people develop relationships to fulfil their needs, and call such relationships friendship. Since needs keep on changing in everybody's life, such people also have to change their friends based on their changing needs and priorities. So, they keep changing 'friends' in their life, depending on who can fulfil their needs best in different stages in life.

12. Is there any change in friendship with age?

Real friendship gets better and stronger with time. It is true that activities, priorities, and status change the nature and amount of time that we spend with our friends. But, friendship as a relationship always grows with time.

Practice Questions:

1. Describe your friends.

---

2. Compare your nature with the nature of your best friend.
3. What things have you learnt from your friends?
4. What type of activities do you do with your friends?
5. What do you prefer more — going out with your friends, or family members? Why?
6. Do you share everything with your friends?
7. Have you had any bad experiences with a friend?
8. Was there any occasion when your friend helped you?
9. Have you had any memorable experience with your friend?

GAMES, SPORTS, SPORTS CELEBRITIES

1. Which games/sports are popular in your area/country?
Popular games/sports of my country are cricket, hockey, football, tennis, table tennis, billiards, volleyball, and badminton. People pursue these activities according to their interest. However, the most popular game/sport among all is cricket. I can say that cricket is not just a game, but a cult in India.

2. Do women get equal opportunities to men, to participate in all games in your country?
Yes, women get equal opportunities to participate in all sports activities at state, national, and international levels. The government gives grants to various sports associations which encourage women to participate in sports.

3. What is the importance of playing games?
Playing games is very useful to people of all ages. Through games, children develop various virtues like teamwork, sportsmanship, planning, fitness, physical development, and strength, and working people get a good break in which they can get exercise, relaxation, and enjoyment with their friends and family members.

4. Do schools in your city give the required importance to sports?
Most schools do give the requisite importance to sports. They develop some area of their campus for sports related activities. School authorities also encourage students to participate actively in sports. They also send their teams to state level tournaments. However, many schools in some big cities don't have enough space for their students to practice and learn sports. I recommend that these schools make some alternative arrangements to support sports activities of their students.

5. What are the benefits of participating in sports activities at school levels?
Participation in sports activities helps in sharpening skills and honing talents. A candidate can be identified and selected by sports authorities for further training if he has real talent, provided he participates. In addition, participation in sports gives benefits like physical fitness, improved reflexes, better understanding of sports, and respect in the society.

6. What is the difference between games and sports?
The difference lies in the motive behind the activity. A game is an activity that can be played by anybody, at any place, and at any time for the purpose of enjoyment. A sport is an activity that can be participated in by athletes or sports persons at state, national, or international levels with the motive of representing a club or a nation. For example, the

cricket that we play in the streets is better classified as a game, whereas the cricket that our national team plays can be called a sport.

7. How important is hard work in getting success in sports?

Hard work is essential in sports. Sportsmen should work hard at all levels to ensure success. They should maintain their physical fitness by regular exercise. They should also keep on practising to sharpen their skills and to develop innovative styles based on the requirements of their sport. Apart from this, psychological conditioning for sports people is equally important. They should learn to stay calm and optimistic even under pressure. To develop such an attitude they should make extra efforts under the guidance of sports psychologists. I can say that toughness of mind works better at times in getting victory, than just playing skills.

8. Does luck play any role in sports? Why?

I believe that luck is actually the result of hard work and positive mental attitude. We often see that persistent people become successful in the end. I accept that some people are gifted in sports, but, they cannot reach the top if they don't work hard, or if they are pessimistic.

9. Should sportsmen accept modelling offers, or not? OR Should sportsmen endorse brands?

Popular sportsmen and sportswomen are role models for many people. In this case, companies take advantage of their popularity by signing them as their brand ambassadors. However, sports celebrities should take care of two issues. Firstly, they should stay away from endorsing tobacco and alcohol brands. Secondly, they get the privilege of endorsement because of their success in sports, only. So, they must not neglect their sports for money from modelling, during their career.

Practice Questions:
1. Which games are children's favourite?
2. Which games/sports do today's youngsters/teenagers play?
3. How popular is your favourite game/sport?
4. Are there any games that are played only by men, or only by women? If yes, what are they?
5. Is there a difference in the liking of games between men and women?
6. When and where do you play games?
7. With whom do you play games?
8. Do you think sports activities should be encouraged among children?
9. Do you think we should ban those sports persons for life, who get caught using performance enhancing drugs?
10. Should the government spend large sums of money on sports events?
11. Do international sports events play any role in improving relations across countries?
12. If given a chance, which game or sport would you like to learn in the future, and why?

GIFTS, PARTY

1. On what occasions do people of your country give gifts?
People of my country gift each other on various occasions like birthdays, ceremonies, anniversaries, and festivals. In addition, they also give gifts to others on various achievements in life like promotions, expansion of business, and inauguration of new premises.

2. Which types of gifts make you happier when you receive them?
Any unexpected gift certainly makes me happier than a gift I have expected for an occasion. That gift can be a flower, a pen, or anything small. I don't always expect expensive gifts, because I value the intention behind a gift. In that context, a card is more precious to me than a watch, if the card is given with genuine emotions.

3. Which days do you celebrate with your family?
I celebrate birthdays, anniversaries, and all of mine and my family members' achievements. I celebrate such events mostly with my family, but we also invite our friends and relatives if the celebration is planned on a larger scale.

4. Where do you like to give a party — at home, or at a hotel/restaurant. Why?
I prefer giving a treat at a hotel or at a restaurant, because I believe that all the members of my family should enjoy the party to the fullest. Many of my family members have to take care of the food and arrangements if I host such celebrations at home. Then, they cannot take an active part in the celebration because of their duties as host.

Practice Questions:
1. What type of gifts do you prefer to buy for others?
2. Which days do you celebrate with your friends?
3. Do you like to attend parties?
4. On what occasions do you give parties?
5. Do you prefer to send greeting cards to your friends/relatives?
6. What are the advantages and disadvantages of giving greeting cards to others?
7. How do you celebrate your birthday?
8. Why are today's elders reluctant in permitting their children to go to parties?
9. Do you visit discotheques/dance floors? Why?

HEALTH, ALTERNATIVE THERAPIES

1. What is more important to you — health, or wealth? Why?
Both are important in our life. But I believe health is more important, because a loss in wealth is recoverable, whereas damage to health is often irreversible. So, health is more precious than wealth.

2. How does modern lifestyle lead to health related problems?
There are many variables in our lifestyle which lead to a loss or damage in health. Firstly, increased working hours and changed working patterns like sitting in front of computers

for hours, and stress at work can have adverse effects on our body. In addition, consumption of junk food and packaged food is increasing, as compared to fresh, traditional, and nutritious food. What's more, we now consume higher quantities of soft drinks instead of fresh fruit juices. This reduces the supply of vitamins, minerals, and electrolytes to our body.

3. Do you think it is advisable to go for regular body check-ups?

Yes, it is necessary to go for regular body check-ups, especially when we reach the age of 40, because most diseases like diabetes, hypertension, osteoporosis, and arthritis start setting in around that time. As we all know, early detection of a disease always helps in its treatment. Regular body check-ups can alert us regarding health issues in their early stages, thus helping us treat them better.

4. Who do you think lives a more healthy life — a city dweller, or someone living in a village?

I think city dwellers live with higher health risks because of factors like air, noise, and water pollution. Their lifestyle is often more stressful compared to that of village people. Such factors can lead to the conclusion that people in villages live a healthier life compared to those who live in cities.

5. What should the government do to promote health awareness among people?

The government should open general hospitals and primary healthcare centres where people get counselling along with treatment to make their life healthier. The government should also run health awareness campaigns in the media to impart awareness about the importance of a healthy lifestyle. They should also show the drawbacks of addictions like tobacco and alcohol.

6. What do you understand by alternative therapy?

All treatment systems other than allopathic treatments are considered alternative therapies. Homeopathy, Ayurveda, Yoga, Acupressure, Reiki, Sujok, Naturopathy, and Unani are examples of alternative therapies.

7. Why are alternative therapies becoming popular nowadays?

Alternative therapies are becoming popular because of three main reasons. Firstly, they are much cheaper than allopathic treatment. Secondly, most of these therapies do not have side effects on our body. Finally, they offer better and more permanent treatment options for chronic diseases like arthritis, gouts, asthma, ulcers, and allergies.

8. How many hours a day do you think a person should work?

It depends on the requirements and physical capacity of the individual. However, in normal conditions we should work for 8 to 9 hours a day, so that we can spend enough time with ourselves, and our families, and find time for other social responsibilities. If we work more than 10 hours a day, we cannot balance our life. In addition, we may invite stress and work related disorders.

9. Which exercise helps us the most in maintaining our health, according to you?

There are many exercises that we can do to remain fit like walking, swimming, aerobics, dancing, and yoga. Among all of these, I think, walking is the best exercise, because it can be done by anyone at any time without any equipment and any supervision. It helps in burning excessive calories from our body and keeps us healthy and fit.

Practice Questions:
1. What health related facilities are available in your area?

2. Do you do anything to maintain your health?
3. How does watching TV/playing games or surfing the net affect our health?

HOME

1. Is it the duty of the government to provide housing to all the people?
The government should provide housing to those who live below the poverty line. It comes under the fundamental responsibilities of the government to provide the basic necessities like food, water, and shelter to all the citizens. Poor people live in slums, where they lead miserable lives. The government can build colonies to where these poor people can be shifted, and their standard of living can be improved.
2. How can the problem of housing be solved?
The problem of housing can be solved only when the government takes an active interest in developing infrastructure and basic necessities in all parts of the country. People from underdeveloped areas have to migrate to other developed areas to avail basic facilities. This increases the population density in urban areas, and a housing problem begins to surface. Hence, the government should develop each and every village, so that people stop shifting to urban areas.

Practice Question.
1. Describe your home.
2. Describe the way to your home from the Exam Centre/your office?
3. Do you want any changes in your house?
4. What type of facilities will be available in future houses?

HOMETOWN, CITY

1. Describe your hometown.
My hometown is Ahmedabad. My city consists of a unique combination of history and globalisation. This city of more than 5 million people is located on the banks of the river Sabarmati, and has now developed on both sides of the river. My city can be broadly divided into two parts — the new city, and the old city. The old city was actually a kingdom of the Mughal monarch, Ahmed Shah who named the city 'Ahmedabad'. A huge fort that had 12 big gates was constructed during the reign of this king, to cover the old town. Even today those 12 gates are standing in my city. The old town is made up of narrow streets and terraced houses. The new town that has developed on the western side of the river has grown with wider roads, latest construction, malls, multiplexes, gardens, hotels, restaurants, and clubs. People in my city are cooperative, kind, and have a good business sense. Authorities of the city have now succeeded in developing a ne of

its kind riverfront, known as the 'Sabarmati Riverfront'. This project has garnered a lot of positive attention for my city since its completion.

2. What changes have you seen in the city in the last decade?
I have seen dramatic development in my city in the last decade. My city has swollen in all directions with almost a hundred percent growth in population. Apart from this, the city has witnessed a huge transformation in all aspects, such as infrastructure, roads, public transport, recreation facilities, shopping malls, and bridges. In addition, many companies have opened their branches in my city to take the benefit of the city's economic development. This has created excellent job opportunities in my city. Recently, the city has been declared a mega city. In short, my city has become truly cosmopolitan in the last decade.

3. What are the problems of your city?
The people of my city prefer their own vehicles to commute within the city. Because of this, the number of two wheelers is increasing like anything. This has resulted in traffic congestion and air pollution.

4. How do you think these problems can be solved?
There are two effective solutions for these problems. Firstly, the government should develop an efficient public transport system so that people may avoid using their own vehicles much, which will help in reducing traffic congestion. Secondly, public transport must run on CNG (Compressed Natural Gas), which is cleaner than other fuels like diesel and petrol. This will help in reducing pollution.

5. Is there any history linked with your hometown?
Yes, the history linked to the establishment of my hometown is interesting. In the 15th century, my city was known as Karnavati. At the time, surrounding territories were ruled by a Mughal monarch, Sultan Ahmed Shah. It is believed that once while he was passing through a large forest area in Karnavati, Sultan Ahmed Shah saw a wild dog chasing a rabbit, to kill it. The rabbit rushed towards the banks of river Sabarmati, where it drank some water from the river. After that, to the surprise of the king, that rabbit counter-attacked the wild dog, and forced it to retreat. This incident amazed the king. He thought the waters of Sabarmati must have some mysterious powers which gave a rabbit so much courage. He then decided to develop his capital on the banks of this river. This city later derived its name — Ahmedabad, from the name of the sultan.

Practice Questions:
1. How was your hometown when you were a child?
2. What types of clothes do people wear in your city?
3. Describe the transportation system of your city.
4. Do you want any changes to be introduced in your hometown?
5. Which are the popular places of your city?
6. What is the special feature of your city?

IMPORTANT DECISION

1. What things do you consider before taking any decision?

I always look for the resources required, and resources available for the same, before taking any decision. After that, I envisage its consequences as clearly as possible. Then I take a decision that is helpful not only to me, but also to others who are concerned.

2. What is a tough decision according to you?

Decisions which can have a long-term impact on life are often tough. For example, selecting a career or job, buying a house, getting married, and starting a new business are tough decisions. In addition, quick decisions are often tough because of a shortage of time.

3. Do you believe that decisions made in haste are always wrong?

It often happens that people take wrong decisions in haste, but this is not always the case. There are a few situations in life where we have to take prompt decisions. If they are based on the right analysis and experience, they can be fruitful.

4. Do you consult your family members/friends/spouse while making important decisions?

I always discuss my situation with my family members. I consider their views and analyse them before reaching a decision. Moreover, I always include those who are concerned with the decision, and those who can provide me accurate guidance, in the decision-making process.

5. Do you like others taking decisions on your behalf?

Not at all. I believe that I should take charge of my life. I neither like, nor allow anyone to take decisions on my behalf, because it is likely that others will consider my problem from their point of view while taking decisions for me. This can be harmful to me.

6. Do you help others in taking their decisions?

I help others in their decision-making process only when they ask for the same. I help others by clearing their view on various aspects of the situation. I also motivate others to foresee the good and bad effects of their decision, and more importantly, to listen to their inner voice. I only support and accompany others in their decision making process. I never take control of it.

7. Should parents be involved in the decision-making process of their children?

Parents should involve themselves in all important decisions of their children. Parents can use their experience and skills to help their children in taking appropriate decisions in matters like studies, selecting schools or colleges, taking up new activities, selecting career related courses, and even marriage.

8. What skills are needed to take decisions?

There are four major skills needed to take decisions in life. They are analysis, clarity, vision, and faith. First, we should be able to analyse the situation and its possible solutions. If we are unable to analyse any issue, we should take an objective opinion to make a better assessment. Secondly, we must be clear about our available resources and objectives. People often jump into a task and repent later, because either they were not well equipped, or they had obscure objectives. Thirdly, when we take a decision, we must anticipate its outcome as accurately as possible. This step is conditional, and comes only if the first two steps are taken correctly. The last requirement is faith. Unless we have complete faith in our decisions and ourselves, we may not take the right decisions for ourselves, and if we do, we may change those decisions in the near future.

9. How useful are computers/latest technologies in making decisions?

Technology is very useful in making decisions. It helps by facilitating communication, i.e. we can contact others on the phone or via email, and seek their views on issues. In addition, we can surf the net and gain required information to take decisions. Moreover, computers offer data storage and analysis options. We can use computers to assess big data to take numerous business decisions regarding sales, marketing, administration, and finance.

10. Do you think the decision making process in companies should be centralized or decentralized?

I believe company management should involve both, concerned and experienced employees in the decision-making process. This gives two major benefits. Firstly, employees feel respected and acknowledged, which enhances their commitment towards the organisation and makes their efforts more sincere. Secondly, the gap between management and workers can be minimized. This is very important for the smooth functioning of any organisation.

11. Should the employee be terminated from services if his decisions prove harmful to the organisation?

It depends on the motive of the employee. He should not be fired if he had taken a decision for the betterment of the company. However, if he is proven dishonest, he should immediately be terminated from his services and punished with legal actions so that he may not repeat the same dishonesty in future with other companies.

Practice Questions:

1. Do you think you are capable enough to make tough decisions in your life?
2. How can parents help their children in taking their important decisions?
3. What difficulties can you face while taking a tough decision?
4. What important decisions are you going to make in your future?

JOB, RETIREMENT

1. What are the ways to search for a job?

There are mainly three ways to search for a job. To begin with, we can look for advertisements in newspapers and apply for the job. Then, we can contact recruitment agents and online job portals. The third is for college students; they can appear for campus interviews and get selected for jobs.

2. Are there any new/emerging fields offering more and lucrative jobs?

Yes, there are many emerging fields which offer exciting and promising career prospects. For example, BPO (Business Process Outsourcing), KPO (Knowledge Process Outsourcing), tele-calling, financial advisory for the stock market, mutual funds and insurance, and information technology, all offer more attractive perks compared to other conventional jobs like those of clerks and accountants.

3. Do you think contacts are helpful in getting jobs?

Yes, contacts are often helpful in getting jobs. Although, their importance has reduced a lot in recent years, because now we have more jobs available, even now, if we are looking for a job in a particular field and in a specific company, contacts can help us get considered for that job.

4. Which type of jobs do men and women prefer?

Men prefer jobs that require some travelling, as youngsters like to travel and learn practical lessons of life, while women prefer desk jobs such as being appointed as a receptionist, a computer operator, a telephone operator, a tele-caller, or a secretary. In my opinion, women usually prefer jobs in which they can sit in the office and work, because they often don't feel comfortable doing jobs that require much physical work and travelling.

5. While appraising employees for promoting them, which of the following is more important, according to you; the qualification of the candidate, his experience, or his abilities. Why?

All these factors are important according to me, because a combination of all these make an employee successful. However, there are some posts where one factor may dominate others. In general, I would give a higher preference to talent, because I believe that talented people are highly adaptable. They can give real growth to the organisation. In my opinion, talented people are an asset to a company.

6. Most companies give awards and rewards to their employees. How useful are they in motivating employees?

Awards and rewards always motivate employees to work better. As humans, we all need acknowledgement of our work. If a worker is honoured for his services and achievements, he is likely to work even harder to excel at his job. What's more, his endeavours also inspire other workers to perform better and get acknowledged.

7. How has the working pattern changed in recent years?

The working pattern has seen tremendous changes in all aspects, in recent times. Firstly, working hours have increased. People these days work for 10–12 hours, compared to the 6–8 hours that they worked in the past. Secondly, work places and styles have altered. Now, employees use technological equipment like computers, scanners, internet, and overhead projectors to work more effectively, as opposed to employees of previous generations who had to be involved in a lot of paperwork. Lastly, more field jobs are offered these days, compared to in-house jobs that were in trend in the past.

8. Should we change jobs frequently, or should we stick to one job only? Why?

There is no harm in doing any job for a long time provided we are satisfied with the remuneration and growth of the company. Rather, it is advantageous, because the employee-organisation bond gets stronger with the duration of the service. However, changing jobs frequently may cause instability in an employee's career, because frequent changes don't allow workers to settle down in any work environment.

9. Many people suggest that these days an employee has to update himself regularly. What are the benefits of it?

It is essential for every employee to update himself regularly about jobs, markets, competitors, products, management innovations, and business techniques. Regular updating makes the employee competent and adaptable, which is vital for his career growth. It is believed that companies which don't innovate and change with time, lag behind their competition, and slowly their products start vanishing from the market. This is equally true for employees.

10. In which jobs do employees have to update themselves regularly?

Almost all type of jobs require regular updating. However, some fields like marketing, information technology, software programming, web designing and security, medicine, and engineering, require a faster and higher degree of knowledge updating from professionals.

11. What are the consequences for the employees who do not update themselves with time?

Employees who don't update themselves have two major disadvantages. The first is that they cannot grow at professionally, because their ideas and techniques are no longer competent and effective. This inhibits their career growth. The second is that when they see that their career isn't growing, they may suffer from a lack of confidence and start getting frustrated with themselves. Consequently, such a feeling reduces their efficiency and commitment, and they start seeing the end of their career.

12. Should college students do part-time jobs? Why?

It is advisable that students do some part-time jobs to earn money. Moreover, students become more responsible, mature, and self-reliant by doing jobs. However, some faculties like medicine, engineering, and management are highly demanding. Students who are studying in such streams must give a higher priority to their studies, because one has to sacrifice his studies to some extent if they start doing part-time jobs.

13. Define an ideal employee.

An ideal employee must be honest, hardworking, adaptable, dedicated, and receptive. He should understand the requirements of the company, and should mould himself accordingly. He should follow all the strategies of the company completely and seek clarity where he has doubts. Lastly, he must be dedicated to the company, because no organisation can get benefits from its employees if they are not dedicated towards their jobs.

14. Define an ideal employer/boss.

An ideal employer must delegate work with clear information. He must be a hard worker, a leader, a motivator, and a visionary. In addition, he should acknowledge the skills of his employees and give them enough liberty to grow well. Lastly, he should identify growth areas of the business and lead the team in the right direction, to acquire benefits from various market segments

15. Define an ideal colleague.

A colleague should be friendly, cooperative, and supportive. A colleague should be a team member who is always interested in the growth and betterment of the team, as a whole. He must turn himself away from typical office politics. A good colleague can become a close family friend who is trustworthy and helpful.

16. Should there be any age limit for retirement?

Yes, I think the government should keep some age limit for retirement. This age may be 60 or 65, so that vacancies can float in the job market and youngsters can get absorbed. This is very useful in preventing unemployment, and in supporting the growth of various industries.

17. What criteria should we consider for retirement?

I believe that there should be only two criteria for retirement — efficiency and age. If some workers are capable of working efficiently even after their retirement age limit, we should allow them to hold their jobs for longer. However, there are some workers who lose their efficiency a few years before their retirement age, too. Such workers often exploit their rights and enjoy their redundancy instead of working harder to remain efficient. I think such workers should be urged to take early retirement.

18. When should people start doing jobs according to you?

A few months after graduating, people should start doing jobs, because qualified people get better jobs with higher salaries compared to unqualified workers. What's more, college studies make students more mature and competitive to cope up with their work environments. So, I believe people should start their job lives after completion of their studies.

19. How can we get a higher salary compared to other employees?

Hard work, commitment, and dedication to the job are the qualities which help workers to get higher salaries than their colleagues, because the management often monitors the activities of workers, and if they find someone who is putting extra efforts, they are also inspired to pay extra to that employee. However, some employees think that they can play political games and stay in the limelight just by talking big. They may get success in drawing the attention of the management in the initial stages, but this attention won't last long. I believe in one wonderful saying, 'Actions speaks louder than words'.

20. Name some jobs that can be done in shifts.

There are many jobs in both, manufacturing and service sector industries that can be done in shifts. Many industries have twenty-four hour manufacturing plants, for which they require workers who can work in twelve or eight hour shifts. Service sector businesses like call centres, hospitals, and research laboratories also work round the clock. They also require shift workers to carry on through the day.

21. What are the advantages of shift work to the society?

Both, the industry and the workers derive benefits from shift duties. Industries can continue their production or service work round the clock. This enhances their productivity and profits. As the industry grows, the economy also grows. In addition, some sectors like BPO can work only in shift duties, because of the different time zones they serve. Workers who are in need of money may do more than one job to support their financial requirements, if there is a shift system in place. Moreover, shift work allows other members of the family to adjust their job timings so that the home never remains unattended.

Practice Questions:
1. What types of jobs are available in your city nowadays?
2. What qualifications are required to get such jobs?
3. Do you require additional skills to get such jobs?
4. What type of pay scale is offered by commonly available jobs in your city?
5. What types of facilities are offered by an ideal organisation to its employees?
6. Describe your work place.
7. Do you want any changes in your work place? If yes, what and why?
8. How do the interiors and infrastructure of a work place influence the work efficiency of employees?

9. Describe the first day of your first job.
10. What problems do fresh graduates face in their first job?
11. What do companies do to help youngsters in settling in their first job?
12. What do you prefer — working in a team of colleagues, or working alone? Why?
13. Do you celebrate special days at work? If yes, which are they? If no, why?
14. What problems do people face when they migrate/do a job in a foreign country?

LANGUAGE, ENGLISH

1. What is the basic function of a language?
The basic function of any language is communication. Historically, in the earliest stages of evolution, humans used to grunt and make other similar sounds to express their thoughts and feelings. Later, sounds became words. Words were then structured to form language. Even today, language serves the purpose of communication in both, spoken and written forms.

2. What is the importance of language in our life?
Language differentiates humans from other animals. Humans have a developed brain, which functions through thoughts rather than impulses. It is impossible to generate and express thoughts without language. So, language is very important for the evolution of human life.

3. In today's life, why is it important to learn English?
Learning English has become extremely important in today's time. English is emerging as a global language. Most communications on the internet are carried out in English. Moreover, new inventions in science and technology are documented and published in English only, because it serves as a common language among those who have acquired technical or scientific qualifications. Further, all corporate correspondences are also done in English. Thus, we must learn English if we want to flourish in this English-influenced world.

4. Do you think we should have only one language in the world?
This is a debatable and controversial topic. One common language across the globe can help in binding people in unity and equality. The whole world becomes easily accessible if we have only one language. In addition, many cultural, racial, and territorial disputes can be solved easily. However, it is not possible to implement this because humans need variety in their lives. If we take English as an example, we can find that most English speaking countries have developed differences in the way they use the language, by introducing colloquialisms and creating forms of English, such as British English, American English, Australian English, and so on. Hence, the idea of one language across the globe looks fascinating, but it is not possible in practical life.

5. What are the advantages of learning a foreign language?
Learning a foreign language broadens our mind and makes us more accepting of other cultures and their lifestyles. This can help us gain amazing knowledge of their community, history, and country. As a result, we can take the benefit of the language to

trade with the country, or to settle down there.

6. Would you like to acquire another language in the future? If yes, which one, and why?
I would like to acquire the knowledge of Sanskrit language in future. It is considered as one of the oldest languages of the world. All Indian scriptures and ancient books are written in Sanskrit. The language will surely help me to understand these scriptures. What's more, next to English, I have an innate liking for Sanskrit, too.

7. Can you be proficient in English without living in an English speaking country?
Certainly, it is possible to be proficient in English without even visiting an English speaking country. We can acquire English proficiency through self-study or with help from a coaching centre, and then it is up to us to keep practising spoken and written English in our day-to-day lives, so as to get a grip on the language with time.

Practice Questions:
1. Which is your favourite language?
2. Why do you think so many people are learning English today?
3. What difficulties can we face when we talk to someone who doesn't understand our language?
4. Do you think it is difficult to survive in any English speaking country without knowing English?
5. What difficulties have you faced in learning English?
6. What have you done to improve your English?
7. What should you do to improve your English?
8. Do you think we are ignoring our mother tongue in the rush to learn English?
9. Who plays a vital role in learning our first/second language — teachers or parents? Why?
10. Should we enrol our children in an English medium school or a school that teaches in our mother tongue/native language? Why?
11. How does a coaching class help you in picking up a second language?

LAUGHTER

1. What are the benefits of laughing?
Laughter offers immense benefits. When we laugh, our mind relaxes and we feel fresh. This strengthens our mind; consequently, our body also gains strength. It is said that laughter is the best medicine. Those who laugh have higher immunity, and are less likely to suffer from diseases.

2. Do you ever feel offended when someone laughs at you?
I never feel offended when someone laughs at me, because laughter is the other person's reaction based on his thoughts, and I have nothing to do with them. On the contrary, I think that the person is doing nothing except enjoying my presence. However, here I would like to point out an important factor that determines our reaction. If we are not happy or satisfied with ourselves, we often feel intimidated when people laugh at us,

because our mind immediately associates our deficiencies with that prank. I admit — no one is perfect; so, if anyone laughs at me, I believe he is showing his state of mind. However, my reaction comes from my state of mind, and I never feel offended.

3. Do you feel fresh when you laugh?

Yes, laughter offers prompt refreshing feelings. When we laugh, our mind focuses completely on the situation. As a result, our mind moves its focus away from all tensed thoughts, feelings of anxiety, and worry, towards the happiness that we get from laughter. This shift of focus happens quickly in our mind. So we instantly feel relief washing over us, refreshing us.

4. What are the sources of laughter available nowadays?

I think a truly humorous person doesn't need to look for sources of laughter. However, these days we have many things to laugh at, like movies, comedy serials and laughter competitions, dramas, articles, books, and jokes. In addition, there are many laughter clubs available in many cities, too.

5. How helpful are laughter clubs?

Laughter clubs help people in many ways. They create an environment for us to break our mental barriers and laugh aloud, because, when we are alone or in a social circle, we feel embarrassed laugh aloud without a good reason. In addition, the feeling of laughter actually multiplies when we laugh in a group at the laughter club. Furthermore, laughter clubs are organised in the early mornings in public gardens. The time and location magnify the benefits of laughter.

6. Do you believe that laughter therapy is a useful way to treat people with chronic psychotic/neurotic disorders or diseases?

Laughter is used these days as a therapy for patients who suffer from both, psychological and physiological diseases, because science has proved that laughter strengthens our immunity and enhances the healing process. These factors are very important in treatment. I think such clubs are a welcome development, because patients and members can recover from the shock of their diseased conditions with the help of laughter.

Practice Questions:
1. Tell me the circumstances in which you laugh.
2. Is there any negative impact of laughing?
3. Can you assess someone's personality by observing the way they laugh?

LEISURE TIME, TV, WEEKEND

1. What are your leisure time activities?

My leisure time activities are reading books, listening to soft music, and surfing the internet for websites offering training in English, IELTS, and TOEFL. At times, I also take a short break to have a cup of tea for a change, and then I get back to work again.

2. What is the difference between your leisure time during weekdays and weekends?

The leisure time I get during weekdays is only for a few minutes when I cannot pursue time consuming activities. However, weekends are long breaks where I can go out shopping, or for a picnic, or to watch movies. So, the biggest difference is in the length of time that we get during weekdays and weekends.

3. Why is watching TV the most common leisure time activity nowadays?
It is true that people of all ages watch television more today, than at any given point in the past. This is because it is not always possible for elders and housewives to go out to pursue hobbies or other activities. So, the only option left for them in their free time is watching television. Moreover, working people are tired when they come back home, and they watch TV to get some rest. To top it, TV shows these days cater to the interests of all ages and classes of people.

4. How do you pass your leisure time at home?
At home, I often pass my leisure time with my child. I talk to her about her school, studies, friends, and sometimes I play games with her. I believe that playing with children always makes us feel more energetic, because they are innocent and are full of energy themselves.

5. What recreational sources are available in your city to carry out leisure activities?
There are many natural and manmade places where we can pass our leisure time. We can go to gardens, the riverbank, or other countryside areas near the city to enjoy closeness with nature. On the other hand, we can also go to amusement parks, game parlours, shopping malls, movie theatres, and cyber cafes to pass our leisure time.

6. What leisure time activities according to you will be popular in the future?
It is difficult to say, but I think activities based on technology like playing three-dimensional or virtual reality games, chatting online, and browsing the net will be highly popular in the future.

7. How do you look forward to your weekend?
I work in a six day working week system, where I get only one day a week to relax. This is the reason why most people often wait for weekends, and at times, they make plans for Sundays two–three days in advance. I also look forward to Sunday, because this is the only day when I can complete my pending commitments, and get a good break from work. So, we really look forward to our weekends.

Practice Questions:
1. What is the importance of having leisure time? OR How important is leisure time in your life?
2. How do you spend your weekends?
3. Should we spend more money on weekends, or not?
4. What activities do you do in your leisure time with your friends?
5. What is your leisure time during weekdays?
6. Compare your leisure time activities with those of your friend/family member/ colleague.
7. What is the difference between the way people pass their leisure time now, and in the past?
8. How do people in India/your city/your area pass their leisure time?

MEDIA, NEWSPAPER, MAGAZINE, JOURNALIST

1. What are the advantages and disadvantages of electronic media and print media?
Electronic media like television, radio, and internet are helpful in providing us the latest real time news from the whole world. Moreover, TV and the internet provide us both audio and video coverage of news. However, it is expensive to access this news, as everybody cannot afford televisions and computers. In addition, we require electricity to operate such equipment, which in turn adds to the cost of living.
On the other hand, print media like newspapers and magazines are cheap and convenient. We can carry and read newspapers anywhere. In addition, they also cover all local events in detail to update us about the goings on in our locale. However, they do not provide real time news like the television. Moreover, this medium is for literate people only. Illiterate and visually impaired people cannot access print media.

2. Which media is more effective according to you — electronic (TV) or print (newspapers, magazines)?
I think both media are effective in their own segments. Television is useful in creating a prompt response, and in spreading news quickly among the masses, because it shows live events as and when they happen. On the contrary, print media helps in generating a wave of awareness or opinion in the society. This is a slow and steady process. Hence, electronic media is used to get a quick response from the masses. On the other hand, when it comes to generating intellectual notions and opinions, print media is the choice for spreading gradual but steady awareness among readers.

3. What is the main function of media?
The basic function of media is mass communication. It provides accessible information to the masses, who can then use the knowledge for their own benefit.

4. How can media be helpful to you in your life?
Media is a useful tool to stay abreast with the current events happening in the world. It updates us about various aspects of life, like politics, financial markets, education, business, jobs, management, entertainment, sports, fashion, and lifestyle. We can also stay updated regarding the latest changes in the world around us, with the help of the media. What's more, if we have a message to convey to the society, the media can be extremely useful in fulfilling our objective.

5. Do you think media gives more importance to celebrities?
It is true that media gives more attention to celebrities. However, some people also say that celebrities use the media for their publicity. But, I believe that it is the interest of an average individual in the lives of celebrities that motivates the media to pay more attention to famous personalities.

6. Should the media interfere in the personal lives of celebrities?
No, celebrities are also humans. They have the right to live their lives as they please. The media should not interfere in the personal lives of famous personalities just to get scoops to increase their viewership. This is inhuman, and should be stopped.

7. Should we give total freedom to the media, or should we control the content of the media?
Media has now become an easily accessible tool for many people. As it is used by many, there are chances that some may exploit the power of the media for their personal benefit.

Thus, to avoid any damage in terms of money, morals, or culture, the content of media should be monitored.

8. What are the fundamental responsibilities of the media?
The prime responsibility of the media is to act as a platform to the society from where people can gain knowledge, information, and entertainment. The media should also ensure that it contributes to the constructive growth of society. Lastly, the media should take the onus of improving the lives of people by spreading appropriate awareness in the society, and by preventing the entry of social evils.

9. What are the qualities of a good journalist?
A journalist must be hardworking, honest, a good communicator, and courageous. He must provide unbiased information to the community, and to ensure this, he must have good analytical and writing skills. Lastly, he should use his skills to enhance the dignity of his profession by serving the society, rather than exploiting his skills for personal gains.

10. What is the difference between the working style of a newspaper journalist, and a magazine journalist?
A newspaper journalist is always on his toes. He has to be prepared to go anywhere at any time to cover events, because events occurring on any day need to be printed in the next day's paper. On the other hand, a magazine journalist can plan his work and manage his time as he only has to cover those events which are suitable for his magazine's readers. In addition, a magazine journalist gets more time to prepare his articles, as magazines are not published on a daily basis like newspapers.

Practice Questions:
1. Do you think some people are exploiting the power of the media for their personal benefit?
2. What do you foresee for the future of the media in India?
3. What problems are faced by today's journalists?

MIRRORS

1. Are mirrors useful?
Yes, mirrors are useful. We use them every day to get ready and check how we are dressed, before stepping out of the house. Through the day, also, if we encounter a mirror anywhere, we check our appearance and feel self-assured.

2. Do you spend a lot of time in front of the mirror?
I spend normal amounts of time in front of the mirror. I wouldn't say that it's a lot, but it's just enough for me to get dressed, look my best, and step out of the house confidently. I don't spend hours in front of the mirror, though.

3. Who according to you spends the most amount of time in front of the mirror?
I think teenage girls spend the most amount of time in front of the mirror. For most teenage girls, trying on different outfits and accessories is a hobby and an everyday pastime. They love checking out their appearance and sprucing it up every now and then.

They are also fond of experimenting with different looks in the mirror. A lot of teenage girls have newly been introduced to makeup, so they spend a lot of time perfecting their makeup skills in the mirror, too.

4. Why do women spend more time before the mirror than men?
Women take longer to dress up than men, usually. This is because they wear more number of clothes and accessories on any given day than men. They also apply cosmetics and put on jewellery, which men usually don't. These activities take up sufficient amount of time. So women spend more time before the mirror, perfecting their look, than men.

MOVIES

1. Has the popularity of cinema increased or decreased in recent years?
The popularity of cinema has increased in my country. This can be seen in the form of a rise in the number of films released every year in both, national and regional languages. Moreover, new cinema halls are also being opened in various cities across the nation. Both these developments prove that cinema is a leading form of entertainment for most people in my country.

2. In your opinion, will this trend continue in the future as well?
This trend will certainly continue in the future, because cinema is also changing with time. Present day movies are made to cater to the interests of different groups of people, right from village residents to metro dwellers. Moreover, new multiplexes have changed the perception of cinema from merely a place to watch a film at, to a place for recreation and leisure. Thus, I believe that cinemas will be highly popular in the future, too.

3. Which types of movies are more popular in your city/country?
The people of my country like social films, dramas, comedies, romantic flicks, and action movies. Most of the movies released in my country belong to one of these five categories.

4. It is argued that movies increase violence in the society. Do you agree with this statement?
No, I don't agree with this statement. Movies are actually a reflection of our society. They usually show events that have happened, or are happening in society. If the argument of increasing violence were true, action and violent movies would have been banned decades ago across the world, but, it has not happened, because people who commit crimes are not inspired by movies they've seen.

5. Do you think films on real life events/history should be made?
Yes, movies should be made on real life events. Such movies give viewers an exact idea of the prevailing situations in society. Moreover, realism based movies often inspire people to learn and to implement positive lessons from events depicted in such movies in their lives. For example, movies like Gandhi, Page 3, Lagaan, Lage Raho Munnabhai, Corporate, Guru, Shootout at Lokhandwala, Gangajal, Mughal-e-Azam, and Rang De Basanti have all managed to make lasting impressions on viewers.

6. Should censorship be there, or not?
Censorship is an essential part of cinema. It defines the limits for the content of cinema in

order to maintain the importance of moral values, culture, and tradition in the society. In addition, censorship prevents the release of films that may hurt the feelings of certain sections of society.

7. If given a choice, would you prefer to watch a drama or a movie? Why?

Both have their own peculiarities. A drama is a live performance of actors on a stage, making the story come alive and involving. Acting in a drama is a challenging task for performers because there is no scope for errors. So, for lovers of acting and live performance, watching a drama is a better choice. However, movies give us better sound effects, cinematography, and music. I often opt for movies over dramas, because I like to watch different outdoor locations, new costumes, and innovative storylines. All these things are not possible with dramas.

8. What are the advantages and disadvantages of watching movies on TV and in cinema halls?

Watching movies on TV offers convenience. We have the controls of our television in our hands. We can adjust the volume or change channels as we like, and avoid viewing boring or unwanted things on screen. We can also sit at ease and immediately attend to any emergencies or other important tasks at home. Next, many people together can watch a movie on television at home, and enjoy together, without paying for tickets, like in a cinema hall. However, a television screen is small, so we cannot get the audio visual effects of a cinema screen on TV. In addition, new movies can only be seen at cinemas. Lastly, advertisements are a big disturbance while watching a movie at home on a satellite channel. Apart from an ad-free experience, cinemas also offer comfortable chairs, air-conditioning, high definition sound systems, and a luxurious ambience. All these things make movie viewing a memorable and enjoyable experience. What's more, multiplexes these days offer other facilities like video games, refreshments, restaurants, and shopping outlets. People often visit such places for relaxation, and to get the feel of a picnic, which the television at home cannot provide. However, cinema visits are often costly, so middle class families cannot visit cinemas frequently.

I prefer watching new musicals, action and adventure movies, and thrillers at cinema halls only, because of better sound and visual effects, and facilities.

Practice Questions:

1. How often do you watch movies?
2. With whom do you prefer to watch movies?
3. Do movies influence our behaviour?
4. Do you think we should ban movies showing violence?
5. Do you suggest any changes to the rules of censorship?
6. What kind of movies will be popular in future, according to you?
7. Who is your favourite actor/actress? Why?
8. If given a choice, would you read a book or watch a movie? Why?

The Ultimate Guide to IELTS Speaking by Parthesh Thakkar

MUSIC

1. What is the importance of music in life?

Music is an essential part of our lives. It serves different purposes for different people. Some listen to it for entertainment and relaxation. For some, it is an art that they pursue, either alone or in combination with other activities like dancing. For some, music is their career. And for others, such as Sufi saints and mystics, it is a means to salvation. Music touches us in many dimensions of life. It is impossible to remain untouched by music in our lifetime.

2. How is today's music different from that of the past?

Today's music is fast, and based more on western styles, whereas music of the past was based on classical rhythms and folk tunes.

3. Nowadays people make blends of Indian music and international music. Are you in favour of this practice?

Music is an art which allows people to constantly experiment. There is nothing wrong in mixing classical and western music. If it is good, people will accept it, and if it is not good, it will be rejected by listeners.

4. How can we preserve Indian classical music?

As I said, music is an art which keeps perpetuating itself, and we don't need to preserve it, because those who like the sound of classical music will instinctively adopt it. However, we can promote classical music at the international and national level, to increase its popularity. To support this objective, the government should encourage the introduction of classical music as a subject from the school level. The authorities can also present awards and honours to those who excel in music, because these artists are the only live mediums through whom the art of music can be spread to future generations.

5. What is the importance of traditional/folk music?

The purpose of traditional music is not only entertainment. In fact it carries the legacy of the cultures and traditions to which it belongs. Traditional music that we enjoy on festivals, seasonal celebrations, and ceremonies acts as a reminder of our cultural history.

6. Is the interest of people in traditional music increasing/decreasing? Why?

I think the interest in traditional music is certainly increasing, because these days we even regional and vernacular artistes have started introducing their music albums. Most of these are based on folk music, and many such albums are getting success in the market. This suggests that the interest of people in folk music is in fact increasing.

7. Is music helpful in healing? OR Can music be used to treat diseases?

Yes, music is actually a type of sound generated by an instrument or by an artiste. This sound comes to us as a wave of energy. When our body absorbs this energy, our body reacts to it in a certain manner. So, we often feel relaxed and refreshed when we listen to soft music, whereas, if we listen to too much loud music, we feel disturbed. This sensitivity of humans to music can thus be deliberately used to produce certain reactions in our body, to enhance healing.

Practice Questions:

1. What type of music do you like?
2. How do you listen to music — on the radio, or on a music system? Why?

---

3. How is Indian music different from international music?
4. What kind of music does today's young generation like?
5. At what time do you usually listen to music?
6. If given a chance, which musical instrument would you like to learn, and why?
7. What career options are available in your country for musicians?
8. Who is your favourite musician? Why?
9. What type of music do you think will be popular in future?

NAME

1. In your tradition, who decides the name of the baby?
In my tradition, the name of the baby is decided by its paternal aunt. However, these days the tradition is changing, and many parents themselves name their children. What's more, some parents also go to their religious mentor (Guru), who blesses the baby and gives it a name.

2. It is said that the name leaves its traits on the nature of the person carrying it. Do you agree with this? Why?
No, I don't agree with this. Sometimes we may observe some people possessing a few characteristics of their name's meaning, but, this is purely coincidental. I don't believe we can generate qualities in a person, simply by naming him a certain way.

3. Do you think a name can help us in remembering a person, or is the nature of the person more instrumental in our recall process?
Both are important up to some extent, when it comes to remembering someone. But, I think the nature of an individual is more important, because we can remember the behaviour, attitude, respectfulness, and other qualities of a person more easily as compared to the name.

4. What is more important to you, your name or your surname. Why?
Both are important to me, as both are part of my identity. However, the name is more important than the surname, because my name reflects my individual identity, whereas my surname reflects my social and cultural identity.

Practice Questions:
1. What is the meaning of your name?
2. Will you change your name in future?
3. How are you recognized in your family/friend circle?
4. Do you think a person should have a nick name/pet name, or not?
5. How do people of your city/country generally select names for their children?

The Ultimate Guide to IELTS Speaking by Parthesh Thakkar

NATURE

1. Do you behave differently with different people?
I don't believe in behaving differently with different people, because I feel that I should not hide or mask my feelings in order to extract benefits from others. It looks artificial and feels unnatural. However, at times we should be tactful with others, for their own benefit; for example, with children and subordinate, we may need to talk and behave with a little more discretion than usual

2. Do the good traits of your nature help you in your life? How?
Good traits of their nature always help people in their lives. I think persistence is an important trait of my nature. This has allowed me to never give up, even under the most difficult circumstances of my life. I have observed that persistent people can survive in tough times, and flourish in good times with dignity.

3. How should we treat children — strictly, or softly?
We ought to treat children softly, and in a friendly way. Children are innocent, natural beings. When they make mistakes, they should be explained gently where they have erred. If we treat children strictly, their sense of curiosity and experimentation will be lost, which will result in a loss of creativity, and will build vulnerability in them.

Practice Questions:
1. Tell me something about the positive and negative points of your nature.
2. What changes do you want to bring about in your nature?
3. What is the difference between your nature in the past, and now?
4. Have you had any bad experience because of any negative trait of your nature?
5. Whom does your nature resemble in your family?
6. Tell me something about the nature of your family members/friends.

PHOTOGRAPHY

1. What are the applications/uses of photography?
Photography has various applications. It is useful in capturing and preserving memorable moments, events, and ceremonies of life. It is also used in providing testimony or evidence of a place, incident, or person. This application is highly useful in different areas like government administration, crime investigation, and traffic management, among others.

2. Have you kept any particular photograph in your room?
I took many snaps of my daughter when she was about 10 months old. Some of them were really cute and some were simply outstanding, so I took them to a photo studio, and got them developed and framed. Since then, 2 of her best pictures have been mounted on the wall of my room. Even today, when I see her innocent and joyful face, I feel wonderful, and grateful to God for making me her father.

3. Do you often get photos framed? If yes, what type of photos?
I do get those photos framed, which are special to me. In the past have got some photos

of my daughter, my wife, and my late grandfather framed. Apart from these, there is a family photo that was taken at a ceremony a few years ago, which we have framed and mounted in our drawing room. Lastly, I have had some of my college friends' and school friends' photos framed; now whenever they come home, we look at those pictures and relive old memories.

4. On what occasions do people take photographs?

Most people take photos to capture moments for future remembrance. People take snaps of their friends and family members on festivals, ceremonies, and at parties. Some people take photos of nature, like trees, gardens, landscapes, mountains, and sunsets. In general, photos are taken to perpetuate some physical memory of a moment in time.

5. What developments have happened in the field of photography in recent years?

There have been dramatic changes in the field of photography, since the advent of digital photography. Now we use digital cameras instead of roll film cameras. What's more, digital cameras can now be fitted in mobiles, laptops, and desktops. They let us click high-resolution pictures without the hassles of a roll film. They are cheap, yet superior in quality to conventional roll film cameras. This is the reason why the spread of photography as a whole is increasing in the world.

6. Will still photography be equally popular in the future?

Although the popularity of still photography is decreasing with the introduction of compact and affordable handy-cams and movie recording facilities in mobiles, I don't think it will become completely out of date in future. People are fond of clicking and viewing still photos, and they will continue to do so, because it is not always convenient or possible to use video recordings.

7. If given a choice, would you buy a photograph, or a painting of a given scene/object? Why?

It is indeed a difficult choice to make. A photograph offers an accurate and high-resolution reproduction of the scene or object in question. Photographs can also be edited and stored in our computers for a lifetime. In addition, they are cheap and readily available. On the other hand, a painting is a mixture of the imagination and artistic skills of an artist. It can be very expensive to own, compared to a photograph. So, I would prefer to buy a photograph over a painting.

8. There are cameras fixed at some public places for 24 hour monitoring. What are the advantages and disadvantages of this?

Cameras at public places help the government a lot. They provide easy and effective monitoring of public places, so that any illegal act may be quickly identified and stopped. Moreover, 24 hour monitoring through cameras also helps in catching criminals moving about in public places.

Practice Questions:
1. Do you like your photo being taken by others?
2. What do you enjoy more — clicking photos of others, or others clicking your photo?
3. How do people preserve photographs?
4. Should photography be taught in schools/colleges?
5. What are the misuses of photography?

PRODUCT, ADVERTS

1. What things do you keep in mind before purchasing any product?

Before buying any product, I look for certain information like the manufacturing date, ingredients, manufacturing company, date of expiry if applicable, and the maximum retail price. This is because I like to pay the right price and get the best product. Apart from this, when I buy items like garments, I check them for defects before paying the bill. Lastly, I always demand a bill for my purchase, from the shopkeeper.

2. Do you ever bargain for any product? If yes, for which type of products do you bargain?

I never bargain for any product. If I find a product expensive, I ignore it and look for a better alternative. However, there are some products that we can bargain for, like vegetables, grains, and cereals. Women usually purchase these products more, to cook for their families. So, they know more about the price and quality parameters of these items, making them better equipped to bargain with vendors. I have also seen people bargaining for garments and other items that are sold in open street markets, or by roadside vendors.

3. Are advertisements necessary for products?

Advertisements are used to inform consumers about a product and its distinctive features. It is possible that consumers may overlook the product in store displays, or may remain unaware of its existence, without advertisement campaigns. This can result in a low sales of the product. Thus, advertisements are actually a way to increase the sales of a product.

4. What are the negative impacts of adverts?

Adverts these days often motivate consumers to buy those products that are hardly of any use to them. Most children's products are marketed to tempt them, so that they may force their parents to buy those products. This negative advertising is a bad development for society at large, because children are vulnerable to influential ads and may become habituated to making unnecessary purchases. If they become too spendthrift at a tender age, they may suffer later in life.

5. Do you change brands frequently, or do you stick only to one brand?

I believe in staying loyal to a brand as long as the brand offers me everything I require. However, if I find something wrong with the brand, or if I find another brand that offers me a better product mix, I may try the new brand for a while; if it suits me better, I may gradually switch over to it, too.

6. What are the different ways to buy products?

There are mainly four ways to buy a product. The first is the conventional way where consumers go to shops, malls, supermarkets, and hypermarkets, and buy the product. The second is teleshopping. Some companies sell their products on television. They demonstrate the functioning and benefits of products, and open phone lines for viewers to order them. Chosen products are delivered to consumers' homes. The third is door-to-door selling. Some companies hire sales executives to go to various residential areas of the country, and show their products to people inside their homes. The last and latest way to buy products is e-shopping. We can view and order products online, and the payment can either be made online using a credit card/debit card/online wallet, or cash can be paid on delivery of the object at our doorstep.

Practice Questions:

1. Which type of products do you use most often?
2. What are your favourite brands that you use in day-to-day life?
3. Have you had any bad experience with any product?
4. Do you want any change in your favourite product?
5. What is the difference between the types of products available in the past, and now?

ROBOTS

1. Have you encountered a robot?

Yes, I have seen many toy robots in the market. Many of my friends' children play with these toy robots. In my childhood I have also played with a remote controlled robotic car. During a recent visit to a car factory, I saw robotic arms assemble heavy parts in each car. Apart from this, I've seen robots in movies.

2. Do you think we are ready to integrate humanoid robots in our daily life?

I honestly do not think that as a species we are conscious enough or ready enough to integrate humanoid robots in our daily life. We currently lack the skills required to program a completely safe robot; and we lack the maturity to use a volatile dynamic artificial intelligence in a responsible, safe manner. People are quite capable of misusing humanoid robots, and the risk of robots becoming smarter than humans is not as farfetched as it sounds.

3. How do you think robots can help humans in their daily chores?

I think robots can help humans very efficiently I scrubbing and cleaning the house, vacuuming the furniture, taking out the garbage, chopping vegetables and making basic food items, keeping an inventory of items in the fridge and cabinets, giving health reminders, measuring our body weight and testing our blood regularly, and helping elderly people move around the house securely.

4. Are robot based movies interesting to watch?

A lot of people enjoy watching robot based movies. These movies either place robots in the protagonist's role, or as major supporting characters. The conflict is then built around whether or not robots can be made to feel human emotions and act sensitively when needed. Sometimes, these movies revolve around humanoid robots trying to overpower human beings, following which a battle between man and machine ensues. Such plots are very gripping, making these movies interesting to watch.

ROLE MODEL

1. Should a person have a role model in his life?

I don't think it is necessary to have a role model in life, because each individual possesses unique traits in his personality. Thus, it is impossible to become like another person. It is true, that we can learn many things from those we meet and interact with, but, it becomes next to impossible to completely follow the footprints of any individual in life.

2. Do you think one should adopt each and every trait of his role model?

No, one must not adopt each and every trait of his role model, because he will lose his individuality if he tries to do so. Further, nobody likes to be a shadow of another person. What's more, some traits of one's role model may not be worth adopting in life. So, it is better to lead our lives maintaining our assertiveness and individuality, relying more on our intuition, rather than diminishing our dignity and self-respect by being a shadow of someone else.

3. Who are the role models of today's young generation?

Today's youngsters have sports stars, film stars, or industrialists as their role models. E.g. Amitabh Bachchan, Hrithik Roshan, Sachin Tendulkar, Sania Mirza, Ratan Tata, and Sunil Mittal are role models to many youngsters today.

4. How do role models inspire us in our life?

Role models inspire us in life by their success. They motivate us by showing the approach or strategies they adopted when facing difficulties on their path to success. They also show us how they solved their problems in order to acquire their prestigious positions in life.

Practice Questions:

1. Do you meet your role model?
2. How has your role model influenced you?
3. What is the difference between the role models of past generations, and the role models of the present generation?

◆ ◆ ◆

SCHOOL/COLLEGE

1. What are the applications of your favourite subject in life?

*Please refer to the language topic of this section if you want to speak about English.

2. Is your school as popular today as it was when you were studying in it?

I feel immense pride in saying that despite the growing number of schools in my city, my school (Dewan Ballubhai School, Kankaria, Ahmedabad) is popular even today. My school is well known for its excellent standard of teaching, great infrastructure, and discipline. It is pleasing to see that the school has actually enhanced its qualitative features with time, and I feel fortunate to have studied there.

3. Describe the features of an ideal school?

I think my school was and is an ideal school for any child to study in. It has a big playground with a cricket pitch, a volleyball court, and a separate play area for primary school children. Also, there is a big parking section in the campus for all the students and teachers. Moreover, the classrooms are big and airy, and have comfortable benches. My school has separate buildings for primary, secondary, and higher secondary classes. In addition, it has a huge hall where lots of cultural activities and competitions are regularly organised. To top everything else, the standard of teaching is very high there. The school is known for the successful results of its students in secondary board examinations. Further, the school was established more than a century ago, and is still one of the best schools of my city.

4. Should the approach to imparting education be changed with each consecutive level of education (e.g. primary to secondary to higher secondary)?

It is indeed a good idea. When children grow up, they develop their intellect, and learn to grasp complex concepts with better comprehension. So, the approach to teaching should be highly interactive at elementary stages. Later on, students should be given some independent tasks like assignments and projects, to enable them to implement the concepts in practical applications. In addition, the use of technology like computers, the internet, and projectors should be increased with each consecutive level of education.

5. Is it important for a child to take pre-school education by getting enrolled in a kindergarten, or a nursery?

This is again a debatable question. My experience says that it is not necessary for children to enrol in a kindergarten, a nursery, or a playgroup, because all the things that a child learns there can also be learnt at home with parents and other family members. In turn, this also strengthens the bond between the family and the child. However, for children of working parents from nuclear families, formal pre-school education is a better option, because the child can learn basic life skills such as sharing, eating, playing, and communicating with others, from the pre-school.

6. How beneficial do you think it is, to group students according to their level of ability?

Grouping students according to their levels of ability may help them in learning efficiently, because uniformity in intellect always multiplies the collective comprehension of studies. However, it is my strong belief that grouping must be done after secondary levels only, because primary and secondary children are too innocent and vulnerable to handle divides based on abilities. They may develop an inferiority complex if they feel isolated from their friends, by associating the isolation with their own lack of intelligence. What's more, those who study in more scholarly groups may develop a superiority complex, which can be harmful to their future academic performance.

7. Should any physical punishment be given in schools? Yes, or no? Why?

There should be no physical punishment at all in schools. Physical punishment can have negative psychological effects on children. They may develop a phobia for the school, an aversion to a subject, or fear of a teacher, which may inhibit their learning.

8. Should there be parents unions in schools?

Parents unions are indeed an integral part of schooling. Parents should be brought together with teachers and with each other, in order to interact with school authorities regarding the enhancement of their children's education, and the overall development of the school.

9. What is the importance of organizing parents-teacher meetings at school?

Regular parent-teacher meetings are vital for ensuring children's optimum performance at school. Here, parents can inform teachers about the peculiar habits and outstanding skills of their children. This information helps school teachers a lot in teaching children and motivating them for various extracurricular activities. On the other hand, teachers can also counsel parents about their children's attitudes towards studies, new developments in their personalities, and their weaknesses.

Practice Questions:
1. What types of schools are available in your area/city?
2. How was your favourite subject taught in your school/college?
3. Was there any subject that you didn't like during your school/college time?
4. Which subjects according to you, should be added to/eliminated from the school curriculum?
5. Would you send your child to study in the same school where you had studied?
6. Describe the features of an ideal college?
7. How do schools help in the development of children?
8. If given a chance, which subject would you like to learn in future, and why?
9. How can studies be made interesting for students?
10. Why do you think studying history is becoming less popular these days?
11. What should we do to motivate youngsters to learn history?
12. What changes do you think will come in the schools/colleges in future?

◆ ◆ ◆

SHOPPING

1. When and where do you like to shop?
I prefer to go for shopping during the weekends, as I only get enough time then. I normally opt for shopping malls and supermarkets for shopping, but, at times, I do go to smaller retail shops where I can get better deals.

2. With whom do you prefer to shop?
I prefer shopping with my wife as she has a better choice than me, and a lot of knowledge of various products and new trends in the market. I have noticed that her suggestions work best for me.

3. Who is better at shopping — men, or women? Why?
I think women are better at shopping. Usually, they shop for many household items, so they have a better idea of various outlets, products, and prices, as compared to men. In addition, ladies often share their shopping experiences with their friends, neighbours, and relatives. This sharing also enhances their knowledge about shopping, making women more adept, better informed shoppers than men.

4. Where do today's youngsters like to shop?
Today's youngsters prefer shopping at malls and supermarkets. These places offer an attractive, vibrant, and pleasant ambience for shopping. Next, the latest product varieties and trending fashionable items are first introduced at malls and supermarkets. As we all know, youngsters want to use only the trendiest of things, so they feel tempted to buy from malls and supermarkets as opposed to small retailers.

5. Are any specific skills required for shopping? If yes, which are they?
Yes, shopping is not as easy as it looks. We must have sufficient knowledge of the products we use, so that we can always stay on the lookout for better products. Also, we

must check the reputation of the manufacturers when we buy their products. Moreover, we should examine products carefully before paying for them, to avoid purchasing defective items and being dissatisfied. We should know the various outlets in our area well, and have an idea of their specialities in terms of the product mix they offer. This is important because often the same products are sold at different rates at different outlets.

6. Do you prefer international brands to domestic brands? Why?

I don't buy any product just because it is international or comes with a big brand name. I look at the features of the product and match them with my requirements before I buy anything. I do admit that domestic brands were not as competent as international brands in the past. But, in the recent past Indian companies have made revolutionary changes in their product offerings, making their products equally competent to international ones.

7. What type of products can you buy from the Internet?

These days the internet offers everything we need. We can buy everything from a pen to a house, online. I prefer buying software, books, CDs, and other products that are not available in my city or country. Moreover, I use the internet when I want to gift something to someone who lives in a different country, because there are many companies on the internet, who have come up with overseas delivery options. So far, I have sent books, sweets, birthday cakes, and many other things to my friends and relatives who live in the USA, Canada, and Australia.

8. What are the advantages and disadvantages of buying products from the Internet?

The internet helps us buy products from sellers in other cities and countries. Internet shopping offers convenience; we can buy any product at any time by logging on to the website that sells it. On the darker side, internet shopping might be risky. We often have to use our credit card or other online transaction services for payments, and such details can be misused by frauds and hackers. What's more, we may not get the product quality that we have expected, when we buy things online, because we haven't physically seen them till they reach us.

9. What are the advantages and disadvantages of using a credit card?

Credit cards are very useful in shopping. They offer safety and convenience, as we don't have to carry cash with us all the time if we have credit cards. They also help us in keeping a record of our purchase, for ourselves, as well as for the shopkeeper. Moreover, credit card companies give us a credit period and some rewards for using their card. But, some people often overuse their credit cards, and then pay hefty sums as interest to the credit card companies. In extreme cases, overuse of credit cards may lead to bankruptcy. Next, credit cards can be stolen and misused, which may put accountholders in trouble.

10. What are the benefits and drawbacks of consumerism?

Consumerism always promotes more buying, and higher utilisation of products, from consumers. It helps companies to earn more profits from increased sales. This development supports higher rates of employment, and aids the improvement in the overall standard of living of people, by constantly introducing innovations in products and services. This, in turn, speeds up economic development. However, consumerism always turns people into spendthrifts. People often waste their money and energy in buying trivial things. What's more, the habit of making high expenditures creates the necessity to earn more money quickly. Over time, this leads to the adoption of unethical practices in businesses and jobs.

11. What changes have you seen in retail outlets in recent years?
Retail outlets have dramatically transformed themselves in the recent past. Nowadays, we can see attractive lighting, luxurious interiors, bigger displays, centralised air conditioning, bar code scanning systems, closed circuit television cameras (CCTV), and spacious areas for shopping compared to the small, dull, and mediocre outlets of the past.

Practice Questions:
1. Do you like shopping? Yes, or no? Why?
2. Which are the places where you do not like to shop? Why?
3. Which aspect of shopping do you find difficult?
4. Tell me about your last shopping experience.
5. What changes have you seen in the buying behaviour of people, in recent years?
6. Do you think window shopping is a waste of time?
7. Do you think people in wealthy/developed countries buy more things than they require?
8. Does this also happen in your home country?

TEACHER/STUDENT

1. What is the importance of a teacher in our life?
A teacher is one of the most important persons in our life. The role of a teacher is not limited to teaching academic subjects, only. Consciously and subconsciously, we learn many things from our teacher. A teacher helps us acquire practical life skills that are essential for our development. In many ways, a teacher helps us to lay the foundation for the rest of our lives. Such a strong foundation is capable of supporting our various personality traits and skills as we move forward in life.

2. What are the qualities of a good student?
A good student should be receptive. He should have the ability and the willingness to grasp what is taught to him without any mental resistance to it. He should be adaptable; he should understand and adjust to the progressive nature of the tasks of learning. Moreover, he should be honest, hardworking, and curious. All these qualities, combined, are capable of making a genius student.

3. Why is it important for a teacher to update himself from time to time?
It is vital for teachers to update themselves about the new developments in their subjects, as well as teaching techniques. It is observed that students' learning abilities change with time. Thus, if a teacher stops learning at a particular stage and doesn't update himself, he might not be able to teach his students effectively.

4. Should we remain in touch with our teachers even after the completion of our studies?
It is indeed a good idea to stay in touch with our teachers even after finishing our studies. It is beneficial to both. We get the support, blessings, and guidance of our teachers when we meet them. On the other hand, teachers get inspired to better themselves further, when they receive love, respect, and recognition from their students.

5. Why do youngsters hesitate in taking teaching as a profession? *challenging / tides paying job, pay skill*

Teaching requires a lot of effort, and a lot of commitment goes into getting the best out of others. It is also considered a slow growing job where chances of handsome earnings are less. On the other hand, nowadays there are innovative, challenging, and fast growing job options available in various fields like IT, Banking, Engineering, Accountancy, and Science and Technology. As a result, youngsters often pursue such fields for their careers.

6. Should teachers specialize in one subject only, or should they be versatile?

It depends upon the teacher. He can study and teach more than one subject to students if he has a genuine interest and relevant qualifications for the same. However, I think, at higher levels teachers should excel in one subject only, so that they can give the best and the latest knowledge to their students.

Practice Questions:

1. Are you still in touch with your favourite teacher?
2. What are the qualities of a good teacher?
3. Do you think today's students give less respect to their teachers? Why?
4. Do you like to study with strict teachers, or friendly ones?
5. Do you believe that if required, teachers should take punitive action against students?
6. Why do you think some people like to become teachers?
7. How has the relationship between a teacher and student changed over the years?
8. Have you ever considered taking up teaching as a profession? Why?

→ parent attitudes.
now friendly preschool.
the the every time. the challenge better
lack of respect, on time motion

◆ ◆ ◆

TECHNOLOGY

1. How can progress in science/technology contribute to the progress of the country?

Progress in science and technology has the potential to act as the growth engine of an economy. The country can have better industrial and agricultural yield with reduced cost input, with the help of science and technology. As a result, countries can export these products and technology-based services to other international companies and governments. This development earns direct foreign revenues in the form of profits, and indirect foreign revenues in the form of foreign investments. Consequently, the GDP (Gross Domestic Product) of the country rises, which is the sign of a growing economy.

2. What are the important inventions of the last century?

There have been countless inventions in the last hundred years. Some important inventions in the field of technology are radios, televisions, airplanes, satellites, space travel vehicles, computers, mobiles, and the internet — the list is endless. Many inventions have been made in the fields of healthcare, manufacturing, travel, and communication. In short, we are living in the most technologically advanced era in the history of mankind, so far.

3. How does technology influence the field of transportation/health/business/ communication? (This question is actually a combination of four questions. In your exam you might be asked this question for one of the above mentioned fields.)

The Ultimate Guide to IELTS Speaking by Parthesh Thakkar

Technology is a boon to our life. It has enormous applications in various fields. In transportation, we can use cameras, sensors, and scanners to monitor traffic, and transport of goods. We now have in place online booking systems that enable us to reserve our seats from our home computer. In healthcare, technology helps in both, the diagnosis and treatment of various diseases. We can use X-rays, CT scans, and MRI (Magnetic Resonance Imaging) to detect diseases and disorders at early stages. In addition, technology also helps in research and development, whereby we can invent new and more effective medicines. In business and communication, it helps us to stay in touch with anyone at any time, and to quickly and safely send and receive important documents electronically. Moreover, people these days use video conferencing to communicate with their colleagues who are in different parts of the world. Technology is at the heart of modern business and communication.

4. What are the destructive uses of the technology?
There are some people who spread viruses through emails and text messaging services. Their sole intention behind this is to disturb others' systems, by causing data loss or material loss. In addition, people these days hack websites to derive personal benefits. But, the most destructive use of technology is in terms of the weapons industry. Nuclear, laser, and other destructive weapons are often controlled digitally. Cyber criminals can misuse their technological know-how to engage such weapons remotely; this may destroy entire nations, or even the entire planet.

5. What are the applications of technology in rural areas?
Technology can be very helpful in rural and coastal areas. It keeps these areas connected to the rest of the world. With the help of the internet, farmers can come to know the weather forecast for the season, suitable crops to grow based on the weather, and the market price of their produce, so that they may derive good economic benefits. In coastal areas, technology enables people to know the locations where marine life density is high. Moreover, they can stay well informed about threats like storms or tsunamis, so as to evacuate dangerous places, and shift to safer areas in a timely manner.

Practice Questions:
1. What is the importance of technology in our lives?
2. Which forms of technology are you using at home/office?
3. According to you, what is the future of technology?

◆ ◆ ◆

TIME

1. What is the importance of time in our life?
It is really difficult to describe the importance of time in words. It is our present that holds the events and effects of the past, so that we can shape our future. If we learn to live in the present we can make the best of our time and our life. TIME stands for 'This Is My Efficiency'. If I waste my time, I ruin my efficiency.

2. Do you think time management is a useful tool to improve our efficiency?

Time management enables us to give the desired priority to the tasks on hand. It helps us to develop an objective view of our work. This objective view helps us schedule our time and make the best use of it, which in turn increases our performance and satisfaction.

3. According to you, what is a bad time in life, and how should we face it?

I believe in living life as it is, taking each day as it comes. So I don't have a predefined notion of a good time or a bad time. However, sometimes it happens that things don't go right for us, and we feel frustrated or defeated. For example, at work or in relationships, if we cannot help things shape up as we have envisioned, we have to step back from situations. Such situations can be called bad patches in life. We should face such situations as detached witnesses. I think we often manipulate or magnify our problems by getting emotionally attached to them. If we learn to stay detached, we may find better options, and we may come out of those difficulties. In short, we should be receptive and open to life so that we can accept whatever it gives us.

Practice Questions:
1. What was the best time of your childhood?
2. Which is the busiest time of your day?
3. Do you think we should prepare in advance to face the bad times in life? If yes, how should we prepare ourselves? If no, why?

◆ ◆ ◆

TOURISM, INTERNATIONAL TOURISM

1. What are the latest trends in the field of tourism?

There are two recent trends emerging in the field of tourism. The first involves people visiting hill stations, resorts, seashores, and adventure parks of their country to be one with nature. The second trend involves people visiting foreign countries instead of travelling within their own country. This is done in order to enjoy the experiences a foreign country, its cultures, and its people can offer.

2. What things should we keep in mind before going on holidays?

There are many things that we should consider before going on holidays. For example, the distance of the destination from our town, the climate of the place, the transportation system available, the type of food available there, the local language, popular places to see, and the approximate expenditure are important things to keep in mind. In addition, if we are planning an overseas holiday, we should own copies of local maps, know about the currency used in the places we are visiting, and have a fair idea of the rules of those countries.

3. How can tourism be developed?

Tourism can be developed in two main ways. Firstly, the places of tourism should be connected by road, air, and rail routes to the major cities of the country. In addition, there should be enough hotels, multi cuisine restaurants, and guest houses to accommodate tourists. What's more, such places should be equipped with all the basic facilities like electricity, water, telephones, banking, and currency exchange booths. Secondly, governments should promote tourism in other countries of the world through print and electronic media, to attract international visitors.

4. What are the benefits of international tourism?

International tourism is beneficial in a number of ways. It helps the host country to earn foreign revenue that can contribute to the economy of the country. It also helps local people to get employment as hospitality and other related industries develop in their region. Further, local arts, crafts, and culture become popular in different countries of the world.

5. Do you think international tourism is harmful for the existing culture in the places of attraction?

I don't agree with this statement. It is true that international visitors come with their own culture, and may influence host cultures by their own behaviours. But, their sole purpose is to enjoy the culture and history of the places they visit. In addition, local governments can also take care of such cultural invaders who want to contaminate local culture, and prevent them from doing so. Hence, even though the argument that local cultures may get affected by foreign ones appears strong, it doesn't actually happen in reality.

6. What are the reasons behind the rise in international tourism?

International tourism has seen a big boost because of three main factors. One of them is the entry of new companies in aviation and tourism, making air travel cheaper and accessible to people from all corners of the world. Next, multinational companies have started operating their branches in different countries due to globalisation. This has caused their employees to travel to various countries in large numbers. Lastly, the spread of movies and satellite channels across the world has inspired viewers to visit other countries.

7. Which place do you prefer more — a place rich in natural beauty or manmade construction? Why?

I prefer places with natural beauty like seashores, hill stations, forests, and waterfalls to manmade constructions like amusement parks, multiplexes, and recreational centres. This is because I live in a mega city, which is not close to any naturally beautiful site. So on a holiday, I like visiting natural places to feel one with the elements, and absorb the silence that is characteristic of naturally beautiful areas, which is almost impossible for me to experience in urban areas.

Practice Questions:

1. Describe popular tourist places of your country.
2. Where do you like to go on holidays? Why?
3. What is the importance of tourism in our life?
4. What is the future of tourism in your country?
5. What changes can we see in a person who has visited a foreign country?

TRANSPORTATION, PUBLIC AND PRIVATE TRANSPORT SYSTEM, BICYCLE

1. What are the advantages and disadvantages of public transport?

Public transport systems are cheap and easily accessible to all the people of a city. An efficient transport system always helps in controlling traffic congestion and pollution, because people reduce the use of their own vehicles to commute if public transport systems are good. However, using public transport can be time consuming as public vehicles have fixed routes. Moreover, public transport doesn't offer privacy to the commuters.

2. What are the advantages and disadvantages of private transport?

Private transport offers convenience to us. We can go anywhere at any time using our own vehicles. Also, we can adjust our routes as per our requirements. Moreover, it offers us privacy and comfort. On the other hand, it is expensive. We have to spend a lot in buying a vehicle, and thereafter in fuelling and maintaining it.

3. How can public transport services be improved?

Public transport services can be improved by introducing comfortable, spacious, and attractive vehicles. In addition, public transport buses should run on CNG (Compressed Natural Gas). Next, the route plans of public transport vehicles should reach all the corners of the city, so that all commuters can take advantage of the system. The government should give concessions on ticket prices to daily commuters, and authorities and commuters should also ensure that vehicles remain in good condition.

4. Should the government inspire people to use public transport more? How? What are the advantages of it?

The first step should be to make improvements in the system as stated in the earlier answer. After that, the government should spread awareness among people about the benefits of using public transport, such as pollution control, reduced traffic congestions, and lowering in the frequency of accidents on the roads. The advantage of spreading such awareness is that more people will replace private vehicles with public transport, thereby reducing fuel consumption and helping the environment.

5. What type of vehicles do you think will be seen on roads in the future?

Vehicles using innovative technology to enhance comfort and fuel efficiency will be more popular in future. We may see vehicles that run on electricity, natural gas, solar energy, and even water or wind energy in the future.

6. What are the advantages and disadvantages of using a bicycle?

The bicycle is a green, cheap, convenient, and safe mode of transport. Moreover, it gives us good exercise, helping us stay fit. On the other hand, it is a slow mode of transport that cannot carry load on it. In addition, it is difficult for the elderly, the disabled, and the sick to use a bicycle.

7. If given a chance, would you like to buy a bicycle in future?

I would love to use a bicycle in future because of three reasons. The first is that I have personally liked to ride the bicycle since my childhood. The second is that I can get good exercise by riding a bicycle; this will help me in staying fit. Lastly, I will be able to derive a sense of satisfaction, by knowing that I am doing my bit to support my environment by using a non-polluting vehicle.

8. When and where will you use the bicycle?

The distance between my home and my office is too long. So, if I get an opportunity to use a bicycle, I will use it for short distance travels like shopping or other tasks that can be accomplished by riding to nearby places. In addition, there is a beautiful lake near my house. I will visit that lake every morning on my bicycle to get fresh air and good exercise.

9. Should the government inspire people to use bicycles more? How?

The government ought to inspire people to use bicycles more, because they offer many benefits to both, the government and the people. The government can do this by announcing bicycle day every month wherein all government officials should use bicycles to go to their offices. Moreover, the government should develop bicycle tracks on main roads to give space and safety to bike riders.

Practice Questions:

1. Which mode of transport do you use?
2. Speak about one traffic problem of your city and give solutions for it.
3. What are the recent developments in the public transportation system?
4. How have recent developments in the transportation system helped society?

WATCHES

1. Do you own many watches?

Yes, I own quite a few watches. I have been collecting these since my childhood. My first watch had a Disney inspired cartoon dial, and was quite inexpensive. A friend of mine gifted it to me on my 10th birthday. The next watch I received was when I turned 16. My cousin gifted me a sporty looking watch that year. After that, at 21 my parents gifted me an expensive branded watch with an elegant white dial and dark brown leather strap. I used it for a long time. Following that, I started buying good watches from time to time, for myself.

2. Are you fond of any particular brand of watches?

I am not very brand conscious or brand loyal. So, I am open to exploring new brands, and trying new option, especially when it comes to fashion. If a stylish watch catches my eye, I usually do not base my purchase decision on the brand name. However, I absolutely love watches by Breguet and Audemars Piguet.

3. Describe a good looking watch you have seen in the recent past.

I recently saw the most incredible watch in a magazine. It is known as the Midnight Planetarium Watch. Launched by Van Cleef & Arpels, this masterpiece has a deep blue circular dial inside a rose gold frame. The dial is dotted with tiny white stars, and instead of hands that show the minutes, hours, and seconds, there is a shooting star that shows the time. The dial has gemstone miniatures of Saturn, Earth, Mars, the Sun, Venus, and Jupiter on its surface; and they move in real time, coinciding with their actual positions in the night sky.

4. Do you think a watch is a good gift for someone close?

Yes, I think a watch is a very good gift for someone close. Watches are usually a little expensive, and yet one has the leeway to browse and select from a varied range of brands, prices, and designs, when buying one. A watch is a style statement, so the receiver of this gift is likely to appreciate it and use it. Because watches are usually delicate, people tend to value them a lot, as well.

WATER SPORTS/WATER ACTIVITIES

1. Are you fond of water activities?

I am very fond of water activities. Water parks are a very good picnic destination for someone like me. I enjoy everything from swimming to water slides, to diving boards, and artificial waterfalls. When it comes to water activities in nature, I am very fond of river rafting, surfing, and boating.

2. Which water activity would you like to try in future?

I have not yet had the chance to try out scuba diving. If given a chance, I would definitely like to take a small workshop on the basics of scuba diving, and then give it a go under the guidance of my instructor. The beauty of the ocean enchants me, and the magnificent coral reefs and marine life that live under the sea ignite my curiosity every time I see them in a book or on TV. I want to see them first hand, and scuba diving will enable me to do so.

3. Are water activities risky?

Usually, water activities in water parks and amusement parks are not risky at all, because there are life guards stationed around everywhere, and the scale of these parks is not as huge as a real river or ocean. However, some water activities that are performed without the guidance of a trained instructor, out at sea or in a river can prove to be life threatening. The current of water in large water bodies is very fast, and even trained life guards may be unable to rescue people at times. So, in some cases water activities are risky.

4. Are there any good waterparks in your city?

My city does not have any waterparks. However, there is a medium sized waterpark in a neighbouring district, which organises many fun events on weekends and holidays, such as rain dances and public pool parties. It tends to be a little crowded, but we visit it occasionally, and children tend to enjoy a lot there. Adults in my city usually prefer to enjoy their swim in members-only clubs.

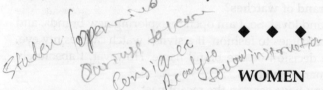

◆ ◆ ◆

WOMEN

1. What is the position of women in today's society?

Women are playing a much better and more effective role in the society, today. They are respected and acknowledged at all levels of the society. Instead of staying at home and taking care of the house and the family, they have upgraded themselves to work shoulder to shoulder with men.

2. What is the difference in the social status of women in the present, as compared to the past?

In the past, the female gender was considered the weaker gender. Consequently, women were expected to stay at home and obey all the decisions of elders in the family. She had to follow many traditions and rules, such as waking up early, cooking food, covering her face in front of other men, and compulsorily fasting on selected days each month, among other things. However, these days, women are taking an active part in the family, society, business, and even politics. Today, they are not perceived as the weaker sex, but as an essential part of the family, who are skilled in balancing their careers and supporting their family, as well as the society.

3. How do you think women should be treated?

Women must be treated with respect and dignity. They are an important part of our lives without whom survival is impossible. I think the idea of 'treating' women a certain way, itself is wrong, and highly chauvinistic. We are here to live life with each other, and to support each other. We have no right to determine any code for the treatment of women.

4. Is crime against women increasing or decreasing? Why?

Crime against women is reducing to a great extent. These days we don't see as many cases of harassment, dowry, exploitation, and domestic violence as before, because women are strengthening their position in society. The education levels of women are rising throughout the world, and governments are also introducing stringent laws to protect women in society. All these factors have contributed to the reduction of crimes against women.

5. How can we prevent crime against women?

There should be strict laws for all types of criminal activities against women. Those who are found guilty should be punished severely to set an example for others. In addition, the government should hire women as police officers, for they can better understand the problems of women in the society.

6. Should married women do jobs? Why?

Loneliness or lack of creative jobs at hand often divert the minds of married women towards trivial activities to kill time, such as watching TV, window shopping, attending kitty parties, talking on the phone for long periods of time, and so on. If they do a job instead, they can support their family financially. Moreover, they can stay in touch with the latest developments in society, which will help them in enhancing their intelligence and quality of life. This is very important, because often, an intellectual gap starts coming in between the husband and the wife after a few years of marriage, if one of them has less exposure to the outside world than the other. This hardens their feelings towards each other. But, if wives do jobs and update themselves regularly, they can have more engaging conversations with their husbands, and lead more creative and satisfied lives.

7. Should married women do full-time or part-time jobs? Why?

I think it depends on the individual. If there is a higher financial requirement, married women should do full-time jobs. If there is no financial burden, they should go for part-time jobs.

8. In which fields do women dominate nowadays?

Women are doing better in many service-based occupations like those of teachers, nurses, laboratory technicians, tele-callers, receptionists, computer programmers, and operators.

9. Do you think men should participate equally in household activities?

Men ought to participate in the household work. Participation in household tasks keeps men aware of their duties towards their families. In addition, such assistance promotes cooperation, teamwork, and warmth for each other in the family. However, the level of involvement can be adjusted by mutual understanding between the husband and the wife.

10. Who according to you plays the more important role in child rearing — the mother, or the father? Why?

Both parents play an important role in child rearing. But, I think the mother plays a better and more important role in parenting. A mother takes care of the child since its birth. She also knows all the subtle changes and developments that take place in the child, so the bond between the mother and the child is stronger in the early ages of the child.

Practice Questions:
1. Is there any difference in the intensity of criminal activities against women in rural and urban areas?
2. Is there any organisation that helps women?
3. How effective are such organisations in improving the position of women in your country?
4. Many people now write their mother's name as their middle name. Do you support them?

◆ ◆ ◆

The Ultimate Guide to IELTS Speaking by Parthesh Thakkar

IELTS Speaking band descriptors (public version)

Band	Fluency and Coherence	Lexical Resource	Lexical Resource	Pronunciation
9	③speaks fluently with only rare repetition or self correction; any hesitation is content-related rather than to find words or grammar ③speaks coherently with fully appropriate cohesive features ③develops topics fully and appropriately	③uses vocabulary with full flexibility and precision in all topics ③uses idiomatic language naturally and accurately	③uses a full range of structures naturally and appropriately ③produces consistently accurate structures apart from 'slips' characteristic of native speaker speech	③uses a full range of pronunciation features with precision and subtlety ③sustains flexible use of features throughout ③is effortless to understand
8	③speaks fluently with only occasional repetition or self-correction; hesitation is usually content-related and only rarely to search for language ③develops topics coherently and appropriately	③uses a wide vocabulary resource readily and flexibly to convey precise meaning ③uses less common and idiomatic vocabulary skilfully, with occasional inaccuracies ③uses paraphrase effectively as required	③uses a wide range of structures flexibly ③produces a majority of error-free sentences with only very occasional inappropriacies or basic/non-systematic errors	③uses a wide range of pronunciation features ③sustains flexible use of features, with only occasional lapses ③is easy to understand throughout; L1 accent has minimal effect on intelligibility
7	③speaks at length without noticeable effort or loss of coherence ③may demonstrate language-related hesitation at times, or some repetition and/or self-correction ③uses a range of connectives and discourse markers with some flexibility	③uses vocabulary resource flexibly to discuss a variety of topics ③uses some less common and idiomatic vocabulary and shows some awareness of style and collocation, with some inappropriate choices ③uses paraphrase effectively	③uses a range of complex structures with some flexibility ③frequently produces error-free sentences, though some grammatical mistakes persist	③shows all the positive features of Band 6 and some, but not all, of the positive features of Band 8
6	③is willing to speak at length, though may lose coherence at times due to occasional repetition, self-correction or hesitation ③uses a range of connectives and discourse markers but not always appropriately	③has a wide enough vocabulary to discuss topics at length and make meaning clear in spite of inappropriacies ③generally paraphrases successfully	③uses a mix of simple and complex structures, but with limited flexibility ③may make frequent mistakes with complex structures, though these rarely cause comprehension problems	③uses a range of pronunciation features with mixed control ③shows some effective use of features but this is not sustained ③can generally be understood throughout, though mispronunciation of individual words or sounds reduces clarity at times
5	③usually maintains flow of speech but uses repetition, self-correction and/or slow speech to keep going ③may over-use certain connectives and discourse markers ③produces simple speech fluently, but more complex communication causes fluency problems	③manages to talk about familiar and unfamiliar topics but uses vocabulary with limited flexibility ③attempts to use paraphrase but with mixed success	③produces basic sentence forms with reasonable accuracy ③uses a limited range of more complex structures, but these usually contain errors and may cause some comprehension problems	③shows all the positive features of Band 4 and some, but not all, of the positive features of Band 6
4	③cannot respond without noticeable pauses and may speak slowly, with frequent repetition and self-correction ③links basic sentences but with repetitious use of simple connectives and some breakdowns in coherence	③is able to talk about familiar topics but can only convey basic meaning on unfamiliar topics and makes frequent errors in word choice ③rarely attempts paraphrase	③produces basic sentence forms and some correct simple sentences but subordinate structures are rare ③errors are frequent and may lead to misunderstanding	③uses a limited range of pronunciation features ③attempts to control features but lapses are frequent ③mispronunciations are frequent and cause some difficulty for the listener
3	③speaks with long pauses ③has limited ability to link simple sentences ③gives only simple responses and is frequently unable to convey basic message	③uses simple vocabulary to convey personal information ③has insufficient vocabulary for less familiar topics	③attempts basic sentence forms but with limited success, or relies on apparently memorised utterances ③makes numerous errors except in memorised expressions	③shows some of the features of Band 2 and some, but not all, of the positive features of Band 4
2	③pauses lengthily before most words ③little communication possible	③only produces isolated words or memorised utterances	③cannot produce basic sentence forms	③speech is often unintelligible
1	③no communication possible ③no rateable language			
0	③does not attend			

IELTS BOOKSELLERS

AHMEDABAD	
Atul Book Stall	25356178
Book Plaza	26440763
Crossword	26424907
New Zaveri Book	25357232
Reading Tree	64501308
Sagar Books	25354250
AMRITSAR	
Sunder Book Depot	2544491
ANAND	
Ajay Book Stall	238237
Rupal Book Stall	237171
BENGALURU	
Prism Books	26714108/3979
Gangaram Book House	25581618
Sapna Book House	22266088
Crossword	25582411
Higginbothams	25325422
Educational Suppliers	26761289
Book Paradise	26637466
BARODA	
Book World	2361012
Bindoo Agency	2438602
Crossword	2333338
Bansal Books Stall	2326109
BHOPAL	
Lyall Book Depot	2543624
CALICUT	
Prism Books	9447884564
Edumart	2372817
TBS Publishers Dist.	2720085
H & C Stores	2720620
CHANDIGARH	
Shivalik Book Centre	2704768
Universal Book Store	2702558
Capital Book Store	2702594/2260
Variety Book Store	2702241
Book Club Enterprise	9815315447
CHENNAI	
Prism Books	42867509
Higginbothams	28513519
COIMBATORE	
TBHPublishers & Dist.	2520491/6
Cheran Book House	2396623
ERNAKULAM(KOCHIN)	
Prism Book Pv1. Ltd.	4000945/2206011
Higginbhothams	2368834
Pai & Company	2361020/025
Educational Publishers	2372817
D. C. Books	2391295
Orient Book House	2370431
H & C Stores	2375649/5563
Surya Books	2365149
Current Books	2351590
HISSAR	
Krishna Book Depot	235678
HYDERABAD	
Universal Book Showroom	24757206
Prism Books	23261828
The Book Syndicate	23445622
INDORE	
Readers Paradise	4075789
SriIndore Book Depot	2432479
JALANDHAR	
Kiran Book Shop	2214170
Subhas Book Depot	2225081
Paramvir Enterprises	2236248
Cheap Book Store	2213183
Literature House	2281055
City Book Shop	2211800
KOLAM	
H & C Stores	2765421
KOZHIKODE	
Cosmo Books	2703487
H & C Stores	2720620/1791

KOTTAYAM	
D. C. Books	2560599
Learner's Books	2567438
H & C Stores	2304351
Pai & Company	2562391
VPublishers Book Stall	2567470
Book Centre	2566992
KOLKATA	
Prism Books	24297957/59
LUCKNOW	
Books & Books	2281417
Universal Book Sellers	2225894
LUDHIANA	
Amit Book Depot	5022930
MUMBAI	
Student's Agencies	40496161
Union Book Stall	24223069
Sterling Book House	22612521
Universal Book Corp.	22078096
NADIAD	
Student Book Stall	2520447
NAVSARI	
College Store	258642
NEWDELHI	
GBD Books	23260022
Jain Book Agency	23416390/91
Om Book Shop	24653792
General Book Depot	23263695
Jain Book Depot	23416101
PALAKKAD	
H & C Stores	2526317
PATIALA	
Goel Sons	2213643
Pepsu Book Depot	2302851
Readers Paradise	2215170
PUNE	
Manneys Book sellers	26131683
Goel Book Agencies	24452176
The Word Book Shop	26133118
Vikas Books	24468737
RAJKOT	
Old & New Book Shop	2466195
SURAT	
Popular Book Centre	23474165
Lucky Book Store	22476530
Book Point	2744231
THRISSUR	
Cosmo Books	2335292
Green Books	2361038/14600
H & C Stores	2421462
D. C. Books	2444322
THIRUVANTHAPURAM	
Prism Books	2365063
Higginbothams	2331622
Modern Book Centre	2331826
D. C. Books	2453379
Prabhus Books	2478397
Academic Book House	2331878
TBS Publishers Dist	2720085/6
Pai & Co.,	2453179
Continental Books	2461426
VALSAD	
Bulsar Book Depot	222377
COLOMBO (SRILANKA)	
C G Associates	4921546/4816726
Sarasavi Book Shop	2821454
Vijitha Yapa Book Shop	2816510
Jeya Book Centre	2438227
Expographlc Books	2787140/41
MALAYSIA	
Crescent Books (K.L.)	61842448
Everbest Media Sdn. Bhd (K.L)	61842003
NEP AL(Kathmandu)	
Ekta Books Distributors	4245787
National Book Centre	4221269
SAUDIARABIA	
Jarir Book Store (Riyadh)	4626000